LUSH LIFE

CLARENDON STUDIES IN CRIMINOLOGY

Published under the auspices of the Institute of Criminology, University of Cambridge; the Mannheim Centre, London School of Economics; and the Centre for Criminological Research, University of Oxford.

General Editor: Lucia Zedner
(University of Oxford)

Editors: Manuel Eisner, Alison Liebling, and Per-Olof Wikström
(University of Cambridge)

Robert Reiner, Jill Peay, and Tim Newburn
(London School of Economics)

Ian Loader and Julian Roberts
(University of Oxford)

RECENT TITLES IN THIS SERIES:

The Multicultural Prison: Ethnicity, Masculinity, and Social Relations among prisoners
Phillips

Breaking Rules: The Social and Situational Dynamics of Young People's Urban Crime
Wikström, Oberwittler, Treiber, and Hardie

Tough Choices: Risk, Security and the Criminalization of Drug Policy
Seddon, Williams, and Ralphs

Discovery of Hidden Crime: Self-Report Delinquency Surveys in Criminal Policy Context
Kivivuori

Serious Offenders: A Historical Study of Habitual Criminals
Godfrey, Cox, and Farrall

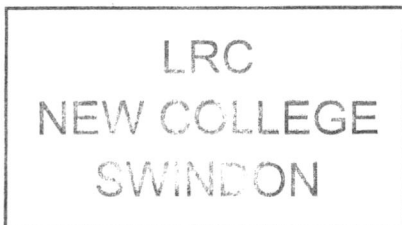

Lush Life

Constructing Organized
Crime in the UK

DICK HOBBS

OXFORD
UNIVERSITY PRESS

OXFORD
UNIVERSITY PRESS

Great Clarendon Street, Oxford, OX2 6DP,
United Kingdom

Oxford University Press is a department of the University of Oxford.
It furthers the University's objective of excellence in research, scholarship,
and education by publishing worldwide. Oxford is a registered trade mark of
Oxford University Press in the UK and in certain other countries

First Edition published in 2013
Impression: 2

British Library Cataloguing in Publication Data
Data available

ISBN 978–0–19–966828–1

Printed in Great Britain by
CPI Group (UK) Ltd, Croydon, CR0 4YY

This book is dedicated to:

Vi Copper of Stepney (1920–2010).
Charlie Porter of Plaistow (1929–2011).
Terry Jackson of The Steamship.
Snowy the Snout for his counsel to those in peril at the Old
Bailey.
All the Jimmy Coopers.

General Editor's Introduction

Clarendon Studies in Criminology aims to provide a forum for outstanding empirical and theoretical work in all aspects of criminology and criminal justice, broadly understood. The Editors welcome submissions from established scholars, as well as excellent PhD work. The *Series* was inaugurated in 1994, with Roger Hood as its first General Editor, following discussions between Oxford University Press and three criminology centres. It is edited under the auspices of these three centres: the Cambridge Institute of Criminology, the Mannheim Centre for Criminology at the London School of Economics, and the Centre for Criminology at the University of Oxford. Each supplies members of the Editorial Board and, in turn, the Series Editor.

Lush Life: Constructing Organized Crime in the UK is an absorbing account of organized crime in the East End of London. Its author, Professor Dick Hobbs, has a distinguished record of research in the field over many decades. His previous books include: *Doing the Business: Entrepreneurship, the Working Class and Detectives in the East End of London* (1988); *Bad Business: Professional Crime in Modern Britain* (1995); and *Bouncers: Violence and Governance in the Night time Economy* (2003). Together his considerable corpus of work has made an important contribution to our understanding of the underworld of professional criminals, the workings of police detectives, and of private security. *Lush Life* has as its particular focus the constructed nature of organized crime and its changing history. However, it continues Hobbs' exploration of themes addressed in his earlier works: not least the operation of illegal markets, criminal entrepreneurship, and the implications of the development of the night-time economy for both. Yet again, Hobbs has immersed himself in the life of the East London neighbourhoods in which he was born and grew up to reveal the myriad ways in which criminal activity is an everyday feature of urban existence in this very impoverished part of the city.

Hobbs amply demonstrates how the historical construction of organized crime has been characterized by a continuing xenophobia about newly arrived immigrants whose closed communities and alien beliefs, customs, and practices seemed to fearful observers to threaten moral chaos. As this book reveals, the very term organized crime has been constructed and reconstructed over time as the structural conditions of its existence change. Successive chapters reveal the changing conditions, patterns, and practices of organized crime, its perpetrators, its beneficiaries, and its victims. Later chapters, grounded in ethnographic enquiry, examine variously the involvement of youth; the rise and fall of violent armed gangs; and the development of organized criminal markets. Although economic reward is clearly a central motivating factor, Hobbs' research also reveals the hedonistic, thrill- and status-seeking aspect to much activity. One particularly illuminating chapter analyses the role of violence, rumour, and gossip in managing reputations, constructing myths, and structuring the environment of illegal markets.

Organized crime is, of course, an umbrella term for any crime committed collaboratively. As such, it is not amenable to statistical record. Instead, Hobbs maps organized criminal activity by tracing the complex associations between offenders or, as he would have it, 'illegal entrepreneurs' over time and exploring their life histories. The result is a densely woven collection of sketches, vignettes, and personal accounts that combine to illustrate vividly the variety, innovation, and entrepreneurial energy of the criminal actors who are Hobbs' chief subjects. Larger themes explored in the latter part of the book include the impact of neoliberalism, globalization, the importance of cosmopolitanism, and of post-industrial decline on the activities of organized criminals. In tracing these influences, Hobbs situates contemporary organized crime within the wider political economy of twenty-first-century Britain.

Lush Life will appeal to students and scholars of sociology and criminology, as well as to the general reader intrigued by the world of organized crime and its actors, from the nefarious to the mundane. It furnishes detailed and powerfully drawn case studies together with a wealth of colourful, first-hand testimony that provide informative tableaux of criminal activity in the East End of London. Most importantly, this book supplies unparalleled criminological insights into the cultural underpinnings and socio-economic processes that inform and animate the hidden world of organized crime.

For all these reasons, the Editors welcome this new addition to the *Series*.

Lucia Zedner
University of Oxford
October 2012

Acknowledgments

During the preparation of this book the following people have helped me by reading individual chapters, providing advice, books, papers, useful references, filling in for my absence in meetings and lecture theatres, and general support. All of this was most welcome and appreciated. In addition, a number of these individuals, both academics and those sufficiently delusional to think they reside in a place called 'the real world', have proved to be loyal friends to my family, and whether this amounted to kind words, or something more practical, thanks, and there will always be a beer in the fridge.

At the LSE: Roxana Bratu, Stan Cohen, David Downes who continues to inspire, Tia Exelby, the late David Frisby, fellow escapee Paul Gilroy, Philip Gounev, Frances Heidensohn who was right, Pat McGovern, Tim Newburn, the indefatigable Paddy Rawlinson, Robert Reiner, and Paul Rock. At Essex: Eamonn Carrabine, Tom Davies, Falko Ernst, Pete Fussey, Christine Jennings, Rachel Kenehan, Jackie Turton, Anna Sergi, Nigel South, and Darren Thiel. At the University of Western Sydney: Mick Kennedy, David Rowe, and Stephen Tomsen, who have all made me feel most welcome.

A number of related research projects allowed me to work with a range of scholars from whom I gleaned a great deal that has undoubtedly impacted upon *Lush Life*. On the night-time economy: Phil Hadfield, Steve Hall, Keith Hayward, Stuart Lister, Kate O'Brien, Louise Westmarland, and Simon Winlow. On organized crime and drug markets: Georgios Antonopoulos, Colin Dunnighan, Petrus van Duyne, Cyrille Fijnaut, Rob (Trigger) Hornsby, Klaus von Lampe, Fernanda Mena, Letizia Paolli, Geoff Pearson who always has a good story to tell, Andy Richman and the staff at Matrix, Chris Rojek, Neal Shover, the late Ian Taylor, and Mike Woodiwiss, who is surely the nicest of History Men. On the 2012 Olympics: Gary Armstrong, Richard Gullianotti, Gavin Hales, and Iain Lindsay.

Many thanks also to Les Back who provided the soundtrack (<http://www.therighttime.co.uk>), Sir Joe Baden of *Open Book*, Greg Condry, who went over the wire, Paul Crace, who taught me all I ever needed to know about hard graft, Bobby Cummines OBE, Nigel Fielding, Graham Hurley, Marshall Jackson, Patsy and Jamie Kensit, Paul Lashmar, Mike Levi, Bob Lilley, who gets younger by the day, Maleiha Malik, Kenny Monrose and his new kidney, the great story teller Terry Morris, Adrian Maxwell and his criminal practice, the late David Robins and his wonderful laugh, Phil Scraton, Heather Shore for her generosity, the resilient Stefan Slater, Anna Souhami (did your mum really say that?), Betsy Stanko, Charlie and Laurie Taylor, whose *Thinking Allowed* provides such a great platform for the largely ignored, Michael Welch, Robin Williams, and Richard Wright. Thanks also to Leslie Gardner of Artellus, Lucy Alexander of Oxford University Press, and Lucia Zedner, General Editor of the Clarendon Series in Criminology.

Special thanks of course to those people who talked to me about various aspects of their skulduggery, and allowed me to glimpse into their lives. With a few notable exceptions, I really enjoyed your company.

And to my family, Sue, Nik, Pat, Lisa, and the Bruise.

Dick Hobbs
London
2012

Contents

List of Abbreviations

AFSJ	Area of Freedom, Security and Justice
EMCDDA	European Monitoring Centre for Drugs and Drug Addiction
FACT	Federation Against Copyright Theft
HMIC	Her Majesty's Inspectorate of Constabulary
INCB	International Narcotics Control Board
NCA	National Crime Agency
NCIS	National Criminal Intelligence Service
NCS	National Crime Squad
NHTCU	National Hi-Tech Crime Unit
OCNS	Organised Crime Notification Scheme
OCTA	Organised Crime Threat Assessment
RARTs	regional asset recovery teams
RCSs	regional crime squads
SCDEA	Scottish Crime and Drug Enforcement Agency
SOCA	Serious Organised Crime Agency
UNTOC	United Nations Convention against Transnational Organized Crime

1

Introduction: Dubious Ideologues and Illegal Entrepreneurs

> I don't want to read none of this glamour, none of this 'my mother never loved me so I was forced to do banks'. I did it for the money, for what I could pour down my throat and put up my fucking nose. For the house, for the cars ... for food on the table. For a life. For a lot of reasons. Will you write that? And all the horrible things that go with it, all the scams and nasty bastard dealing, the full-on stuff when people get hurt/go missing. You gonna write that? (Tony)

While writing this book I came into contact with venal, duplicitous, grandiose individuals whose inflated egos were entangled in morally ambiguous predatory cabals. Their true motives were often shrouded by a façade of renegade posturing behind which lay a deeply reactionary core generating ethically dubious activities that threatened to corrupt anyone negotiating entry to their secretive world. Certainly, I frequently found it degrading to work amongst these chaotic webs of voracious, status-obsessed opportunists—but enough of the British university system. I also spent time with people who were involved, whether full time, part time, temporarily, or peripatetically in criminal activity. I met their families, and drinking and business partners. I went to weddings, funerals, and parties. I sometimes sat in on conversations about their business dealings and mundane issues concerned with sport, family, violence, and the price of almost anything. Some of these people were full-time criminals, some operated businesses that featured illegal activity, while others flitted in and out of illegal activity. Some were violent.

This book connects with my previous work which stressed the way in which specific political economic environments produced cultural interpretations that located market relations as a central driver of everyday life (Hobbs 1988), before looking at how a professional criminal culture emerged from this environment, and how entrepreneurship had come to dominate both legal and illegal markets (Hobbs 1995). While *Lush Life* seeks to continue these themes in relation to both the social construction and practice of British organized crime, there are also continuities with the body of work that emerged from research on the night-time economy. In the context of neoliberal urban governance, these ethnographic studies stress the importance of alcohol-based leisure to post-industrial economies, and the emergence of private security as a form of violent commercial control (Hobbs et al 2003; Winlow 2001), the role of licensing laws in the construction of these alcohol-based leisure zones (Hadfield 2006), and the normality of youthful violence in these new arenas (Winlow and Hall 2006). While the state has proved impotent in imposing regulatory control over these economies, and has utilized legislation to enhance corporate profitability (Hobbs et al 2003; Hadfield 2006), consumers rather than polluters were routinely criminalized by the carnival that never leaves town, and stigmatized by vague categories of disgust such as 'binge drinking' (Hayward and Hobbs 2007). *Lush Life* seeks to continue some of these themes in relation to the social construction and practice of British organized crime during the twentieth and twenty-first centuries, and stresses that this recently concocted concept should be understood within the context of political change, particularly in forms of global governance, post-industrialism, unrestrained consumerism, and the intensity of contemporary illegal trading relationships, which has resulted in UK prisons being 'full of those young men serving long sentences because they got a taste of the good life' (Foreman 1996: 73).

London is the focal point of *Lush Life*, and although I stress crime as a cultural, essentially interactive phenomenon, I have been concerned to situate it within the context of the drastic economic changes that have been inflicted upon a constructed place that I have called 'Dogtown', a conflated cluster of neighbourhoods in East London that is rich only in poverty indicators, and where crime is a deeply embedded characteristic of the local culture. During the course of this research I became acquainted not only with a significant number of highly successful traders in the illegal economy, but also with numerous 'low-hanging fruit' who were routinely harvested by the criminal justice system, as well as those victimized by the market's internal regulatory procedures. The latter included a father who handed over his life savings to two dealers in a car park in an effort to save his indebted son's life. The boy was no more than a naïve user-dealer with fantasies of upward mobility, and fear, shame, and mistrust are now deeply embedded in this family's existence as a form of cultural bankruptcy.[1]

Many illegal practices were beyond my ethnographic range, in particular the multiplicity of activities that make up the white collar wing of enterprise crime and people trafficking. However, some of the social settings inhabited by the so-called 'higher echelons' of active illegal traders (Varese 2012: 240) did become familiar to me, and a considerable number of very successful operatives were interviewed as part of two interview-based studies of drug markets with which I was involved (Matrix 2007; Pearson and Hobbs 2001).[2] However, this is not a textbook on organized crime (see Wright 2006), but a partial, personalized view of the concept's construction in the UK, followed by a discussion of various aspects of the illegal trading that constitutes its enacted environment.

Although a number of people were interviewed semi-formally, for the most part I followed Les Back's suggestion and listened (Back 2007). On occasions this was no great chore as I had known a few of these people for most of my life, and was readily vouched for as I progressed through the field, encountering little opposition or outright suspicion.[3] I am concerned to portray the entrepreneurial culture that is at the heart of our notion of contemporary organized crime as an unremarkable characteristic of contemporary urban life, embedded in the mundane and hedonistic chaos of the city, and located specifically in the fractured rhythms of illegal trading that underpin the pain and pleasure of our increasingly fragmented urban existence. I have tried to retain an ethnographic sensibility during excursions into pubs, clubs, football matches, industrial lock-ups, and living rooms across East London and its

[1] The quest for the 'lush life' generated numerous other casualties, both physical and mental. In particular during the three decades that I have researched this milieu, addictions took their toll on a large number of respondents. However, it was notable that tobacco, lager, and supermarket vodka proved to be more significantly debilitating, and indeed deadly, than any illegal, more exotic substances.

[2] Material from both of these studies, some of it previously unpublished, is referred to in Chapter 7 and Appendix 1.

[3] In nearly 30 years of conducting research I have been searched twice in case I was wearing a 'wire': once by a police officer and once by a man who I subsequently discovered knew little beyond the products of his dull imagination.

periphery, and having previously been fingered by the methods police, I feel obliged to stress that this research did not require me to be involved in illegal activity. However, I find it difficult to understand why, given the time and resources, any urban dweller would not have similar tales to tell, for one of my key points is that so-called 'organized crime' is an everyman performance, and so is the research upon which this book is based. My concern is primarily with deviance as an everyday feature of life, an activity that is integral to urban existence and which I believe justifies academic attention in its own right, without being hampered by any conceits regarding helping the police with their enquiries. For while the police constitute a fascinating object of sociological study in their own right, the view from the backseat of a police car tends to be the back of a police officer's head. Indeed, much academic discourse regarding organized crime avoids analysis of the activity itself, concentrating instead upon commentaries on the policing of this vague concept, and making for easy alliances between academics and savvy law-enforcement agents who are able to present their organizations as exclusive sources of credible knowledge pertaining to the state of criminal play.

Making a Case

> the study of organised crime—part science, part gossip, part theology (Lacey 1991: 367)

Organized crime is a category of transgression that invokes extraordinary levels of hype, excitement, and anxiety, and with little consensus regarding its definition (van Duyne 2003);[4] it festers in numerous, self-contained historical, journalistic, legal, and criminological silos. Lacking (in the UK) a discrete offence category in its own right, it is difficult for scholars of organized crime to plunder official statistics to create some of the more simplistic mathematical-based assumptions that plague the study of crime, and as a consequence there is 'an immense amount of conceptual confusion about the idea ... [but] there are plenty of experts firmly convinced that there are important truths' (Hacking 1999: 131–2).

---

[4] As Levi notes, problems in defining organized crime have done little to inhibit assertions regarding the scale of the problem (Levi 2002: 879).

This book emphasizes that criminal collaborations generate chaotic sets of personal and commercial affiliations featuring fluid and often unpredictable interchanges that are ill suited to the sociometric analysis favoured by police and police science (Sparrow 1991; Coles 2001). Interpreting data that are the result of the actions of control agents although they represent real criminal activity or criminal trends, and creating theoretical frameworks based solely upon such data can give the impression of a stable, 'mappable' community, rather than a volatile, market-based series of fluid and mutating collaborations (Natarajan 2000; 2006). Beyond the computer-generated network charts that are designed by the police primarily to freeze-frame and simplify complex interactions with a view to gaining convictions, there is a chaotic emotional world of loyalty, distrust, wealth, debt, cold business calculation, fierce hedonism, and impulsive risk-taking (Gambetta 2009), and those accustomed to the neat narratives created by law enforcement data, or by the entertainment industry, may be confused or disappointed by the unruly disjointed episodes (Reuter 1984), and 'overlapping and interrelated social relationships' (Potter 1994: 116) that are presented in this book.

The Cache of Association

As Morselli neatly illustrates in his analysis of life histories, social networks are important in understanding illegal entrepreneurs, and researchers are not obliged to embrace law enforcement-generated data in order to unravel the overlapping relationships of illegal markets (Morselli 2005). The complexity of motivation found within illegal markets is far more complex than either the selective précis of police case files or the equally selective, often codified, deliberations of transcribed wire taps can possibly express, and mere association with law-enforcement targets can be enough to bring an individual into the law-enforcement net. A wide range of interactions and relationships are ill served by scholars relying upon case file analysis, the subjects of whom may be little more than 'gofers' running petty errands for those with more obvious criminal clout and receiving little or no monetary reward in exchange,[5] but who are content with friendship or basking in the

---

[5] Sammy was a driver who had worked in various capacities including bouncer, barman, and decorator for his boss, who owned a number of clubs. Although he

glow of the power of more charismatic or influential players;[6] while others are just unlucky.[7]

In addition, as this book will indicate, the loose-knit relationships generated by illegal trading will generally fall outside the parameters of criminal justice-generated 'data' that have been designed to designate, categorize, and convict. For if our interests are in the culture of illegal trading we must look beyond case files in order to interpret the actions of those individuals who not only carry drugs and weapons, but who also open doors, laugh at jokes, phone for cabs, pick up take-away meals, and whose reward is merely the cachet of association.[8]

knew that there were drugs in the boot of the car when he chauffeured his boss from club to club it did not bother him, as anyone working in that sector was aware of the full range of pharmaceuticals stoking the business. When the police stopped the car one night and found a large quantity of cocaine in the boot he realized that a prison sentence was likely. However, while his boss got two years, Sammy was sentenced to 17 years, and he believes that his boss 'did a deal' with the police, providing information in exchange for being presented as a bit-part player.

[6] Abe and Barry had been friends since childhood and had lived in the same town all of their lives. Both had worked in labouring and driving jobs and Abe started using heroin in his early twenties, while Barry stuck to alcohol. Within a year Abe became a dealer travelling by motorway to a nearby city every week to buy drugs. Barry would often accompany Abe on these trips, and later would 'babysit' Abe's stash in a rented flat. Barry at no time accepted money from Abe, but once a year would be taken on an all-expenses-paid holiday to Spain in exchange for his time and labour. However, through the law-enforcement lens he appeared to be a key cog in Abe's middle market operation and received a ten-year sentence.

[7] Sid was accompanying his older brother and a friend on a night out. They took a detour to wait in a supermarket car park for a business connection who was to pass over a package of drugs to the two older men. The connection was made, the police pounced, and the car in which Sid was a passenger rammed a police car injuring an officer. The not-entirely innocent, but apparently inactive, backseat passenger received a five-year sentence.

[8] For instance a semi-retired extortioner who returned to the old neighbourhood every Friday afternoon to use the local Turkish bath was met by an elderly bath attendant providing him with extra towels, a member of the kitchen staff refilling his teacup, and a queue of men waiting to play cards, while in the hot room there were no shortage of willing masseurs volunteering to lay hands on the wizened skin of this one-time neighbourhood predator. Two men in their twenties followed the gangster everywhere, mimicking the bodyguards they had seen on TV, carefully attending, laughing, fetching, and carrying. When they left they were rewarded by an invitation to a 'celebrity golf day', as well as the considerable kudos to be gleaned from their association with a genuine cashmere-coated local icon of the now-defunct underworld.

Driving, socializing, or actually performing some relatively minor function can place an individual on a database and flagged as a target, and when the distorted lens of law enforcement focuses upon a crime group, members of the entourage can often be placed in a frame that instantly raises their status, making 'association rather than action...the crime' (Naylor 2003: 95). Cases constructed by law-enforcement personnel do not constitute an accurate picture of the quality or intensity of relationships of those implicated in illegal trading; they are not supposed to, it is not their job. However, there is no excuse for researchers making exaggerated claims based upon data designed to gain convictions. Law-enforcement-based research seldom reveals the organizational decisions, assumptions, and prior knowledge that impact upon their selection and sampling, and as a consequence research derived from these sources should always carry a disclaimer that 'the content of this file are the fruits of police activity' (Kituse and Cicourel 1963).[9] It is therefore important, particularly in relation to the chaos and disorder of illegal markets, that we heed Matza's warning that although 'The aim of writing is to create coherence...[t]he risk is that coherence will be imposed on an actual disorder and a forgery thus produced' (Matza 1969: 1).

Lush Life

After this introductory chapter, Chapter 2 interrogates the construction of organized crime in the UK, and the institutions and practices that constitute its governance, before Chapter 3 considers precursors to the concept of organized crime in the UK and the development of racial stereotyping in relation to acquisitive crime. In Chapter 4 the connection between the industrial neighbourhood and territorially based extortioners is mapped with particular reference to some of London's principle crime groups of the twentieth century, while Chapter 5 looks at the shift of crime groups and the cultures that sustained them out of the old neighbourhood and into the suburbs. Chapter 6 extends this consideration of territory to youth groups in an attempt to unwrap the nascent trading cultures of both the industrial and post-industrial eras. Chapter 7 looks at the rise and fall of violent robbers as prominent denizens of the

---

[9] For detailed analyses of the research methods employed in the study of organized crime, see Hobbs and Antonopoulos (2012).

industrial era's underworld, and Chapter 8 considers the influence of entrepreneurially based trading cultures. Chapter 9 is concerned with violence, gossip, and rumour as forms of control within crime groups, and Chapter 10 considers the importance of cosmopolitanism in our understanding of contemporary marketized criminal relations. Chapter 11 concludes with an attempt at a more nuanced view of illegal trading cultures in post-industrial society via the concept of a community of practice.

It is 'easier to assume structure than to document it' (Gottfredson and Hirschi 1990: 207), and, as I will stress throughout this book, particularly from the perspective of law-enforcement agencies, it is the nature of organized crime 'to be blurred' (Young 2004: 25–6). However, the concept is usually ordered into several types of illegality: transit crime, which includes 'drug trafficking, smuggling illegal immigrants, human trafficking for sexual exploitation, arms trafficking, trafficking in stolen vehicles' (van Koppen et al 2010: 2); money laundering and organized fraud (Gold and Levi 1994; van Duyne and Levi 2005); and serious (that is to say competent and successful) theft and robbery collaborations (Matthews 2002). While these activities may be self-contained or linked via pragmatic, ethnic, or family ties, they differ significantly from the systems of alternative governance that are associated with the big brand names of organized crime (Fijnaut and Paoli 2004: 603–21; Kleemans 2007; Paoli 2003: 71), who loom ominously, slavering with malicious intent outside the gated community of the nation state. Some have evocative names; some wear tattoos.

As Lacey explains, 'Many of the criminals themselves are fantasists' (Lacey 1991: 394), and indeed, while researching this book, I found that fantasists were not uncommon. However, by staying attached to the field for such a long period of time, stories could be checked against precedents established within the culture. For instance while sitting in a pub, one man told me a story of how he had recently faced down a violent drunk who had threatened him. He explained that 'I don't know what it is about me, but people do find me intimidating'. When he left to visit the toilet one of his friends said, 'Take no fucking notice of him. I have known him all his life and he aint had a fight since he was about nine.' While another companion explained that 'the most intimidating thing about him is the hair growing out of his ears'. This put me on my guard, and indeed when I interrogated some subsequent claims, both the intimidator's business acumen and even his family status were proven to be bogus. Another man rejoiced in the nickname 'Bilko', believing it to be a tribute to his skills as a ducker and diver, when actually it referred to his haircut and its similarity to that of the bald actor Phil Silvers who played Sergeant Bilko in the vintage TV series of the same name.

Personal Archives: Being Lucky

All ethnographers should bring their biographies to the research table, and in this respect I am no different. Like millions of others I was brought up in a household that had been severely affected by both the Second World War and the poverty and insecurity of the 1930s. My parents' generation were a bombed-out people who had experienced too much violence, chaos, and insecurity, and just wanted to be left alone in a world where working-class families could be warm and well fed in a welfare wonderland where the doctor no longer charged for home visits, false teeth and glasses were free, and widows no longer wore black in perpetuity. Security was everything, crime was bad, and the police were worse. Criminals 'thought the world owed them a living', took the little earners and fiddles 'too far', and, worst of all, got caught, opening the door not to avuncular *Dixon of Dock Green* types, but to ex-military men who did not wipe their feet, who wanted information on neighbours and workmates, and who would 'knock you about'.

Yet amongst my parents' generation there were enormous ambiguities regarding attitudes to crime, violence, and the police. Mild-mannered men who had fought fascists on the streets of London and in Africa, mainland Europe, and Asia, would periodically flare up at some real or imagined indignity, for violence had been hard-wired to their sense of self. They had short fuses and were not afraid to 'raise their hands' to anybody threatening their home, their family, or their dignity, and it never occurred to anyone to call the police. At the age of 14 I was knocked down by a car and a police constable brought me home from hospital. My mother answered the front door to be confronted by my bloody and bruised face accompanied by a large smiling policeman and, assuming that I had been a victim of police violence, attacked the bemused officer. The police were to be avoided.

This knowledge had been acquired the hard way, and fragments of the quasi-Dickensian lives of older relations, in particular that of my grandfathers, peppered my childhood. From them I overheard fragments of conversations concerning booth-boxing at Mile End Waste, fights in Victoria Park, knuckle dusters and pickpockets, Jackie Spot,[10] and coin-tossing rings, dodgy bookmakers at Brighton races, the police horses at Cable Street, rat-baiting in Brick Lane, 'coming off worst' in a fight with two pimps during the war, and of a detective's unsuccessful attempt to blackmail my maternal grandfather. We seldom saw the police in our street. They were not hated, but they were not wanted. There were plenty of examples of police violence and intimidation; down the generations memories whispered what the police were capable of, and if you took liberties you got caught, and if you got caught they would 'ruin you'.

But all around people were taking liberties. Handfulls, pocketfulls, and lorry loads went missing from the docks; the local pub sold more meat than the butchers; and friends, family, and neighbours unceremoniously spiced their lives with the odd roll of cloth, box of shirts, or leg of lamb. At school the best-dressed kids were dockers' children, some of their parents drove cars, owned caravans in Clacton, and every Friday night the local pub featured bespoke tailoring, silk ties, and crisp white collars. Somebody was taking liberties and nobody seemed to get caught.

Two policemen were shot dead just a mile from our home; there were late-night fights when the pubs closed; and when I found a small sheath knife in the gutter, an elderly uncle shook his head in disgust and exclaimed that 'in our day we only used bike chains'. Often wielding weapons, little crews/mobs/firms created mayhem, and walking through hostile adjacent neighbourhoods late at night I became accustomed to dealing with the hazards of teenage nightlife. Easing uncertainly into adulthood, boys in steel-toed boots sang a song in praise of a police killer, and an acquaintance bled to death on the floor of a pub when a sliver of glass pierced his jugular. For some, thieving became a way of life, and as we acquired money we enthusiastically entered the market for cheap clothes, records, and— for the few for whom middle-class culture was a lure rather than a taboo—drugs. A young man who lived three doors away was imprisoned for theft; a man with whom I had been at primary school was convicted of armed robbery; and a friend waiting at a bus stop was inadvertently hit by shotgun pellets as a group of robbers fled from a bank. Watchful, immaculately dressed 'Faces' and laughing, off-duty robbers dressed in swathes of glossy mohair boosted the local

---

[10] See Chapter 4.

pub's old-age pensioners' Christmas fund, thus ensuring all kinds of community compliance. Get caught? I don't think so.

I worked for a time in a warehouse, and for a month I was asked to come in every Saturday morning in order to 'clear a backlog of orders'. Along with two other young men I spent three hours loading lorries and was paid cash-in-hand by a grateful foreman who was arrested a few weeks later for stealing thousands of pounds' worth of goods. The managing director of the firm he had ripped off had been convicted for dealing in black-market goods during the Second World War. Working on building sites, I watched as workmates diverted lorry-loads of bricks and copper piping to projects being run by friends and relations. Stealing, fiddling, and dealing was a way of life and integral to an insolent style that luxuriated in the self-confidence afforded by full employment; and while the intense commitment of some placed them in a rarefied annexe in the shape of a quasi-glamorous underworld, and exposure to some of the illegal economy's more visceral exponents was inadvisable, total abstinence was the exception and deviance was normal (Taylor et al 1973: 282).

Shortly after leaving school, during a routine visit to a pub, there was a muffled explosion from the bank next door, and a would-be safe-cracker and three policemen stumbled smoke-blackened, coughing, and spluttering into the bar from the adjoining toilets. As the safe-cracker passed us he burst out laughing and tried to order a beer before being hustled away by the police. This was a scary, exciting world where all of the whispers of violence, anger, police, and thieves had started to make sense; a world where 'be good' had morphed into 'be lucky'.

However, the term 'organized crime' was not part of our vocabulary, for these thieves, dealers, and 'Faces', even the publicity-hungry gangsters, were situated either among the general population or within a few highly accessible smoky alcoves, and organized crime remained an alien concept associated with Hollywood, Al Capone, Tommy Guns, and *The Untouchables* on TV. Indeed, American cultural products have been enormously influential on the imaginary construction of organized crime (Rosow 1978; Grieveson 2005; Schatz 1981: 86–95; Saviano 2007: 244–8), creating 'an infinite hall of mirrors where images created and consumed by criminals, criminal subcultures, media institutions and audiences bounce endlessly off the other' (Ferrell 1999: 397). The glamorous social capital of the gangster provides an enduring urban narrative that has shaped both our understanding of organized crime and the careers of many self-conscious criminals (Gambetta 2009: 251–74), for whom the gangster film provides the 'cultural emotional and sensual parameters that…constitute the foreground of criminal activity' (O'Brien et al 2005: 243; see Napper 1997; Larke 2003). From the iconic gangster films of the prohibition era, via *The Godfather* trilogy and its portrayal of embedded corporate gangster culture (Langford 2005), the visceral commerce depicted in *Goodfellas* and *Casino*, and the unsettlingly familiar domesticity and hedonistic economics of *The Sopranos* (Fields 2004), these urban parables are imbued with 'the city's language and knowledge, with its queer and dishonest skills and its terrible daring' (Warshow 1948: 131).

Yet America's influence over the social construction of organized crime extends beyond the imaginary, and its political construction is rooted in immigration, migration, and patterns of urbanization (Woodiwiss and Hobbs 2009). From the perception of organized crime as a distinct association of gangsters in league with corrupt officials (Landesco 1968), via the cold war era's stress upon hierarchical models of essentially foreign syndication (Cressey 1969), to the emergence of 'The Drug War Industrial Complex' (Chomsky 1998) that has provided a vehicle for the promotion of foreign policy objectives under the emotive cloud of transnational crime, the agenda has been dominated by the US (Sheptycki 2000: 214). American law-enforcement orthodoxy established its prominence as 'the source of the greatest number of exported ideas and practices…in the field of crime control' (Newburn and Sparks 2004: 5), and as Europe developed its own fears and paranoias in response to political shifts and movements of population, an American-dominated consensus regarding the source and nature of transgressive threats permeated global institutions of governance (Andreas and Nadelmann 2006). As we will see in Chapter 2, the menace emanating from those who are politically and socially marginalized has been exacerbated by embracing the equally murky and indistinct phantoms of terrorism and state security (Solana 2004), and this 'criminology of the other' (Garland 1996: 461–3) created an enforcement orthodoxy that, when the global political economy made a degree of homogeneity possible, was exported like a criminal justice version of Starbucks.[11]

---

[11] For a concise overview of the evolution of the notion of organized crime in the US, its political impact both at home and abroad, and the key American theories that have underpinned academic studies, see Hobbs and Antonopoulos (forthcoming).

2

A Malady of Modernity: Constructing Organized Crime in the UK

There was nevertheless a calm confidence that the rest of the world would see the American light....Every country must go through recognition at its own pace (Kempe et al. 1980: xvi–xvii; cited in Hacking 1999: 148)

In the summer of 2010 ex-Commissioner of the Metropolitan Police, Sir Ian Blair, bemoaned the fact that the British Police had not been subjected to a Royal Commission for nearly 50 years, and proceeded to list the changes that had taken place in policing since 1962: 'The police didn't even have radios, there was no terrorism, there was no organised crime' (BBC, *Today Programme*, 25 June 2010). This neatly sums up the British attitude to the concept of organized crime, which is presented as a distinctly contemporary phenomenon, a malady of modernity, and the consequence of recent human activity.

When Ian Blair referred to the non-existence of organized crime in 1962, he was actually talking about the perceived lack of threat to the UK state that was offered by criminals half a century ago. This chapter will argue that UK law enforcement agencies and their political masters currently perceive organized crime as a major threat, and this shift in perception is a direct consequence of a particular reading of globalization and its attendant attributes, in particular the expansion of illegal economic activity and its cosmopolitan associations. Consequently, organized crime is considered here as 'a powerful idea being moulded before our very eyes...in a matrix of very different types of elements' (Hacking 1999: 127), and is not therefore concerned with the 'reality' or otherwise of organized crime, but with its institutional evolution, and particularly the train of institutional formations and their attendant political drivers that have taken us into a transnational orthodoxy that has contributed to fundamental alterations to the manner in which we perceive risk, social problems, and impending catastrophe (Alexander et al 2003; Ungar 2005; McCright and Dunlap 2000).

Elements of criminal organization involved in either predatory or entrepreneurial activities have been features of UK society long before the term 'organized crime' was to emerge as a key prop of law-enforcement rhetoric (Sharpe 1999), and historians have explored precursors to the late twentieth century's interest in crimes for profit and the cultures that spawned them. For instance, much of the establishment and maintenance of British colonies was carried out by pirates who were licensed to plunder Britain's commercial competitors before being rewarded by entry to elite Elizabethan society (Sherry 1986). Historical research should also be credited with highlighting the crucial role of the market, not only in those urban areas where regimentation of the emergent working class was at its most ineffective (Stedman Jones 1971), but also in coastal, rural, and provincial areas (Styles 1980), where activities such as poaching (Munsche 1981) and smuggling, which was described by Hill as a 'national sport' (1969: 238),[1] were by the eighteenth century firmly embedded in British society. Dealers in stolen goods, 'fences' (McMullan 1984), were vital to the corrupt environment that became integral to urbanism, requiring 'some degree of a division of labour, an intelligence and information system, and a sophisticated network for distributing the goods in question' (Sharpe 1999: 151). Klockar's depiction of the iconic Jonathan Wilde as a highly competent enabler at the centre of a network of robbery, corruption, and the fencing of stolen goods (1975) indicates the kind of emergent urban criminal collaborations that were later to become familiar during the industrial era. In particular, the concept of an underworld is a long-established staple of British historical writing (McMullan 1982; Shore 2007), providing a vital link with urban ecology, the economy, and both formal and informal social control.

However, until recently organized crime in the UK was largely missing from political, or indeed law-enforcement discourse, and has seldom been contemplated as an international or indeed

---

[1] Hobsbawm's (1972) notion of 'social banditry' remains valuable here. For a critique of the concept, see Blok (1972) and Lea (1999).

national issue. At its worst it was periodically regarded as a 'substantial local problem facing particular cities' (Levi 2004: 825),[2] and historically the British police responded by creating special squads to counter specific forms of criminality (Wright et al 1993; Morgan et al 1986). For instance, the Metropolitan Police's Flying Squad was formed in 1919 to work across divisional boundaries gathering intelligence and arresting burglars, house-breakers, robbers, and pickpockets. Often visiting pubs and clubs on the home turf of the usual suspects (Wensley 1931), the originally named 'Mobile Patrol Experiment' gained notoriety for the close relationships that its members fostered with active criminals—a notoriety that was to prove a consistent feature of the Squad's operational culture until relatively recent times (Cox et al 1977; Mark 1978: 121; Hobbs 1988: 68–75). The local accountability of individual constabularies was sacrosanct, and there was a traditional resistance to 'continental style', centralized state policing (De Polnay, 1970), and although the 1962 Royal Commission on Policing considered establishing a national detective agency, this was regarded as politically unacceptable. However, the increased mobility of criminals[3] created a need for a degree of flexibility within the police organization, and the Commission recommended that elite detective work be organized at a regional level. Consequently, regional crime squads (RCSs) were formed in 1964 with a capability to operate across police boundaries, but with a regional rather than national agenda (Booth 1969; Mawby and Wright 2003: 189; Critchley 1967: 257–8).

RCSs were followed by the establishment of criminal intelligence branches in each of the regions (Dorn et al 1992: 154) and operational 'drug wings' in the mid 1980s (ACPO 1985). As the rhetoric regarding organized crime emanating from mainland Europe became louder, and the perception that the RCS framework was unable to cope with a threat which was increasingly international, in 1974 the Metropolitan Police inaugurated the influential Central Drugs and Immigration Unit, which morphed eventually into the National Drugs Intelligence Unit as a joint

---

[2] This is precisely the point made by Sicilian Mafiosi Antonio Calderone, who claims that although in Palermo there are more than 50 Mafia families, each one is 'autonomous in its own territory' (Arlacchi and Calderone 1992: 35).

[3] '[T]he advent of the car and the development of roads and highways to accommodate them…developed rapidly in the 1950's and 1960's in UK' (Garland 2001: 84).

police and Customs intelligence-gathering organization (Dorn et al 1992: 154).[4] Although the nine RCSs (reduced in 1994 to six) remained largely rooted in a specialized local knowledge base, and although police action was aimed more commonly at British indigenous criminals,[5] special legislative measures were periodically taken with regard to particular problems associated with immigration that highlighted various forms of vice and stressed a racial pathology that located certain ethnic groups as being culpable for the corruption and degradation of vulnerable members of white society (see Chapter 3). A key feature of this demonology is that these transgressive, essentially alien activities were enabled by collaborations featuring some form of international reach, and it was the prospect of foreign criminality imposing itself upon the UK that formed the core of what was to evolve as the UK government's policy on organized crime.

Here Comes the Nice

> The hell of dope addicts is that, to get their supplies, they MUST go to the underworld. A boy must steal—a girl must learn to pay in sickening ways for the handful of dried leaves, the pinch of white numbing powder, the chunk of deadly brown gum, without which their bodies writhe and brains bleed (Fabian 1954: 43)

As Lippman noted, traditionally, and in stark contrast to the US, Europe was 'tolerant of human appetites, and far too worldly to seek to condemn absolutely what it seems impossible to abolish' (Lippmann 1967: 63–4), and in the UK occasional moral panics concerning vice (Greenslade 2008) or American-style 'gangsterism' (Hobbs 1988: 46–61) were the exceptions to this rule until the latter part of the twentieth century. For instance, rather than prohibit the sale of alcohol, the British restricted where and when it could be bought and 'Gambling was also regulated in ways intended to discourage it. Similarly when there was awareness of the use of drugs such as heroin, cocaine and cannabis, the response was either to

---

[4] See Kelland (1996) 241–61 for a discussion of the internationalization of drugs policing in London.

[5] See Sillitoe (1955) for an example of local police operations against violent gangs in Sheffield during the 1920s (59) and in Glasgow during the 1930s (122–35).

make the use of these drugs a public health issue or, more usually, to turn a blind eye to behaviour so long as it only harmed the consumer' (Woodiwiss and Hobbs 2009). Consequently, although Britain had a long history of moral panics, these had little direct influence on the policing of organized crime until the second half of the twentieth century.

Self-styled master sleuth Robert Fabian had identified 'coloured men' as the cause of Soho's drug problem in the 1930s (Fabian 1954), and Jamaican Edward Manning, a jazz-drumming opium and cocaine dealer, was regarded by Fabian's mentor, a hard-bitten constable close to retirement, as 'the worst man in London' (Fabian 1954: 36). As UK society became increasingly hostile to unearned pleasures (Young 1971), the criminal justice system started to regard drugs as uniquely destructive of personalities, social order, and morality, taking away 'human agency, autonomy and reason; people will be driven to degradation, crime and the abandonment of moral principle and social obligation' (Bancroft 2009: 22). Subsequently, the rise in recreational drug-use in the 1960s inspired a deluge of horror stories, and the US provided the model and inspiration for the subsequent response by British law enforcement.

In 1969 US President Richard Nixon declared war on drugs, claiming that drug-use was the most serious peacetime threat to the well-being of the nation (Gavan 1985; Woodiwiss 1988: 221–2). By the 1980s President Reagan was also using metaphors of war in his anti-drug speeches, contributing considerably to a powerful moral panic (Hawdon 2001: 419–45) that demanded action: 'The important thing is we're hurting the traffickers...they can run but they can't hide...Drugs are bad, and we're going after them...we've taken down the surrender flag and run up the battle flag. And we're going to win the war on drugs' (*Presidential Radio Broadcast*, 3 October 1982).[6]

Three years later in 1985 the UK's House of Commons all-party Home Affairs Committee warned that drug abuse was 'the most serious peacetime threat to our national well-being', and the

---

[6] In the US the chair of a commission to investigate 'traditional organized crime' and 'emerging organized crime "cartels"' described the phenomenon as 'a pervasive cancer spreading throughout all levels of society' (President's Commission on Organized Crime 1983: 4–6), and these external threats justified America's intent to internationalize the wars on drugs and organized crime (Nadelmann 1993: 470; Sheptycki 2003: 127).

Committee's chairman, Sir Edward Gardner, added, 'Every son and daughter of every family in the country is at risk from this terrible epidemic' (Gavan 1985). The report mimicked the rhetoric of Nixon's and Reagan's war on drugs (Woodiwiss and Hobbs 2009) and recommended a range of American-inspired policies, including the interception of suspected drug-carrying ships and the confiscation of the drug traffickers' profits (Hencke 1985), while Prime Minister Margaret Thatcher echoed Reagan's warning to traffickers that 'We are after you. The pursuit will be relentless. We shall make your life not worth living' (Woodiwiss 1988: 222).

As Hacking notes, 'The fusing of events with little "commonality" made it easy to create a popular front...' (Hacking 1999: 138) and by the 1990s a range of diverse criminal practices became placed in the omnibus category of organized crime (Edwards and Gill 2003: 266), which gradually evolved into a high-profile UK policy concern, much of which focused upon the activities of foreigners in the shape of an American-style alien conspiracy,[7] for instance 'Black Mafias' in the shape of 'Yardies' (Murji 1999) who sought 'domination of all criminal activities, irrespective of who controls them' (Gardner 1987). The source of this revelation was the National Drugs Intelligence Unit, and much of the subsequent rhetoric on organized crime emanated from that organization and its successor, the National Criminal Intelligence Service (NCIS), which presented organized crime as 'a newly noticed kind of human behaviour' (Hacking 1999: 136).

Elephants with Tentacles: You Will Know It When You See It

> The British public desperately wanted a Mafia, but they also wanted an Elliot Ness to catch them and lock them up (Richardson 1992: 93)

The UK formally embraced the notion of organized crime in 1993 at a conference at Bramshill Police College where it was announced that 'Organised crime has many definitions; this may be because it is like an elephant—it is difficult to describe but you know it when you see it', and the subsequent threat featured 'some of the most

---

[7] For an overview of this highly influential concept, see Hobbs and Antonopoulos (forthcoming).

brutal international criminals ever known'.[8] By this time the NCIS was already in its first operational year as Britain's first centralized policing acknowledgement of organized crime, which until then had been dealt with on a local or regional basis (Hobbs and Dunnighan 1998a), and although by the 1990s police intelligence units with both national and regional rubrics had been created to deal with specific problems, the NCIS was established prior to any plausible data collection on organized crime (Gregory 2003). The role of NCIS was to integrate existing databases and create and maintain national indices in relation to such diverse practices as counterfeit currency, drug trafficking, money laundering, football hooliganism, organized crime, paedophilia, kidnapping, and extortion. The NCIS was also tasked with the provision of strategic analyses on changing trends and patterns in organized and serious criminal activities, and early threat assessments confirmed its remit to prevent harm to the UK from external threats, and as a consequence concentrated upon a roll call of usual suspects from a global central casting office (NCIS 1993a, 1993b; Anderson 1994: 302).

Although a former Director General of the NCIS described British organized crime as emanating from 'its bases around the world (and) tends to spread its tentacles and those tentacles reach the United Kingdom' (Hobbs 2004), there was considerable initial scepticism amongst the British political classes regarding the NCIS definition of organized crime,[9] and in particular the stress upon its essentially foreign nature (Home Affairs Committee 1994). Indeed, the Home Affairs Committee placed an emphasis on 'professional' as opposed to 'organized' criminality, and the Association of Chief Police Officers referred to organized crime as 'serious crimes committed by career criminals who network with each other across the UK, across Europe and internationally' (Home Affairs Committee 1994: 16–17), a definition effectively divested of the apocalyptic terminology favoured by both the UK's most senior police officer and the Home Secretary of the day (Condon 1995; Howard 1996).

---

[8] See van Duyne (2011).

[9] 'Any enterprise or group of persons engaged in continuing illegal activities which has as its primary purpose the generation of profit irrespective of national boundaries.'

With an annual budget of £31.8 million and employing 562 staff drawn from the police service, Customs and Excise, the Civil Service, and other agencies, the NCIS was also the coordinating authority for Security Service activity in the prevention and detection of serious and organized crime, and with the cold war a fading memory, a number of MI5 personnel were seconded to the NCIS in an intelligence-gathering role, and MI6 diverted some of its resources to combating drug trafficking overseas (Hobbs and Hobbs 2012). The impetus accompanying the formation of the NCIS made further institutional expansion inevitable, and in 1997 the Police Act created the National Crime Squad (NCS), which took over from the existing regional crime squads in England and Wales in April 1998, and joined HM Customs and the police as a strategic partner of the NCIS, generating a degree of police centralization that had been unthinkable merely a decade earlier (Dorn et al 1992: 203; von Lampe 1995: 2).

Further institutional developments quickly followed, and the Bank of England, the Financial Fraud Information Network, the Securities and Investment Board, the Insolvency Service, and the Serious Fraud Office created groups such as the Joint Action Group on Organised Crime, and legislation was created requiring banks to inform the NCIS about suspicious financial transactions. However, joint operations targeted at organized crime generally resulted in agencies complaining of a lack of coordination and resources (Dunnighan and Hobbs 1996; Hobbs and Dunnighan 1997; Burrell 1996) and, partially in response to these complaints, the new Labour administration kept a promise made prior to the 1997 General Election to follow the lead of the US and set up an 'overlord' or 'Tsar' to coordinate 'the war against drugs'. In 1998 the Chief Constable of West Yorkshire Police, Keith Hellawell, took up the position, but resigned in July 2002 over the government's reclassification of cannabis from a Class B to a Class C substance (Hellawell 2002).

A Global Orthodoxy

The UK's discovery and subsequent inflation of organized crime did not take place in a vacuum and there had been a long and often sordid history of attempts to colonize or control the international drug trade (Hanes and Sanello 2003). In 1909 the Shanghai Opium

Commission normalized drug prohibition and established a principle bound by international law forbidding the production, trade, and consumption of drugs.[10] However, this first attempt at global prohibition floundered as a result of protectionism (Mena and Hobbs 2010; MacAllister 2000: 31–2), and only a handful of countries ratified the first international drug control treaty that emerged from the Hague Opium Conferences of 1911, 1913, and 1914 (see Willoughby 1976).[11]

After the First World War the League of Nations became the organization formally concerned with drug prohibition, although its initiatives were weakened by a lack of support from the US, which never took part in the League (Knepper 2009). However, the advent of the United Nations in 1945, and the establishment of drug control as one of its priorities, paved the way for the 1961 Single Convention on Narcotic Drugs, which was ratified by 98 per cent of nations, and combined with the 1971 Convention on Psychotropic Substances and the 1988 Convention against Illicit Traffic in Narcotic Drugs and Psychotropic Substances to fashion the current system of drugs prohibition (Chatterjee 1981). The 1961 Convention created the International Narcotics Control Board (INCB), which monitors the implementation of UN Conventions on drugs (Bancroft 2009: 117), and a decade later the 1971 Convention was settled as a result of growing concerns over synthetic drugs (amphetamines, barbiturates, and LSD). A further convention in 1988 tackled drug trafficking and introduced the requirement that each signatory to the Convention make the possession of drugs for personal consumption a criminal offence (Bewley-Taylor 1999: 173).

In 1987 the United Nations announced a new international treaty against drug trafficking, and in 1988 a G-7 task force suggested international action against money laundering and the confiscation of drug-trade profits. In December of the same year, the G-7 countries incorporated these proposals into the 1988 UN Convention

---

[10] This global orthodoxy has been reiterated by periodic reviews of international drug policy carried out first by the League of Nations and then by its successor, the United Nations (Nadelmann 1990; Levine 2003; Miron 2004; Bancroft 2009; Barrett and Nowak 2009).

[11] Dikotter (2003) notes that in China 'the commodity that most benefited from prohibition was the ready-made cigarette', a market dominated by the US and the UK (Mena and Hobbs 2010).

Against Illicit Traffic in Narcotic Drugs and Psychotropic Substances (Friman 1991: 880–2), which further internationalized American drug prohibition policies by introducing measures against trafficking and money laundering and strengthening cooperation between countries (Woodiwiss and Bewley-Taylor 2005: 17–21). Ignoring the Convention risked condemnation by the US-led international community, and the possibility of forfeiting future gains from cooperation (Keohane 1984: 94), and by 2005 173 countries had signed up to the Convention, changing their codes of criminal offences and policing structures accordingly (Bewley-Taylor 1999: 171–4).[12]

Security in the Shadow of the Skyscraper

By 1994 a Washington DC conference of high-level American law-enforcement and intelligence-community personnel was able to assert that 'Global organized crime is the world's fastest growing business, with profits estimated at $1 trillion' (Raine and Cilluffo 1994: ix). The keynote speaker at the conference, FBI Director Louis Freeh, warned that democratic society was at risk from 'the ravages of transnational crime', which 'constituted the gravest long-term threat to the security of the United States'. This was followed by the Director of the CIA, who contended that 'the threats from organized crime transcend traditional law enforcement concerns...affect critical national security interests...Profits from drug trafficking alone—some $200 billion to $300 billion a year—dwarf the GNP of virtually all the 170 nations in the international system' (Raine and Cilluffo 1994: 135).

This conference was rapidly followed in the same year by the United Nations World Ministerial Conference on Organized Transnational Crime, which marked a distinct merging of interests between the US, the member states of the European Union, and the internal politics of the UN itself (Edwards and Gill 2003: 8–9; Elvins 2003: 28–41). The United Nations Secretary claimed in his opening address that 'Traditional crime organizations have, in a very short time, succeeded in adapting to the new international context to become veritable crime multinationals' (Woodiwiss and Hobbs

---

[12] For discussions of the related historical development of global anti-money laundering regimes, see van Duyne and Levi (2005) and Naylor (2007).

2009). The 1998 Birmingham G-8 Summit emphasized the links between transnational organized crime and globalization, stressing the need for international cooperation (Scherrer 2008), and in 2000 over 100 countries met in Sicily to sign up to the United Nations Convention against Transnational Organized Crime (UNTOC), which came into force in 2003 with a manifesto based upon American anti-organized crime policies. Global drugs prohibition created black markets regulated by violent entrepreneurs which, particularly in developing countries where there is a lack of economic opportunities for the poor, often constitute the only feasible employment options (Zaluar 2001: 370). Consequently, prohibition, and in particular the militarization of its enforcement, has hindered the advancement of democracy and has led to violence and increases in human rights abuses (Barrett and Nowak 2009; Mena and Hobbs 2010).

Meanwhile, the UK was becoming a key player in countering this major threat which, until just a few years previously, it did not know existed, and in NCIS press releases the 'foreignness' of new threats received a greater-than-ever emphasis.[13] By 2001 the NCIS was able to claim that 'Organised criminality underpins at a very high level a lot of the criminality that goes on in this country…drugs…cigarettes and alcohol which have evaded the proper duties, it is the means by which illegal immigration takes place in growing numbers'[14] (Woodiwiss and Hobbs 2009). The NCIS collated, processed, analysed, and evaluated this apparently global threat, and posted officers overseas to exchange information and intelligence with local agencies. The NCIS International Liaison Unit was linked to the worldwide Drug Liaison Officer network managed by HM Customs and Excise, and the NCIS was also the contact point between UK police forces and foreign police agencies through Europol and Interpol. In 1996, Britain became the first member state of the European Union to ratify the Europol Convention, giving Europol legal status and enabling information exchange between law-enforcement agencies of member states and the analysis of information (Harfield 2008).

---

[13] For example, the *Times Online* announced that 'Albanian gangs…already run most of the country's off-street prostitution' and were about to challenge the Turkish gangsters 'who run the trade in heroin' (Tendler 2002).

[14] Roger Gaspar, Director of Intelligence at the NCIS, *BBC News Online*, 2001.

Inventing Organized Crime in Europe

> You do not have organised crime (in the UK). We have it, we
> know what it is (Italian academic at organized crime confer-
> ence, Aix en Provence, 1995)

The first crucial move towards European cooperation on organized crime was in 1975 when the TREVI group, composed of the
Justice and Home Affairs ministers of member states, was formed.
However, cooperation took a considerable step forward with the
signing of the Schengen Implementing Convention in 1990, which
opened up the EU's internal borders. Before the 1990s, with the
exception of Italy and, to a lesser extent, Germany (von Lampe
2001), European states had considered themselves largely unaffected by organized crime (Paoli and Fijnaut 2006). Although there
were discussions regarding organized crime within both the Council of Europe and the European Parliament before the 1990s, these
were not concerned with its extent or nature, and, most importantly, organized crime was not regarded as a generic threat to
stability (Gachevska 2009: 104).

However, 1991–2001 was the decade when the internationalization of American law enforcement found favour after the cessation
of the cold war had opened up political and security space in Europe
(Edwards and Gill 2003: 264), and organized crime began its rapid
assent in importance within political discourse.[15] The EU was
about to open up its borders and establish a free market, and the
assassinations of Italian Judges Falcone and Borcellino brought the
threat of organized crime to the attention of otherwise unconcerned
EU policy makers (van Duyne 2011). Member states were required
to report on this previously unnoticed threat, and at the aforementioned Bramshill Conference in 1993, the audience was told by a
representative of the Metropolitan Police that 'In five years time
there is no doubt that the major threat confronting the inner cities
of the United Kingdom will come from central, eastern European
and Russian countries' (Kirby 1993). These remarks prompted a
spate of Russian Mafia stories over the next few years (Sweeney
et al 1996), driving both politicians and media into a frenzy of hype

---

[15] Gachevska reports that the *Guardian* newspaper in 1992 mentions 'organised
crime' once. By 2000 the term was mentioned 184 times and by 2007 364 times
(2009: 106).

concerning the former Soviet Union.[16] However, after Russia had joined the G-8 Group in 1998, the threat magically declined to the extent that by 2000 the NCIS was able to state that 'Judging from current intelligence, the UK is not facing an "invasion" by a "red mafiya"' (NCIS 2000).

Particularly after the United Nations Convention against Transnational Organized Crime in 2000, European states began to redefine their internal crime problem via the concept of organized crime (Gachevsksa 2009: 109–13). However, as in the US in the 1960s (see Hobbs and Antonopoulos (forthcoming); Woodiwiss 2012) policy was not evidence based but dominated by 'the strong opinions of experienced police officers, public rumours, sensational incidents and, of course, electoral interests' (Fijnaut 1989: 76). Best (1990: 58) has highlighted 'the rhetorical advantages of broad definitions' when constructing social problems, and the eventual EU definition of organized crime—'a mosaic of national law enforcement and legal responses' (Mitsilegas 2003)—consisted of 11 characteristics which, in common with so many official definitions of organized crime,[17] were deliberately vague (Verpoest and Vander Beken 2005) as the EU looked increasingly for an external threat to define the problem, and so to build a common policy (Loader 2002).

Eastern Europe's transition to a market economy involved 'opening new areas of cooperation: foreign and security policy, as well as internal security and home affairs with a focus on fighting organised crime' (Gachevska 2009: 57–8) and, bolstered by pressures from the US and the UN (Woodiwiss and Hobbs 2009), the notion of security was invoked to cope with uncertainties emanating from the demise of the Soviet Bloc. With a growing perception that globalization had multiplied international linkages and created powerful transnational sites located beyond the nation state (Mann 1999: 238), non-state actors now constituted the key threat to Western interests (Gachevska 2009: 69), and the 'New Evil Empire' of transnational organized crime was regarded in some quarters as

---

[16] 'The children of the West are about to pay back the capital on the mafiya's dirty Russian money, with interest', *Observer*, 15 December 1996, 16–17; see also Edwards-Jones 1994: 8–10.

[17] See Klaus von Lampe's list of organized crime definitions at <http://www.organized-crime.de/contactpage.htm>.

a greater danger to international security than the communist threat of the cold war era (Raine and Cilluffo 1994).

Cooperation on policing and immigration was ingrained in the Maastricht Treaty of 1992, which established Justice and Home Affairs (JHA) as one of the EU's 'three pillars', followed by the European Monitoring Centre for Drugs and Drug Addiction (EMCDDA) in 1993, Europol in 1995, and in 1997 the EU action plan against organized crime. The European Anti-fraud Office was established in 1999, followed by the European Police College in 2000. The EU has become a crucial source of policy transfer with regard to the policing of organized crime, and now rivals the US in terms of the pragmatics of policing this most flexible of problems. One of the most notable products of the EU's attention to organized crime is the EU Organised Crime Threat Assessment (OCTA), which is formulated from the threat assessments of member states (see Edwards and Levi 2008; Vander Beken and Verfaille 2010), and is a key tool in the continued development of the Area of Freedom, Security and Justice (AFSJ), a collection of policies focusing upon security, rights, and freedom of movement within the EU, which coordinates not only Europol, but also Eurojust (cooperation between prosecutors) and Frontex (cooperation between border control authorities). The EU also operates the Schengen Information System, a common database for police and immigration authorities throughout the Schengen Area, and has legislated in areas such as extradition, for instance the European Arrest Warrant.

European policing systems merged, amalgamated, and mutated within a maelstrom of political and legal jurisdictions (Sheptycki 1995, 1998) as a result of the emergence of new, flexible, non-state threats that required non-military or *soft* security (Buzan et al 1998), based upon inter-state cooperation in the form of transnational bureaucracies (Aldis and Herd 2005). In turn, this created a security space where the rag-bag of activities that constitute 'organized crime' were reconfigured and tailored to fit (Edwards and Gill 2003: 265).

The Normal Run of Things

Although post 9/11 the quality of outputs from the NCIS, and later from the Serious Organised Crime Agency (SOCA), undoubtedly improved, the tendency to generalize the nature of any threat emanating from such a wraith-like concept as organized crime exposes the political nature of police work, and when data is properly addressed, huge fissures between the rhetorics and the realities of the 'organized crime problem' become apparent (Hamilton-Smith and Mackenzie 2010), particularly in relation to threats emanating from a pervading alien conspiracy. For instance, in Gregory's analysis of the Organised Crime Notification Scheme (OCNS) (Gregory 2003), the majority of the core members of organized crime groups were 'white European', with 85 per cent of crime groups based in the UK. Regarding the issue of transnationality, Gregory found that of those groups with known bases, only 1.7 per cent were based outside the UK and, of these, 79 per cent were based in Europe. In addition, just over 40 per cent of organized crime groups were active outside the UK, and less than 8 per cent active in at least three continents. Even after taking into account Gregory's acknowledgment of the statistical failings and general methodological shortcomings related to this data, the global/transnational obsession that has dominated recent British organized crime discourse is difficult to justify.[18]

However, while concerns regarding the creation of a 'British FBI' (Burrell 1996) and the threat that its accompanying centralized architecture of anti-organized crime policing had once posed to police accountability (Uglow and Trelford 1997) had become '"re-normalised", perceived as part of the normal run of things' (Zizek 2003: 160), the menace embodied by organized crime was made explicit by a government report (Home Office 2004) which also announced the creation of the SOCA (see Harfield 2006: 7). A non-police agency boasting considerable designated powers, and a partner, along with the UK Border Agency, HM Revenue and Customs, and the Association of Chief Police Officers in the Organised Crime Partnership Board, the SOCA was governed by a non-executive board and answerable directly to the Home Secretary, thus sidestepping any of the political processes associated with transparency and traditional local democratic accountability (Bowling and Ross 2006: 1025).

Operational in 2006, the SOCA combined the National Crime Squad, the National Criminal Intelligence Service, the National

---

[18] Even the NCIS 2000 Threat Assessment noted that of the 938 leading organized crime groups, the vast majority were made up of 'British Caucasian' working-class criminals.

Hi-Tech Crime Unit (NHTCU), the investigative arm of HM Revenue and Customs on serious drug trafficking, and the Immigration Service's unit dealing with people trafficking. The SOCA adopted a number of explicitly American-inspired approaches (Travis 2006) in order to target the 130 'Mr Bigs' of UK crime. With over 4,000 staff, and a budget of more than £400 million, the agency was headed by Sir Stephen Lander, an ex-Director-General of MI5, an appointment that confirmed the view that organized crime and new regimes of soft security enabled 'old Cold war experts (to) simply re-qualify and become the new soft security protagonists' (Gachevska 2009: 75). Lander admitted that the SOCA's priorities would be partly based on the amount of space that newspapers afforded to different forms of organized crime (Woodiwiss and Hobbs 2009), and subsequently the SOCA was accused of inefficiency, a perceived lack of democratic oversight, and insulation from normative public scrutiny (Lashmar 2008; O'Neill 2008; Barrett 2008), not to mention the strong whiff of George Lazenby-period James Bond that pervaded the SOCA's public presentation during its formative years, as it established over 100 overseas field officers in 'problem' parts of the world.

Mapping and Ordering

> A driver is lost in the darkest depths of the countryside trying to find his way back to the hotel where he is staying. In desperation he pulls over to ask directions from one of the locals. 'Excuse me', he says, 'Can you direct me to the Hotel please?'. The local looks at him for a moment, sucks his teeth and says 'I wouldn't start from 'ere if I were you' (a very old joke)

The year 2009 was marked by a flurry of official outpourings regarding organized crime in the UK. In April Her Majesty's Inspectorate of Constabulary (HMIC) reported that there were 2,800 criminal gangs active in the UK, of which 10 per cent had an international dimension (HMIC 2009). In June a mapping exercise by the Scottish Crime and Drug Enforcement Agency (SCDEA) reported that 367 organized crime groups were making £2.6 billion a year, and in May 2009, the 2008/2009 SOCA Annual Report stated that 'the number of organised criminals known to SOCA and placed on record grew significantly to over 5,000' (SOCA 2009: 24), while two months later a 'comprehensive' map of organized crime in the UK claimed that between 25,000 and 30,000 criminals were involved in organized crime (Cabinet Office Strategy Unit 2009). The report's mapping of organized crime conducted by the Association of Chief Police Officers uncovered England's 'major hubs' of organized crime in 'London and the South East, the North West and the West Midlands', the nation's major urban centres, and the location of approximately 55 per cent of England's population.

This report, *Extending Our Reach* (Cabinet Office Strategy Unit 2009), acknowledged both the local consequences of organized crime and the importance of local agencies as part of strategies of enforcement, marking a partial shift back towards a more regionally orientated policing strategy to deal with a problem that been increasingly regarded as an international issue (O'Connor 2005). However, pragmatism had already ensured that many large urban forces were already operating squads dedicated to locally defined notions of organized crime-related activity. For instance, the Metropolitan Police formed the Specialist Crime Directorate in 2002, which now encompasses ten operational command units dealing with murder, shootings, armed robberies, drug and people trafficking, life-threatening kidnaps, child abuse and paedophilia, organized prostitution, extreme pornography, computer crime and fraud, and rape and serious sexual offences. The Directorate also provides a range of surveillance and undercover technical and IT services and intelligence products.

Also notable were the police-led multi-agency teams and the regional organization of the Assets Recovery Agency (established by the Proceeds of Crime Act 2002, which began operating in early 2003), which were also precursors to the 'new' local orientation suggested by *Extending Our Reach*. Indeed, much of the new rhetoric regarding countering organized crime focused upon the recovery of assets gained through criminal activity, and in 2003 the West Midlands Regional Asset Recovery Teams (RARTs) became the first of five RARTs formed from officers and staff seconded from police, HM Revenue & Customs, the Asset Recovery Agency, the Crown Prosecution Service, and the SOCA. The aim of the RARTs was to disrupt organized criminal enterprises and promote the increased use of financial investigations and the recovery of 'illicit assets' via confiscation orders.[19]

---

[19] In 2007, the Asset Recovery Agency was merged with the SOCA.

A key function of *Extending Our Reach* was an attempt to placate those branches of law enforcement that felt increasingly excluded from the agendas set by the SOCA, and the report recommended that regional intelligence units be tasked with identifying organized crime groups operating 'below the radar' of local police forces, and suggested that each policing region be required to dedicate a unit or taskforce to respond to serious organized crime.[20] This directive inspired a new-found bullishness in the provinces where such units were already dealing with segments of the illegal marketplace (Pearson and Hobbs 2001; Kelly and Regan 2000), as well as with operational problems emanating from locally defined law-enforcement priorities fitting broadly into the flexible template of organized crime.[21] *Extending Our Reach* reinvigorated this tendency, and with an extremely broad remit, and exploiting organized crime's definitional ambiguity, these new 'ways and means' units dealt with troublesome youths, football hooligans, low-level drug dealing, or any local policing problem that could be targeted by a high-profile dawn raid and large numbers of black-clad police officers accompanied by the local media.

The cloak of transnationality that was used to establish the threat of organized crime was being cut to fit local conditions, which does not indicate a radical reassessment or downgrading of the severity of the threat, nor a return to the low-key localized policing of the Regional Crime Squad era. Rather, this emphasis upon a local policing capability (Home Office 2011a, 2011b) appropriates the fear, loathing, and fascination integral to the organized crime brand by valorizing both the mundanity of everyday transgression and the policing of the usual suspects, and is apparent within routine sce-

---

[20] See also <http://inspectorates.homeoffice.gov.uk/hmic/inspections/thematic/get-organised-report/>.

[21] For instance: 'A New police squad to tackle organised crime', *Newcastle Chronicle*, 2 June 2009; 'Three more arrests in Operation Landslide', *Northampton Chronicle and Echo*, 26 March 2009; 'North East drug raids nets a £500,000 haul', *Newcastle Chronicle*, 12 February 2010; 'Five arrested in crackdown on organised crime in Northampton', *Northampton Chronicle*, 3 June 2009; Elderly being targeted by "organised crime gang"', *Rutland and Stamford Mercury*, 9 June 2009); 'Leeds arrests blitz is the biggest yet', *Yorkshire Evening Post*, 4 June 2009.

narios of shattered front doors and the familiar pixellated faces of the usual suspects being ushered into the back of a police vehicle.

Although the British public remained generally indifferent to the 'abstract' notion of organized crime (van Duyne 2011: 31),[22] *Extending Our Reach* confirms that the concept had nonetheless become established as a key component of UK home and foreign policy. However, budget wars were now being fought in a credit-crunched UK, an environment where the very existence of a centralized anti-organized crime agency was being questioned. Coinciding with the publication of *Extending Our Reach* in 2009, Sir Ian Andrews, a civil servant who had spent his career at the Ministry of Defence, was appointed as Lander's successor, and proceeded to lead a public relations campaign where an extraordinary range of media crime stories from across the globe featured the cooperation of the SOCA. In a public relations effort entirely at odds with the secretive era of Lander, the SOCA increasingly attached its sobriquet to any media account of a successful law-enforcement operation featuring the term 'organized crime', emphasizing 'partnerships' with UK or international agencies, and making claims regarding potency and competence that were impossible to confirm.[23] Subsequently, the SOCA was accused of exaggerating drug seizures and its role in anti-importation operations,[24] and the Home Affairs Select Committee highlighted that the Agency had only recovered £78 million of assets from criminal networks despite costing the taxpayer £1.2 billion—amounting to around £1 for every £15 in the SOCA's budget.[25]

---

[22] In an Ipsos MORI poll of 1919 adults in England and Wales, only one in three regarded 'serious organised crime' as a problem where they lived (Gottschalk (2009)). See Bullock et al (2009).

[23] 'Royal Navy Warship Intercepts Yacht Carrying Cocaine Worth £4m Conor Shields, a Serious Organised Crime Agency (Soca) officer seconded to the Lisbon narcotics centre as head of joint operations co-ordination, said: "It is with these collaborative, concerted efforts against common objectives we continue to target the organised crime groups which cause so much harm to our communities"', *Guardian*, 30 August 2010.

[24] 'Class A drug confiscations at ports and airports have tumbled for the last four years and serious question marks are now being raised about the ability of the UK's "FBI", the Serious Organised Crime Agency (SOCA), to combat drug smuggling', *Independent on Sunday*, 25 November 2007.

[25] 'Britain's "FBI" Soca spending £15 for every £1 it recovers', *Telegraph*, 23 June 2009.

Criticisms of the SOCA's costly emphasis on upstream activities were beginning to bite, and in July 2010 the newly elected Conservative Government announced its intention to abolish the SOCA in favour of a new UK-wide National Crime Agency (NCA) whose responsibilities will include organized crime, border policing, and the child exploitation and online protection centre (Home Office 2010). According to a strategy document designed to give some details of the new agency, which becomes operational in 2013, there were by 2011 around 38,000 organized criminals in the UK and around 6000 organized crime groups. Despite the drastic cuts in public service budgets announced in 2011, the new agency will be 'strengthened by investment in communications interception capability, cyber security and the use of technology to secure our borders' (Home Office 2011b). The NCA was to adopt a multi-agency approach heavily nuanced towards the utilization of developments in 'lawful interception capabilities' (phone tapping). Citing The Strategic Defence and Security Review, the projected strategy for the new agency blurs still further distinctions between cross-border crime and counter-terrorism, and places much emphasis on the importance of sharing intelligence between regional intelligence units, conventional law-enforcement organizations, and disparate agencies such as Trading Standards, the Driver and Vehicle Licensing Agency, the Gambling Commission, the Environment Agency, and the Federation Against Copyright Theft (FACT): 'The NCA will collect and analyse its own and others' intelligence, building and using a comprehensive strategic and tactical picture . . . it will harness the latest technology to ensure that, subject to robust safeguards, its intelligence gathering and analytical capabilities match the threat posed by criminals who seek constantly to evade detection' (Home Office 2011b).

This future strategy appears to be markedly reliant upon an all-too-familiar 'technological fix' (Manning 1997: 122; Marx and Corbett 1991), and the defence industry has shown particular interest in entering this expanding national security market, which is enveloping the domain of organized crime under the umbrella of securitization. Companies such as Detica and Raytheon have become prominent in lobbying and sponsoring events that promote the militarization of technical solutions to the organized crime threat, and the latter company in particular has utilized ex-US specialist military personnel to actively promote their products at events in London in the build-up to the formation of the NCA, indicating a distinctively commercial element to both the creation of the illusion of security (Nordstrom 2007) and to the social construction of organized crime.

Although in its death throes, the SOCA had appeared to be having some impact, it remained, like its predecessor, hugely unpopular amongst a law-enforcement community generally resistant to change, and in particular to centralization. The SOCA was expensive[26] and its close association with the security services, particularly in its early days, served to mystify organized crime and emphasize a growing interconnectivity between acquisitive crime and terrorism (Makarenko 2004),[27] establishing a labyrinthine bureaucracy that can inspire nostalgia for simpler days when organized crime was accepted as part of the local order, and was managed by local detectives drinking in the same pubs and often from the same trough as local villains (see Hobbs 1988; Taylor 1984).

Outside of Normal Bounds

Extending Our Reach also marked an inevitable net-widening, embracing most forms of serious illegal acquisitive crime and featuring threats as diverse as the Taliban, Somali pirates, and 'delinquent youth gangs'. In the wake of 9/11, foreign terrorism morphed with foreign organized crime, seamlessly blending the 'social deviant and the political marginal' (Horowitz and Liebowitz 1968: 113–14; Morgan et al 2010), as the Home Office Organised Crime Strategy Group, which included membership of the security services, the Anti-Terrorism Crime and Security Act 2001, and the Proceeds of Crime Act 2002,[28] combined to finesse the problem of organized crime into a major securitized threat (Mitsilegas et al

[26] 'Our broad estimate is that in 2010/11 SOCA, UKBA and HMRC will spend between £779 million and £829 million on organised crime, on top of what is spent by the police service' (Home Office 2011b: 33).

[27] Although post 9/11 the British state has been surprisingly quiet about the relationship between UK-based acquisitive crime and political violence (Silke 2000).

[28] For fulsome overviews of these innovations, see Elvins (2003) and Levi (2004, 2010).

2003), justifying actions 'outside the normal bounds of political procedure' (Buzan et al 1998: 23–4).

Via its conversion into a national security problem (Findlay 2008), the nature of organized crime and the appropriateness of law-enforcement strategies became de-politicized (Zedner 2009: 45) and difficult to debate. This was made apparent when in March 2008 the British government published *The National Security Strategy of the United Kingdom: Security in an interdependent world*, which identified 'transnational organised crime' as a 'security challenge' (Cabinet Office 2008: 4; Zedner 2009: 85). In turn, this enabled the 2010 Strategic Defence and Security Review to state that 'organised criminal activity poses a significant and persistent threat to the UK public and economy' and predicted 'it is likely that the threat from organised crime will increase over the next five years, in particular as new technologies make it easier for criminals to hide or disguise their communications and exploit new opportunities', while the National Security Risk Assessment found a 'significant increase in the level of organised crime affecting the UK'.

Fear of foreign or alien attack or infiltration remains an ever-present 'gold standard' for British organized crime[29] where 'global trends, technological developments and the increasing ease with which people, goods and ideas can move around the world, have all created opportunities for organised criminals to exploit' (Cabinet Office Strategy Unit 2009: 59). The threat now lies with globalization itself, albeit an insidious, menacing version of globalization (Findlay 2008: 151–2), whose abstract nature enables it to be used as a conduit for alien conspiracy-inspired moral panics which 'suggest that righteous citizens are being perverted, intimidated, and forced into vice by alien forces (which) is far more palatable than suggesting that "native" demands for illicit drugs, sex, and gambling invite the creation of organised crime groups' (Potter 1994).

Although national political cultures retain a degree of sovereignty in the formulation and implementation of specific policies (Nellis 2000; Jones and Newburn 2002), with regard to the official British stance on organized crime, policy convergence is now very much the norm. The insidious adoption of alien conspiracy theory (US Senate 1951; Moore 1974; Albini 1971; Smith 1975) and the iden-

---

[29] 'Foreign gangsters behind most of organised crime in UK', *Daily Mail*, 29 January 2008.

tification of foreign forces at the virulent core of the problem suggest a considerable emulation of America's concerns (Bennett 1991: 23), which were rooted in the conflicting moral orders of urban America (Woodiwiss and Hobbs 2009). American law-enforcement orthodoxy has permeated global institutions of governance and was influential upon Europe as a global consensus regarding the source and nature of transgressive threats was reached. The coincidence of these threats emanating from those who are politically and socially marginalized (failing for instance to identify fraud as a form of organized crime unless it is performed by working class gangsters (Levi 1981)),[30] has been exacerbated by merging crime with threats related to the equally murky and indistinct phantoms of terrorism and state security, lending a global dimension to the fear of crime (Walklate and Mythen 2008).

In terms of developing an understanding of how the trope of transnationalism has so rapidly impacted upon the law-enforcement institutions and socio-legal cultures of the UK, globalization should be understood as 'the universalization of the particular characteristics of an economy embedded in a particular history and social structure, that of the United States' (Bourdieu 2003: 87). However, despite the hegemony over global organized crime policy achieved by the US, the policing of British organized crime has its own, very distinctive characteristics, which similarly feature a fear of strangers and a growing tendency to embrace political solutions that scapegoat and exclude the most vulnerable at times of crisis. Since the mid 1990s, British politicians, particularly during New Labour's first administration, shifted their focus from Europe to the New Democratic policies of the US (Sparks 2001:165), and while uniquely European collaborations on organized crime are self-evident (Elvins 2003), the influence of the US has proved to be as dominant in the UK as it has, often in conjunction with the United Nations (Mena and Hobbs 2010), in the rest of the world.[31]

---

[30] The estimated damage to the UK economy in 2010 from tax evasion and fraud was £42 billion (*Guardian*, 27 October 2010).

[31] Indeed, amongst recent rhetoric stressing localized responses, the following crucial statement is vital: 'The UK will continue to work with our US partners through the new senior level UK/US organised crime contact group which met for the first time in January 2011. This group was established to support enhanced strategic and tactical cooperation against the most significant geographic and thematic organised crime threats to the UK and the US' (Home Office 2011b: 31).

As Best indicates, 'Rhetoric is central, not peripheral to claims-making. Claims-makers intend to persuade, and they try to make their claims as persuasive as possible' (1990: 41), and the blend of America's concerns with alien conspiracies and European anxieties with political violence, immigration, and freedom of movement (Bigo 2000) have proved a potent rhetorical brew in the development and subsequent fortification of neoliberal governance (Garland 1996, 2001), which in turn coalesced 'around the new global pluralist theory of the security threats posed by ethnically defined criminal groups' (Edwards and Gill 2003: 268). As a consequence, the 'organized criminal' now epitomizes the 'dangerous other' of late modernity, requiring global interventions to ensure the exclusion of these collaborations of otherness, whose presence is identified across the neoliberal orthodoxy.

Conclusion: On the Global Beat

> Criminal justice policy is largely the creation of a cabal of bureaucrats and police officials who, with the benefit of co-operative elements of the media, mass market a problem, pronounce a diagnosis, then connive a prescription that naïve or opportunistic politicians cooperate to pass into law (Naylor 2004: xi)

Despite the 'failure to demonstrate beyond all doubt the existence of substantive criminal networks in the United Kingdom' (Coles 2001: 580), by late in the twentieth century the term 'organized crime' had become part of the UK's political discourse, and rapidly morphed into a platform for a global conversation concerning a vast and expanding crisis which, up to that point, had been hidden or manifested as an alternative form of social problem. The destruction of national boundaries, and in particular the redundancy of cold war narratives, has enabled an enormous growth in concern regarding transnational organized crime (Godson and Olson 1993; Labrousse and Wallon 1993; Williams and Savona 1995; Sterling 1994; Calvi 1993), a term which, as van Duyne notes, was first used in a 1974 United Nations working paper to describe the victimization of developing countries by multinationals, before being diluted, 'bleached' (van Duyne 2011: 21), and rapidly morphing into a 'hat stand concept upon which (researchers) could hang all sorts of threatening criminal phenomena' (van Duyne 2011: 22; van Duyne and Nelemans 2011; Spenser and Broad 2010).

The term 'organized crime' now usually relates to crime 'that violates the laws of more than one state' (Jamieson 2001: 377), although it is routinely thrown into the same lazy mix as international or global crime, and it tends to be connected with the propensity of criminals to seek out trade routes that are associated with commodities, groups, and individuals located in a territory called 'abroad'—somewhere beyond the banality of our own backyards. As Best has noted, 'claims need to be compelling if they are to be successful' (1990: 17), and the shift towards the global drastically ratchets up the seriousness of transgression and focuses upon crime groups who are influential beyond their national borders, and who are often described as constituting a 'threat' to the nation state. The philosophical foundations of the notion of organized crime remain firmly entrenched in the US, and the rhetorics of American law enforcement formed the backbone of the UK's increasingly politicized anti-organized crime policies (Andreas and Nadelmann 2006). The US has been the prime mover in the establishment both of the concept of organized crime and of the use of the concept in its attempt to establish a global hegemony in which law enforcement became little more than a front for a government-backed central casting agency, stereotyping both heroes and villains. As Hacking notes, 'Once we have the phrase, the label, we get the notion that there is a definite kind of person...a species' (Hacking 1999: 27), and moral panics are especially effective when they are linked to the presence of resented minorities and their associated hedonism (Woodiwiss and Hobbs 2009).

In the absence of any kind of rational discussion concerning the legislative frameworks that prop up the various trading cultures which constitute much of our contemporary understanding of organized crime (Nutt 2009, 2010), these doomed but politically embedded wars against transgression will continue.[32] Played out

---

[32] 'Colombian President calls for global rethink on drugs: Juan Manuel Santos stresses vital role of Britain, America and the EU to "take away violent profit of traffickers"', *Guardian*, 12 November 2011. However, as Currie has noted, calls for deregulation ignore the 'multiple pathologies of drug use' (1993: 68), and to a great extent follow in the tracks of neoliberalism by seeking yet another market-led solution.

particularly in drug, people, and weapons markets, global crime does not override locality, but highlights the feasibility of globalization as a key facet of the local social order (Robertson 1992, 1995; Hobbs and Dunnighan 1998b; Hobbs 1998). The subsequent local/global dialectic (Giddens 1990: 64; 1991: 22) creates locations based on local readings of global markets (Robins 1991), and global forces can only be operationalized through local identities and sensibilities (Bauman 1998), for the global/local are not mutually exclusive zones (Hobbs 1998). Yet the reduction of the policing of organized crime to a succession of legal treaties backed by transnational enforcement units constitutes a simplistic response that manifests in practice as little more than a series of chaotic institutional hybrids that challenge social democratic orthodoxies of national sovereignty and police accountability (Sheptycki 2004).

The pressures brought by powerful forces of global governance to coordinate categories of transgression have been central to the emergence of organized crime as a social problem in the UK. Leading this drive are institutions reconfigured by notions of threat formulated in American cities and police precincts as well as in policy arenas dominated by American interests, accompanied by a complementary discourse from the evolving European community for which organized crime had become inextricably linked to the multitude of threats emanating from the East. Indeed, it is via the recognition of new threats and the recalibration of others that the domain of organized crime is expanded, and the threat kept fresh (Best 1990: 65).

Anti-organized crime strategies function as vehicles for the repressive, racist, and increasingly global governance of urban life via 'the colonisation of democratic states by the penetration of political institutions' (Woodiwiss and Hobbs 2009). This does not deny the transgressive tendencies and hedonistic drives that lie at the heart of so much of urban life, but grouping these enterprises, vices, and pleasures into the emotive and politically charged category of organized crime implies a coordinated threat far more powerful, ominous, and extensive than is justified (Goode and Ben-Yehuda 1994: 36). Crime is experienced, enjoyed, acted out, and suffered locally, albeit, like the rest of late modern human existence, as the result of pressures that can be partially attributed to ebbs and flows on trade routes whose myriad of networked connections can be typified as global. However, excluded communities featuring refugees, asylum seekers, and immigrants are especially vulnerable to demonization as a result of moral panics linked to vague concepts such as organized crime (Balcaen et al 2006), and the organized criminal/folk devil has been located as an external threat (Cohen 1973), marginalizing the importance of the indigenous generation of demand, the creation of local markets, and the enthusiastic engagement of local criminal labour.

The construction of organized crime in the UK is a prime example of 'domain expansion' (Best 1990), the process through which 'the contents of a previously accepted social problem expand' (Loseke 1999: 82), and particularly since the 1980s this domain has became increasingly broad. Via the hegemony of the US, and the insecurities that have accompanied new political formations in Europe, fresh problems were piggybacked onto what was originally an undefined cluster of malignant cosmopolitanism (Chapter 3) infused with local mutant proletarianism (Chapter 4), and the term organized crime came to encompass a plethora of globalized transgressions. This reconceptualization enabled the domain of organized crime to expand and attain a powerful cultural dynamic that in less than two decades had moved from being a non-existent to a widely recognized problem, and confirming that, '"somewhere", "somebody" is pulling all the complicated strings to which the jumbled world dances' (Bell 1961: 140–1).

In a remarkable period of activity, the UK state has, via the use of ordering, mapping, and actuarial devices, endeavoured to manage the unpredictable (Bauman 2000: 3), enforcing the rational in an attempt to suppress the chaotic, contingent, transgressive groups and individuals who embrace illegal markets. The term 'organized crime' corrals and systemizes an often disparate range of hedonistic and entrepreneurial activity, denying ambivalence, homogenizing chaos and disparity, and suppressing variety in an attempt to universalize social order. For, as we will see in Chapter 3, incomers, particularly those associated with diasporas who become disempowered segments of the working class, are rendered neither insiders nor outsiders (Marotta 2002: 44–5), but as hybrid strangers (Bauman 1991: 58), whose transgressions are associated entirely with their ethnicity (Ruggiero and Khan 2006; Silverstone and Savage 2010), as they are counted, categorized, and corralled, enabling anti-organized crime strategies to emerge as a 'form of control of dangerous classes' (Christie 1993: 62), obscuring both the complexity and the normalization (Lea 2002: 135–60) of deviant activity in a veil of malevolent exoticism.[33]

---

[33] From the point of view of attempting to carry out empirical research, securitization has enhanced the mystique that has increasingly been associated with organized crime, and police officers will often signal where knowledge ends and ignorance sets in by claiming that they cannot comment further as there are national security implications.

3

Malignant Cosmopolitanism: Precursors of Organized Crime

> If Great Britain could sweep out and keep out the non British element of her criminal world, the taxpayers burdens of the public expenses would be lowered by half (Fitch 1933: 195)

Based historically upon US attempts to police the morals of the poor (Woodiwiss and Hobbs 2009), alien conspiracy theory engineered the identification of key threats to the normative order as emanating from alien, essentially hostile sources rather than from within its own backyard. Similarly, the British response to alien transgression also emphasized the deviant pathology of strangers and new arrivals, a pathology that was extended to entire communities and was related in particular to the infectious allure of vice and transgressive leisure.

Marotta has noted that 'the stranger comes to symbolize the very ambivalence that the ordering impulse is attempting to destroy' (2002: 42), and in organized crime discourse, boundaries between natives and 'foreigners, lower class, ethnic offenders or a combination thereof' (van Duyne 2011: 2) constitute a demarcation between criminal and non-criminal via the vehicle of othering (Agozino 2000).[1] Current trends in the study of organized crime express both the concept's global nature and the redundancy of any perception of organized crime that does not embrace the trope of transnationality, although the identification of aliens as a principal threat to British society pre-dates the creation of the organized crime menace and its subsequent institutionalization. These precursors

---

[1] A senior British police officer explained to me in 2009 that 'Importing cannabis is the white man's crime, Turks do the heroin, and the Trident boys (a term increasingly used as a shorthand for Black British and Caribbean) do cocaine and shoot each other.'

comprised sections of the UK population who were subjected to the process of othering on the grounds of transgressive ethnicity, a device that excluded the British from confronting their own vices and highlighted a jingoistic emphasis upon the tainting of Albion by foreign criminality.

Precursors

Prone to hooliganism

Irish nineteenth-century immigration to Britain had been met with widespread indignation and opposition (O'Day 1996; MacRaild 1999: 155–84), and the perceived habits and lifestyle of the Irish community were often cited as contributing to a broad range of social problems (Mayhew 1861 (1981): 296–301; Engels 1987: 124). However, the role of the Irish community in creating the industrial infrastructure of the UK (Bermant 1975: 43) and the ability of the Irish to find crucial niches in the production process that did not require 'steady methodological application, inner motivations of sobriety, forethought, and punctilious observation of contracts' (Thompson 1974: 473), resulted in their begrudging acceptance, albeit as part of an unruly 'lumpen subclass engaged in unpleasant manual occupations to which the English were no longer suited, either physically or temperamentally' (Hobbs 1988: 96). Casualized, heavy, dirty work constituted the lived reality for the bulk of the Irish community in nineteenth-century England, and in London the key to their assimilation can be found within the capital's distinct economic base, and in particular the docks, for 'the vast majority of Irish immigrants were farm labourers and dispossessed peasants' (Feheney 1983: 322), and the experience of agricultural subsistence labour could be replicated in the casualized employment market that dominated dock work (Hobbs 1988: 94–8).

While some commentators attributed Irish criminality to the fact that they were 'unacquainted with any industrial occupation' (Mayhew and Binney 1862 (1968): 403), their over-representation in court and prison records (McManus 1994) can be linked to offences traditionally associated with poverty, in particular alcohol-related offences, amongst a population rooted in rural cultural traditions (MacRaild 1999: 162–3). 'The Irish give infinitely more trouble, and are infinitely more riotous and disorderly in the streets than any other class of persons, or than all others put together; they make a great deal of noise, they are in fact more accustomed to a country than a town life' (*Report on the State of the Irish poor in Great Britain* 1836: 495; cited in Feheney 1983). The Irish who were distributed across proletarian London, albeit within distinct settlements, for instance in St Giles and Whitechapel, were regarded, even as they assimilated, as being rowdy and prone to hooliganism (Pearson 1983: 74–5), and were not associated with 'professional vice or villainy' (Pollard-Urquhart 1861: 747). Consequently, the subsequent racism to which they were consistently subjected through the nineteenth and twentieth centuries was related to the stigma of poverty, religious bigotry, and the dregs of colonial attitudes (Hickman 1995), rather than to any perception that the Irish were prominently involved in organized or professional crime.[2]

However, beyond their propensity for getting 'quite drunk and fighting with their shelalahs' (Feheney 1983: 321), the Irish were nonetheless deemed to require special policing measures beyond the mundane social control offered by the 'Blue Locusts' of the Metropolitan Police. In a response to the Fenian bombings of 1867–8 and 1881–5, the Met formed the Special Irish Branch in 1883 (Porter 1987), which evolved into the Special Branch as the unit's remit expanded to take responsibility for all political threats. By the turn of the century its brief included attending to the apparent risks posed by individuals of eastern European origin.

Beyond the Pale

By this time Whitechapel in East London had established itself as a destination for the poor, displaced, and politically marginal, and by the turn of the twentieth century, during an era when radical ideological affiliations often bled into each other, revolutionary politics, in particular anarchism and Bolshevekism (Knepper 2008), had become closely associated with the area, and an apparently powerful link between immigration and political subversion (Fishman 1975) became conflated with the various nationalities arriving in

---

[2] This perception has since been belied by numerous prominent professional criminals of Irish descent including the self-styled 'Boss of Britain's Underworld' (Hill 1955).

Whitechapel from eastern Europe. In 1909 a group of Latvian anarchists committed suicide after killing a police officer and a ten-year-old schoolboy, and wounding 27 others in a botched armed robbery in Tottenham. The following year at a failed burglary by Latvians, three police officers were shot dead; 18 days later, on 2 January 1911, the remaining members of the anarchist group were traced to a house in Stepney, and the 'Siege of Sidney Street' commenced. The anarchists fired over 400 shots from state-of-the-art, semi-automatic weapons at lightly armed police who were reinforced by a company of Scots Guards from the nearby Tower of London, while the top-hatted Home Secretary, Winston Churchill, took direct control and an estimated crowd of 100,000 looked on (Rumbelow 1973). When the siege ended seven hours later, a police officer had been wounded, a fireman killed by a collapsed wall, and the bodies of two of the anarchists were found in the burnt-out shell of the building.[3] The Siege of Sidney Street contributed greatly to the conflation and demonization of 'anarchists' and 'aliens',[4] which was confirmed by the tailors' strikes of 1906 and 1912, in which Jewish anarchists were central (Kershen 1995; Fishman, 1975). Although the British political class were primarily concerned with subversion seeping into the country from eastern Europe, both British nationalists and the emerging Labour movement focused upon the threats that Jewish immigrants posed to indigenous employment, pay, and conditions.

The anxieties being fostered by these fears made no distinction between 'native, nationalised and immigrant Jews' (Kadish 1992: 44); the Jews of Sephardic origin who first arrived in Britain during the seventeenth century (Cesarani 1994) were 'socially, culturally

---

[3] The association of eastern Europeans with crime and violence which was triggered in the public imagination by the Siege of Sidney Street lasted for many years. My grandmother had joined the huge crowd that gathered to watch the spectacle, and well into the 1960s, as a means of imposing domestic order, would intone solemnly that 'Peter the Painter', the alias of Janis Zhaklis, one of the besieged anarchists whose remains were never recovered, 'will come and get you'. In 2003 William Fishman, one of the contributors to a London Weekend Television documentary about the Houndsditch murders, described Peter the Painter as 'the Osama Bin Laden of his time'.

[4] Nine years after his controversial showboating at Sydney Street, Winston Churchill argued in the *Illustrated Sunday Herald* that Jews were part of a 'worldwide conspiracy for the overthrow of civilization and the reconstitution of society on the basis of arrested development' (Kadish 1992: 137).

and economically' (Knepper 2007: 72) integrated, and were as dissimilar from the 160,000 poor, displaced Yiddish-speaking new arrivals who arrived in the East End of London from the Pale of Settlement between 1880 and 1914 (Lipman 1990; Newman 1981) 'as the English aristocracy were from factory workers' (Henriques 1968: 127; cited in Knepper 2007). By the time they joined the 40,000 Jews already living in the two square miles of what was to become the Jewish East End, these newcomers had experienced political and religious repression, as well as a severe loss of social status as a result of the industrial revolution (White 1980: 252; Hobbs 1988: 98–101). The Jewish elite had long been concerned to establish a state of self-sufficiency within the Jewish community in order to 'reduce the pariah or scrounger image so often attached…to the Jewish immigrant' (Hobbs 1988: 98). To this end a range of charities and self-help organizations, including the Jewish Board of Guardians, were formed to provide basic welfare for the 'strange poor' (White 1980: 250), enabling newly arrived Jews to avoid competing with the indigenous population for scarce resources, or becoming a burden on the state.

The Labour movement, along with the proto-fascist East London-based British Brothers League, expressed their disquiet at these 'might-be paupers and would-be workers' (Knepper 2007: 63), and with the large majority of Jews arriving in a London borough where over one-third of the population were 'living on or below the margin of subsistence' (Fishman 1988: 12), inciting anxiety was an easy task. The entire might of the non-Jewish Labour movement lined up to advocate controls against Jews (Bermant 1975: 138–63), and Fabian luminaries such as Beatrice Potter mixed her concerns for the 'British worker' with a conviction that Jews were 'deficient in social morality' (Brustein 2003: 147, 228, 229) as objections to the sweating system and fears concerning unfair competition (Booth 1889: 481–97) evolved into rabid anti-Semitism.

There was a long tradition of linking vice to foreigners, and this fresh outbreak of anti-Semitic fervour enabled old stereotypes concerning moral degeneracy to come to the fore (Lebzelter 1981: 93). While British crime was generally associated with drunken disorder (Knepper 2007: 64), Jews were increasingly linked with 'foreign associations with vice' (Slater 2007: 53), and by the time of the 1903 Royal Commission on Alien Immigration, 'the "white slave" trade, and living upon the earnings of women, (were) now two of the regular professions of the alien Jew' (Marks 1996: 38). Although the Anglo-Jewish establishment in the form of the Board of Deputies of British Jews and the Federation of Jewish Organisations rejected suggestions that Jews had a detrimental impact on the workplace, wages, and employment, they accepted the link between the eastern European Jew and crime, and in particular Jewish involvement in white slavery (Knepper 2007: 66). The new arrivals 'presented a stereotype (that) Anglo-Jewry had spent two centuries trying to erase, that Jews were strange menacing and dangerous' (Knepper 2007: 72). The Jewish establishment were eager to campaign against every crass racist allegation made about East End Jews except those relating to crime, as they colluded in propagating an insidious criminal stereotype which located London at the centre of the international illicit sex trade (Jewish Association for Protection of Girls and Women 1908: 16; cited in Knepper 2007: 71).

Of course crime was not unknown within the East End's Jewish community (Samuel 1981: 125–45), but the cultural isolation of first-generation immigrants meant that most of this crime was targeted at the parent community (Zorbaugh 1929: 170–6). For instance, at the turn of the twentieth century rival gangs of immigrant Jews—the Bessarbians and the Odessians—fought over territory and the extortion of immigrant businesses (Morton 2000: 39–43; Sims 1911), and while they were of some concern to the police (Cornish 1935; Leeson 1934), their low-level, intensely local gangsterism failed to excite the imagination in the same way as white slavery, 'a crime which is usually initiated in one country and consummated in another' (Jewish Association for Protection of Girls and Women 1898: 23; cited in Knepper 2007: 68).

The four-month killing spree of Jack the Ripper during 1888 had provoked the East End's most prominent newspaper to announce that 'no Englishman could have perpetrated such a horrible crime…and that it must have been done by a Jew' (*East London Observer*, 15 October 1888; cited by Fishman 1979: 84–5). *The Times* contributed with a theory emanating from its eastern European correspondent, who linked the murders to an alleged ritual of German Jews that involved making candles from the uterus (Bermant 1975: 112–13). More seriously, when a leather apron was found adjacent to one of the corpses, a number of Jewish craftsmen were cast under suspicion (Bermant 1975: 114), Odell noting that 'A ritual slaughterman steeped in Old Testament law might have felt some religious justification for killing prostitutes' (Odell 1965: 153). The official description of the killer—bearded, wearing dark clothes, and speaking with a foreign accent—was that of 'a Jew in a Jewish ghetto' (Hobbs 1988: 107), and the unsolved crimes of the Ripper were still fresh in the minds of the British public when the Royal Commission on Alien Immigration reported in 1903.

Although the Commission found no data supporting the notion of a Jewish crime wave, nor of any detrimental effect of Jewish immigration on health or employment amongst the indigenous population, statistical data from the Prison Commissioners were used to confirm racist assumptions regarding Jewish criminality, and the existence of synagogues at Wormwood Scrubs, Parkhurst, and Pentonville Prisons were cited as examples of an increase in the Jewish prison population (Knepper 2007: 65). Although in subsequent testimony to the Commission this interpretation was contested, the notion of a signature Jewish crime, built upon the ability to 'carry out and conceal their crimes using their own language' (Knepper 2007: 64), was presented as especially insidious.

The 1903 Commission laid the foundations for the Aliens Act of 1905, which was targeted specifically at Jews and introduced immigration controls and registration for aliens, defining some groups of migrants as 'undesirable' and making entry to the UK discretionary rather than automatic (Gainer 1972). The Act was primarily designed to stop paupers or criminals from entering the country, and set up a mechanism allowing magistrates to deport foreigners convicted of offences linked to prostitution (Feldman 2003; Pellew 1989).[5] The context of the Act was the perception of the Jewish community as prone to morally reprehensible, un-English criminality. Despite the failure of the 1903 Commission to make any link between Jews and white slavery, the dirt stuck, and the Act's emphasis upon 'returning' criminals, particularly prostitutes, to the country of origin, clearly locates a key social problem of the day with an identifiable alien type. This racialization of the provision of vice did not mark the end of the link between Jews and white slavery (Bland 1995: 301; cited in Knepper 2007), and in 1912 the Criminal Law Amendment Act, known as the White Slave Traffic Bill, was passed after being promoted heavily by the Jewish Association for Protection of Girls and Women. As Knepper has noted, within 20 years the leaders of the Anglo-Jewish community, although acknowledging the past involvement of some Jews in white slavery, were claiming

---

[5] However, if a woman was to marry a British citizen this could be avoided, creating a vibrant trade in arranged marriages (Slater 2007: 56–9).

that, thanks to Jewish pressure groups and the 1912 Act, Jewish-run trafficking was now a thing of the past (Knepper 2007: 70).

The criminally immoral Jew, operating internationally and capable of making money from organizing the corruption of vulnerable women, was a moral outcast who would become part of a narrative contributing to the overall history of British organized criminality during this precursor period. While the term 'organized crime' was not used, the notion of a transgressive international trade infecting the wholesome skullduggery of the indigenous population is a pervasive theme that perfectly mirrors much of the evolution of organized crime in the US, including the political institutionalization of moral entrepreneurship. Perceiving Jewish immigration as a criminal problem connected to the vice trade was as functional to the Anglo-Jewish establishment as it was to British politicians, and although the subsequent controls were largely bureaucratic and had little immediate impact upon immigration, the precedent of using crime as a means of othering sections of the population, and the racialization of a social problem using the mystification and exaggeration of criminal activity, was established.

The transformation by the state of both protectionist drives and fears of moral contamination into ground-breaking immigration policy set a tone that has been maintained by periodic emphasis being placed upon the integral degradation of cosmopolitan urban settings. This tainted locale is typified by the toxic leisure habits of the settlers, a toxicity that is intensified by exaggerating its commercialization. This has laid the foundations for British organized crime policy, linking the trade in illegal leisure not with an evaluation of harm or damage to the social fabric, but by implying a contamination of indigenous purity whose degraded origins lie far away in a dangerous and unfathomable 'Otherstan'.[6]

Chinatown: Sex, Dope, and the Other

Then she drifted down to China Town—

And you all know where that is—

Where slitty-eyed Chinks take 40 winks

---

[6] Anti-Semitic conspiracies of this era stand close comparison with those that emerged as part of the post 9/11 anti-Muslim moral panic concerning the alleged Islamic colonization of Europe, and the development of 'Eurabia' (Carr 2006).

And she's known as Lime house Liz

And she lives on dope and tarry rope,

She'd never have started the racket

But one day she went on a charabanc ride

And 'One Lung' gave her a packet!

Limehouse Liz, a popular music-hall song
(cited in Witchard 2009)

The Chinatowns of Britain's port cities (Ng 1968), and in particular the tiny enclave that evolved in London's Limehouse which, by the end of the First World War, numbered less than 300, created a micro-economy based around the food, shelter, laundry, and recreational requirements of Chinese seaman who docked in London (Seed 2006). These latter requirements often included premises for gambling and opium smoking, and the opium den, with its focus upon luxuriant hedonism, had long proved a source of fascination and revulsion for the affluent intent upon exotic voyeurism (Kohn 1992: 18–19; Witchard 2009), but was generally regarded as largely non-problematic, often standing in contrast to the 'white squalor' of East London as an oasis of order (Bancroft 2009: 37).[7] Victorian Britain was willing to fight two wars in order to enforce opium trafficking (Hanes and Sanello 2003), while back in 'Blighty' the louche dilettantism of imperially formed self-indulgence ensured that, as long as the working classes refrained, opium smoking could be regarded as an issue of taste (Walton 2002), which did not warrant prohibition (Berridge and Edwards 1981).

In 1914, the House of Commons passed the Defence of the Realm Act—a catch-all 'ways and means' law that was utilized to impose a wide range of authoritarian measures, including restricting the opening times of licensed premises, which in turn created a booming illegal nightlife. The Act made the possession of both opium and cocaine illegal in the wake of growing fears concerning off-duty soldiers being plied with drugs (Berridge 1978), driving both the trade and its consumption underground.

---

[7] See James Greenwood's wonderful account of his visit to a Shadwell opium den and his initiation into opium smoking (Greenwood 1883).

While it had long been regarded as an acceptable vice, particularly by ex-colonialists and London's literary elite (Hayter 1968), in the wake of the jingoistic and anti-foreign sentiment instigated by the First World War, opium now became associated with illegal nightlife, and in particular the seduction and degradation of white women by non-whites (Kohn 1992: 27–8; Wade 1900: 306). The unique social and economic conditions that had emerged during the war had produced a confidence and self-assertedness amongst British women liberated by war work, newly visible in public spaces, stylish and independent, who were creating a stir that inevitably led to a patriarchal backlash (Kohn 1992: 45–56). In London, in particular, the chorus, ballet, and cabaret girl could enjoy a transgressive social life that featured new and essentially 'foreign' commodities, which until then had been the preserve of upper class men, and both opium from the East and cocaine originating from pharmaceutical factories in Germany became popular. The vulnerability of women to drugs and seductive orientalism became an ideal platform for the re-establishment of pre-war patriarchal values. 'The principal theme of the British discourse upon its Chinese communities in the first quarter of the twentieth century was the intrinsic evil of sexual contact between the races' (Kohn 1992: 57), echoing some of the terrors generated by images of Jewish sexuality discussed above; for both drugs and white slavery involved 'international traffic…controlled by a criminal conspiracy' (Kohn 1992: 32), and the moral panic regarding the Chinese 'clearly provided a prototype for the idea of international drug trafficking conspiracies' (Kohn 1992: 32).

The death of actress Billie Carleton in 1918 brought public attention to focus upon 'the far end of Bohemia', a hedonistic demi monde featuring 'neurotic men' and young women whose identities had been destabilized by inappropriate levels of liberty, alcohol, and drugs. A society fop and a Limehouse-based Scottish woman married to a Chinese man were convicted of possession and supplying opium at a party that Carleton had attended. Carleton's death was almost certainly due, at least partly, either to heroin, which was not at the time illegal, or a hypnotic that had been prescribed for a bout of influenza, yet it was Carleton's cocaine intake that was formally recognized as the cause of death (Kohn 1992: 85–104). The Carleton case was prosecuted under the wartime emergency auspices of the Defence of the Realm Act and set the scene for subsequent drug legislation. The moral panic that ensued sought scapegoats for the corruption of British women while their men-folk were suffering in the trenches. Popular fiction and cinema had for a number of years been busy developing a Chinatown genre which at its core presented the Chinese as embodying a capacity for 'sophisticated clandestine organization' (Kohn 1992: 19), featur-ing the evil oriental mastermind Fu Manchu (Rohmer 1998), a crass racial stereotype that became embodied in the form of real-life, evil, oriental folk-devil, businessman, and restaurateur Peter 'Brilliant' Chang, who became the focus of a media campaign that barely hid the revulsion it was stoking with regard to drugs and racial and sexual degeneration (Murphy 1993: 10–13).

Chang was a successful socialite, a denizen of London's semi-legal post-war nightclub scene, and an associate of club hostess Rachel Kempson, who died in 1922 from a cocaine overdose. Two of Chang's cooks were convicted of dealing cocaine, and the opi-um-related death in Cardiff of a Chinese man whose body was found with three unconscious white women added to an anti-Chinese frenzy (Kohn 1992: 144–7). Intense pressure was placed upon the foreign enclave of Limehouse, and arrests for smoking opium became common. When Chang opened a nightclub he was harassed by the police, and gave up the business after just six months. Although there was little evidence to suggest that Chang had supplied drugs to anyone other than his girlfriends, a convic-tion was secured, and he was deported in 1924 after serving 14 months in prison. Meanwhile, unemployment amongst ex-service-men led to racial unrest, and with distinct echoes of the anti-Semit-ic sentiments noted above, the Labour movement responded with demands for protectionism (Kohn 1992: 63–4).

The opium moral panic, and the Chang affair in particular, illus-trate how a particular merging of socio-economic forces can create a demand for action on behalf of the state. As with the Jews, moral degradation, manifested as an alien and particularly threatening form of sexuality, was presented in terms 'vectors of vice' (Kohn 1992: 63), a degenerate network with nodes that spread beyond British cultural jurisdictions, and requiring emergency measures in order to re-establish a sense of moral order based upon traditional notions of class and gender (Houlbrook 2007). Both the eastern European Jews and the Chinese were regarded as pollutants of pristine urban spaces whose indigenous population was managed by a combination of policing and the corralling of transgressive potential into the rigid strictures of the industrial process and their

associated institutions of assimilation. By the early twentieth century white slavery, prostitution, and drugs threatened the moral
order in a way that the habits, vices, routinized disorder and intra-
class violence of London's working-class communities were no
longer capable of doing.

French Lessons: Inter-war Soho

> Soho is the place for its area has the worse record for blood or
> violence and for darker forms of vice than any other in Great
> Britain…the scum of continental gutters (*John Bull*, 23 May
> 1936, cited in Slater 2007: 54)

During the years between the World Wars there was little evidence
of white slavery in Britain (Slater 2007: 66) although prostitution
remained an activity commonly associated with non-British protagonists (Slater 2007: 55), inspiring a sexual fascination grounded
in the exoticization of the other (Walkowitz 1992). Then, as now,
the male demand for commercial sex was regarded as largely
unproblematic (Farley et al 2009; Matthews 2008; Sanders 2008)
and the policing of prostitution was concerned with containment
via informal cooperation between the police and the pimps controlling prostitute women (Watts 1960). The French took over from
the Jews as the perceived main players in this 'non-English' activity,
and Soho, 'London's Latin Quarter', with an estimated three-
quarters of the prostitute workforce (Slater 2007: 60),[8] came to
represent a tainted cosmopolitan exotic (Walkowitz 1992: 65).
Soho flagged a physical and moral boundary which marked the
limits of the normative moral order, and as a consequence 'Soho's
cosmopolitan reputation as the habitus of foreigners and a den of
vice, combined with the convergence of London's sex trade within
its environs, led to increased public fears about these supposed
salacious and illicit parts of the city' (Slater 2007: 67).

The capital provided an ideal environment for entrepreneurs of
prostitution, and French, Maltese, and Italian pimps, along with
overseas sex workers, were increasingly targeted by the police
throughout the inter-war years (Slater 2007). They were visible and
suitable targets, and the occupational culture of policing assured a

---

[8] There are structural reasons why French prostitutes may have been attracted to
the London market (Slater 2007: 62).

ready supply of usual suspects, as quotas were met and zones of toleration established (Slater 2009). 'Exemplary prosecutions' against foreign prostitutes and their pimps were commonplace, with the 'un-English' nature of this activity to the forefront of the moral outrage, which, as Slater suggests, was influenced heavily not only by racial intolerance, but also by a series of panics related to imperial decline, female mobility, an inability to curb domestic prostitution, and the continuing influence of the Home Office's anti-alien policies (Slater 2007: 66–7).

Vice Lords? The Messina Brothers

> Not my kind of gangsters…sleazy imports (McDonald 2002: 285)

After the Second World War public attention focused even more intensely upon the role of foreigners in the provision of vice. Despite a lack of evidence, there was a general perception that prostitution had increased from the levels of the 1930s (Slater 2009), and post-war full employment and the introduction of the welfare state meant that 'economic causation no longer carried the same weight as an explanation for prostitution' (Slater 2009, 2010). Communities attempting to cast aside the stigma of visible signs of depression-era poverty campaigned to eliminate prostitution, while simultaneously expressing concerns regarding immigration (Smart 1981: 49–50). These concerns were reflected in police practices, which were affected by an increase in manpower and the 'payment of overtime…which paid officers up to 14/- for attending court the morning after an arrest' (Slater 2010: 354).[9] However, the policing of prostitution was concerned largely with containment (Emsley 1996: 75), and, like so many areas associated with vice in London, was enabled by routinized police corruption (Kelland 1986: 49).[10]

Yet again it was exoticism situated within an alien conspiracy that attracted attention, and in 1953 *People* journalist Duncan Webb, working under the protection of gangster Billy Hill, ran a

[9] During her 19-year period working as a prostitute in London, including 15 years spent working for the Messina brothers, Marthe Watts claimed to have accrued over 400 convictions for being a 'common prostitute' (Watts 1960: 11).

[10] Foreigners were also blamed for that other 'non-English' activity police corruption, particularly in relation to the preponderance of French- and Italian-owned nightclubs in Soho (Slater 2007: 65; Hobbs 1988: 43).

six-week exposé of the Messina brothers' involvement in post-war prostitution and marriage-of-convenience rackets (Webb 1953). Allegedly 'the most complicated and certainly the most powerfully organized gang of vice this nation has ever known' (Webb 1953: 149), the five Messina brothers 'controlled vice in London for a period of over ten years' (Read and Morton 1991: 136) and ran a 'vice empire' (Kelland 1986: 27). Although conveniently labelled as Maltese (Dench 1991: 69–70),[11] the Messinas were of mixed Egyptian, Sicilian, and Maltese descent, and had operated brothels in Sicily, Malta, Egypt, Morocco, and Spain (Webb 1953: 128–69), before turning their attention to London in the mid 1930s, and they were active throughout the profitable war years when 'Time was short, money was loose, morals were out' (Watts 1960: 169).

A violent dispute between the Messinas and another group of Maltese in 1947 led to demands in the House of Commons for the establishment of a commission to look into organized vice in London. When the Home Secretary, Chuter Ede, denied this request,[12] an MP claimed that the Messinas were making £500,000 a year from their business.[13] Although they were paying off the police (Watts 1960: 207) as well as extortionists such as Billy Hill and Jack Spot, Webb's investigations eventually led to Alfredo Messina receiving two years' imprisonment and a £500 fine, while the remaining four brothers fled to mainland Europe, and their profits were couriered across the channel (Watts 1960: 214–29). A series of prosecutions, deportations, and relocations followed over the next decade, and remnants of the Messinas' increasingly fragmented London interests continued into the late 1960s (Morton 1993: 194–203; Murphy 1993: 105–12).

The 'Despicable Brothers' received an astonishing amount of attention, much of which reiterated the general assumption of the brothers' dominance of vice in London. However, as Slater's careful research has shown, in what is a truism of illegal markets generally, 'no group "controlled" prostitution in London' (Slater 2009: 28), and the trade is best understood in terms of loosely connected indi-

---

[11]   For an important discussion of the association between Malta, the white slave trade, and prostitution during the inter-war years, see Knepper and Azzopardi (2011).

[12]   *Hansard*, Vol 439, 3 July 1947.

[13]   Watts estimated that she was personally responsible for making £150,000 for the Messinas.

viduals operating in small networks (Slater 2007: 57–9). Further, these 'emperors of a vice empire in the heart of London'[14] had, at the peak of their careers, only 20 women working for them (Slater 2009: 27). The Messinas' notoriety is clearly unconnected to the existence of an evil empire, an all-pervasive, transgressive network, or indeed to any actual criminal hegemony. They were exotic and photogenic, prospering during the career of a publicity-hungry crusading journalist at a period in British history when, in a repeat of the racism that singled out the degenerate threat of alien sexuality in the aftermath of the First World War, traditional conservative forces were trying to reassert themselves. In this period of post-war austerity, the public were titillated and appalled by Webb's exposure of the Messinas, which 'had established a clear link in the public mind between white slave trading and Maltese ethnicity' (Dench 1991: 69). As in the USA, moral entrepreneurs laid the ground for a panic featuring the perverse sexual drives and allures of foreigners who threatened the white indigenous-gendered order (Woodiwiss 1988; Woodiwiss and Hobbs 2009)—an order that had been disrupted by the violence and exigencies of war.

In the post-Second World War years, vice became directly associated with 'Cypriots, Maltese and coloured British subjects' (Scott 1954: 66; cited in Gilroy 1987: 80), and with the demise of the Messinas, other entrepreneurs of vice, a number of whom were Maltese,[15] prospered in connection with Bernie Silver, a Jewish ex-paratrooper (Kelland 1986: 112–16). In his autobiography, Commander Bert ('The Old Grey Fox') Wickstead, in a blatant borrowing of American crime hyperbole, christened this group 'The Syndicate, the multi-million pound Mafia-style vice organization which had ruled Soho for eighteen years' (Wickstead 1985: 114).[16] Wickstead, who is comfortable throughout his book to use the term 'organized crime', eventually secured the convictions of a number of men for conspiracy to live on immoral earnings, and most of the main players, including Bernie Silver, received sentences of up to six years (Wickstead 1985: 114–50). Before its apparent demise, the

[14] *The People*, 3 September 1950.

[15] Maltese also featured in prosecutions connected with prostitution away from the seedy glamour of the West End of London (Dench 1991: 70–4).

[16] Read provides an alternative and somewhat more nuanced description of this 'syndicate', in the form of a 'co-operative, running clubs and near beer and clip joints' (Read and Morton 1991: 119).

Silver/Maltese group had segued effortlessly into pornography via 'businessmen' such as James Humphreys (Kelland 1986: 160–217), and although it can only be conjecture, I suggest that especially after the Street Offences Act 1960 took prostitution off the streets and into premises, the real money made by these 'emperors of vice' and 'vice kings' was from investments made in the West End property market.[17] Foreigners involved in the vice trade were in the minority (Slater 2009: 28), and the most enduring criminal firm during this era was the Metropolitan Police, whose greed contributed to making the sexual exploitation of women in the West End of London such a prosperous business (Cox et al 1977: 140–210; Hobbs 1988: 62–83).

Conclusion: An Exclusionary Logic

In a mid-1950s article on the cannabis trade, *The Sunday Graphic* reported that:

Detectives on this assignment are agreed that never have they had experience of a crime so vicious, so ruthless, so unpitying and so well organised…The victims are teenage British girls and to a lesser extent teenage British youths. The racketeers are 90 percent coloured men from the West Indies and the West Coast of Africa.

The reporter then quoted from a girl called Jesse to impress upon the readers the real danger of black/white, drug-induced dance floor intimacy in West End clubs: 'The days will come when this country will be all mixtures if we don't watch out' (Tyler 1985: 6; cited in Woodiwiss and Hobbs 2009: 118).

The association of alien forms of crime and hedonism (Gilroy 1987: 101) invoked the threat of racial, sexual, and cultural contamination, and the response of the state—particularly in the form of immigration and anti-drug legislation—racialized the sex and drug trades by implicating foreign forces at work, and provided precedents for a problem yet to receive the potent label of 'organized crime'. Amongst the chaotic people-trafficking, drug dealing,

---

[17] For example, sex impresario and pornographer Paul Raymond, who died in 2008, appeared annually in *The Sunday Times* Rich List, and his property empire, which in 2007 owned 60 of Soho's 87 acres, was thought to be worth some £650 million (Willets 2010). See also 'Paul Raymond: Self-styled "King of Soho" who built a successful business empire from property and pornography', Obituary of Paul Raymond, *Independent*, 5 March 2008.

cash for coupling, and pornography of the last century, the enduring names who are presented as being inextricably linked to vice-related activity are foreign (Finmore 1951; Morton 1993: 185–228; Sharpe 1938; Murphy 1993: 105–12; Read and Morton 1991: 117–29; Campbell 1994: 177–95). White-slaving Jews, opium-smoking, dope-dealing Chinamen, black drug-dealing pimps, and sleazy Mediterranean pimps and ponces have, regardless of their actual competence, power, potency, or criminogenic significance,[18] combined to create an anti-alien discourse that links foreigners to degeneration (Cesarani 1993: 27). As the century progressed, predatory sexuality emerged as a primary threat, and specific forms of criminality were increasingly presented as emblematic expressions of culture (Gilroy 1987: 109), enabling racist interpretations of cosmopolitan cultural forms to dominate British understanding of transgressive collaborations.

The targeting of newly arrived migrants as a grave threat to Britain's moral order, and the construction of legislative tools ensuring the exclusion of morally degenerate foreigners, pre-empted the use of the term 'organized crime' and its accompanying institutionalization. The state, particularly when in flux, found suitable enemies amongst poor, vulnerable populations seeking refuge and respite from religious and racial persecution, war, poverty, and economic chaos. Their transgressions were subject to exaggeration and elaboration, and their difference magnified. Further, as we can see from this discussion of the precursors of British organized crime, the 'boundary creating processes and the social construction of threat' (Tsoukala 2008: 139) have a lineage somewhat older than the National Criminal Intelligence Service, which, although an important marker as an institutional recognition of 'the tendencies leading Europe to submit to transatlantic powers' (Bourdieu 2003: 48), was the extension of an exclusionary logic with origins established in previous times of crisis, when the world seemed to spin a little too fast, and the order of things threatened to transmute into a fearful miasma of moral degradation.

---

[18] A nice inversion of these racist assertions can be found in the common habit of those relatively low-level villains who 'manipulate ethnic reputations to protect, justify, or promote themselves' (Bovenkerk et al 2003: 24) by exaggerating their connections to one of the alien organized crime 'brands'.

4

Mutant Proletarians: Class and Territoriality

They were not the smartest kids in the neighbourhood. They were not born the richest. They weren't even the toughest. In fact they lacked almost all the necessary talents that might have helped them satisfy the appetites of their dreams, except one—their talent for violence (Pileggi 1987: 42–3)

Marquee Criminals

As we can see from Chapters 1 and 2, xenophobic anxiety informed the evolution of the organized crime threat, and much of the response to this threat is an attempt to staunch the flow of 'matter out of place' (Douglas 1966: 36) by the suppression and exclusion of the 'other'. However, before the term 'organized crime' became fully operational, these foreign coalitions sat alongside the largely home-grown concept of 'the underworld', a construct commonly used to describe violent parochial networks of working class men active across a range of illegal markets. This chapter will look at the emergence of some of the iconic names of London's underworld who retrospectively became associated with twentieth-century organized crime in London, the authenticity of some of the claims made regarding these marquee names of British crime, and the veracity of their enduring criminogenic legacy.

What is normally referred to as 'the underworld' relates to the West End of London, Soho, during the late 1930s to the early 1970s, and to extortion and the economic relations of prostitution, gaming, and illegal drinking clubs. It is here that groups from deprived urban industrial neighbourhoods created a narrative featuring chaotic, fractious networks where personal, territorial, and family conflicts were as likely to fester and burst internally as amongst strangers, enemies, or competitors.[1]

Racing Certainties: The Sabinis

> Giovanni's world was a confusion of plots and counter-plots, his chief preoccupation was with vague hosts of 'enemies' whose dark schemes must be frustrated by schemes still darker, and his principle ambition was to make an infernal machine (Benney, 1936: 53)

The slippery concept of 'organization' appears to gain some credibility when applied to the racecourse gangs who extorted the horse racing betting industry, and were major features of British life in the first half of the twentieth century (Chinn 1991: 197–200). In the years after the First World War there was a boom in horse racing (Huggins 2003; Divall 1929: 185–99), and with street gambling illegal, many who wished to gamble were drawn to the opportunities for lawful betting at racecourses. However, groups of men with violent reputations rented the betting pitches at extortionate prices, and monopolized the market in chalk, stools, and other paraphernalia of on-course bookmaking (Greene 1943; Lucas 1969: 19–27; Samuel 1981: 175–86; Bean 1981; Greeno 1960: 17). The more powerful and competent of these local coalitions of violent men are significant for their willingness to pit local reputations within a national arena, and the dominant racecourse gang during the early part of the century had emerged from Birmingham, the 'Brummagems', led by Billy Kimber, a bookmaker (Samuel 1981: 182–3). Kimber, a south Londoner who had moved to Birmingham as a deserter during the First World War, was a long-time racetrack operator who, in collaboration with Charles 'Wag' McDonald, combined his Birmingham-based men with a large and powerful group from the Elephant and Castle in South London, and established extortionate control over the major southern England racecourses (see Emsley 2005: 34–5). However, it was their key

---

[1] This iconic era had been neglected and half forgotten until in 1994 the BBC televised an excellent series, *The Underworld*, which, along with the equally excellent accompanying book by Duncan Campbell (1994), established the time line of this transgressive trajectory, and most importantly reintroduced to a surprisingly voracious public the entire cast of London-based blaggers, thugs, pimps, and dealers in all their wide-lapelled, impudent majesty.

competitors, the Sabini family from Clerkenwell, who eventually emerged during the inter-war period as the most notable of the racecourse gangs.

In the 1880s mass migration, as a result of an agrarian crisis, led to Clerkenwell becoming the centre of the Italian community in London, and its largely male population were employed in occupations that often involved a degree of transience, such as street entertainment, organ-grinding, and costermongering (Stedman-Jones 1971: 61–2). The Italians also dominated a number of precision trades such as clock-making (Sponza 1988: 22), as well as exploiting British workers' dislike of low-paid, heavy, hot work by populating the ranks of pavoirs, asphalters, and road workers who helped configure the capital (Sponza 1988: 88–90). Immigrant communities are often marginalized from hostile host cultures and institutions, and fall back upon familiar practices and cultural comfort blankets creating 'well-defined Little Italies, and within these colonies they tended to congregate with others from the same province and even the same village' (Ianni and Ianni 1972: 44; Whyte 1943: xviii; Zorbaugh 1929: 152). Migrants transpose key cultural elements that are typical of the country of origin, and Italian migrants brought with them a suspicion of official institutions, and in particular a lack of trust in the police (see Landesco 1968: 108–109) that had been forged in feudal poverty, and replicated in the cultural and economic maelstrom of working-class London.

The 1905 Alien Act required potential immigrants to be vouched for by a current UK resident who could provide lodgings and a job, which reinforced chain migration between the settled Italian community and their villages of origin. Along with the importation of Italian food, this created infrastructures that maintained village connections, and supported a desire for self-proficiency that was vital in providing a way out of the deprived and disease-ridden area of London that had once been used as a model for the thieves' den in *Oliver Twist* (Beames 1852: 44–68).[2] British society was becoming more affluent, and the Edwardian fashion for eating out assisted Italian integration into the economic mainstream (Sponza 1988: 94–115), as Italian ice-cream making and selling along with provision-dealing and catering forged a way into the previously French-dominated district of Soho. However, integration was not

---

[2] Field Lane, where Dickens situated Fagin's den, was demolished in slum clearance in the mid-19th century.

achieved without considerable struggle, and both a reliance upon kinship and a distrust of authority continued to mark the Italian experience (Sponza 1988: 247).

Indigenous concerns with the deviance of the Italian community were considerable, particularly in relation to the perceived immorality of the immigrants' leisure pursuits. The Italians were regarded as being prone to use knives (Sponza 1988: 234, 242; Shore 2012: 4), a tendency that was central to a 'disorderly character' which embraced 'perversions and vice' (Sponza 1988: 235). Further, as many of the migrants were sojourners seeking to make money before returning to Italy, Clerkenwell took on a somewhat temporary character where single men, off-duty waiters and cooks, along with artisans, labourers, costermongers, and street entertainers, gathered in drinking and gambling clubs amenable to leisure hours that did not conform with those of the corralled and settled sections of the host community. A number of these clubs relocated to Soho and were frequented by 'low class Italians, immoral women, bullies and thieves, beer and wine were served, cards and dominoes played for money' (Sponza 1988: 256). The Italian clubs became vital props in a culture largely bereft of permanent foundations based on long-term family structures (Sponza 1988: 248), and provided for the needs of migrant workers who were self-contained, increasingly employed in Italian businesses, and locked firmly into the ever-expanding London consumer market. This was a community of hard endeavour, whose deeply rooted individualistic character was ideally suited to the disrespectful entrepreneurial bedrock laid down by the indigenous working class of London (Linebaugh 1993: 122–3). It was also an insular yet fragmented community with little formal internal cohesion, and where a 'rough and individual-self justice' (Sponza 1988: 251) thrived.

Entrepreneurship and rough justice suited the Sabini family, who emerged from the Italian clubs of Clerkenwell. Led by Darby Sabini, a man with a background in boxing and what has become known as 'door security', the Sabinis established themselves as core defenders, both of the territory of Little Italy and of the integrity of the 'Italian' culture of Clerkenwell. For instance, in 1920 Darby Sabini administered a beating to Elephant and Castle stalwart Thomas Benneworth, allegedly due to the latter's assault on an Italian woman, and this in turn led to a revenge attack by the south Londoners which merely cemented the reputation of Darby Sabini as a heroic protector of Little Italy (McDonald 2000: 80). The racecourses offered the richest prize to any group who could transcend the restricted opportunities offered by the working-class territory that forged their reputation, and to enable this transcendence the Sabinis first fought, and then formed alliances with, Jewish bookmakers and criminals such as 'the Jewish Al Capone' Edward Emmanuel, Alf Solomon, Bobby Levy, and Bobby Nark (Samuel 1981: 316–17; Greeno 1960: 166). As Arthur Harding noted, 'all the Jewish terrors worked with the Italian mob on the racecourse' (Samuel 1981: 133) in challenging the Birmingham/Elephant and Castle alliance. However, although Kimber resisted (Samuel 1981: 183; Chinn 1991: 201), as Billy Hill ruefully notes, 'Somehow the Sabinis always seemed to win' (Hill 1955: 3).

Nonetheless, the Sabinis never achieved the kind of total hegemony portrayed by Hollywood renditions of organized crime, and violent opposition was a constant reality. In 1922 the Sabinis faced challenges from within Clerkenwell as well as from Hoxton, Birmingham, and south London. The Cortesi brothers formed a breakaway group that was crucially backed by a number of Jewish bookmakers, and in November 1922 the Cortesis took over the Sabini operation at Sandown Park Racecourse. Consequently, George Cortesi was attacked and a number of members of the Sabini firm were convicted of attempted murder; Harry Sabini was shot by the Cortesis at the Fratellanza Club in Clerkenwell, resulting in prison sentences for Enrico and Augustus Cortesi (McDonald 2000: 77–8; Fraser 1994: 9).

Effectively this was the end of the Cortesis, but beatings, shootings, and a number of murders marked the era as 'The Sabinis and their rivals fought for supremacy on street corners, on trains, on the roads, and at the race-courses' (Morton 1992: 16). In April 1922 there were four racetrack-related stabbings and a beating in Soho, before the Sabinis were charged with a shooting in Camden Town, although the complainants later failed to identify their assailants (Morton 1992: 16). A youth connected to the Sabinis was then stabbed to death in a central London club, and another thrown on a fire (Morton 1992: 16), as Sabini/Brumagen violence was reported at Doncaster, Yarmouth, and Cardiff. Kimber was shot after a meeting at the Sabinis' home that had been arranged in order to negotiate a truce (Morton 1992: 15).

By taking control of the Racecourse Bookmakers and Backers Protection Association, the Sabinis and their allies gained employment as racecourse stewards, and were able to use the Association and the power and access it afforded as a platform against Kimber. When the Sabini firm was sacked by the Association in 1922, Sabini and Kimber came to an agreement to split England's racecourses; Kimber left the south of England tracks to the Sabinis, while he continued to prosper in the Midlands and the north of England (Chinn 1991: 202). In 1925 the Home Secretary, largely in response to exaggerated press coverage (Shore 2012), declared 'War on the Race-gangs' (Chinn 1991: 203; Morton 2000: 125) and joint action by the Flying Squad and the Jockey Club, combined with the order imposed by the Sabini/Kimber monopolies, reduced racecourse violence (Chinn 1991: 202–3). Meanwhile, the reputations of the Sabinis, which had been further enhanced by their role in resisting the extortionate demands of their long-time rivals in Hoxton and Hackney, opened the way into the West End, and 'Bottle parties, clubs, public houses, cafes, restaurants, even ordinary shops had to pay protection money to the Sabini extortionists' (Hill 1955: 5; see also Chinn 1991: 202). Although profits from racetrack extortion were enormous (for instance, Arthur Harding claimed that the Sabinis would glean £15,000–£20,000 on Derby day (Samuel 1981: 184)[3]), by the mid 1930s there were a number of warning signs for the Sabinis. Some Sabini firm members with strong allegiances to Italy were influenced by the rise of fascism in their homeland, and were expressing unease at working with Jews. In turn, the alliance with Edward Emmanuel had ended a number of years earlier, and influential Jewish collaborators such as Alf Solomons were showing independent tendencies (Samuel 1981: 204–5).

While generally the scope for racecourse extortion had been radically reduced by police action and the regulatory regime of the Bookmakers and Backers Protection Association, a handful of courses were difficult to enclose and remained vulnerable. In 1936 an infamous battle between 50 armed men at Lewes Racecourse was sparked by a member of the White family from King's Cross

[3] The likelihood is that Harding's career situated him merely at the fringes of groups such as the Sabinis. Raphael Samuel's life history of Arthur Harding, although acquiring iconic status, needs to be read with certain reservations. Harding was active in territorial violence and a range of criminal activities, served time in borstal, and contributed to the Royal Commission in 1908. However, there is no evidence of Harding being a prominent criminal during the inter-war years, and there is nothing to link him to the Sabinis, which suggests that he would be unlikely to possess knowledge such as detail relating to Sabini finances (thanks to Heather Shore).

having his throat cut at London's Liverpool Street Station. The Whites were now pressing for independence from the Sabinis with whom they had been allies for many years, and the Lewes attack by a coalition from King's Cross, Hoxton, and Hackney was led by Jimmy Spinks,[4] a notorious street-fighter who drank, fought, and avoided work, while occasionally acknowledging ancient territorial alliances. However, the Sabinis had tipped off the Flying Squad, and although the recently independent Alf Solomons and his clerk were injured in the subsequent affray (Greeno 1960), 16 of the combatants received sentences totalling 43 years (Thomas 2003: 3–4). In the aftermath of the Lewes attack, the Whites reached an accommodation that their own territory around King's Cross would be out of bounds to the Italians (Fraser 1994: 46), and at the start of the Second World War the White family took over much of the racetrack business, which was severely limited by wartime restrictions (Thomas 2003: 5).

Although by the outbreak of war Darby Sabini was a semi-retired resident of Brighton, the Sabinis, under the direct control of Darby's younger brother, Harry, should still have been ideally situated to exploit the unprecedented criminogenic possibilities that sprang up during the war years. However, many of the key players whose surnames ended with a vowel were interred as enemy allies on the outbreak of war (Sponza 1993), and the Sabinis never fully recovered their power. In 1940 Darby Sabini was arrested at Hove dog track and subsequently interned under Defence Regulation 18B. His file in the National Archive contains material from MI5 as well as the police, and he is described as a 'dangerous gangster and racketeer of the worst type', with fascist sympathies, who was 'liable to lead internal insurrections against this country' at the behest of an occupying power'.[5] He was released, but in 1943 was sentenced to two years' hard labour for receiving stolen goods (Fraser 1998: 1). It is interesting that one of the Sabini police files contains a somewhat mitigating report from the Chief Constable of Brighton claiming that Darby Sabini had not been a criminal force for 20 years (HO 45/23691). However, the Chief Constable's letter is more likely to reflect the perception that 'the Sabinis ingratiated

---

[4] In addition to being idolized by the Kray twins (Pearson 1973), Spinks was bare-knuckle celebrity Lenny Mclean's adored uncle (Mclean 1998).

[5] Darby Sabini's only son Harry had joined the Royal Air Force, and was killed in action in Egypt, aged 21.

themselves with the law so much that they more or less had things
their own way' (Hill 1955: 4), a point supported by Arthur Harding, who stressed that it was the Sabinis' corrupt relationship with
the police that had defeated the Brummagens (Samuel 1981: 183).

Despite making some inroads into the West End, the Whites faced
fierce competition from groups of young men from every corner of
the capital (Hill 1955: 6–7) and the beating that Alf White received
from a Stoke Newington firm at Harringay dog track in 1939 hardly suggests the emergence of an all-powerful crime supremo (Murphy 1993: 34). Further, the Whites' collaboration with the remnants
of the Sabini firm and a number of the young emergent Italians
from Clerkenwell was hampered by the anti-Semitism of some of
the Italians. This culminated in 1941 with a clash between the
'Yidisher Gang', who were aligned with the Whites, and a group of
Italians, which resulted in the murder of 'Little Hubby' Distleman,
and the conviction and death by hanging of Antonio Mancini
(Morton 1992: 28–9).

Although racecourse-related violence was regarded as something
essentially 'unEnglish' and potentially dangerous (Shore 2012:
3–4), in response to 'the Italian mob' the police 'did not automati-
cally draw on tropes of "otherness" and "foreignness"' (Shore
2012: 24), and resorted neither to a US-style alien conspiracy theory nor to its accompanying moral panic. Territorial alliances were
always more important to the Sabinis than their part-Italian heritage, for they were born in the capital and they neither visited the
homeland nor spoke Italian (Humphreys 1946: 147–8). Although
they allegedly imported violent Sicilian labour (Samuel 1981: 183),
the Sabinis were distinctly a product of working-class London. The
Sabinis and most of their cohorts came from a very specific part of
Clerkenwell in Saffron Hill, which, by the start of the twentieth
century, was mainly home to workshops and warehouses, and was
in the process of demolition (White 2001: 108). The significance of
the 'Italian firm' is that of a powerful criminal group who transcended their immediate neighbourhood and briefly succeeded in
dominating a wide territory that included most major English racecourses, as well as the honey pot of the West End of London. As
Chinn has noted, 'There was no other gang in Britain that could
compare with that of the Italians for their cohesion organization
and longevity' (1991: 207), and as a consequence Darby Sabini was
'the nearest Britain got to an organising gangster' (Pearson 1973:
30), whose bread and butter was the 'dollar in the pound' extorted

from bookmakers (Ward 1974: 21).[6] However, the Sabinis failed to establish any organizational longevity, and as a step on the 'queer ladder of mobility' (Bell 1953), crime did not prove significant for the Italian community of Clerkenwell, who 'filled tiny gaps in the London labour market' (White 2008: 147) and whose penetration of the West End came about via catering rather than extortion: the source of their prosperity was the ice-cream cone, pasta, and hard work, rather than the cut-throat razor.

Thieves' Paradise: London in Wartime

> The War organised criminals. Before the war thieving was safes, jewellery, furs. Now a whole new world opened up. There was so much money and stuff about—cigarettes, sugar, clothes, petrol coupons, clothing coupons, anything. It was a thieves' paradise (Fraser 1994: 18)

The isolation of Britain during the early years of the Second World War led to shortages in a wide range of products, from building materials to food and clothing (Thomas 2003: 160–82; Smithies 1982). This scarcity lasted for some commodities well into the 1950s and created a black market that touched even the most law-abiding citizen (Thomas 2003: 353–76).[7] As Frank Fraser explained, 'now everyone was crooked. Mums, they'd want to buy extra eggs for their children and a bit of extra meat...Everyone was involved. It was wonderful' (Fraser 1994: 18). Rationing led to widespread abuse by otherwise law-abiding citizens, and the combination of shortages, the blackout, and a fragmented civilian population created an environment where theft and the trade in stolen goods was normalized. 'It was a wonderful time to be a thief. I will never forgive that Hitler for surrendering when he did.'[8]

---

[6] Shore suggests that the dominance of the Sabinis began to fade as early as 1926 when, as a result of a 1924 Sunday newspaper article profiling him, Darby Sabini sued for libel, failed to turn up for court, and was ordered to pay costs of £775, the 2009 equivalent of approximately £35,000. This bankrupted 'Britain's Godfather' (Hart 1993), who was reputed to be earning £20,000 to £30,000 per year (Shore 2012: 22; Murphy 1993: 34; Hart 1993: 201).

[7] By 1945 there had been more than 114,000 prosecutions for black market activities, including 'legitimate' businessmen who regarded the government as fair game for a range of frauds (Thomas 2003).

[8] Frank Fraser interview, May 1995.

Territorially based criminals had for generations regarded the centre of London as a prize, and with the onset of the Second World War, individuals with reputations acquired via violent exploits as racetrack enforcers (Divall 1929; Bean 1981; Greeno 1960; Samuel 1981; Hart 1993) or as thieves and extortionists (Hill 1955) began to ease into this booming marketplace. As the war progressed Britain played host to thousands of young men far from home preparing for D-Day, many of whom descended upon the capital in search of recreation. Consequently, as during the First World War, the alcohol licensing laws of the day created a demand for illegal drinking venues, and prostitution thrived (Watts 1960) as allied servicemen were attracted to Soho and its environs: 'They were loaded with dough...They flung it about the West End like ticker-tape paper on Broadway' (Hill 1955: 117). Crime amongst servicemen also thrived, and an estimated 20,000 deserters who were unable to gain legal access to ration books and identity cards were forced to commit crime to survive (Mannheim 1955: 113–14).

Going up West

> Some of them are broken nosed and razor-slashed. All have police records (Robert Fabian 1954: 89)

Although embedded acquisitive criminality was not limited to London (Janson 1959; Bean 1981), it was the excesses of the capital's criminals that were to provide the post-war focus for the nation's concerns about crime. Much of this concern was couched in a concern with the Americanization of British society, and as the 1940s gave way to a 1950s of full employment and a new era of working class prosperity (Hoggart 1957), the West End of London became the focus of a number of high-profile, violent disputes (Janson 1959; Hill 1955; Murphy 1993: 121–31). As we can see from the discussion of the Messinas in Chapter 3, the West End of London was synonymous with vice, and well-tailored extortionists with a prison pallor policed the market at a price. During the immediate post-war era they were joined by some powerful criminal collaborations who emerged in response to a new expanded marketplace that had been shaped by a regime of shortages and strict rationing that lasted until the early 1950s, and their broad-shouldered presence, and blatant borrowing from the stylistic templates of a Hollywood central casting agency, moulded an image of organized criminality to which both villains and the general public enthusiastically invested their imaginations.

The convergence of thieves and gangsters upon the West End of London both during and after the Second World War contrived to create criminal collaborations that have remained influential to this day (Pearson 1973: 84–99; Fraser 1994). Two men in particular were of note: Billy Hill from Camden Town via Seven Dials, a thief who, by the end of the war, already had 20 years' penal servitude to his name, and Jack 'Spot' Comer, a Jewish street fighter and extortionist from Mile End, who had served an apprenticeship with legendary bookmaker Moshe Cohen. Hill and Comer combined to take on the Whites in what was seen by some as a way of ending the dominance of the racecourse gangs, for although their heyday was in the past, there was still money to be made from a trade that remained studded with violent practitioners. While bookmakers on official pitches were bound by Jockey Club rules, the 'freeground' adjacent to the main course still offered ripe pickings. However, Hill in particular was more concerned with the incursion of the racetrack gangs into Soho, as he explained in language more fitting to a High Court judge: 'The generations of repression, extortion and blackmail were remembered vividly by the sons of men who had spent years in gaol because of the race gangs. At last they saw a chance to revenge themselves for their fathers and uncles and grandfathers. I saw at last a chance to clean up the West End' (Hill 1955: 10. See Pearson 2001: 61–5).

Billy Hill was a knife- and open-razor-wielding thief (Hill 1955: 27–8) whose reputation had been forged during the Second World War when he established an extraordinary network of thieves and receivers from a base in a barn in Hertfordshire. Spot, on the contrary, was something of a throwback to the street-fighting thuggery of the nineteenth century, and worked his way up from providing 'protection' for Jewish shopkeepers and stallholders, to burglary and fairground scams, before working for Moshe Cohen. However, the key to Spot's reputation lies in his claim to have valiantly attacked and beaten Oswald Mosley's bodyguard at the Battle of Cable Street in 1935 (Janson 1959). Despite no evidence for this heroism (Morton 2000: 162–77), Spot traded on this attack for the rest of his life, and on his discharge from the Army in 1943, his heroic status enabled him to operate in and around the Jewish communities of a number of northern provincial cities before returning to London in 1947 and clashing with the Whites in a West End club

(Fraser 1994: 47). The Whites' patriarch, Alf, was aging, and his sons did not relish taking on either Hill, who despised the race-course gangs, or Spot, who had retained control over the freeground at Ascot Racecourse before moving in to Soho. The Whites faded from the scene, and the armies and vast arsenals that both Hill (1955: 10–14) and Comer (Janson 1959) claimed to have assembled were disbanded and discarded.

Hill had a talent for planning and organizing project crime (Hill 1955: 162–8), developed interests in gaming clubs and extortion, and invested in legitimate business opportunities. 'I had a fancy goods business and several restaurants, and I went into demolition in a big way. Bought up buildings where they stood. At one time I owned the old Earl's Court Exhibition Building, and the Roth-schild Mansion just along from Apsley House' (Pearson 2001: 64). Spot, however, who was particularly at home on the racetracks, which were cleaning up their act in preparation for the legalization of the betting industry, found club life problematic and remained rooted to old practices and arcane enmities, and was rapidly losing power and influence.[9]

Hill had been particularly astute in absorbing the talents of asso-ciates of the Italian firm whose careers had been delayed by intern-ment, war service, and the emergence of the Whites. 'Italian' Albert Dimes (Alberto Dimeno) was an associate of the Sabinis, and apart from his part in the murder of Harry Distelman (see p 65), was reputed also to have killed a man in a street fight in 1939 (Fraser 1994: 81). With two killings and some first-class criminal connec-tions on his CV, including that of being Hill's bodyguard, Dimes was a vital link with a group of Italian bookmakers who had sided with Hill against Spot. In a 1955 knife fight between Spot and Dimes, dubbed the 'Battle of Frith Street', both men were seriously injured, and although after a bizarre court case both were acquitted (Murphy 1993: 122–31), the following year Spot was attacked by a number of Hill associates including Frank Fraser and Bobbie Warren, resulting in the ex-black-shirt basher needing 78 stitches and a blood transfusion. Fraser and Warren received seven years each for the assault (Fraser 1994: 92–5), and while Spot faded into

[9] Frank Fraser insists that this was due to the emerging knowledge that Spot had been an informant since the late 1930s (Fraser 1994: 81). Spot was also jealous of Hill's claim to be 'Boss of Britain's Underworld' and broke the arm of Duncan Webb, Hill's biographer.

obscurity, Hill was assured a peaceful retirement in Spain by mentoring his successors.

The Low Spark of High-heeled Boys: The Krays

> Violence was natural to them. It fuelled them…It was routine. A familiar exercise. Their eagerness to attack and the fact that people were aware of their strutting brutality were the key to their power (Pileggi 1987: 43)

The Kray twins emerged during this post-war era, and by the 1960s had established a powerful, enduring, and heavily stylized narrative suggesting a potency that is disproportionate to either their economic success or the power they wielded. Their iconic status is only partly connected to the thriving mini-publishing industry that is based upon their lives, crimes, and imprisonment (Pearson 2001), and it was the Krays' ability to mix elements of the post-war spiv, teenage teddy boy, 1930s Hollywood gangster,[10] and ferocious unpredictable violence into a package bonded by traditional working-class community and solidarity, that created a curious legacy for two murdering twins whose 'legendary' empire failed to extend much beyond their own backyards (Hobbs 1988). However, in an era that has seen British society fragmented, and traditional, pragmatic working-class communities decimated, the well-tailored, impudently upwardly mobile, white organized crime that the Kray twins represent has proved to be a nostalgic comfort blanket for the public, the media, and the police. The imagery of the post-war gangster as a predominant form of British organized crime, firmly ensconced in a defined working-class neighbourhood and extorting elements of big city vice, is crucial to this imagery, and the Kray twins came to embody this emphasis via a peculiar, but enduring focus upon style rather than economic power.

---

[10] In particular, the twins slavishly mimicked the style and sartorial swagger of the classic stable of screen gangsters: Edward G Robinson, James Cagney, Humphrey Bogart, and particularly George Raft (Pearson 1973: 71; Read and Morton 1991: 92–3). In a 1960s' article for the *Sunday Times*, Francis Wyndham wrote that 'To be with the Twins is to enter the atmosphere (laconic, lavish, dangerous) of an early Bogart movie' (Pearson 2001: 109). Pearson also reports that 'when Ron (Kray) started shaving as a teenager he copied his Mafia hero Al Capone, and like a true Italian gangster had the local Italian Barber come each morning to the house to shave him' (Pearson 2010: 288).

Reg and Ron Kray grew up in the East End of London amongst a vibrant squalor that had changed little since Dickens' day (Hobbs 1988). The family's cultural inheritance prized toughness, individuality, and a heavily localized mutant entrepreneurship, and boxing and various forms of self-employment were crucial props in the upbringing of these two young men growing up amongst poverty and the violence and social dislocation of the Second World War. Their father, Charles, worked door-to-door as a second-hand trader in clothes and jewellery, and the early years of the twins and older brother Charlie were marked by the relative affluence that the family enjoyed as a result of their father's entrepreneurial skills (Pearson 1973: 16–18, 27–8).

However, on the commencement of the Second World War, Charles declined to join the hostilities and went 'on the trot' for the duration, leaving the task of bringing up the twins to their mother, Violet, who created in their home in Vallance Road, Bethnal Green a fiercely protected safe haven from a hostile world that was always threatening to impose itself upon the self-contained, largely self-policed area that Jack London once christened 'the awful east'. The Kray brothers were brought up in a family of fiercely independent men, and powerful resourceful women. For, while Charles senior was away from home 'on the knocker', their mother Violet and her sisters May and Rose became important influences upon all three brothers, and in particular upon the twins (Pearson 1973: 34–5). During the war, Violet and her sons were evacuated from the East End, which was sandwiched in between the two prime targets of the docks and the City of London, and rural Suffolk proved a temporary refuge from the Blitz, before invasion scares drove the family back to bomb-scarred Bethnal Green (Pearson 1973: 30).

Violence was always a lure in an area that was home to legendary neighbourhood hard men and fighters such as Jimmy Spinks, Dodger Mullins, and the brothers' grandfathers, Cannonball Lee and Jimmy Kray, and boxing was an obvious outlet for the twins who followed their talented older brother into the ring. However, their reputations were derived from the sheer viciousness and ferocity they displayed as street fighters, which ensured that their potential would eventually come to the notice of powerful forces beyond the confines of the East End's bomb sites, street markets, and boxing clubs. By the time they became professional boxers at the age of 17, Reg and Ron Kray had already taken on and beaten the criminal justice system at the Old Bailey when serious assault charges against them were dropped (Pearson 1973: 38–9), and although both twins fought briefly as lightweights, with Reg showing some natural ability (Kray and Sykes 1977: 66–71), only Charlie was to emerge as a contender. However, the boxing careers of both twins were effectively ended after Ron assaulted a young police constable, and the PC's colleagues gained revenge in the traditional manner, leaving Ron bloodied in a cell. Reg immediately sought out the same police officer and punched him in the face, and following the intervention of a local priest the twins were given probation (Pearson 1973: 39–40).

National Service beckoned, but a penchant for direct confrontation, and total disregard for military authority, ensured that the twins' brief military career ended in the guardhouse after just 15 months, most of which was spent AWOL (Kray and Kray 1988: 20–6). Nothing was to get in the way of the locally based entrepreneurship that had evolved from the territorial disputes of their adolescence, and by the age of 20, the Kray twins had taken over a billiard hall and entered that contentious grey zone between security and extortion. A group of violent sycophantic young men attached themselves to the twins,[11] and 'the firm' extorted money from thieves as well as from legitimate businesses, feeding Ron's dream of forming a powerful criminal force capable of dominating London. Although Reg was very much part of this visceral world of vendettas and extortion, of cuttings and punishment beatings, the clubs were his natural habitat, and it was in this environment that Reg perfected the 'cigarette punch', offering a cigarette with one hand and breaking the man's jaw with the other (Pearson 2001: 43).

The Krays' criminal careers were initially propelled by their successful involvement in extorting money from bars and clubs (Donoghue and Short 1995: 23–4; Lambrianou 1992: 32–3, 36–7; Pearson 1973: 80–1; Ward 1974: 152). Under the mentorship of Billy Hill they moved up market into London's West End, providing 'security' for illegal gambling clubs (Pearson 1973: 124–5). Yet having penetrated this market, and despite the legalization of gambling in 1960, they continued to use their regularly enhanced reputations for extreme violence to extort clubs, pubs, and legitimate

---

[11] Pearson 2001: 65 describes the Kray firm as 'threadbare gangsters', and Webb claims that even at the peak of their powers members of the firm were only earning £30 a week, 'plus free drinks' (Webb 1993: 170).

businesses (Pearson 1973: 133–4), as well as successful thieves (Donoghue and Short 1995: 58–75; Pearson 1973: 80; 2001: 45), who, along with lesser predators, '[paid] to stay in business' (Schelling 1984: 185), accepting extortion as an informal tax.

The Krays also enthusiastically engaged in long firm fraud, where an apparently legitimate wholesaling business was set up, initially paying for goods on time, and creating a good credit rating with suppliers (Levi 1981). Ultimately, however, the fraudsters had no intention of paying for the goods, and when their credit limit was reached by purchasing large consignments of goods from multiple suppliers, they sold up and disappeared, often leaving behind a 'patsy' or front man to face the consequences (Levi 1981: 63–4). Much of their success can be attributed to a successful professional fraudster who used the Krays' violent reputations to underpin these frauds (Payne 1973), and as Levi explains in detail, the violence that underwrote these enterprises was coupled with a general ignorance regarding everyday business practice, for 'Despite their brief but profitable venture into the world of fraud, the Krays remained above all racketeers and extortionists' (Levi 1981: 67).

Ron thrived on conflict, and the Krays' business interests in the West End suffered as his unpredictable bouts of violence became more savage (Pearson 1973: 53–6). However, this did little to stifle Reg's ambition, and by the time gambling was legalized in 1960, the Krays had established themselves as fashionable and generous hosts in an East End fiefdom where criminals, film stars, and the aristocracy played out a brief Brechtian fantasy against the classless backdrop of 'swinging London' (Pearson 1973: 152–3). At this point the already bizarre story of the Krays becomes fantastic, and Ron's exotic connections amongst politicians and the aristocracy that resulted from his membership of London's homosexual underground (Pearson 2001: 73–102) rendered the twins untouchable and free to commit murder, as the political classes distanced themselves from the possibility of a scandal that threatened both the government and its imminent successors (Pearson 2010: 100–37).

Apart from one half-hearted failed attempt (Pearson 2010: 138–63; Read and Morton 1991: 89–116), the police abandoned ongoing operations against the Krays who, in the wake of the Profumo scandal, had become a hot potato, and the twins were free to revel in the social and commercial opportunities on offer, as the photographer David Bailey made the twins cold-eyed icons of 1960s' London (Pearson 2001: 68–70, 109–110). As the 1960s progressed the twins became more impudent in their confrontations with authority. For instance, as an expression of their power, Frank 'Mad Axeman' Mitchell was sprung from Dartmoor Prison and secreted in an East End flat, before being murdered by Fred Foreman on behalf of the Krays when he became an inconvenience (Dickson 1986: 64–107; Donoghue and Short 1995: 139–60; Foreman 1996; Pearson 1973: 185–200).[12]

George Cornell was an alumni of Stepney's Watney Street Mob who had once beaten up Ron Kray (Webb 1993: 143–4; Pearson 2010: 188–9), and had made derogatory remarks about his sexuality (Kray and Kray 1988: 70–1; Pearson 1973: 183–4). Cornell, who had married and settled south of the Thames, worked with the Richardson brothers in the provision of security for illegal pornographic clubs in the West End (Fraser 1994: 146). When Ronnie Kray approached Cornell at a West End nightspot asking for a slice of this lucrative business, he was publicly insulted, and in March 1966 Ron Kray shot George Cornell dead in the saloon bar of the *Blind Beggar* in Whitechapel (Dickson 1986: 26–34; Kray and Kray 1988: 67–77; Pearson 1973: 183–4). Despite details of the killing rapidly entering East End folk-law, no witness could be found to identify the assailant to the police (Pearson 2010: 177–92).

The Krays flirted with American organized crime (Pearson 1973: 175–6), hosting Mafia associates in London (Anastasia 1991: 53), and looked abroad to expand. However, Ron's mental condition was deteriorating, and although responsibility for the firm fell to his twin (Pearson 1973: 201–2), the suicide of his wife in the summer of 1967 sent Reg, and therefore the firm, into free fall (Pearson 1973: 189), resulting in a series of shootings and knifings. Ron urged his twin to prove his manhood by committing a murder of his own, and Jack 'The Hat' McVitie, a fringe member of the Kray firm who had recently proved unreliable and disrespectful, was lured to a flat where Reg butchered him in front of several associates. (Dickson 1986: 118–28; Lambrianou 1992: 7–17; Kray and Kray 1988: 85–94; Kray and Sykes 1977: 197–202; Pearson 1973: 212–21). Witnesses to the killings of both Cornell and McVitie were found following a police operation which initially took the

---

[12] The twins were later acquitted of Mitchell's murder (Read and Morton 1991: 208–14, 260–2).

Krays off the streets as the result of evidence provided by an agent provocateur working for the US Secret Service (Pearson 2010: 251–64).

At the subsequent trial in 1969, and with a few notable exceptions such as the Lambrianou brothers and Charlie Kray, in exchange for leniency the firm crumbled and turned against the twins (Read and Morton 1991: 228–57). The Krays' trial was a show trial for the 1960s. There was a perception in the beleaguered 'Establishment' that the old order was disintegrating, and as a result the twins' sentences of life imprisonment were out of proportion even to the horrendous murders of which they were found guilty. There followed frequent campaigns to get them released, numerous books, and a film of their lives. They were idolized by many as icons of safer, predictable days, exploited by hangers-on and ridiculed by a few ex-gangsters. But it was all irrelevant to Ron, who at the trial had called the prosecuting counsel 'a fat slob' before he disappeared into the prison system. He was certified a paranoid schizophrenic in 1979 and served out his sentence heavily medicated. In 1995 Ron Kray died of a massive heart attack having spent the last 20 years of his life in Broadmoor Hospital (Hobbs 1995).

Reg spent the years of his sentence writing autobiographies, books of poetry, and keeping fit, while various old friends orchestrated campaigns to get the twins released. In 1998, 30 years after his arrest, Reg Kray expressed at a probation assessment some remorse for the murder he had committed, and in August 2000 he was diagnosed with bladder cancer, the Home Secretary, Jack Straw, ordering his release on compassionate parole only weeks before his death in October 2000 (Hobbs 2000a).

Charlie Kray was one of the few members of the Kray firm who did not appear as a witness for the prosecution, and he received 10 years for his role in disposing of McVitie's body, a role that some writers and ex-members of 'the firm' have since questioned. Charlie rebuilt his life by dedicating himself to campaigning for the release of the twins, whilst simultaneously exploiting the Kray name to the brothers' best advantage. However, when, in 1996 his son, Gary, died of cancer, he did not have the funds for the funeral expenses, and Reg, who by that time had been incarcerated for 28 years, paid the bill. That same year Charlie was arrested following a bizarre police sting operation, and in June 1997 he was sentenced to 12 years' imprisonment for supplying two kilograms of cocaine and promising to supply cocaine to the value of £39 million. Although he had never seen the cocaine, what was probably just another scam cashing in on the family name this time had dire consequences, and he died in prison in April 2000 (Hobbs 2000b).

As John Pearson explains, 'With most celebrities, their fame dies with them, but long before they died, the Twins were already as firmly part of criminal mythology as Bill Sykes, Dick Turpin and Jack the Ripper' (2001: 231). The potent mixture of money, violence, sex, madness, and nostalgia that characterized the life of the Kray twins has ensured that they will not be forgotten. When he was a child, his aunt Rose had told Ron that he was 'born to hang', and although this proved not to be the case, his incarceration ensured that the decline of two of Britain's most notorious criminals was suspended in front of a voracious audience in a cruel parody of a public execution.[13] The Kray twins served 28 and 32 years in prison for two killings, yet 'what truly mattered to the Twins was their image and their legend' (Pearson 2001: 233), which was 'part black farce, part cockney tragedy, part sick saga in the overheated culture of celebrity' (Pearson 2001: 221).

The Kray twins were not the most successful of criminals, and they were far from the most violent. They were glamorous gangsters—mother-loving murderers who contributed to local charities. The Dickensian East End, of which the Kray family and their ilk were among the last remnants, has gone for ever, and a merchant bank has been built on the site of the *Bluecoat Boy* pub, where in the 1970s, after serving his time for disposing of McVitie's body, Charlie held court, tanned, suited and booted with a navy blue cashmere overcoat draped artfully over his shoulders.

Particularly now, with the material base for traditional, urban working-class communities all but erased, and with crime located overwhelmingly within loose collectivities of ad hoc groupings, the emphasis has shifted to the deification of key individuals as functional touchstones of competence and honour (Hobbs 1997) whose task is 'recycling old trade names, refurbishing old properties, and laying claim to the production of classics...their image is inten-

---

[13] The peak period of the Kray twins' career featured some of the UK's key legislation of the twentieth century. In particular, the Betting and Gaming Act 1960, which legalized gambling, the Murder (Abolition of Death Penalty) Act 1965, and the repeal of the Sexual Offences Act in 1967, which decriminalized homosexuality, provide a somewhat remarkable context framing their rise and fall.

sively marketed on the strength of an aestheticized version of the past' (Samuel 1994: 78). It was near-full employment and the consolation of living in tight-knit communities, rather than the activities of a pair of hapless criminal businessmen, tainted by mental illness and with a flair for violence, that were the sources of stability and prosperity for the east London of the 1960s. Yet the Kray twins are often regarded as symbols of safer, predictable days, when white working-class tough guys in sharp suits ruled their manor by hard but fair means, and, particularly during their long incarceration, they morphed into icons of a brief 'golden age' of the post-war era, epitomizing a particular brand of photogenic proletarian hegemony.

The Richardson Brothers: Scrap and Metal

> He (Charlie Richardson) was a genius, not like a Professor who might know about art and paintings, but as a money maker.[14]

Charlie and Eddie Richardson were much more than the sum of their parts. Born into a traditional south London working-class family, like their east London counterparts the brothers endured a wartime childhood, enjoyed the vibrant street life of working-class London, and developed as talented young boxers and prominent street fighters. According to folklore, and generations of pub-talk, the Richardsons were the south London nemesis of the Kray twins, but rather than faithfully reworking that story here, I will quickly outline the important place that the Richardsons have in British organized crime narratives.

Unlike the Krays, both Charlie and Eddie Richardson had a penchant for hard work, and made good money from the post-war scrap metal trade, in particular plundering the remnants of abandoned wartime airfields. With an astonishing entrepreneurial zeal, which a generation later could have seen them receiving knighthoods, they moved into a number of disparate commercial areas, including wholesale chemists and mineral mining, as well as extortion and, notably, long fraud. The honeypot of the West End brought them into contact with the Krays, and although the east London firm along with its associates claimed to be preparing for outright

---

[14] Interview with Frank Fraser, May 1995.

warfare, there is little to suggest that the Richardson firm took the Krays seriously. The Richardsons could boast amongst their associates some of London's most violent and feared men, including one of the celebrated 'Chainsaw Robbers' Jimmy Moody, George Cornell, an East Ender who had clashed with the youthful Krays when he was a member of the Watney Street mob, and Frank Fraser, whose affiliation to the Richardsons was described by Mickey Bloom, an associate of north London's Nash Brothers, as 'like China getting the atom bomb'.

Fraser summed up the south London firm's attitude to the Krays: 'Using racing terms, there would be no race...The Richardsons were miles in front, brain power, everything' (Campbell 1994: 91). In their dotage both Charlie and Eddie Richardson have expressed a degree of contempt for the Kray firm: 'There was never any direct threat from them...They were playing at being gangsters, like you see in the movies' (Richardson 2005: 91).[15] Although skirmishes and casualties were not unknown (Mason 1994: 186; Fraser 1994: 147), while the Krays, and in particular Ron, fantasized over Chicago-style gang wars (Donoghue and Short 1994: 110–15), the Richardons diversified into long firms, gaming machines, pornography, five scrap metal yards, a perlite mine in South Africa, control over car parking at Heathrow, and more. However, the very idea of a self-contained Richardson 'firm' is problematic, and in a telephone conversation with Eddie Richardson he explained to me that he had not worked directly with his brother since 1962, when Eddie and Frank Fraser, assisted by Albert Dimes and part funded by Billy Hill, set up Atlantic Machines. This was a business providing gaming machines to licensed premises (Fraser 1994: 192–6, 199–203; Richardson 2005: 77–81) all over the UK, a business where anyone disrupting its smooth running was invariably subjected to violent sanctions (Parker 1981: 151–4).

Like the Krays, the Richardson brothers, and Charles Richardson in particular, enthusiastically engaged in long firm activity (Levi 1981: 76–7), and like the Krays their violence both underwrote and contributed to the demise of these enterprises. Charlie Richardson would impose himself upon both legal businesses and nascent long firms and surrounded himself with businessmen and long firm spe-

---

[15] John Pearson also stresses that the notion of a forthcoming 'war' between the two firms is a myth (Pearson 2001: 119).

cialists. The latter included ex-professional boxer, pickpocket, and cohort of Charles Kray senior, Jimmy Kensit.[16] Described to me by Eddie Richardson as a 'plausible rogue', Kensit first worked with Charlie Richardson in 1962 when he was invited to invest £150 in a company concerned with 'hire purchase in boats'. After this maritime excursion, Kensit then moved to another Richardson-run company, 'Central Supplies', a wholesalers where he worked as a salesman on a commission basis, and it was during this period that he witnessed an associate being beaten after complaining about Charlie Richardson frequently plundering the stock. Kensit was one of a number of men sent by Richardson to Milan to place orders with several manufacturers for stockings (see Levi 1981: 68–75). On arrival in London the stockings were sold by mail order, but with both money and goods leaking from the business, and with the Italian creditors pressing, Charlie Richardson told Kensit to ensure that he had an alibi for the following night. Jimmy Kensit kept the ticket stubs from the cinema that he visited with his wife, before going on to the high-profile Astor Club. That night Central Supplies burnt down.

Richardson then set up a new company, LR Gray, based in Mitre St in the City of London, and it was one of Kensit's tasks to pay £25 per week to a police officer at nearby Bishopsgate Police Station in exchange for any information relating to the company. Several more associates were beaten for allegedly stealing from the long firms, before LR Grey also 'had a fire'. Kensit then broke away from Charlie Richardson for three years, during which time his wife had a minor car accident, allegedly as a result of her brake cables being cut. After three years Jimmy Kensit worked with Richardson again, joining a legitimate chemical company, Warren Stanley Ltd, for £25 per week plus commission. The firm followed a familiar path, building up credit, before going bust. Kensit then ran a football pools company where few people were actually paid the prizes due to them, before the business suffered a break-in one night and closed down. Jimmy Kensit then worked from home 'buying and selling', until he was arrested in July 1966 on a charge of warehouse breaking. He was described by police as a 'minor criminal', 'A man completely under the domination of the

[16] This material on Jimmy Kensit was gleaned from an archive kindly given to me by the family of the late Superintendant Gerald McArthur, who, as head of No 5 Regional Crime Squad, led the Richardson investigation (see Hobbs 1996).

Richardsons', and while in Lewes Prison he gave evidence against the brothers.[17]

In 1966, in a shooting at Mr Smiths Club in Catford, an associate of the Krays was killed and five men were wounded. Eddie Richardson and Frank Fraser were arrested, Fraser for murder (Parker 1981: 273–80). The following night Ronnie Kray murdered George Cornell (Pearson 1973: 183–4). Meanwhile Charlie Richardson had taken to attacking a number of fellow fraudsters whom he suspected of stealing from his long firms. The resulting 'torture trial' in 1967 featured bizarre allegations of the use of pliers to remove teeth and fingernails, and the attachment of electrodes to genitals. A distinct lack of physical evidence to support some of the more extreme allegations did not deter the judge[18] from imposing huge sentences on the entire firm. Eddie was sentenced to ten years' imprisonment with another five for the Mr Smith incident, and Charlie Richardson received 25 years. Frank Fraser, who had been acquitted of the Catford murder, received five years for affray, and an additional ten years for some deviant dental practices at the Richardsons' Peckham scrapyard (Campbell 1994: 103–5; Morton 1992: 123–8). Charlie Richardson summarized his trial as follows: 'I was actually charged with a bit of long firm fraud and five counts of grievous bodily harm. Nobody was dead, maimed or even bloody scarred…I had slapped five hooligans around and had defrauded large companies …' (Richardson 1992: 215–16).

The sentencing policy with regard to the so-called 'torture' cases was far more savage than that applied to the Krays, who were undoubtedly guilty of murder, and whether this was due to the upsurge in fear of American-style 'organized crime' or linked to Charlie Richardson's alleged relationship with the South African Secret Service (Parker 1981: 239–53), remains, over 40 years later,

---

[17] 'I want to say that any association I have had with Charlie Richardson was because I have been scared and terrorised and worried because of my wife's safety. I have seen how violent he can be and I have heard about many other cases. My wife has been worried out of her life for me and herself and the baby. She has gone in fear ever since the break cutting incident. I have known times, late at night when car lights have shown in the bedroom, when my wife has been terrified, got up, and looked out to make sure the car went right past.' (Kensit File).

[18] The son of a prison governor, the trial judge, Mr Justice Lawton, was, in 1936, adopted as the British Union of Fascists' candidate for Hammersmith North. When called to the Bar he acted as pupil-master to the young Margaret Thatcher (Morton 2001).

rather difficult to unpack. Official files relating to the Richardsons have been sunk deep into the long grass of British officialdom.

London Boys: Making an Underworld

> Memory is always the enemy of structure (Saul 1992: 14)

> ...and all to create the myth of a gangland London to make England proud (Richardson 1992: 223)

Commander Bert Wickstead was given the job of tidying up the East End after the Krays were convicted, and proceeded to apply a tactic that has proved to be popular in police circles. He exaggerated the threat. Wickstead asserted that the Dixon brothers and publican Phil Jacobs were about to step into the shoes of the Krays, and along with his newly formed squad of 'Untouchables' gained successful prosecutions for extortion and theft (Wickstead 1985: 76–87). Similarly, the Tibbs family were designated as 'a highly organised gang' by Wickstead despite no evidence other than their violent feud with the Nicholls family, who were 'a loose collection of criminal friends' (Wickstead 1985: 95). This hyping-up of any post-Kray, family-based collaboration, particularly those emanating from east London, was an early indication of the political cachet to be gleaned from being tough on organized crime, and should be noted in terms of the exaggerated threat that white working-class families involved in crime were deemed to pose in this era before drugs came to dominate the marketplace (Wickstead 1985: 87–102).[19]

The quest for criminal organization, or indeed any kind of neatly delineated social or economic order amongst a London working class whose very character was forged in disorder, disharmony, and, most importantly, 'the Hustle: wit, mental toughness, the impulse to autonomy and an extreme materialism' (Robson 1997: 14) is at best doomed to simple parody. The era discussed above created highly marketable criminal identities, featuring careers marked by levels of flexibility that mock any notion of organized crime based upon rigid territoriality or formulaic hierarchies. For

---

[19] Of particular interest is Wickstead's assertion that on the conviction of the Tibbs family, 'some measure of tranquility had been restored to the streets of the East End' (Wickstead 1985: 102)—which was news to the citizens of East London.

instance, Saffron Hill's Albert Dimes, whose diplomatic and net-working skills earned him the title of 'The League of Nations in Soho' (Richardson 2005: 79), helped stymie the West End ambitions of the Krays, while simultaneously working with Kray mentor Billy Hill, and staying close to south Londoners Frank Fraser and Eddie Richardson in setting up Atlantic Machines.[20] Frank Fraser, a south Londoner, had no regard for the symbolic barrier of the Thames, and considered Soho as the place where he grew up. His long and bloody criminal career commenced as a ten-year-old bucket boy wiping down bookies' blackboards for Darby Sabini, and Zelig-like, he worked for Islington's Billy Hill as a young man, was courted by the Krays, collaborated with south London's Richardson brothers in Peckham and Soho, and retained connections all over the capital, including amongst the Italians in Clerkenwell.[21]

Although Billy Hill found Camden an ideal base for his early forays into theft and violence, his criminal imagination enabled him to consider possibilities not just beyond the local neighbourhood, but beyond Britain's shores (Hill 1955: 181–216), marking him an extremely innovative practitioner way ahead of his time. Similarly, Charlie Richardson, while affiliated to working-class territory in south London, was able to shift seamlessly between legitimate and illegitimate enterprise, and embrace exotic intrigues beyond the streets of Peckham, whilst never acknowledging the territorial boundaries that legend insists existed between east and south London. Indeed, one of his most lucrative long firm operations was in Mitre Street, about a mile from the twins' base in Vallance Road. The Krays, however, never really made the grade outside of the old East End; as criminal businessmen they were star-struck disasters who were comfortable making their money the old-fashioned way—from extortion and intimidation in the style of Dickensian hard men such as Jimmy Spinks and Dodger Mullins. Yet it was the Krays who attracted the attention of society photographers, and who had contacts in Parliament, the House of Lords, and show business, and it is the Krays, in their mimicry of a Hollywood-cloaked mafia, who contrived Britain's most enduring

[20] For a unique account of Dimes's enduring influence on Soho in particular, see Connor (2003) 141–51.

[21] For many years Fraser could be seen enjoying the annual procession that takes place around the Italian Church in London, St Peter's of Clerkenwell, which is organized by the Italian community.

imagery of organized crime: a pretend firm, a make-believe mafia which, on its destruction, left behind the tight-knit, neighbourhood-based Dixons in the old East End, the evergreen Nashes in north London, the Tibbs in West Ham, and umpteen neighbourhood firms yet to acquire a brand marketable beyond their own back-streets.

Bad Manors

> These were the neighborhoods where local wiseguys felt safe, where racketeers had become an integral part of the social fabric...(Pileggi 1987: 43)

An enduring aspect of London's urban criminal collaborations are their rootedness amongst parochial family and neighbourhood networks whose territories feature marked variations in levels of cosmopolitanism. This is partly due to the fact that immigrants arriving in London were not equally distributed across the capital, and in 1931 it was possible to regard south London as 'more genuinely and thoroughly English than any other part of London' (Garbett 1931: 7). The lack of cosmopolitan influences in pre-war south London made it easy for locals to gather under quasi-territorial flags of convenience, such as the Elephant Boys (McDonald 2001), which provided an enduring collaborative model well into the 1960s throughout an era of considerable non-white settlement. Conversely, territorial and ethnic allegiances elsewhere in London, and in east London in particular, were complex, and although there is no evidence to suggest criminal dominance on the part of new arrivals from the Pale of Settlement, Jews were clearly features of the capital's criminal life in the first half of the twentieth century (Samuel 1981: 125–45).

Working-class London was made up of 'a social patchwork of intensively localist culture and sentiment' (Robson 1997: 7), which lacked the homogeneity and repressive paternalism that is a feature of cultures created by a single mode of production and of mass employment on a single site (Hobbs 1988: 87). London's economic base was diffuse, and as a consequence the capital's proletariat evolved as a complex and highly individualistic amalgam of multiple, albeit class-specific, identities gleaned from localities sharing little in common with their neighbours other than socio-economic deprivation (Sennett 1994: 322). Even dock work, upon which vast swathes of south and east London were reliant, created working cultures dependent upon semi-autonomous groups of workers hired by the day before shifting to another cargo, possibly on another ship, maybe in a different dock (Hobbs 1988: 109–11). The localism of Londoners manifested itself in a tendency to regard territories beyond their own with deep suspicion, and an inclination to embrace the familiar and maintain exposure to the strange habits of those residing in adjacent neighbourhoods to a minimum.[22]

New Cross Boys fought with their rivals from the Elephant, and a loose-knit group of violent men from Hoxton engaged with the Italians in neighbouring Clerkenwell, while the inhabitants of Watney Street, adjacent to the Thames in Stepney, who were notable for the number of marriages between Jews and Irish in the early twentieth century (Samuel 1981: 131), became traditional enemies of 'the ancient villains of Bethnal Green' (Pearson 1973: 97). This Jewish/Irish mix was at the core of the violent resistance to fascism during the 1930s, which gave added spice to the Watney Streeters' ongoing feud with the Krays and others from the Mosleyite stronghold of Bethnal Green (Samuel 1981: 276; White 1980: 136–7). However, although never a coordinated entity, Watney Street could boast amongst their violent alumni men such as Timmy Hayes and Dodger Mullins. Both 'ignorant as hell and brutal with it' (Samuel 1981: 132), they proved to be remarkably flexible, and showed no long-term affiliation to Watney Street's loose-knit alliance. For instance, as products of dockland and supposed 'members' of an organization consisting largely of dockworkers, both worked as strike-breakers during the 1926 General Strike. In addition, Mullins was both an associate and an adversary of the Sabinis (Fraser 1998: 12; Morton 2000: 109), and, despite the Watney Streeters' long-term conflict with the Krays (Pearson 1973: 128–9), in his later years he became an ally of the twins (Kray and Dineage 1994: 20).

---

[22] During the late 1950s and early 1960s, slum clearance in Custom House resulted in families being re-housed less than three miles away in Plaistow, where new flats had been built by the local council. This resulted in anxiety on behalf of some Plaistow residents, who were convinced that the incomers were rough and prone to violence. The stigma lasted for a number of years until the realization that the incomers were no more rough and prone to violence than the rest of the population, many of whom had originally moved to Plaistow from the heavily stigmatized, inner East End areas. Ten years later similar fears were being expressed by Plaistow residents concerning the possible impacts of West Indian newcomers.

Although the 'Watney Street mob' had many dockworkers amongst its ranks who enjoyed the abundant fruits of the riverside stolen goods trade, it is important to resist imposing an organizational logic upon this chaotic informal market (see Morton 2000: 286–93), for the sheer size of the docks and the scale of the stolen goods trade made it unfeasible to create a criminal monopoly. Further, the logic of territoriality dictates that any attempt to control such a vast market would be met with violent resistance amongst communities established in tight-knit riverside parishes close to the dock gates. Dock work often featured networks of friends and families (Ross 2010), but I could find nobody amongst the mass ranks of ex-dockers now living in Essex who regarded river-based crime to be coordinated. Ed, now in his 80s, explained, 'It's not likely is it. There was over 20,000 men working in the dock, and you worked with your people, your gang. Whether you was at it (theft), and a lot were, or not, somebody in Stepney never had no control over a couple of blokes working out the Royals. You had your little…scam…you kept your head down…put the money away, got your beer money. As for getting somebody work, that did happen and it was all through the Union and the main man round our way was.…and he was a magistrate…there was money flying about for a bit. He was in with (local) councillors and all them people…(but) he was just one man getting backhanders.'

A Special Competence

> We are a country of nuanced tribal relationships, not top-down power. Building local trust is everything (Gary Trudeau, *Doonesbury*)

Based in neighbourhoods defined by poverty, families such as the Brindles, Garrets, Carters, Richardsons, and Roffs fought through rumbustious adolescence, before channelling their feuding into more aspirational pursuits. Chaotic theft, stolen goods, and extortion networks emerged to create clusters of collaborations that defy orderly underworld narratives, and conjure diverse interlocking networks of relationality (O'Byrne 1997; Strathern 1995: 179). The ability of certain individuals, groups, and families to move beyond the confines of the orthodox and somewhat banal confines of the working-class neighbourhood mark out the groups discussed in this chapter. Once they had exhausted the full economic potential of their own locale through the imposition of a monopoly of informal violence, new territories were sought out and colonized. As we can see from the careers of the marquee criminals, extortion was a career entry point that created 'protected enclaves' (Arlacchi 1986: 195) within the working-class city, and the ability to guarantee compliance (Jacobs 1999: 118) constituted a potent form of economic power that lent the criminal entrepreneur a special competence (Katz 1975: 1381).[23]

As entrepreneurs of trust, albeit a trust that was underwritten by violence, the careers of the marquee criminals were reliant upon the maintenance of a viable threat as a vehicle for consolidating territorial control (Falcone 1993: 116; see also Behan 1996: 110–12), and the competent, occasionally extravagant application of violence can monopolize the entire market within a given territory. As Gambetta explains, 'He who beats hardest not only does away with the beaten competitors, but advertises himself as an adequate protector' (1988: 140), which highlights the dynamic role of extortion in our understanding of both entry-level transgression and the bedrock of a notion of organized criminality that is linked not to a racialized pathology, but to the predatory principles underpinning class society.

However, in relation to crime and criminal collaborations, some unpacking is overdue, and these family connections and working-class territorial imperatives situated within traditional locations, and linked to traditional practices (see Knight 1990: 213–14), need to be addressed as much in terms of their limitations as for their attributes as fundamental props in establishing allegiance and maintaining loyalty. Many of the accounts of this iconic era feature a self-conscious local patriotism and partisanship, and while this may play itself out as south London versus east London or vice versa, it can also feature, particularly in dealing with Italian

---

[23] This special competence is shared with the police, who can invoke the coercive power of the state in order to negotiate with illegal businesses (Whyte 1943: 128–9). For instance, during the 1960s and 1970s businesses dealing in pornography were extorted by the 'dirty book squad' in exchange for allowing the pornographers to continue their activities (Cox et al 1977). Criminal entrepreneurs seeking an advantage in the marketplace a high premium on having police officers 'on the firm' (Richardson 1992: 93), converting police power into an explicitly commercial entity.

and Jewish criminals, a pervasive odour of racism. For instance, while both McDonald (2001) and Divall (1929) stress the superiority of south London's Elephant Boys, their accounts stand in direct opposition, both morally and descriptively, to that of Hart (1993), who relies upon a one-time Sabini enforcer as well as a senior police officer to construct his florid account of Darby Sabini's career. As earlier emphasized in the comments on Arthur Harding, biographical material, particularly relating to hidden histories and shrouded criminal trajectories, should be contextualized wherever possible, for the gaze from the periphery of serious crime networks is invariably partial, obscured by the actors' distance from an ever-shifting centre and by the sheer chaos that is integral to illegal markets.

This gives rise to the question as to whether we would have heard of Hill or Spot if they had not courted the attention of biographers Duncan Webb and Hank Janson. And why was the apparently powerful Billy Howard almost totally ignored until his biography emerged some 20 years after his death (Connor 2003)? If Howard had commissioned a biographer while still active, as did the publicity-hungry Hill, Spot, and Kray brothers, our popular history of what has come to be regarded as the British underworld could have been very different. Indeed, there are plenty of candidates for being the 'real' boss of London's underworld circa 1920–70, for example Bert Marsh, who, as an alumnus of the Sabinis, prospered in gambling, clubs, protection, and receiving, and according to Frank Fraser was the low-key criminal success story of the era (Fraser 1998: 38–40). But some of the less-glamorous badlands of London surely house dank archives that cry out for attention. Step forward the transgressive emeritus of Paddington, Shepherds Bush, Upton Park, and Canning Town with stories of ferocity, bravery, and, crucially, unacknowledged superiority.

Integral to the way that 'organised crime is experienced, perceived, and reported' (Lacey 1991: 394) is an underworld fantasy where bravery, honour, and chivalry are afforded precedence over market pragmatism in an attempt to conjure some order from an essentially imaginary community (Hobbs 1995). This eternal recurrence of themes related to an underworld constitutes a quest for order (Bauman 1993: 1–17) within an enacted environment whose contours have been bent out of shape by the collapse of working-class territoriality and the industrial culture that defined traditional neighbourhood crime groups. However, these marquee criminals serve not only as forefathers and cultural chaperones of contemporary, loose-knit, urban elites, but as predators whose modus operandi has proved an enduring bridge between the exclusive underworld that evolved as an annexe of working-class culture, and the inclusive community of practice that has blossomed amongst the barren wastelands of post-industrial society.

5

The Houses in Between: The Neighbourhood Firm on a Shifting Terrain

Oh! it really is a very pretty garden

And Chingford to the Eastward could be seen

With a ladder and some glasses

You could see to Hackney Marshes

If it wasn't for the houses in between

(Edgar Bateman/George LeBrunn 1899)

Crime seems to change character when it crosses a bridge or a tunnel. In the city, crime is taken as emblematic of class and race. In the suburbs, though, it's intimate and psychological/ resistant to generalization, a mystery of the individual soul (Ehenreich 1990)

The Empty Kennel

The pick-up is from a scrapyard where the plasma TVs are being stored as a favour by Tony and Terry who run the yard. Terry has sold some of the TVs and is due to hand over £8,000 to Charlie and Phil who have placed the stolen goods in a number of safe stores around the edge of Dogtown. Tony had been a van driver working for a building firm before he built a lucrative sideline dealing in stolen copper piping and set up a series of legitimate businesses, subsequently serving a five-year prison sentence for 'something to do with drugs'.

On arriving at the scrapyard for what seemed like a routine meeting, a relaxed Charlie and Phil get out of the van and stub out their cigarettes before entering the yard's office, a Portacabin set back against an old brick wall. The yard is immaculate. A small pile of neatly stacked car doors and a couple of unidentifiable lumps of elderly industrial machinery appear suspiciously symbolic. Three nondescript, recent-model family cars sit in the yard next to a pristine flat-back 4x4 with a ladder and two large plastic drums in the back. Most scrapyards have dogs, but in this yard there are none.

After about ten minutes Charlie and Phil emerge from the office looking grim, and as they walk silently back to the rented van the door of the office opens and Tony, Terry, and another man leave the office and begin to walk to their cars. Charlie starts to get into the van, hesitates, and walks back towards the 4x4 where the three men stand lighting cigarettes. While Charlie engages with Terry in an intense, but sotto voce conversation, Tony and the other man deliberately disconnect themselves, taking a few lateral steps away from the conversation, the volume of which is rapidly increasing as Terry can be heard explaining, 'No money now, knock it all out and divvy up on Wednesday.' An exasperated Charlie loudly repeats this excuse and gets into Terry's face, prompting Tony and his colleague to stare apprehensively at Phil, who, although he has quickly halved the distance between the van and the 4x4, is standing very still and showing no intention of intervening. Phil is standing closest to Tony and after a few seconds the two men, who have known each other from Tony's days as a copper bandit, nod to each other in recognition.

The conversation between Charlie and Terry becomes extremely heated, their faces are touching, and as they grab each other's sleeves, their knees and ankles are entwined and their balance becoming precarious. At this point Phil, hands held palms outwards at head height, and maintaining eye contact with Tony, walks very slowly towards the scuffling pair. The third man, who has been standing partly in shadow, puts down a metal tool box and steps forward a couple of slow paces, while Tony remains static, his eyes fixed on Phil, who tentatively approaches the struggling pair just as their words have deteriorated into gargled renditions of 'fuck, money, cunt'. Phil places his hands gently Charlie's shoulders and commands in a clear but even tone, 'leave it, let it go', before carefully peeling back Charlie's clenched fingers from Terry's cotton bomber jacket. Unaided, Terry reciprocates in instalments, his left hand reluctantly releasing his opponent's collar only when he is totally free of Charlie's grasp. The long stares are broken as Phil and Charlie turn their backs, get into their van, and reverse past the car doors, the old machinery, and a previously unnoticed empty dog kennel into the main road that links Dogtown with Essex.

The object of this chapter is to illustrate some of the changes that have taken place in and around the 'Family Firm' (Jenks and Lorentzen 1997), a product of industrial working-class culture which has adapted, like the working class itself, to a radically altered cultural and economic terrain. As we can see in Chapter 4, the designated territories of these crime 'firms' corresponded with distinct and defined working-class neighbourhoods whose political economies generated enduring fiefdoms that were crucial cultural props of traditional working-class communities (Bean 1981; Samuel 1981; Stedman Jones 1971). Having established in Chapter 4 the way in which variations in working-class criminal fraternities are impacted on by normative social and economic drivers that reside beyond the scope of criminal justice considerations, this chapter will argue that tendencies associated with the organization of legitimate labour are reflected within crime networks (Hobbs 1997; Ruggiero 1995), and involve the generation and nurturing of local interests, albeit interests that are located across a range of post-industrial locales.

Once Upon a Time in Dogtown

> The Golden Age of the post war settlement with high employment, stable family structures, and consensual values underpinned by the safety net of the welfare state has been replaced by a world of structural unemployment, economic precariousness, a systematic cutting of welfare provisions and the growing instability of family life and interpersonal relations (Young 2007: 59)

The essence of Dogtown during the industrial age was a very distinct set of pragmatic adaptations that encompassed key aspects of a highly localized, working-class disposition (Hobbs 1988), and a tough, independent entrepreneurship emerged as a practical logic that constituted a general habitus (Bourdieu 1997). With a history of poverty and municipal socialism (Hobbs 2006), as well as casual labour and its accompanying crime (Meier 2011: 57), industrial-era Dogtown had established itself as a bastion of proletarianism, and the immediate post-Second World War period when communities were entrenched and stable offered a unique respite from the extreme and very particular economic forces that had forged the East End (Gavron et al 2006).

However, the East End's halcyon era in the wake of post-war economic resurgence was short lived, and the area's decline commenced with the decade-long demise of the timber and furniture industries between 1961 and 1971, which resulted in the loss of over 26,000 jobs (Hall 1962: 72), and the loss of 40,000 jobs in London's clothing and footwear industries which were centred in the East End (Hall 1962: 44–5). Yet it was the slow death of the London Docks (Ross 2010) that marked the end of this classic period of entrenched, pragmatic working-class community. Throughout the 1960s containerization and new handling methods reduced the demand for manual labour in the docks (Hill 1976), and massive capital investment in the modernization of Tilbury, where the width of the Thames could accommodate the new containerships, and with adjacent land sufficiently cheap and plentiful for the storage of containers, clearly signalled the imminent demise of the old East End. By 1971 the Port of London's workforce had shrunk to 6,000, and the five Dockland boroughs (Tower Hamlets, Newham, Southwark, Lewisham, and Greenwich) lost 150,000 jobs between 1966 and 1976, mainly in transport, distribution, and food and drink processing, all sectors closely associated with port activity. This represented 20 per cent of all jobs in the area, and was in contrast to a decline of 13 per cent in Greater London and just 2 per cent in Great Britain. Thus, after a very brief period of unparalleled labour autonomy and spectacular industrial strife that accompanied the end of dock casualization (Hobbs 1988: Ch 6; 2010), the London docker, and the communities that nurtured him, were no more. And Dogtown took a distinct turn for the worse.

When the docks closed, the younger generation of dockers moved eastwards to work at Tilbury, while older workers also moved to Essex, but into retirement. It is hard to articulate the importance of the pervasive presence of both dockworkers and ex-dockworkers at work and play in and around Dogtown through the 1950s, 1960s, and 1970s. They were a constant reminder of the contested nature of the regimes of work[1] that routinized power relations, responsibilities, and obligations, creating 'an arena of empower-

---

[1] The missing fingers or fingertips on the hands of veteran dockers, like the 'blue tattoo' of coal dust under miners' skin, was a constant reminder of the price paid at the more visceral end of the manual labour market.

ment' (Sennett 1998: 43) where narratives of resistance and negotiation lent coherence and dignity to everyday life (Ross 2010). However, the ensuing chaos of the free market established a bitter competitiveness in British society from which it has never recovered. Especially in London where property values were high, the results were astonishing, particularly as a result of the sanctioning of the sale of two million local council-owned homes in the UK. This sale of public housing overheated the housing market, and resulted in working-class council tenants buying their homes at a massive discount before selling at a profit and heading for London's periphery, which, combined with deindustrialization, effectively drained working-class London of much of its human capital, as well as its cumulative memory.[2]

The long-established social order of neighbourhoods fractured as dock workers and their families took their severance pay and moved out of London, taking with them a fierce local patriotism based upon the everyday realities of class antagonism. They were not aspiring to join the middle classes, but responding to the emptying-out of a cultural and economic space where the restraints on individualism that had been guaranteed by trade union membership and municipal socialism had been abandoned. The shrewd, imaginative 'ducking and diving' of generations of East Enders that eased the pressure close to the rump of class society was transformed into a fiercer set of strategies based upon the new gloves-off entrepreneurship of market society. For while Prime Minister Margaret Thatcher deregulated Britain's commercial zones, removing traditional restrictions and restraints and valorizing business, she also effectively deregulated the criminal marketplace and normalized entrepreneurship in all of its manifestations. The fragmentation of working-class populations and the decline of extended family networks have been extensive, and the dilution of the legitimate employment market has redefined criminality in the context of the new decentered, unpredictable trading economy created by the harsh post-industrial thrust that has laid waste to traditional communities 'emptied out' of marketable labour and traditional forms of governance (Pakulski and Waters 1996: 110).

---

[2] This retreat of the state has continued, but rather than develop a Nirvana of home ownership, private landlords now dominate the Dogtown housing market.

The Political Economy of the Family Firm

> Margaret Thatcher made a lot of people a lot of money.
> Wonderful woman in my opinion (ex-armed robber Danny
> Woolard)

The fragmentation of both traditional working-class neighbourhoods and the local labour markets upon which they were dependent (Beck 1992; Pakulski and Waters 1996) made it difficult for the
family-based units described in Chapter 4 to establish the kind of
parochial dominance they once enjoyed (Hobbs 1995: 67; Stelfox
1996: 18). As a consequence, working-class crime became relocated more than ever within ad hoc, loose-knit, flexible, adaptive networks whose scope exceeded circumscribed terrain and which were
characterized by an ability to splinter, dissolve, mutate, self-destruct,
or simply decompose in response to the uncertainties of the
marketplace.[3] Men and women on the edge of the East End's stolen
goods trade, thieves, van and lorry drivers, football hooligans, and
bouncers joined armed robbers and established family crime firms
in a criminogenic free-for-all. Duckers, divers, burglars, bit-part
players, and the runts of dysfunctional litters came to the fore, making easy money merely doing what came naturally—buying and
selling. Chaotic, unruly broods became 'crime families' merely on
the strength of their ability to pick up a chunk of dope or a parcel
of white powder and sell it on at a profit, before festooning their
homes with CCTV cameras, steel plating the front door, putting
bars on the windows, and decorating the family seat with dogs
called Tyson. In the post-industrial void created by the destruction
of traditional industries and their syncopated cultures, the elevated
status of these families and their embeddedness in the former working-class city is due to their manifestation as symbols of material
success in insecure neighbourhoods festering in the shadow of
Canary Wharf, where four-wheel-drive, gold-toothed consumerism is one of the few real alternatives to diazepam and daytime
television.

These 'individualist marauders on the periphery of empire' (Earle
2004: 146–7), while occasionally playing shamelessly on the ico-

---

[3] For instance, a group dealing in amphetamines splintered into both legal and
illegal enterprise when a key member was arrested for a crime totally unconnected
with their business. They dispersed and adapted, bonded not by some exclusive
freemasonry but by the promise of pecuniary reward (Hobbs 1995: Ch 6).

nography of the underworld, had little need for the staunch comfort of a prison cell, or a smoke-infused illegal drinking club. In the 'conflictual web of beliefs, symbols, modes of interaction of values and ideologies' (Bourgois 1995: 8) that constitutes the chaotic milieu of illegal markets, particularly those situated close to the retail sector, the availability of weapons and the surplus of cheap labour willing to use them contributed to a maelstrom of disordered, fragmented entrepreneurship unencumbered by the professional protocols of practitioners concerned with mere 'business imperatives' (Hallsworth and Silverstone 2009: 362).

As Block has noted, 'Feuds and vendettas are endemic' (1994: 33) within the serious crime community, and it is inappropriate to attribute economic rationality to all of their violent activities. In Dogtown, a murder that was formally attributed by the media to be a revenge attack resulting from another killing linked to a high-profile market dispute was actually carried out by a man who was having an affair with the wife of his victim (see Falcone 1993: 97–8). As Hallsworth and Silverstone explain, 'This is a parochial social order populated by young, volatile men who dwell in dangerous street settings where many also strive to earn a living in the least lucrative but most violent part of the criminal economy. This is a street world where rules that might delimit violence rarely exist...where the injunction to retaliate is an obligation' (2009: 362), and where, as in a previous era of individualistic violent entrepreneurship played out on a lawless frontier, there is 'no duty to retreat' (Brown 1991).

Amongst the killings, punishment beatings, and kidnappings that became commonplace in Dogtown, one identifiable group stood out. Ex-armed robbers, often bitter at their loss of status to mere dealers, and smarting from the effects of heavy doses of incarceration as a result of the state's clampdown on 'blaggers', brought a fierce professional vitality to this chaotic marketplace, playing out their mid-life crises to a soundtrack of shotgun blasts as 'the world composed and recomposed itself in an endless process of dissatisfaction' (Doctorow 1989: 135). With reputations forged 'across the pavement' in high-profile banditry, and freed of the restrictive protocols of the 'underworld', some ex-robbers made up for lost time by threatening, shooting, robbing, and swindling the motley crew that constituted Dogtown's criminal residue.

Robbing drug dealers became particularly prominent in the 1990s, and one group with networked connections across London and into the suburbs created chaos by alternating between paying cash on the nose for drugs and stealing the entire consignment. Dan attempts to explain: 'It happened over and over...nobody knew if they was paying or not. When they had the money it was on the table and thanks very much. But then another time they would just not pay. And from what I heard, shooters or heavy stuff weren't always needed. Just "fuck off it aint happening" and they walk out with the gear...that was when it seemed like everybody was getting tooled up with something and there was talk of shootings, kids with guns out riding their bikes at night...then there was all the street robberies going off.' This created a decline in trust across the local marketplace, and street-level dealers found the ensuing instability infectious, often indulging in bouts of non-lethal shootings that had only a tentative connection to instrumentality.

The local order had been seriously disturbed, and the atmosphere became noticeably predatory. Merging with the ongoing post-industrial decline in Dogtown, the resultant atmosphere of suspicion and insecurity played itself out as an increase in racial tension, with youths from Dogtown's myriad of global diasporas being blamed for a wide range of problems, from late-night nuisance and noise, to burglary and street robbery. Meanwhile, the less public, adult criminal collaborations became intertwined with violent criminal entrepreneurs whose enacted environment regularly transcended rationality (Katz 1988: 181–5), composing an environment of confusion and disorder and negating the cliché that organized crime is merely a distorted reflection of normative business. In such an environment murder mixes all too easily with personal grievances, robbery, and the drug trade (Zaluar 2001: 375),[4] and while a few of the old faces paid dearly as cheap labour was employed to settle old scores, some made it to the suburbs and beyond.

Shifting Terrain

> Essex is the nearest thing we have in this country to New Jersey in the States. We should honour the fact (Wobble 2009: 19)

---

[4] For instance, see the career of ex-armed robber Tommy Hole, *Observer*, 19 March 2000.

The relocation of significant parts of London's working-class population to suburban and rural locales, which had commenced after the Second World War (Young and Wilmott 1957: 121–99), marked a fragmentation of traditional communities that was subsequently accelerated by deindustrialization (Cohen 1972; Hobbs 1988: 126–30). As these communities fragmented they took with them those remnants of traditional culture that retained some pragmatic utility, and the result is the transformation of the local criminal firm during the second half of the twentieth century from traditional, family-based associations, deeply entrenched in working-class parochialism, to a networked system partly displaced from the resonance of nostalgic criminal locales. The transformation of the traditional family firm into either individualistic mutations or disorganized teams of deviant scavengers reflects the dramatic economic changes sustained in the post-war period, which removed the industrial contours that had shaped and structured community life, fracturing its material base and creating new, blurred, socioeconomic coalitions. This has enabled the dissolution of traditional criminal coalitions that were so reliant upon the industrial landscape, rendering as meaningless any interpretation of organized or serious crime restricted to the languid boundaries of traditional cultures and subcultures (Horne and Hall 1995).

You get…scruffy kids sitting on the wall with hoods up, then a £60 grand BMW will stop off in the middle of the fucking road, park up and have a chat, gear changes hands and off they go. How they are not nicked I don't know, but old bill are not bothered about street dealing, they don't live round here, and neither do the boys who do the dealing. Meanwhile all the real hounds, white, black, Paki (Asian) all of them, they are long gone out to Essex and away…They are still at it but they aint got to hang around this shithouse to make a few bob. (Jim)

The impacts of both local housing policies and markets are crucial in understanding the distribution of individuals engaged in serious crime, and the emergence of potent post-industrial forces that have 'emptied out' marketable labour from communities formed around the assumptions of traditional cultures (Wilson 1987; cf Ruggiero and South 1997: Ch 6; Bursik 1986) have relocated criminal coalitions within decentred, unpredictable, relatively fragile economies, spread over a wide, and at times seemingly inappropriate, terrain. By the late 1970s the traditional neighbourhood had been decimated by various clumsy attempts at regeneration, and most of the traditional family firms had become at least partly ensconced within London's periphery, establishing new business ventures, and in particular engaging with the drugs trade, an enterprise that often involved little more than the application of the family name to an activity centred on a transport yard.

Post-industrial society is a disordered, inchoate, and episodic place with 'no rules, where cheating, lying, and stealing (are) accepted, even expected' (Anastasia 1991: 279), and where cultural chaperones such as the family firm are imbued with a sense of retrospective order that resonates of traditional working-class community and preserves an illusion of an enduring expert system. Indeed, those aspects of traditional culture that retain some viability within post-industrial markets are vital in nurturing and generating deviant collaborations, for as Lambrianou reminds us, 'if you didn't have a family of brothers with you, you were nothing. Brothers were your strength' (1992: 29). Although blood ties retain considerable power, particularly as generators of trust relationships, over several decades traditional, neighbourhood-based hegemony based on violence gave way to interlocking, ever-mutating networks that utilize cultural inheritance, legend, and myth to populate trade routes forged both by forbidden leisure and the suburban colonization of post-industrial urban and rural landscapes. By this time the various ancient feuds that had inspired the family firm for so long had begun to tail off, and as re-housing and the early 1980s' housing boom saw Dogtown relocate and reinvent itself in the flatlands of the commuter belt, members of the family firm became minor icons and symbols of traditional, insolent bandit enterprise (Sassen 2006: 74).

Trade between ex-denizens of locales rich with their own banditry and legendary atrocities are now common, as ancient antagonisms based upon largely redundant notions of territorial dominance fade like an old tattoo. The territorially based dimensions of the old firms' activities that were based purely upon reputation made control and surveillance of the firms' activities relatively easy, and in many ways mirrored the informal controls and conservative tendencies that were prevalent in industrial working-class culture. Within the family firm these controls, which channelled profits and discouraged members from instigating break-out enterprises, are no longer operational, and family members and associates are free to engage in buying, selling, importing, and wholesaling a wide range of goods 'according to the circumstances of the business cycle and (their) own family needs' (Castells 1996: 161).

The sense of 'retrospective unity' (Bauman 1992: 138), which is exploited by relocated crime firms, is reliant upon a generalized recipe of locality (Robertson 1995: 26) that is neither structural nor hierarchical, but is a highly durable yet flexible system of transposable dispositions, from which emerge practices organized into strategies that reproduce 'the objective structures of which they are the product' (Bourdieu 1977: 72). The contingency that is apparent in the flexibility of contemporary crime collaborations licenses engagement with new markets part populated by powerful individuals and proven practices from previous eras. However, contemporary criminal entrepreneurs do not inhabit a culturally constituted world (McCracken 1988), and while they may be steeped in traditional criminal cultures established and maintained by the precedents of indigenous markets, crucially they are not restricted by the parameters of specific neighbourhoods. While no longer determined by territorially driven notions of a local hegemonic order, economic viability is now established by syncopations of consumption, circulation, and exchange, inherited and adapted from the traditional indigenous socio-economic sphere (Block 1983: Ch 2), as criminal collaborations are obliged to roll with the punches of economic change while voraciously seeking out new arenas in which to perform.

Indeed, the shift to the suburbs or to a semi-rural retreat has created new entrepreneurial opportunities located around activities requiring real estate (construction, quarries, industrial estates, transport yards, container depots), along with enterprises based on non-urban land offering the prospect of profit as London's periphery continues to expand (see Barnes et al 2001).[5] The rural suburbs also offer coastal facilities for the movement of goods and people, barns and farm outbuildings for thieves and highjackers, and an excellent road system linking rural space to a ravenous marketplace, as goods are filtered across a wide territory defined

---

[5] The *Guardian*, 1 July 2009, reports that football clubs are the perfect vehicles for laundering money; many clubs are managed by amateurs and can easily be acquired by dubious investors; and criminals may use ownership of a club to forge legal business ties and win lucrative construction contracts. The report cites several examples of clubs in financial difficulties whose deficits were funded by suspected criminals.

by market logic rather than by networks grounded solely in local precedent.

The post-industrial drift of London's traditional working-class communities away from its urban heartlands was enabled by both public housing policy and the private housing market, and resulted in the colonization of rural space, bloating the periphery with new towns and extending the suburbs with a rash of housing projects. Those involved in criminal enterprise were merely part of this migration, and the key to understanding their change of address rests not with their criminality, but with their status as part of a proletarian diaspora whose trajectories out of Dogtown could encompass a six-bedroomed period residence with paddocks and outbuildings, an extended bungalow down a country lane, a three-bedroomed terraced house in a New Town, or a one-bedroomed flat in a tower block on the outskirts of a Victorian seaside resort.

However, the shift out of the old neighbourhood is seldom total, for the restructuring of the heartland created opportunities for money-making that would have been rude to ignore. For instance, a wide range of legitimate opportunities cry out for capital, and pubs, clubs, and gyms make good investments that will always benefit from being associated with an old established brand. Gyms and pubs are ideal bases for drug and robbery networks that benefit from considerable input from the suburbs, but such investments also engender rivalry and competition with other criminal commuters, as well as with the increasingly bitter remnants of the old order harbouring grudges and long memories; fatal shootings have occurred in Dogtown which were inspired by incidents that took place a generation ago.

Each phase of urban regeneration to which Dogtown has been subjected has witnessed suburbanized crime firms returning to the old neighbourhood to purchase land and property that has been subjected to compulsory purchase orders by either the local authority or government quangos. Hundreds of thousands of pounds were at stake a generation ago when crime firms used threats to purchase slices of Dogtown's backstreets standing in the way of new road development. Millions of pounds are now the prize for ex-Dogtown crime firms returning in order to plunder the public purse by either cashing in on their investments or intimidating property owners standing in the way of the relentless shift eastwards of London's financial sector. Competition amongst both legal and illegal entrepreneurs has led to a return to territorial conflict where the prize is no longer trading rights, but the value of land which has a ready-laundered return.

Remnants of the working-class city's old underworld are now attached to fragments of entrepreneurial opportunism that are networked across the former industrial areas into the semi-rural suburbs of London's periphery and beyond. Further, as geographical location becomes a somewhat ambiguous concept around which to base an illegal business, criminal labour itself, far from being linked to rigid hierarchies of local, familial, and highly specialized loyalties, takes on transient characteristics that underpin the essential instrumentality of the illegal marketplace. The pool of labour for these enterprises mirrors its legitimate counterpart in that it is negotiated within networks of small flexible firms 'slashing payrolls, flattening hierarchies, marketing aggressively' (Brzezinski 2002) and characterized by short-term contracts and lack of tenure (Lash and Urry 1987), where the workforce can be 'hired/fired/ offshored, depending upon market demand and labor costs' (Castells 1996: 272).

The contemporary neighbourhood firm is essentially a constantly evolving social system made up of 'patterns of relationship among individuals, which have the force of kinship' (Ianni 1971: 35), and its strength and longevity is derived from the sense of proximity and continued identification with a locale that retains a deep and enduring well of historical sentiment. For even when the material base for such a community is removed, and crime is located within loose collectivities of ad hoc groupings, the regard for apparently remote and non-instrumental protocols and methodologies, via 'selective remembering, misremembering and disremembering' (Douglas 1995: 13), establishes remnants of the traditional family firm as functional touchstones of competence and honour (Hobbs 1997). As a long-term admirer of one enduring family brand that has relocated to the suburbs explained, 'They are fucking old school…There was a load of people around like that who would fight you if they thought you was having a go. Every street had them, they was fighting people who would fight anybody who stuck their chin out.'

Understanding how violence is implemented within this marketplace makes it possible to stress that the suburban/rural shift does not constitute the reconfiguration of non-urban space as a mere base for criminal operations; the family firm has impacted on its new habitat by utilizing violence in a number of ways. Repayment of debts accrued as a result of legitimate business activity is demanded via threats, aggravated burglary, and stabbings. Drug debts can result in extreme violence, and there is always a catalogue of vendettas resulting from personal slights, perceived insults, or simply being barred by a bouncer from entering a club. The personal reputations, as well as the business activities, of the family firm and its cohorts ensure that forms of violent action traditionally associated with the inner city are now common in the swathe of suburban neighbourhoods that constitute London's increasingly ambiguous periphery.[6] This effectively shifts the notion of criminal territory away from an emphasis upon youth, poverty, and ethnicity, and focuses instead upon the 'bourgeois utopias' (Fishman 1987) of the suburbs, from where the family firm can join its neighbours and commute into the city, or exploit the new territory of the periphery.

Indeed, some of the new criminal firms are able to prosper incognito in suburban settings, and a fine example of the new hybrid form of suburban criminal governance concerned with market, as opposed to territorial, domination can be found in the lucrative ecstasy and cocaine market of London's periphery, which is closely associated with the volatile world of door security (O'Mahoney 1997, 2004: 73–100, 115–45; Leach 2003: 33–51). Operating within small disintegrated firms, located some way removed from the inner city alcoves which served to nurture the traditional family firm, vast sums of money were made in a very short time without having any significant impact upon the local social order beyond the world of clubs, drugs, and security. For instance, a near neighbour of one such entrepreneur became aggravated by the constant barking of the man's dog. Unaware of his neighbour's criminal status, or of the fact that he often carried a handgun, the middle-aged civilian, with no connection to gangsterism or the dark culture generated by the drug trade, was threatening to 'go around and sort

---

[6] 'Since the beginning of the year, there have been four execution-style murders in Essex. In one, a father of two was shot on his doorstep in full view of his family in Grays. In August two bouncers were shot after wading into a brawl outside a popular Essex nightclub. A man opened fire with a handgun...In the most recent incident earlier this month, Kenneth Kenny, a notorious villain, was shot three times in a hospital car park in Romford. Police are still hunting his killer, but believe he may have been killed as part of a continuing drug feud': *Observer*, 26 November 2000.

him out'. However, before he could register his complaint, the body-building heroin addict was killed in a highly publicized triple murder (O'Mahoney 1997; Rugby and Thompson 2000). While all three victims had violent criminal careers, their influence was upon local trade, their territory defined by the whims of a predominantly youthful market, and the normative local order remained relatively unaffected and unknowing.

Freed of the territorial restraints of the traditional neighbourhood, the enacted environment of the family firm is a blend of the local and the global (Cooke and Morgan 1993), and is a crucial and effective vehicle enabling individuals and groups to move between these two interlocking spheres. For, as the above examples indicate, criminal career trajectories are no longer restricted to highly specific and essentially redundant geographic and cultural spaces within an urban 'underworld', but are located 'all over the main streets and back alleys of the global economy' (Castells 1996: 168) and infused with the 'compulsory amnesia' of the suburbs 'where you eradicate slumland memories' (Sinclair 1997: 83).

Suburban Life

> Kenny lives in a nice street, and as far as he knows, his neighbours are nice people. He bought his bungalow 15 years ago before the motorway came, linking a semi-comatose retirement village to the pin-striped portals of the City. The ensuing commuter hell pushed up house prices, but not before Kenny had purchased the small parcel of land that backed onto his garden…Kenny is a businessman. He owns a video hire shop, and has a share in a used car business. Kenny also deals in amphetamines and cocaine, until five years ago he regularly imported pornography into the country, and his girlfriend is currently in prison for her part in a major conspiracy involving forged foreign currency…He is virtually indistinct from the under-managers, plumbers and insurance salesmen with whom he shares the stone clad certainties of a well earned suburban cul-de-sac, hewn from the remnants of post-industrial society. (Hobbs 1995: 60)

Serious crime should be understood in terms of interlocking networks which are metaphors for relationality (O'Byrne 1997; Strathern 1995: 179), expressed as amalgams of family, neighbourhood, region, and nationality, and which merge with purely instrumental commercial coalitions. Kinship in particular should be regarded as a highly instrumental trust variable, assuring loyalty by appealing to something other than self-interest (Gambetta 1988; Reuter 1985), and 'If a group all speaks the same language, has the same village roots, possesses the same myth and culture norms, then it can function as a unit with greater trust and understanding' (Lupsha 1986: 34). This is particularly relevant to the family firms' continued use of violence, for despite their involvement in the legitimate economy, violence is never entirely abandoned, but remains a tactic of the increasingly blurred personal and commercial domain (Ruggiero 1996: 25–45), and its continued relevance highlights the importance of trust, since 'Where violence is paramount, interpersonal ties must necessarily be strong, intense and affectively connoted' (Catanzaro 1994: 273).

The family firm is far from obsolete, and its role in generating and enabling criminal activity should be considered alongside numerous collaborations whose identities are not dependent solely on hegemonic territoriality, and whose configurations have changed in accordance with post-industrialism and subsequent relocation (Ruggiero 1993). The family firm trades in legitimate and illegitimate spheres, and various mutations in between, operating in the 'inherited basic architecture' (Castells 1996: 146) of the old neighbourhood where the family name is a legend, in its new suburban idyll where the displaced are reconnected to their origins (see Young and Willmott 1957: Chs 8–12), and across regional, national, and international boundaries. The family firm is the embodiment of Rose's belief that the individual 'can within the limits permitted by the culture define for himself somewhat new patterns suggested by the variation among the old ones' (1962: 14).

Peripheral Vision

Compared with the 'family businesses' of days gone by, today's organised crime networks are more agile and inventive, quick to embrace new technologies and seek out new markets and supply routes (Cabinet Office Strategy Unit 2009: 1)

'Organized crime', despite the global conspiracies of a growing number of political scientists fearing redundancy in the post-cold war era, is enacted within the cultures of class society, and localized crime collaborations, often in the form of 'family firms', have long been central to the economies and cultures of traditional working-class communities. These communities have undergone massive changes as a result of deindustrialization, and as a consequence the territorial base upon which so many informal and formal institutions were dependent has drastically altered. However, this chapter clearly indicates that, like working-class culture itself, organized crime has evolved rather than expired, and flourishes in post-industrial nooks and crannies that are inconvenient or inaccessible to the gaze of flâneurs, reformers, or nostalgic gangster groupies.

Traditional family firms were based upon the extortion of both legal and illegal local businesses; they were neighbourhood based and protected their territory from imperially inclined families from adjacent 'manors'. In exceptional cases, as detailed in Chapter 4, forays beyond their circumscribed territory were conducted in pursuit of larger prizes. However, 'The same processes that destroy autonomy are now creating new kinds of locality and identity' (Wilk 1995: 130). The scope of activities engaged in by contemporary organized crime groups is far greater than that of their one-dimensional predecessors, and the family firm's ability to prosper unrestrained by territorial imperatives shows that the same forces of deindustrialization and fragmentation that have ravaged traditional communities have created new notions of locality and identity, and fresh markets to plunder.

In Dogtown, because of housing policy and housing markets, patterns of immigration, the mobility of the workforce, and the sheer diversity of both legitimate and illegitimate markets, the traditional neighbourhood has largely disintegrated. In this environment serious crime networks, some containing 'remnants' of the traditional 'firm', operate as fluid, flexible marauders, engaging with 'a whole variety of relationships of adoptive or artificial kinship and instrumental friendship' (Arlacchi 1986: 133), which, as local social systems, are no longer reliant upon forms of parochial dominance previously enjoyed by the feudal warlords of the 1950s and 1960s.

In every major urban conurbation, the family firm can be observed as a constantly evolving social system whose potency is derived from a sense of proximity and continued identification with locales that retain a deep and enduring sense of place and source of cultural commitment (Blok 1974: 212). Traditional criminal firms are based upon family ties and neighbourhood dispositions, and gaining an allegiance to such a firm can be highly beneficial to a fledgling gangster or drug dealer. The illegitimate economic sphere is constituted by interlocking networks of small, flexible firms, and while criminal careers are no longer restricted to the dark, smoky alcoves of an urban 'underworld', the family firm remains a crucial and effective vehicle enabling individuals and groups to move between the inter-reliant spheres of the local and the global. Local crime families are long-established urban institutions whose survival is due to an ability to operate not only in the old neighbourhood, but also across regional, national, and international boundaries, operating from the suburbs, from a regenerated inner city, from foreign parts, or perhaps from a prison cell. Retaining links with the family seat in the ruins of Britain's industrial past is crucial, and blood ties remain as important in British crime as they are amongst the British aristocracy.

Situated within social networks that are not exclusively transgressive, these collaborations utilize powerful urban histories as a way of affording structure to a terrain that is no longer fixed (Chaney 1994: 149). The culture of this new terrain, along with the cultural inheritance of traditional criminogenic locales (Arlacchi 1986: 227), feature gossip, rumour, and violent folktales that provide some certainty and illusion of structure to an environment that is fluid and in a state of constant mutation. Rather than pontificate upon such intangible panic-riddled and potentially racist notions as 'transnational organized crime', we might glean more from considering the permutations of old established brands, who continue to form the cultural and economic bedrock of what is often understood as British organized crime and who bring a real meaning to the term 'family values'.

The Wrong Un

The Wrong Un is a wine bar in Dogtown High Street where middle-aged escapees to the suburbs return to ruefully stroke fading scars while recalling deals gone by and honouring those who are absent without leave, 'doing a ten', or living in Lanzarote. The Wrong Un used to be a carpet shop, and while it would be indiscreet to delve too closely into how it was granted an alcohol licence, its atmosphere of shaven-headed, nostalgic collusion makes a comforting alcove for an ageing clientele resentful of the seemingly arbitrary character of the streets that once nurtured and confirmed their deviant essences. Leaning on the bar of The Wrong Un in the mid afternoon and dressed for the golf course, a glass of lager, a plate of pie and mash, perhaps a seat at the football or a visit to the boxing, are the allures of the old neighbourhood for any working-class escapee, and the family firm and their cohorts are no exceptions.[7] This is a reaffirmation of an identity forged by predatory entrepreneurship, and confirmed and strengthened by the same global forces that have shredded the old neighbourhood.

The prized residues of industrial culture that pock mark the fragmented landscape are burnished with pride and expectation. Somebody is investing in buy-to-let properties, the Olympics are coming, and West Ham United have got a young Italian striker on loan. The family firm is regularly drawn to the backstreets and estates where they made their names, and although they may retain commercial interests in Dogtown, the visits are nostalgic confirmations of identities created as much by the bricks and mortar of Dogtown as by the activities that enabled their escape.

But the family firm pays a price for life in suburbia. When they were the local lord of the manor, integral to the cultural mechanics of the community, life was simple and challenges to their hegemony were rare. The middle classes did not wish to colonize Dogtown, and opposition from adjacent territories was as negligible as it was predictable. Local police generally left the family firm alone, citing informal order maintenance, and the relative security and predictability of industrial-era, working-class community was replicated in the world of the family firm. However, the old certainties are no more: the fine-grained protocols of the taken-for-granted social order have disintegrated; long-established hierarchies have disappeared with the docks and its confident unionized workforce; and despite the underworld legend dictating that violence is the prerogative of a small gladiatorial elite who 'only hurt their own', even the family firm is now vulnerable. As one man who used education to leave the life behind noted, 'Now you get somebody who is a Chap gets shot, look in the paper when they nick who did it. Nobody would have heard of him, he won't be a Face, it'll be some young

---

[7] 'A spokesman for the National Criminal Intelligence Service said: "You can take the boy out of the East End, but you can't take the East End out of the boy. Even when they move out to Essex, they still want to attend boxing matches and go to dog racing. There is a huge social network that has sprung up to cater for these people and allow them to continue with many of the activities they were involved in back in London."': *Observer*, 26 November 2000.

boy with no record who's been bunged a few quid and given a gun.'[8]

As with the very notion of an 'underworld', the concept of a specialist 'shooter'—a respected and much-feared man whose willingness to carry and use a firearm either during the course of a robbery or in order to enact personal or professional retribution—is a relic of industrial-era urban culture, no longer a highly revered specialism, no longer remarkable. Consequently, an overt presence back on the streets of Dogtown could be tempting for some traditional rival with an ancient grudge, or to a disrespectful freelancer with no sense of history. Discretion is the key, and it is only the avuncular superstar dinosaurs of the old underworld chasing another book contract who encourage publicity. An anonymous, electronically gated, half-timbered chunk of mock Tudor festooned with CCTV cameras situated in one of the leafier alcoves of London's periphery is a far more appropriate address.

The family firm is no longer reliant upon the exploitation of local markets; it makes money from a range of local and regional activities that are increasingly informed by opportunities with global connotations. Like the children and grandchildren of the dock and processing workers, the ship suppliers and repairers, and other workers once reliant upon the global trade that focused upon the Thames, the family firm has shifted its residence to London's periphery. Increasingly, this is where its business is carried out, and where the fruits of that business are enjoyed.

Chez Cash

You can eat quite cheaply in the restaurant; two local men in their thirties cook and local students wait on tables for a clientele that is a microcosm of twenty-first-century Britain. Commuters from the recently rural executive developments and dressed for the nineteenth hole are explicitly casual diners, mixing with special-occasion, displaced, second-generation refugees from the urban overspill estates celebrating birthdays and anniversaries. Pastel

---

[8] 'The country's youngest professional "hitman" has been convicted of murder at the Old Bailey. The teenager, known as Riot on the streets of north-west London, was 15 when he was paid £200 to kill a young woman in Hackney, east London…The hitman in this case was the fourth young black man to be used in this way in 12 months': *Guardian*, 23 May 2011.

Pringle sweaters and battleship grey chicken Kievs swirl; the microwave goes into overdrive and the coffers of Constable country brim with their skim from City deals, used car sales, traditional sweat, relentless tedium, and sometimes something darker.

The locals are no longer yokels, and fields vie for space with suburban developments of houses, off-licences, hairdressers, and supermarkets, as the electrification of the London rail link and an improved road system has merged town and turnip, cockney and country. But Mr Cash still manages to turn a glance into a stare, adding a glaze of menace to the rural idyll of the prints adorning the paisley walls. The merging of powerful working-class histories and increasingly cosmopolitan urban remnants with rural space and suburban anonymity constructs a terrain of opportunistic alcoves and enterprise trails that recalibrates the logic of criminal commerce carrying few suggestions of topographical orthodoxy. Any attempt to ascertain a sense of order and structure, or to locate where individuals are situated in relation to such a complex, flexible, or illusory terrain, must be acquired through engaging with the interface of culture and economics rather than by gazing through the lens of law and order. But in the meantime, 'we are not only without an adequate cartography of global capitalism, we lack political maps of our own backyards' (Cooke 1988: 489).

6

Small Faces: Entrepreneurial Youth and the State of Dogtown

> In some areas, there are links between the serious violence perpetuated by delinquent youth gangs, and the existence of more organised criminal groups (Cabinet Office Strategy Unit 2009)

This inability to map the post-industrial terrain that has realigned the neighbourhood firm has contributed to an ignorance of working-class deviant collaborations and the cultures that nurture them. As Chapter 4 clearly demonstrates, London's marquee criminals did not arrive in the marketplace fully formed, but had their origins firmly established in territorial imperatives that were established during their youth, suggesting that UK youth collaborations deserve to be considered seriously when seeking to comprehend the evolution of illegal market engagement.

As discussed in Chapter 2, the rapid expansion of the British state's definition of organized crime has encompassed a wide range of disparate transgressive collaborations that includes youth gangs, marking a significant, and very recent, shift in the state's reaction to youth deviance.[1] Like organized crime, youth gangs are a 'newly noticed kind of human behaviour' (Hacking 1999: 136) in the UK, and, as with organized crime, the term requires new and suitably vague definitional boundaries in order to accommodate contemporary social conditions (Klein 1995). According to the influential

---

[1] In 2007 the Home Office established a specialist subgroup, the *Tackling Gangs Action Programme*, overseen by a Task Force on Gangs and Guns and chaired by the Home Secretary to develop policies designed to deal with the problem of gangs. However, Hallsworth and Young locate a 2008 report as the formal acknowledgement of the British gang problem (Home Office 2008), and point out that most of the attention focused upon the British gang has been concerned with violence, and in particular the increased use of weapons (Hallsworth and Young 2008: 176).

definition of Klein (2005), 'A street gang is any durable, street oriented youth group whose own identity includes involvement in illegal activity', which is so inclusive as to be virtually useless, lacking even the 'veiled expressions of bourgeois disapproval' (Ball and Curry 1995: 227) that mark most academic definitions, suggesting an imprecision (Hancock 2006: 180) that renders much gang research 'an argument over the correct description of a ghost' (Katz and Jackson-Jacobs 2004). Indeed, the absence of any relatively precise definition, combined with the British state's aforementioned conflation of gangs with organized crime, has made it difficult to find a youthful form of transgressive collaboration that cannot be designated as 'gang related' (Armstrong et al (in progress)).

Clean Living under Difficult Circumstances: The British Orthodoxy

Until recently the British academic orthodoxy has been to maintain that gangs did not exist in the UK (Young et al 2007: 36–8), and with one notable exception[2] the British experience was that 'Gangs are always present in the next district or they existed last year, never here and now' (Gibbens and Ahrenfeldt 1966: 83). The pivotal British academic study of youth was carried out by Downes (1966), whose work stood in direct opposition to influential American theories by Cohen (1955) and Cloward and Ohlin (1960), which were based upon the American 'corner boy's' reaction to failure within a fiercely aspirational culture that produced a frustration that was channelled into gang membership. Downes found an absence of aspirational culture amongst working-class boys in east London, and instead stressed dissociation, the process by which all aspects of middle-class life, and in particular the primary engine of aspirational culture—education—is rejected (see Willis 1977; Corrigan 1976). The boys' 'expectations and aspirations are centred on the

---

[2] Patrick's (1973) is therefore an exceptional study of an exceptional area, presenting an insider's account of fighting gangs based on territory—a network of area-oriented violent action that conforms in many ways to Thrasher's structured gang, with its leadership and defined roles. However, the loose membership and image of the group as a collectivity based on spontaneous violence, is indicative of Yablonsky's 'Violent Gang' (Yablonsky 1962). An inter-locking network of inequality had produced an enduring gang subculture hinging on dissociation from middle-class norms and survival in a climate of socio-economic hardship that had narrowed the possibilities for action (see Fraser 2011).

world outside the factory' (Downes 1966: 237) in 'loose collectivities or crowds within which there was occasionally some more structured grouping, based on territorial loyalty' (Cohen 1973:128) and who congregated on street corners and committed petty crime and nuisance. Downes wrote of a white, working-class culture of cafes and bomb sites, and of a two-tiered state education system from which most youths exited at age 15, the elite of whom entered into three-, five-, and seven-year apprenticeships, while the bulk were destined for unskilled, low-paid manual work (Davies 2008).

For Downes and the scholars who followed him, structural inequalities within working-class communities were cross-generational, and working-class youths took over traditional practices behind which lay traditional values (Parker 1974; Gill 1977). This, along with an awareness and general acceptance of the low pay and poor conditions on offer in the job market, were integral to cultural transmission. The boys regarded the world in terms of class, 'of "Them" and "Us" rather than in terms of success and failure' (Downes 1966: 235), and young men generally matured out of street-corner deviance to take their places in a society of peers, where, if horizons were low, they were visible and attainable.

Throughout the industrial era, generations of youths thrived more in harmony than in conflict with their locale, forging reputations in defence of the neighbourhood (Suttles 1968). Groups of young men would regularly drift into adjacent hostile territory in order to provoke violence which routinely involved weapons, yet these groups emanated from a domain that was shaped, refined, and restrained by elements of social control that were lodged in the pragmatic realities of the local political economy and its associated cultures and institutions. As a consequence, for most participants these were temporary collaborations before engagement with the local employment market enabled maturation into an unambiguously proletarian society, where crime was normal and 'everyone was at it (but) some were at it more than most. They were the professional criminals' (Hobbs 1988: 8) who 'undertake crime as a vocation' (Hallsworth and Silverstone 2009: 362).

Steve: On and On

As a young man, I would guess what, between 14 and 17 (mid to late 1960s), I was out every night. And every one of those nights was spent expecting to fight. We were out of Dogtown and we would do dances mainly...[as I became] older, pubs came into it, and weapons. I think back and there were stabbings. I got stabbed in the back, and I had (to go to) hospital when I had my jaw broke by a chisel outside a pub on Kingsland Road...two of my mates were stabbed and one nearly died after he got chased in Bethnal Green...Oh I carried a tool [weapon], I had a little sheath knife for a while, screwdrivers, anything really...Yes used them, hurt people. For a while our little mob put ourselves about, we would go over Hackney, Stepney and have full-on rucks [fights]. Then they would come over to us and do the same thing. If you had time then you'd rob what you could once they was on the floor, go through pockets and wallets...Go mob handed into the cloakrooms and grab leathers and sheepskins [coats]...I fucking loved it. You was taking on an area, a whole area, it was exciting. But people were starting to get really hurt, and when a boy, just a boy, got murdered at Stratford, it pulled me up a bit. I knew him, not well, but I started thinking that it was getting serious. It wern't funny no more. Then you started watching people getting put down [prison], stabbed up, one of the boys I was at school with lost an eye. I just eased off bit by bit. I was married at 19, but some of those boys went on and on.

Steve named a number of his old friends who had gone on to make names for themselves as professional criminals, several of whom had served long prison sentences. However, the bulk of his friends, including some of the most aggressive, had, like him, eased away from violence and had entered a job market still buoyed by the post-Second World War economic boom. These boys were able to mature into adult members of communities yet to be decimated by deindustrialization.

As we can see in Chapter 4, the strictly defined territorial parameters of industrial working-class communities produced clusters of youthful collaborations who utilized neighbourhood identity as a vehicle for recreational transgression (Pearson 1983: 188). McDonald (2000) details growing up during and immediately after the Second World War, and of particular significance is his description of the relative ease with which the street-based play of childhood evolved into hedonistic, often violent delinquency (Shildrick and MacDonald 2007), before morphing seamlessly into adult pursuits which for some had potentially deadly consequences. This 'playfulness' of much territorially based transgression was recognized by

Thrasher (1927: 46), who established youth collaborations as quasi-institutions in the emerging social ecology of the industrial era. Thrasher also emphasized that conflict had a major role in integrating collective behaviour (Thrasher 1927: 46) and, as Simmel notes, 'The extent and combination of antipathy, the rhythm of its appearance and disappearance, the forms in which it is satisfied…produce the metropolitan form of life in its irresolvable totality; and what at first glance appears in it as dissociation, actually is one of its elementary forms of sociation' (Simmel 1955: 20).

Youthful conflict was crucial in forming identities, creating reputations, and moulding communal distinctiveness in the face of opposition. These territorially based groups occupied spaces or interstices between sections of the urban fabric frequently situated within 'delinquency areas', where youthful deviant collaborations were organized around working-class territorial imperatives defined by the experiences of low income, poor housing, and poor health (Shaw and McKay 1942). Here, criminal careers were nurtured and youth formulated criminal associations (Yablonsky 1962: 147–8). As described in Chapter 4, a minority would commodify their violence by exploiting local entrepreneurial opportunities and addressing vulnerable targets in adjacent territories (Whyte 1943: 10).

In working-class London, neighbourhood-based groups abounded, and territorial imperatives featuring individual, local, and family reputations were forged in youthful combat that was ideal preparation for the world of acquisitive gangsterism (McDonald 2000). These fractious networks were evolving in south London, in particular the riverside areas of Bermondsey, Deptford, Southwark, Lewisham, and Lambeth; across the Thames in Hoxton, Hackney, Whitechapel, Bethnal Green, Aldgate, Mile End, Stepney, Stratford, Walthamstow, Upton Park, and Canning Town; in north London in Islington, Kilburn, the Angel, and Clerkenwell. Working-class enclaves in west London, such as Shepherds Bush and Notting Dale, also produced groups of young men whose main preoccupation was the joy of violent confrontation. A loose-knit coalition of south London's youth went under the generic name of the 'Elephant Boys', which referenced the Elephant and Castle district (Fraser 1998: 1–4); others had exotic sobriquets such as the long-standing 'Titanics' from the northern edges of the City of London, while the loose-knit Irish in Camden Town, or the early twentieth century's Russian Jewish, Whitechapel-based 'Bessarabians'

(Leeson 1934: 147) were founded on ethnicity. These territorial-based groups sometimes morphed into adult crime collaborations that were ideally situated geographically, culturally, and, in its wider sense, organizationally, to engage with 'night-clubs, protection rackets, extortion, gambling, dog and horseracing pitches, horse thieving, car thieving and beatings. Complementing these activities were receiving, safe-breaking, black marketeering, smash and grab, burglary, high-jacking, jump-up, robbery and wages grabs' (McDonald 2000: 9).

Whether or not they proceeded to segue into adult crime, these youthful collaborations must be understood as products of industrial-era spaces and places. However, the constantly mutating character of the post-industrial political economy has ensured that many of the traditional theoretical props upon which scholars have framed their work are no longer reliable tools. In particular, within academic discourse, gangs and subcultures had coexisted as contrasting views of working-class youthful collaborations maintained by the socio-economic differentials that typified and divided British and American cultures. However, these differentials were created within the context of the codes, protocols, and assumptions of industrial society, and this context has changed. As the old order that generated the relationship between deviant youth and the relentless continuation of production-based cultures has disappeared, it may be time to reassess.

The State of Dogtown

As described in Chapter 5, the post-war period featured full employment for the first time in Dogtown's history, which generated an unprecedented stability and confidence within this tight-knit community. This was the world that once enabled subcultural membership to bloom as a temporary bridge between childhood and the adult world, and where dissociation from middle-class culture enabled maturation into an exclusively proletarian adult lifecourse. Downes' boys accepted their proletarian occupational futures and looked forward to traditional forms of leisure, where transgressive experimentation was largely restricted to liminal episodes dominated by the ecology of the working-class street and the hegemony of a single-class social structure built upon the firm foundations of unionized manual labour and the extended family (Cohen 1972).

Yet this period proved to be little more than a fleeting moment. The world of single-class manual communality, where middle-class culture was remote and irrelevant and consumerism underdeveloped, is gone, and Dogtown is now a socially fragmented area of high unemployment and low income. Dock work, upon which Dogtown was founded, is now a distant memory, and the trade unionism that had once dominated social and political life in the area has drastically declined, along with social housing and high-quality technical education (Hobbs 1988, 2006). The fragmentation that has occurred as a result of deindustrialization, and in particular the shift from metropolitan-based production to the financial, corporate, and service sectors, has produced in Dogtown, which is situated in the shadow of London's financial centre, a brittle, often fractious working-class culture made up of vulnerable and increasingly disposable 'contingent workers' (Persaud and Lusane 2000: 26) living alongside the ethnically diverse remnants of long-established families with roots entwined in the decaying social and political fabric of the area.

The fragmented reality of contemporary social and economic life means that easy connections between youth and a single-dimensional version of the parent culture can no longer be made. There are many versions of youth and just as many parent cultures. The subcultural assumptions of industrial society are inadequate tools with which to explore post-industrial youth who are 'separat(ed)...from the kind of work that could include them securely in community life' (Currie 1985: 278) and who, often encumbered by the exclusionary logic of racism, cannot assimilate into a unitary working-class culture that no longer exists (Horne and Hall 1995). As a consequence, the sense of continuity with a parent culture embedded in pragmatic communities based upon the certainties, restraints, and conflicts of the manual working class central to the subcultural thesis is missing, creating a strategic space in which nihilism can thrive.

What is clear is that in post-industrial society, youth collaborations are increasingly market orientated (Hobbs 2012), and, as discussed below, all of the new studies of British gangs acknowledge, although to different degrees, that the drugs trade offers an accessible alternative sphere of enterprise to declining opportunities in traditional male employment. However, although, as illustrated in Chapter 4, youthful collaborations of the industrial era were ideal adaptive devices for converting territorial dominance to market supremacy, not all of the more recent youthful forays into enterprise culture have attracted the gang sobriquet.

The People's Game

As we can see in Chapter 4, the shift from neighbourhood street violence to neighbourhood entrepreneurial violence was as important in the creation of British crime collaborations as it was in enabling urban American street gangs to exploit the Volstead Act in order to move on to greater things (Hobbs and Antonopoulos (forthcoming)). The young men of the Sabinis' Clerkenwell street gang, the loose-knit territorial coalitions who formed under the flag of the 'Elephant Boys', the Richardsons, the Krays and countless other working-class street predators, commodified their violent reputations to exploit opportunities offered by variations of extortion. The British working classes have continued to engage competently with economic opportunities that arise inadvertently on the periphery of market society, and the shift of the football hooligan elite into entrepreneurial pursuits was noted by Gilman (1994), who locates football hooliganism within the British subcultural tradition, but also notes that the hedonistic youth culture of the late 1980s situates drugs, and therefore drug markets, at its very centre.

Enterprise culture proved to be a seductive adventure, and hooligans, who just a decade earlier were presented by many as heroic luddites resisting the commodification of the people's game (Taylor 1971), had become, in the words of screenwriter Al Hunter, '1980's Thatcher's eagles'.[3] Football culture in the 1980s fully embraced the fetish for expensive aspirational sportswear (Lloyd 1988; McLaughlan and Redhead 1985), and enthusiastically engaged with markets for counterfeit and stolen casual clothing (Thornton 2003). In addition to their lurid mimicry of tennis stars and golf pros, these working-class wide boys were also heavily influenced by local black culture, and elements of the nascent acid house/rave scene were borrowed from the peripatetic clubs of local black colony culture. 'Most of these white working class boys started moving around with blacks and the music/rave thing started. Blacks did illegal raves—blues (parties), shebeens, for years cos they couldn't

---

[3] Al Hunter wrote the screenplay for Alan Clarke's remarkable 1989 film *The Firm*, which used West Ham United's Inter City Firm as its inspiration.

get legal premises to hire…empty flats…would be used, set your own bar up, £5 to get in, and make a bomb. These "illegal" do's had flyers printed and were advertised on black pirate radio.'[4] Pirate radio stations such as the Dread Broadcasting Corporation, which first broadcast in 1979, brought these events to the attention of listeners, creating an influential precedent for the West Ham Inter City Firm-connected Centre Force, a 24-hour station generating its own illegal music events (Collin 1997: 133–7).[5]

By the end of the 1980s the peak years of hooliganism were over, and the national game had embarked upon its task of gentrifying what once had been the property of the industrial working class (Collin 1997: 124–5). Most of the senior members of these now infamous groups of hooligans were in their late twenties, and some were ensconced with the music scene and various related legitimate and semi-legitimate business ventures. These were not unknowing dupes of capitalism, but young men who had matured along with enterprise culture itself and 'The same geezers who would be standing across the road, throwing bricks and having silly fights over football, had realised there was no money in football' (event promoter and ex-hooligan Joe Wieczorek, in Collin 1997: 131). The fashionable drug ecstasy was closely linked with the underground dance and music scene, and the emergent entrepreneurs of rave culture looked to the old neighbourhoods for the necessary muscle to provide security at illegal dance events ('I'd already got a reputation as a hardcase West Ham supporter and they knew I could handle myself. Fancy it? I took to it like a duck to water' (Leach 2003: 28; see Pennant 2003: 390–92)) before morphing into gatekeepers to the events' drug trade, and then direct involvement with the drug trade itself (Rietveld 1993: 41–78; Leach 2003: 252. See Ayres and Treadwell 2012).

As we can see in Chapter 4, the triumvirate of twentieth-century 'Crime Lords', the Sabinis, Krays, and Richardsons, confirmed the euphemism of 'protection' as a central activity within the informal urban economy, and in industrial society those fields of leisure prohibited or licensed by the state, for instance gambling or the supply of alcohol, were especially vulnerable to extortion. The decline of the British manufacturing base created an economic crisis which prompted British towns and cities actively to pursue forms of city

---

[4] Kenny Monrose: personal correspondence.
[5] For a vibrant summary of this era, see Broughton and Brewster (2009).

centre regeneration, and the night-time economy—that 'previously marginal zone of space and time'—was 'being promoted as central to the image of a modern "European" city' (O'Connor and Wynne 1996). This, in turn, created a demand for security which, during the industrial era, had been dominated by the police's monopoly of violence (Hobbs et al 2003; Hadfield 2006). However, since the state was unable to provide a level of security commensurate with the very specific hedonistic protocols of this new economy, 'Bouncers' emerged as both protectors and extorters (Hobbs et al 2003: 211–42), normalizing violence (Winlow and Hall 2006) and embedding violent potential in the socio-political structure (Arlacchi 1986: 115) via 'systems of accumulated expertise' (Giddens 1991: 3) which were based within traditional criminogenic locales (Arlacchi 1986: 227).

Door-security firms oscillate between security and protection, enhancing interlocking individual and commercial reputations (Hobbs et al 2003: 241–2; Mclean 1998: 75) while operating an informal system of taxation (Winlow 2001: 147–53). As Bauman indicates, 'Cultural authorities turn themselves into market forces, become commodities, compete with other commodities, legitimise their value through the selling capacity they attain'(Bauman 1992: 452), and the development of extortion and its entrenchment and normalization within the night-time economy enhanced market stability (Gambetta and Reuter 1995: 116–35). Private security blossomed not only in alcohol-based venues, but also in venues whose commercial feasibility depended upon a controlled supply of illegal recreational drugs (Hobbs 1995: 74–80; O'Mahoney 1997; Hobbs et al 2003: 228–9), where bouncers operated as 'gate-keepers' and extorted money from dealers seeking to trade (Silverstone (forthcoming)). While legitimate businesses, 'faced with the constant threat of cut-throat competition are subject to easy temptation to pay gangsters for protection against competitors' (Lippmann 1967: 61), and 'where the state is weak or its rationalizing minions are held in contempt' (Courtwright 1996: 29), 'the forces of law and disorder' (Wilson 2002: 223) have, like the Sicilian Mafia (Blok 1974; Gambetta 1993; Catanzaro 1992), become both defenders and exponents of the dominant economic order.

As the night-time economy evolved in the 1990s the demand for security at legal venues placed a high premium on muscle backed by local reputation (Hobbs et al 2003; Leach 2003: 114), and 'What earned these men "respect" was, first their capacity to coerce with physical violence and thus invoke fear in others' (Blok 1974: 62). Many of the reputations forged in football violence and their cumulative networks remain commercially relevant to this day and not only in the field of door security, for ex-hooligans have made their mark on the music business, the building and property industries, catering, and a whole range of disparate enterprises (Sugden 2002); while for others, football hooliganism served as an introduction to legal and illegal security work, debt collection, and the kind of generic violent support services so vital to the modern entrepreneur (see Stewart in Chapter 9).

Located at the intersection of culture and the market, football hooliganism is merely one example of how the violent potential of working-class youth, which has its origins in urban play, the quest for excitement, and 'a source of status where other sources have dried up' (Slaughter 2003: 194), can offer an alternative career trajectory. They were street-savvy entrepreneurs making money from a prohibited youth market, and, like generations of streetwise entrepreneurs before them, the violence upon which their reputational platforms were built was ushered from the territorial and recreational spheres and into the marketplace via a regulatory vacuum created by prohibition. As discussed in Chapter 4, the use of territorial dominance as a training ground for major criminal careers is a common feature on the CV of professional criminals (see Fellstrom 2010), their violent entrepreneurial delinquency maturing into the epitome of the successful tough, independent, working-class businessman totally in harmony with the local habitus (Robson 1997).

However, while generations of working-class youth, including the ex-football hooligans discussed above, have engaged in this commodification of violence and territory, it is the current generation who have become the focus of 'Britain's Gang Problem'[6] and who constitute a threat so apparently serious that the actuarial expertise of the state is required to define, order, and quantify it.[7] As Van Duyne has noted, 'forms of crime not stemming from "others" do not sufficiently touch the right emotional chord' (2011: 2). Thus,

---

[6] 'LA Gangs take over UK streets', *Sun*, 15 April 2010.

[7] BBC News, 21 February 2007, 'Police identify 169 London Gangs'. However, variations in official estimates regarding gang membership across UK police areas are almost certainly due to 'the relative amount of effort each force puts into collecting intelligence about gangs': Newburn, Taylor, and Ferguson (2011).

could it be that the youthful entrepreneurship stemming from the enduring 'visceral habitus' (Hall 1997) which preceded the UK's gang problem was not generally regarded as a serious threat warranting dedicated government intervention because, with few notable exceptions, the protagonists were white?

Gang UK

> ...boys aged between fifteen and twenty, with drape suits, picture ties and an American slouch (Hoggart 1957: 203)

As discussed above, subcultures dominated the British academic literature on youth for 40 years,[8] at which point the previously inconceivable notion of the British gang began to seep into the public consciousness, resulting in the abandonment of the nuances of subcultural analysis in favour of the frightening novelty of yet another form of essentially alien transgression (Hobbs 1998). As neoliberal policies have bitten deep into the proletarian heartlands, we are faced with the possibility that the social conditions that have nourished gang membership in the US are being replicated in the UK.[9] If this is the case, then the benign relationship between deviant youth and the parent culture, a relationship that has framed British subcultural studies, may be all but redundant. Further, for this youthful minority, albeit a minority that impact significantly upon the local community (Pitts 2008), the fissures created by economic policy afford them interstitial status, a status described so vividly in the classic work of Thrasher, and Shaw and Mackay, and reinforced by much contemporary work in the US.

In the US, the post-industrial destruction of traditional working-class areas (Fagan 1989; Moore 1991) has eroded the presumption of upward mobility that was a central prop of the aspirational culture of the US (Hagedorn 1988). As the shift from the formal to the informal economy was compounded[10] and traditional forms of

---

[8] For an excellent overview, see Campbell and Muncer (1989).

[9] It is worth pointing out that the Mod vs Rocker 'battles' of the mid 'sixties were a minority sport, and that, as Stan Cohen's (1973) work clearly indicates, the numbers involved were tiny: perhaps as small as the 6 per cent of youths estimated to be members of contemporary 'delinquent youth groups' (Sharp, Aldridge, and Medina 2006).

[10] 'On the Books: Can tapping into the informal economy improve the lives of the urban poor?', *American Prospect*, 18 January 2010.

working-class organization were made redundant (Schneider 1999), the gang was elevated to the cutting edge of entrepreneurial strategy (Hagedorn 1998; Davis 1990: Ch 5), evolving as an increasingly commercial entity (Sanchez-Jankowski 1991) for youths suffering 'multiple marginality' (Vigil 1988). This normalization of the drug trade should be understood not in terms of pathology, but in terms of a predatory logic (Williams 1989, 1992; Mieczkowski 1990; Hamid 1990), where individualism and pecuniary advantage reign over communal priorities (Bourgois 1995), taking contemporary youth and the communities that spawned them into the realm associated with organized crime, a realm that only the most naïve of urban observers would continue to regard as a rarefied deviant zone (Simon and Burns 2009: 183). Consequently, in the US the 'youth problem' has become increasingly redefined in terms of the drugs trade (Taylor 1990; Padilla 1992; Waldorf and Lauderback 1993), featuring strategies that are not implicitly distinct from those found in a fiercely unforgiving mainstream society. In this respect, entrepreneurial gangs show close similarities with the street gangs of the early part of the twentieth century, who, on developing rudimentary structures based upon ethnicity, class, and territory, evolved via the Volstead Act into some of America's principal crime groups (Lacey 1991).

Nearly a century on, conditioned by poverty and economic marginality (Brotherton and Barrios 2004) and with the comfort blanket of industrial society now permanently removed, the gang constitutes a rational attempt at countering ethnic and class marginality via 'local patriotism' (Sanchez-Jankowski 1991: 99) to emerge as 'an institutionalized bricolage of illicit enterprise, social athletic club, patron to the poor, employment agency for youth, substitute family, and nationalist, community, or militant organization' (Hagedorn 2007: 23). As the street gang mutated into a local entrepreneurial institution, merging markets with territories, young men continued to use violence as a tool with which to create their own masculinity; but now they insisted on getting paid (Bourgois 1995).

'Let's go get paid' (Sullivan 1989: 163)

However, the lives of British, post-industrial urban youth are rather more chaotic and less conveniently ordered (Hallsworth and Silverstone 2009; Winlow and Hall 2006) than is suggested by the literal transplantation of urban narratives from the US, and the youthful collaborations of twenty-first-century London bear little relationship to the gangs described by Thrasher (1927) in Chicago almost a century ago, or to the alternative institutions of contemporary American cities (Pitts 2008: 13).

Recently, engaged scholars have tended to approach the emergence of British gangs with empirically informed caution.[11] Hallsworth and Young (2008) in particular warn against the adoption of an inappropriate 'hegemonic interpretation' of the chaotic, occasionally violent lives of a minority of urban youth, while Aldridge and Medina (2008) avoid over-prescriptive definitions and retain much of the emphasis upon the cultural continuity that was a feature of the classical British subcultural tradition, steering a careful path between Hallsworth and Young's (2008) scepticism and Pitts' (2008: 110–25) identification of disadvantage as the context for the embeddedness of entrepreneurial 'supergangs' coordinated by organized crime groups.

With an emphasis on traditional, often conservative, features of industrial society, Downes' notion of subcultures was not based upon the emerging youth consumer market, but upon communities based on family, work, and distinctively working-class leisure pursuits, and where the solutions to everyday problems were always pragmatic, and never magical (Hall and Jefferson, 1976).[12] However, contemporary youth have been moulded by a logic generated by consumer capitalism (Hallsworth 2005) and have little hope of incorporation into the nihilistic mainstream unless it is via the consumption of the teen-specific cultural products of 'orchestrated rebellion' (Hall et al 2007) fashioned in the 'global gulag of factories' (Ferrell et al 2008: 14). The void created by post-industrialism has 'promoted a culture of intense personal competition, and spur[ed] its citizens to a level of material consumption many could not lawfully sustain' (Currie 1985: 278), and as the drug trade became normalized (Coomber 2006: 156), 'the lifestyles of British youth became inextricably bound up with criminal activity' (Collin 1997: 131), and the streets 'home to a tired collection of bit-players

---

[11] Goldson's (2011) outstanding edited collection brings together a range of scholarly perspectives on the British gang.

[12] See Clarke (1982), Cohen (1980), and Hall (2012) for critiques of the Birmingham School.

struggling to make their shot within the confines of the drug culture itself' (Simon and Burns, 2009: 182).

Drug dealing is now an everyday part of Dogtown's fabric; it is unexceptional, and youthful collaborations are part of the community of practice who are seeking to eke profit from this chaotic and fluctuating market. However, it would be a mistake to brand these entrepreneurs with the single-dimensional master status of gang member. For instance, a group of young men who are enthusiastically involved in violent conflict with rivals in the north of the borough also have a thriving business selling crack cocaine in a leafy suburb many miles from Dogtown. The success of this enterprise is due to their ability in seeking out a market where there is little competition, where they are unknown to the local police, and where their locally acquired reputations as territorially orientated gang members are irrelevant. Yet to Dogtown police their enterprise constitutes 'gang related drug dealing', and is a prime example of gang imperialism (Armstrong et al (in progress)).

In Dogtown, generations of informal networks of fiddlers, dealers, scammers, and planners have laid the foundations for the teenage drug dealers who represent 'a sphere of *continuity* in the life of the area' (Robson 1997: 9). Their physical toughness and sharp business acumen are enduring attributes of a cultural inheritance which is not demeaned or corroded by engagement with the drug trade, and which constitutes one of the few enduring connections with Dogtown's historical 'ragged-arsed' capitalism. The adoption of trading opportunities thrown up by the local political economy lends an entrepreneurial edge to the traditional youthful hedonism of working-class youth, and wheeling and dealing in the drugs trade is no more or less liberating than the catalogue of 'little earners' that enhanced the lives of previous generations of Dogtowners (Hobbs 1988).[13] In short, encumbering young, occasionally violent street dealers with the full emotive weight of the organized

---

[13] For instance, Dogtown railway station, is periodically designated by the local police as a hotspot of street crime, and houses rush-hour beggars, purveyors of magazines, and cigarettes sold singly. However, late at night cannabis, and during winter 2006/7 cocaine, were on offer from a variety of youthful, bright-eyed 'Jack the lads' keeping the East End dream alive, who were in competition with older, fiercely friendly vendors with dirty trainers and a mouthful of polythene-wrapped product. CCTV and Transport Police shifted this street market to another venue, and Dogtown station returned to being a centre of excellence for mobile phone thieves.

crime brand, global or otherwise, as suggested by the Cabinet Office Strategy Unit in *Extending Our Reach*, is simplistic, and understates the complexities of territoriality, post-industrial urban identities and pervasive entrepreneurship, as youths seek to locate alternative means of constructing identity, and along the way gain status and respect, generate excitement, have fun—and make money.

One for the Money

The youthful collaborations that went on to form powerful entre-preneurial crime groups around variations on extortion discussed in Chapter 4 were exploiting market opportunities which happened to ripen during their era, and the drug trade is merely the current crime *du jour*. In considering the drug trade, the moral economy of intoxication and the 'political economy of social suffering' (Bourgois 2003) often merge into especially disturbing narratives that can distract from the attempts of young men attempting to sidestep the exclusionary logic of capitalism by commodifying their leisure and establishing dominance over territory that will otherwise dominate and demean them (Bourgois 1995).

Since the early 1990s two of Dogtown's community centres have served as bases for consistently violent, loose-knit groups of young men, a number of whom dealt drugs. Neither of these groups has a name or brand, but in time-honoured fashion are associated by their proximity to street corners at the crossroads of a set of back-streets on the periphery of a pleasant council estate. One of these groups worked with some middle-market dealers from north London operating one step away from importation, and the Dog-towners proved to be effective when another group of violent entre-preneurs from outside the area set up a dealing business in a local council flat. Guns were wielded and there were a number of stabbings. Several fringe members of the Dogtown group left the area, as did the outsiders, and the Dogtowners' reputation was assured. Some of the Dogtown group stored and protected drugs in exchange for product, which enabled a number of older youths to go into business in their own right, becoming central to local 'alternative circuits of survival [which] can be seen as articulated with more general systems of economic decline...high unemployment, poverty...and shrinking resources in the state to meet social needs' (Sassen 2006: 188).

While this enterprise was undoubtedly enabled by group solidarity, the label of 'gang related drug dealing'[14] valorizes mundane territorial disputes with the mythic glamour of market-led predation (Thornberry et al 2003) for individuals no longer empowered by the options provided by industrial society, and adds an illusory, somewhat glamorous façade to what was a routine entrepreneurial conflict related to the lower rungs of street drug markets (Stanko 2009; Reuter 2009: 281). However, now that the majority of cannabis available on the British market is being produced domestically (Metropolitan Police Service 2010),[15] levels of violence previously associated almost exclusively with Class A drug markets (Bowling 1999) are now clearly apparent amongst cannabis dealers, 'and such a sea change in the market, with decreased barriers to entry to a high level—and hence profit—supply/manufacture, and a seemingly insatiable demand for the product may—when placed in the context of continuing high levels of unemployment, discrimination and deprivation—create a market that is deemed "worth fighting for". Further, this market may have a particularly detrimental effect on the youth populations of deprived neighbourhoods' (Davies (in progress)).

Of course, industrial society, particularly in Dogtown, never constituted an even, albeit proletarian playing field, and during its brief post-Second World War industrial heyday, Dogtown, like Downes Poplar, was a predominantly white area, significant black and Asian settlement not taking place until over a decade after the commencement of the area's industrial decline (Butler et al 2008). The parents and grandparents of contemporary black youth seldom had a stake in the 'ordered and respectable working class life' (Rustin 1996: 4) which awaited white, East End youth as a reward for ending their brief dalliance with deviant subcultures. Consequently, black and Asian youths did not enjoy the relative luxury of temporary subcultural membership before maturing into a parent culture which offered, via local and familial networks born of longstanding settlement, unionized manual work in dock-related employment, in local wholesale markets, in the building trade, or

---

[14] As Alexander notes, age and ethnicity are often sufficient to warrant the label 'gang related' (2008: 5).

[15] Decorte et al (2011) report that worldwide decreasing amounts of cannabis have been seized at entry points to countries associated with drug importation. See also Potter (2010a, 2010b); ACPO (2012).

any of the multitude of proletarian options over which the local white population had acquired some measure of control.[16] The interracial world so vividly described by Hebdige (1979: 53–4) was seldom apparent outside of a small number of West End clubs and some remarkable venues in south London (Hobbs 1988); particularly in east London, black youths were largely excluded both from subcultures and from the world of work into which members of subcultures segued (see Fieldhouse 1999).

Although the 'tough and violently macho' (Bourgois 1995: 142; cf Willis 1977) characteristics that were integral to traditional masculine work cultures are inappropriate to the 'public subordination' (Bourgois 1995: 115) of the low-paid, non-unionized, post-industrial service sector, they are ideally suited to predatory illegal trading cultures. While youth styles have traditionally been influenced by criminal subcultures (Hebdige 1979: 81), post-industrial consumerism has reacted with consummate precision in promoting 'market masculinity' (Taylor 1999: 77). In particular, the appropriation across Dogtown's multiple ethnicities[17] of 'African-American street culture, which has an almost complete hegemony over style in the underground economy' (Bourgois 1995: 45) should be understood within the context of an essentially insolent working-class dandyism (Mercer 1987: 49) designed to defy and delay the inevitable tedium and associated trajectories of maturity once crucial to the logic of the industrial project. While in Dogtown there are few signs of the supportive alternative institutions described by some of the more engaged American gang researchers (Brotherton and Barrios 2004), the visual ambiguity of street style can be difficult to unpack, as children on bikes wearing hoodies may be runners for local drug dealers, kids 'playing out', gang members, school kids, or all of the above. However, what is not ambiguous are the patterns of violence and predatory interaction (Pitts 2008: 80–3) that have become normalized, and wearing the wrong-coloured

[16] Gunter stresses the essential fluidity between subcultural options that see black youths adopting the traditional masculinist identities associated with white working-class culture, and white youths enthusiastically engaging with 'road culture' as a result of 'interracial friendships and alliances' (Gunter 2010: 95).

[17] 'In the early hours of an unusually warm October morning in Poplar, I observed a 2 hour running fight between some Kosovan men and a younger coalition of white and Bengali youth. The Kosovan battle cries were in English with Jamaican accents (See Zorbaugh's quote from a newspaper report of a fight between Persians in Chicago (1929: 15))' (Hobbs 2006).

t-shirt in the wrong part of the borough can inspire a stabbing, and tit-for-tat beatings, knife attacks, and ripples of reprisal are constant features of life in Dogtown (Armstrong et al (in progress)).

Violence serves both to secure and to define membership of these groups, providing a consistent mode of response to interlocking, market-related disputes, territorial threats, and personal slights (Hales et al 2006; Pitts 2008). Local territory is often the only element of their lives over which many of these youths have any control, in an area where urban regeneration is a constant threat to stability as Dogtown's politicians and planners, in collaboration with local, national, and global commercial forces, seek to distance this once proud, self-confident area from its grubby industrial past. As part of this process of regeneration, Dogtown has rebranded a number of its neighbourhoods and parks, while a large secondary school, ensconced in the local community for nearly half a century, has been relocated to the other side of the borough, necessitating the daily transportation of hundreds of young men into a neighbourhood that for decades had been regarded as hostile territory. The result has been an ongoing 'Slow Motion Riot' (Blauner 1992), the occasional major incident, and the subsequent embedding of the 'gang problem' in Dogtown's schools, as official, anti-gang protocols were established by police officers toting their high-profile new specialism and 'tooled up' with fresh bespoke powers.[18]

Economic explanations isolated from the cultural contexts in which business is carried out are inadequate tools with which to explicate the complexity of motivations that lead to violent action. Most transgressive youth groups are not initially formed out of commercial motivation, but to resist other groups (Decker and Van Winkle 1996) in socially excluded areas (Hagedorn 1998) that are typified by an 'ecology of danger' (Fagan and Wilkinson 1998) and where 'repeated displays of "nerve" and "heart" build or reinforce a credible reputation for vengeance that works to deter aggression and disrespect' (Anderson 1999: 11). This 'respect'-based violence (Wacquant 1994) has continued to take precedence over entrepreneurship in Dogtown, and while most (but not all) claims of fortunes being made from the drug trade were the result of 'romantic reconstruction' (Medina et al 2011), the inevitable prison sentences and emotional burnouts have assured that, to date, group struc-

---

[18] BBC News (2011), 'Gang Injunctions Launched in England and Wales', available at <http://www.bbc.co.uk/news/uk-12311184>.

tures have proved as impermanent and fluid as everything else in this part of London.

While some local youthful entrepreneurs play a key role in the drug market, particularly at street level (Lupton et al 2002), monopolies are rare (Maxson and Klein 1995; Howell and Gleason 2001), and in some parts of Dogtown young men from outside of the area, and unaffiliated to any branded youth groups, run flourishing, street-corner enterprises unopposed by local collaborations. For instance, in one, physically difficult-to-access neighbourhood of social housing, the same two young men have operated a cannabis and cocaine street operation for over a year. Nobody knows where they come from, but they are not local. They retail from a vantage point in a backstreet that affords excellent views of approaching traffic, adjacent to a patch of grass that appears never to have been mown, and on the rare occasions that they are approached by police their product is flung into the grass and retrieved later. The business is overseen by two men who drive an expensive 4x4 and who visit most days to check on their investment. The reason that they are unopposed is because this is Dogtown and not *West Side Story*, the area has a population churn of approximately 30 per cent per year, and few of the residents stay long enough to develop any form of local patriotism.[19] Further, those residents that do stay have been subjected to the full force of unleashed market forces, which in turn have had a significant impact upon the way that notions of community, threat, and risk are constructed.

Buy to Let

Bourgois romantics should spend a day in Dogtown or in any of its mouldering, post-industrial doppelgängers that pit the UK, for the world of *Passport to Pimlico* and *How Green is my Valley* is no more. In contemporary working-class communities pockets of con-

---

[19] A number of local residents expressed how intimidated they felt by this business being carried out on their doorstep, and when their feelings were made known to Col, a known and respected thief with a violent reputation, he decided to approach the youths. 'I couldn't tell them not to do their dealing, that wouldn't have worked. But I explained that the older people didn't like it, and it would be handy if they toned it down a bit.' The youths were polite and respectful to Col, and agreed to carry out their business with minimal disruption to local residents, always discreetly acknowledging him when he walks, exuding not a little menace, past their dealing patch.

viviality are forged in places of worship, at the school gates, and in other tiny alcoves that seldom embrace the industrial era's essential formula of work, family, and the street (Cohen 1972). As a consequence there is 'no common sentiment, no common interest' (Zorbaugh 1929: 180).

A middle-aged, white drinker assaulted a 14-year-old Somali boy who had beaten up his nephew, and the 14-year-old has allegedly recruited a group of older boys to gain revenge. When Sarah looks out of the window of her pristine maisonette, the boys dressed in t-shirts and tracksuit bottoms stare at her until she withdraws behind her curtains. Sarah has two girls at primary school and she cannot let them play in the small patch of grass at the front of her home as she is frightened of the boys. She had a cousin who was a heroin addict and had spent time in prison for theft, and she felt that one of the flats opposite her home was being used for dealing drugs because 'the people look like my cousin. Shuffling and that'. When the boys eventually move away from Sarah's fence at about 11pm, she quickly gathers in the garden toys that her daughters have not been able to use. None of the boys appeared to be Somali, Sarah knew none of their names.

Elaine is now in her early 50s and is of mixed Caribbean and Irish descent. Her walls are lined with the DVDs that she watches every night when she gets home from her work as a care assistant. With her children grown up and with families of their own, she finds the local streets 'running alive with the gangs', who play football up against her outside walls and 'shout, swear, and take drugs over in the playground'. Elaine is especially concerned with the Asian kids who 'speak cockney English when they want but when other people are around talk their own language...Some have got cars.' Such voices are usually reduced to a muted media backcloth, or to paragraphs of timid, inarticulate data in a 'fear of crime' report. Yet Elaine has very rational feelings of being intimidated by a group whose youthful transgressive behaviour is magnified by racial difference. She uses the term 'gang' as a device to express her isolation and confusion regarding the state of her world, and the unfamiliarity of the streets where she has lived for her entire life. She has few human resources to whom she can turn and express her fears and anxieties, not because of half a dozen kids playing football and smoking dope, but because she, like so many of the residents of Dogtown, are strangers to each other.

Of the 14 houses at Elaine's end of the street, one contains residents who arrived five years ago, one is home to a family who moved in eight years ago, two houses have occupants who arrived ten years ago, and one house has had the same occupants for over 50 years. The remaining nine houses were bought by speculators as rental investments, creating an environment of constant tenant rotation. The introduction of assured shorthold tenancies by the Housing Act 1988 offered less security of tenure for tenants, and enhanced the power of landlords to evict. Along with the introduction of specialist mortgage products, the Act brought new investors into the property market who were attracted by rental incomes, rising capital values, and a perception that the housing sector entails a lower risk than for equity-based investment. Buy to let created a new breed of landlord attracted by rising property values and taxation rules that allow them to deduct the taxable portion of their rental income and the interest portion of their mortgage repayments as well as maintenance costs on the property. In London, buy to let has had a huge impact: one in three new properties are being bought by investors,[20] contributing significantly to a sense of instability and uncertainty, particularly in cheaper areas such as Dogtown where entire neighbourhoods are now dominated by short-term tenancies.

Although one of Elaine's immediate neighbours is a long-term resident, she works long hours and Elaine seldom sees her. The house on the other side has had more occupants during the past five years than Elaine can estimate, but they have included a doctor and his family, and several groups of students. Currently, she thinks that her next-door neighbours are eastern Europeans, and has become friendly with one of the young men who helped fix her front gate. But we must not dismiss Elaine on the spurious grounds of racism. She does not care who lives next door to her. She just wants somebody to stay there, to know the kids who are playing football up against her wall so that she can complain to their parents, and to understand a world over which she feels she no longer has any control. Gangs are an ideal metaphor for this lack of control and the decline in Elaine's environment.

It is not gangs or organized crime that have created the unarguable deterioration of life in Dogtown for citizens such as Elaine and Sarah. Drink, drugs, or wall-to-wall DVDs are entirely rational

---

[20] *Oxford Economics*, August 2007.

responses to a fearful predatory space where 'There is history but no shared narrative of difficulty, and so no shared fate' (Sennett 1998: 147). Dogtown will never recover the sense of negotiated communality and the possibility of conviviality that existed when it was part of industrial society.[21] Deindustrialization, road building, and attempts at regeneration have turned contemporary Dogtown into an increasingly stigmatized atoll of multiple deprivation, a 'dreadful enclosure' (Damer 1974) where bored youths, entrepreneurs, and would-be gangsters alike have become embedded in the fissures between households, neighbourhoods, and generations.

Post-industrialism has fractured the links between working-class youth and the parent culture, and unpacking the complex matrix of identities that constitute the new working-class city is difficult for local residents suffering a 'loss of control of public space' (Bourgois 1995: 10). The resultant suspicion and palpable sense of insecurity has inspired 'gang talk' (Hallsworth and Young 2008)—a racialized shorthand for transgression (Pitts 2008; Alexander 2000, 2008) that is evoked, often via rumour and folklore, to provide an urban narrative which creates an illusion of structure in a world that is unstructured and ambiguous (Bauer and Gleicher 1953: 297–310). Consequently, much youthful transgression is initially typecast by the default categorization of 'gang related', before investigation invariably produces a more nuanced explanation (Stanko 2009).

Enter the Dragon: Neoliberal Related

> My line back then was that class allegiances and institutions were strong enough to hold the dragon of anomie at bay. But that if those weakened, and a more individualistic success or failure culture took hold, we would see a shift towards more structured gangs (David Downes, personal correspondence 2009)

The gang genie is out of the bottle; like organized crime it has become institutionalized and embedded in the discourse of local and national governance. The best that sceptics can do is to remind community workers, schools, anti-gang enforcement units, politicians, and the rest of the burgeoning gang industry of the possible

---

[21] For a wonderful description of how the apparent isolation and alienation of a contemporary London street is negotiated, see Miller (2008).

consequences of imposing a phenomenon that merits close comparison with some of the far from benign youthful collaborations of previous generations. As we see in Chapter 4, numerous London-based professional criminals of the pre-drug era were active members of violent juvenile subcultures who were able to utilize their territorially honed violence as platforms from which to exploit the illegal markets of their era. Youth collaborations remain 'the fabric that binds organised criminality' (Toy 2008: 27), but we should consider their contemporary manifestation in the context of the downgrading both of the industrial base of advanced urban economies and the cultures that service them (Sassen 2006: 196), which dictates that it is still the working class neighbourhood that nurtures criminal collaborations (Young et al 2007), whatever their nomenclature.

The dragon of anomie that Downes warned about above is now amongst us, and a 'toxic blend of hyper-individualism, consumerism and resentment' (Pountain and Robins 2007), along with a 'free reign to acquisitiveness' (Lasch 1979: 10), mark a new dark era of narcissism (Hall et al 2007; Ryder 2009). From the dandified strut of Manchester's Scuttlers (Davies 2008), to the bespoke, hyper-commodified bling that pockmarks the aspirational edges of the post-industrial landscape, each successive generation of youth has embodied essential essences of both resistance and adaptation. However, in post-industrial society the trajectory of dissociation is accelerated, and the subculture evolves into social forms that no longer function as platforms for maturation into the parent culture. Instead, we are faced with a distinctly post-industrial, youthful transition that threatens 'the symbiotic relationship between the youthful and adult world' (Hobbs 1988: 138) that was taken for granted in the industrial era.

Dogtown's phenomenal population churn includes groups of young African, European, and Asian men escaping war and economic trauma, who are drawn to Dogtown by cheap housing. When a small number are associated with street robbery, public disorder, or street dealing, they are attributed with emotive and hard-to-shake monikers (ie the Somali/Algerian/Portugese Mafia), and become the property of the newly formed Dogtown police gang unit. Fitting perfectly with the net-widening imprecision of the term's contemporary use, here the term 'gang' suggests a level of competence and organization somewhat removed from the rootless, chaotic street life of these young men for whom the term 'exclusion' could have been invented (Armstrong et al (in progress)). For Dogtown's young, fluid, and constantly churning population, territories established in the industrial era that were built upon a strong, cross-generational sense of neighbourhood patriotism no longer have the same relevance, resulting in an increasing reliance upon artificial or symbolic territorial boundaries (Katz 1988:146). A vast, new shopping centre, on the site of what had been, during the industrial era, the location of thousands of both skilled and unskilled jobs, has created a site of exclusion for local youth (Sibley 1995: xii), a 'non-place' (Auge 1992) with no history, designed by global capital to give the impression of being beyond context and devoid of any preordained territorial identity. Consequently, for Dogtown youth this pristine territorial vacuum is an exciting allure (Armstrong et al (in progress)), creating a contested space with fresh opportunities for invasion and colonization, and exacerbating the existing range of problems which for administrative convenience can be placed into the category of 'gang related' (Armstrong et al (in progress)).[22]

Against the backdrop of an irretrievable economic decline that has impacted particularly upon youth (Davies 1998) and the implementation of punitive policies designed to shrink welfare provision for working-class youths (Pitts 2008), the area's fragmentation has inspired an intense localism and emphasis upon territoriality. The result has been a fragmentation of working-class youth transitions to adulthood that no longer feature relatively simplistic linear maturation from school into the world of work, working-class family, and community (Johnston et al 2000), and there is now a complex field of transitional possibilities featuring markets offering something more interesting than 'Mc Jobs' (Craine 1997; MacDonald 1997, 1998), and more immediate than the promissory notes written on the back of a student loan. Dogtown's population had endured generations of poverty before less than two decades of hard-won, relative economic peace and security created an impression of confident proletarian affluence and consensus. When the brief hegemony that had been enjoyed by organized labour during its post-war compromise with industrial capital (Dumenil and Levy 2004) was swept away, it was not the convoluted abstracted logic

---

[22] 'Man dead in Olympic shops brawl. A man dies after being stabbed during a fight at the Westfield shopping centre next to the London 2012 Olympic park', <http://www.bbc.co.uk/news/uk-england-london-18653961>.

of global capital that was blamed for the area's subsequent decline, but the 'Hedonism and dangerousness' (Gilroy 1987: 101) of the black criminal, coded under the guise of 'street crime' and 'gangs'. By pathologizing race and creating the illusion of a terrifyingly unfamiliar dystopia, a correlation was established between crime and ethnicity that had not been noticed when the thieves, receivers, street fighters, and gangsters were white, and crime was subsumed into the pragmatic consciousness. Racializing the problem is akin to blaming the potato famine on the Irish.[23]

The importance of local conditions to the formation of youth collaborations cannot be overemphasized (Sandu 2003), and even within the chaotic conditions created by post-industrialism, there is often an overlapping of historically linked, territorially based family affiliations and branded local gangs where youthful acquisitive crime is a long-standing cultural expectation spanning eras, rather than a product purely of neoliberal forces (Medina et al 2011; Aldridge et al 2009, 2011; Ralphs et al 2009). Gangs are not a grotesque creation of late modernity that has no precedent (Young 2009: 14). The evisceration of the UK's industrial core and its accompanying cultures has created a complex and fractious urban hinterland where illegal activity has become normalized, where gangs are 'not the product of youth culture, but of working class culture turned upside down' (Schneider 1999: 50). The gang has been valorized by prurient, obsessive media coverage, and established as a social problem by the absorption of specialist counsellors, police, and community workers into the ever-evolving governance of youth. This, along with the conflation of the gang problem with a wide range of activities including those that are counter-intuitive to any notion of organization,[24] has afforded the

---

[23] Disputes between youth gangs, especially when they are made up of non-whites, frequently capture the imagination of media investigators, one of whom described to me in a telephone conversation the emergence of 'murdering super-gangs dealing drugs across the world from the Caribbean to Afghanistan'. As convicted heroin smuggler Suleyman Ergun explained, 'They're only little kids who don't respect anyone. In my opinion they are just idiots who think that selling a bit of brown and having a gun means you're a gangster...these youngsters...are selling it on the street, and that's where the war is coming from...It's just a price war or the usual stepping on one another's toes that's where all this fucking mix-up is': *Guardian*, 25 October 2009.

[24] For instance, the urban riots in the UK during August 2011 were partly attributed by the Prime Minister, David Cameron, to 'opportunist thugs in gangs': *Guardian*, 11 August 2011. See also the response by Hallsworth (2011).

UK gang a prominence never acquired by the more common, embedded, yet more opaque concept of subculture, a deficiency due partly to the concept losing its analytic power as it morphed into a lazy shorthand for youth style.

While post-industrialism has generated marked changes in the nature of youthful deviance, in particular the fracturing of work-based cultural continuities with the parent culture, working-class youth collaborations remain as crucial to the generation of networks of illegal trade and commerce in the twenty-first century as they did during the era of the marquee criminals. As legal alternatives have diminished, there is no shortage of potential labour for the complex overlapping urban networks that are located in a web of 'Multiple group-affiliations' (Simmel 1955: 136), featuring predatory entrepreneurs cashing in their class inheritance whilst utilizing the full range of market-orientated infrastructure. Whatever transgressional sobriquet is applied to them, these urban youth groups are part of the constellation of collaborations that constitute a community of practice responding to interpretations of global markets operationalized via local identities and sensibilities (Bauman 1998).

Yet while globalization has undoubtedly impacted on the connectedness between street cultures and serious crime groups, the phenomenon of industrial-era youth progressing into professional crime via subcultures has received insufficient attention. For if we continue to ignore deviants of the industrial era, many of whom also chose a life that offered more attractive cultural and economic returns than a life of 'unmanly obedience' (Schneider 1999: 174) at the rump of the job market, and dismiss lessons from the past as meaningless nostalgia (Lasch 1979: xvii), we create a world of recurring novelty, where the academic wheel is constantly reinvented and the brutal adaptability of those born at the back of the queue regularly comes as a nasty surprise (see Appendix 1).

7

Populating the Underworld: Armed Robbery

'And sometimes a person from the underworld?'

'Yes' said the witness, 'some might drop in'.

'Pimps and thieves and things?' queried the judge.

'Possibly so' replied the gambler (Landesco 1968: 72)

Armed Robbery

The consciousness of a common way of life among thieves is very, very old (Maurer 1955: 199)

As discussed in earlier chapters, there were precedents for British organized crime long before the term was formally established as a vehicle of governance. Racism and post-imperial angst merged with the class-specific ecological logic of urban exclusion to produce an underworld where collaborations of criminality were located and consequently policed. This chapter will examine a crime that, before entrepreneurial serious crime came to dominate illegal markets, had emerged as particularly representative of 'the underworld', and which operated within networks that imbued transgressive action with a significance that has since all but disappeared. Indeed, armed robbery carries with it a romantic aura of maverick specialism that traditionally occupies a unique position in the hierarchy of professional criminality, and lends a piratical aura to what is usually a crude act, albeit one riddled with overtones of fantastical banditry.

Craft

McIntosh's seminal work (1975) introduced the notion of craft crime as typified by the safe-cracker (McIntosh, 1971, 1975) and suggested a distinct parallel with the world of industrially organized employment, where aspiring safe-crackers were often apprenticed to older villains (Hobbs 1995: 18; Macintyre, 2007: 7). Craft criminality also features informal hierarchies based upon competence rather than formal organization, and their practice lacked the territorial imperative so central to extortion and the identity of the gangster.

During the immediate post-Second World War years, professional burglars plundered the homes of the rich and famous (Scott 1995; Reynolds 2000: 239) as well as cinemas and departmental stores and other cash-based businesses which kept their takings overnight, and factories and warehouses, particularly on the night before pay day (Hobbs 1995: 13–19). Although safes were vulnerable to 'picking', drilling, cutting, or having their doors or backs levered,[1] these tactics were exceptionally time-consuming, a fact which, along with improvements in lock technology, led to an increase in the use of explosives (Chambliss 1972; Letkemann 1973: 56–86).

During the pre-terrorism era explosives were easily obtained: 'we rented a car…and drove down to Mousehole in Cornwall and broke into a quarry to get gelignite and detonators' (Reynolds 2000: 128; Hobbs 1995: 14–15). A top safe-cracker of the era explains:

It's called Polo Ammond (Polar Ammon Gelignite) and it was like mincemeat, red with all little red globules in it and it was powerful enough to knock a door off a safe. The detonators were of a size that just used to fit into the keyhole of the safe so you would take the baffle plate off the safe, load it up with enough explosive, put it all round in the lock. Then you press your detonator in, run the wires off if it had wires, or if it had a fuse you just light the fuse and get out the way and the explosion occurs and you run back in. The door's usually laying on the floor…(Hobbs 1995: 15; see also Chambliss 1972)

Bruce Reynolds vividly explained the sensual enjoyment to be gleaned from a successful attack on a safe: 'I couldn't believe the buzz blowing a safe gave me. It was the ultimate power trip. Unless you've been there, you can't understand how a little block of gelly and a handful of detonators can make you feel almost omnipotent. I couldn't wait to try again' (Reynolds 2000: 130). Yet this was a

---

[1]   <http://www.safeman.org.uk>; <www.peterman.org.uk>.

hard-won sensation: 'I discovered that it was far more technical than most people imagine. So many things can affect it—the atmosphere, the temperature, the positioning and the vagaries of metal' (Reynolds 2000: 158). Technological innovations made safe-blowing difficult and time-consuming (Letkemann 1973: 86–9): 'They used to cement them down so you'd blow the door off. But if they weren't cemented down, 20 minutes you could have the back off. So Milner, who I could open their safes quite easy, joined up with Chatsworth Milner, and they now had a safe which was virtually blow-proof. In fact when you blew it, you blew it and it set off on springs a secondary mechanism so the bolts were shot home again. You'd made a lot of noise so you couldn't blow it again, you had to get out of there ... lot of effort, lot of noise'(Hobbs 1995: 18).

Alternatives such as the thermic lance and oxyacetylene cutter were tried, but they required vast amounts of heavy equipment (Walsh 1986: 171; Punch 1991): 'Our equipment included about six suitcases and several oxyacetylene gas bottles weighing two hundredweight each' (Foreman 1996: 105). The gradual shift away from a cash economy towards a security-conscious, more risk-averse society also had an impact: 'The cash targets who had made their lot during and after the war were changing with the times, becoming more accustomed to using banks and safety deposits' (Reynolds 2000: 239). These innovations accelerated the passing of craft crime, and hastened the emergence of team-based project crime (Mannheim 1965: 656–9; McIntosh 1975) as 'It was quicker to go and get it out with a shotgun, and they used to take all the money. That was the easy way ...' (Hobbs 1995: 18; cf Punch 1991).

Enter the Blagger

With full employment and a post-war consumer boom, workers were usually paid in cash on a weekly basis, which made the wages clerk an attractive and easy target as he departed the bank carrying a bag full of cash (McVicar 1979: 181; Fraser 1994: 48–9). Some of the more ambitious wage snatchers were already interested in larger hauls of cash, and began operating in teams (Reynolds 2000: 247–50, 269–76), although armed raids, albeit raids that seldom featured firearms, captured a great deal of media attention (Hill 1955: 162–7, 217–19; Murphy 1993: 95–7) as violent predators turned their attention to banks (Mannheim 1965: 657; McClin-tock and Gibson 1961; Ball et al 1978).

The nascent security industry reacted by confronting robbers with constant technological advances, which in turn led to further violent innovation. Glass screens in banks resulted in the increased use of sledgehammers, and when the glass was hardened the money was also attacked 'over the pavement', as it was being delivered or removed by security guards who had been issued with protective helmets and batons. This instigated pitched battles with robbers armed with pick-axe handles and ammonia sprays, and when the guards were then issued with visors for their helmets, a gun, usually a sawn-off shotgun, became an essential tool to intimidate guards, bank staff, and custom-ers. A blast from a sawn-off into the ceiling of a bank, shouts, threats, and in less than two minutes a huge haul of used notes was stolen (Cox et al 1977: 11–17). When banks continued to improve their security further, the money was attacked in transit (Gill 2001; Matthews 2002), and when the van makers responded by inventing airlocks and inter-locking doors, robbers turned to chainsaws and increased levels of brutality (Clarkson 2004).[2] By the summer of 1972 armed robberies in London were being committed at the rate of one every five days. Crowbars, pick-axe handles, and other blunt instruments had given way to firearms, a trend not entirely welcomed by all members of the professional criminal fraternity (Reynolds 2000: 203); robbers had become prime targets for the police: 'For a policeman to catch a bank robber is like a fisherman catching a 20lb trout' (bank robber, quoted in Taylor 1984: 76). Consequently, the risks associated with carrying out armed robbery had increased, although robbers continued to work at their trade (Ball et al 1978) despite the heavy sentences being dished out.[3]

Skill (Inciardi 1976), craft (Mcintosh 1971), and competence (Shover 1973) are the everyday qualities inherent in the committal of crime as work (Letkemann 1973) and, in the case of armed rob-

---

[2] For an illuminating overview of this contest between robbers and the security industry, see the TV programme *How to Rob a Bank* (RDF Television, transmitted Channel 4, March 2003), which lends vivid evidence to compliment: Matthews (2002).

[3] Although no guns and only minimal violence were used during the £2 million plus 'Great Train Robbery' in 1963 (Reynolds, 2000: 329–30; Campbell 1994: 129–30), the 30-year sentences imposed on the robbers were similar to those given to murderers (Campbell 1994: 140).

bery, merge to create 'a superior competence to control the interaction' (Katz 1988: 170). This performance of competency is echoed in Luckenbill's (1981) study where a sequence of transactions is closely managed by the robber involving his victims in the accomplishment of four interrelated tasks. The robber establishes his presence with the victim, the interaction is transformed into 'the robbery frame', the loot is transferred to the robber, and finally the robber leaves the scene. The creation of 'the illusion of impending death' (Wright and Decker 1997) is the key to this sequence, and is designed to scare victims into a state of total compliance without the threat being carried out.[4] However, there is often a 'Russian roulette' aspect to armed robbery (Cook 1987: 300) which is related to the victims' levels of resistance, as well as to the assailants' momentary murderous impulses and the type of weapon used, all of which have implications for the potential degree of injury and lethality (see Matthews 2002: 68–74).[5]

Talking and Walking: Supergrasses

> You couldn't do a worser crime (Frank Fraser)

Convictions for armed robbery were rare, and the loot was seldom recovered, while the culture and organization of the police did little to alleviate the problem. During this era CID officers were entrepreneurs of local knowledge, which was usually acquired from drinking and wheeling and dealing with local villains (Hobbs 1991); as a consequence the gap between corruption and practical policing became extremely narrow (Short 1991; Foreman 1996: 144–5). This was compounded by the tendency of the CID and its various specialist squads to jealously guard the intelligence they had acquired, for intelligence is the currency of detective work and is not given up lightly (Hobbs 1988).

Thriving on the insularity of these CID fiefdoms, armed robbers such as Bertie Smalls were able work across police boundaries,

---

[4] For an in-depth exploration of the maintenance of compliance, see Goffman (1952). See also Schur (1957) and Katz (1988: 176–9).

[5] O'Donnell and Morrison report that in the UK the majority of robbers choose to carry replica or imitation firearms (1997: 265). These findings are supported by Taylor and Hornsby (2000), who report that victims of armed robbery were unable to differentiate between real and replica handguns (see also Wright and Rossi 1985).

plundering banks all over London and the South East. In the mid 1960s Smalls was at the forefront of the switch from coshes and pick-axe handles to firearms, and was a key figure amongst the high-spending, hedonistic, robber fraternity. Although he had been questioned by the police a number of times in relation to armed robbery, Smalls always had a decent alibi, and his only adult convictions were relatively minor, such as living off immoral earnings and a fine for possession of a loaded gun. A raid on the National Westminster Bank in Palmers Green had netted just £10,000 which was then split four ways, and Smalls promptly put together a seven-man team who, in 90 seconds inside the Wembley branch of Barclays Bank, stole £138,000 before decamping to Torremolinos with their families (Hobbs 2008).

Back in London a specialist Robbery Squad with officers from previously competing units such as the Regional Crime Squad and the Flying Squad was formed, and despite interviewing some of the robbers and visiting Spain, the 25-strong squad had no further success as the case floundered against a traditional wall of silence. However, Smalls' name was increasingly being linked with a portfolio of robberies across London, and eventually his house was raided and the family's au pair gave the police an address in Northamptonshire owned by Smalls' brother. Bertie Smalls was arrested, and in the car back to London he offered to 'do a deal', which the police refused. Within a month he offered to give up 'every robber in London' in exchange for immunity, and again the police showed no interest. At the committal hearings in March 1973 Smalls was served with papers indicating some very strong evidence against him in relation to the robberies at Palmers Green and Wembley, as well as a Hatton Garden robbery that netted £296,000 in cash and jewels (Cox et al 1977).

Faced with the probability of a 20-year sentence, Smalls again offered to 'do the royals', or offer Queen's Evidence in exchange for immunity. This time the proposal was put before the Director of Public Prosecutions, a deal was struck, and the term 'supergrass' entered the public lexicon. Smalls confessed to 15 robberies, and named 32 bank robbers and a number of associates. The Wembley robbers were sentenced to a total of 106 years, and over the next 14 months a further 21 men received sentences totalling 308 years. Smalls also secured the release from prison of one man who had been falsely imprisoned for his part in the 1970 raid on Barclays Bank in Ilford that had netted £237,000 (Cox et al 1977).

The Chief Superintendent of Wembley CID was accused of stealing £25,000 from the safety deposit box of one of the robbers; the subsequent police investigation cleared the officer, who then retired from the force. A related inquiry into accusations that the Chief Superintendent and another senior officer had 'fiddled' a reward claim for the provision of information that named two of the Wembley robbers also found in favour of the accused officers. The second policeman promptly left the police to become a security officer for Barclays Bank. By 1973 two officers a week were voluntarily leaving the Met as a result of a general anti-corruption purge led by Commissioner Robert Mark, and in the same year the number of bank robberies in London fell from 65 in 1972 to 26 (Jennings et al 1991: 48–57; Mark 1978; Hobbs 1988: 62–83).

Until Smalls broke rank, the notion of an underworld code had prevailed (Benney 1936: 194), and although Lord Chief Justice Lawton subsequently decreed that the arrangement between Smalls and the Director of Public Prosecutions should not be repeated, other 'supergrasses' quickly followed Smalls' example.[6] Bertie Smalls died of natural causes in 2008, after spending the rest of his days with an assumed name living under police protection (Hobbs 2008).

Wining and Dining: Robbery as Subculture

> The money they made they spent in harbour as quickly as they could—gambling, drinking whoring—until they had nothing left, and had to go to sea again (Kuhn 2010: 36; cited in Parker 2012: 47)

As illustrated by the reaction to the 1963 'Great Train Robbery', which was a prime example of McIntosh's project crime thesis (Reynolds 2000: 320; Read 1978: 291–312), robbery was frequently attributed with military levels of precision and efficiency (Mannheim 1965: 656–7; Reynolds 2000: 320; Read 1978: 291–312). Coupled with a tendency to regard spectacular robberies as requiring both conception and direction from a 'Mind' (Fordham 1965: 29) or 'Mr Big' (Read 1978: 12; Biggs 1981: 217–23), these

---

[6] Maurice O'Mahoney was a notoriously violent armed robber who dubbed himself 'King Squealer' after passing on more than 150 names to the police in return for a five-year sentence served in Chiswick police station with a free supply of alcohol and conjugal visits with his girlfriend (O'Mahoney and Wooding 1981).

concepts shift the public gaze away from the essential ingenuity of proletarian practitioners who often originated from working-class neighbourhoods that had been bypassed by the disciplining functions of industrial society (R Smith 2005; T Smith 2005; Hobbs 1995: 47; Mason 1994: 126–33). Despite the highly organized imagery of armed robbery, working arrangements were often casual, with little planning and a disregard for detail in respect to either the robbery itself (Hobbs 1997) or in dealing with its aftermath (Knight et al 2003). Unlike the craftsman, the self-identity of the robber was located not in skill or in the acquisition of an intricate arcane craft, but in personal, idealized masculine qualities (Hobbs 1995: 21) featuring elements of physicality, fortitude, and endurance often located in industrial work. The violent potential and instrumental physicality of industrial cultures is ideally adapted to armed robbery, lending little credence to either the military metaphor or the 'Mr Big' assertion (Hobbs 1995: 47) amongst a subculture featuring rationales that are hedonistic rather than commercial (McVicar 1979: 158; Reynolds 2000: 116).

The sensual delights of 'irrational consumption' (Katz 1988: 198) singled out professional armed robbers from the mundane rhythms of working-class employment and its attendant routines. 'Restaurants were prompt in their attention, a twenty-pound note to the *maître d'* ensuring that there was never any problem getting a table. Pruniers in St. James's, Bentleys, and Sheekeys were our fish places…Wheeler's in Duke of York Street off Jermyn Street: you could have a small dining-room to yourself there, very private and intimate. The Rib Room at the Carlton Towers was an innovative fashion for a while, serving great beef at a time when beef was synonymous with strength: we all ate plenty of that, thinking that we needed it for our work' (Reynolds 2000: 241). From contemporaneous accounts, there is a sense of a criminal fraternity populated by committed hedonists: 'There were nights when we would be celebrating at the Astor or the Embassy and we would spy another group of crims supping magnums of champagne. Bottles would be exchanged as we toasted each other's success amid much rivalry. It was exciting. This was the recognition I had always craved' (Reynolds 2000: 194).[7]

---

[7] Smith writes of his ambition as a young man to be recognized as a 'face', a respected man whose defining characteristic is his nerve: 'The Great Train Robbers, John McVicar, the Wembley bank Robbers, John Dillinger and Willie Sutton…they

The narcissistic drive that is implicit in a 'Life lived without a safety net' (Pileggi 1987: 39) and 'life as party' (Shover and Honaker 1992) confirms the centrality of 'earning and burning money' (Katz 1988: 215) which authenticates the commitment to a subcultural identity defined by conspicuous consumption, and funded by crime (Hohimer 1981: 19). The emphasis placed upon reckless consumption as 'masculine capital' (Mullins 2006: 69) is alluded to by Freddie Foreman when looking back at his career as an armed robber: 'You could go from one club to the other and see the same faces. We could easily tell which pavement firm had a touch on a particular day by the way they were celebrating in the afternoon. They'd be walking around with bottles of vodka or scotch. Money just flowed' (Foreman 1996: 93). The professional criminal cited by Taylor sums it up; 'well I'm a natural. I mean, I am a natural. I love it, I love the high life...I love the...going out to wine and dine, the fucking champagne and the birds, and living it up, and first class on the airplanes. Champagne fucking Charlie. You know. Ducking and diving; and, you know, wining and dining' (Taylor 1984: 121).[8]

The straight world did not offer comparable financial rewards nor the same frisson of excitement and exclusivity, and the armed robber became immersed in the ambience of 'spontaneity, autonomy, independence and resourcefulness' (Shover and Honaker 1992: 283) integral to outlaw status. Hedonism also plays a part in the committal of the crime, and is exemplified in the following quote from Bertie Smalls: 'The nervous tension I used to feel before a job didn't stay with me all the time, only till I got started. Once I start I feel completely calm, one hundred per cent, everything comes brilliant to me...I might be fogged up a minute or two before but the minute it's on it's like the sun coming out from behind a cloud' (Ball et al 1978: 183).

Armed robbery was a form of edgework (Lyng 1990) which sat nicely with the hedonistic opportunities that could be purchased with the proceeds. The clarity and sensual awareness identified above by Smalls (see also T Smith 2005: 148) bear close compari-

were violent robbers who controlled their violence and used just enough to get the prize' (R Smith 2005: 59).

[8] Ex-armed robber John McVicar (1979) had much to say about the relationship between masculinity, professional crime, and hedonism many years before academics, and criminologists in particular, had colonized the territory.

son to the experiences of participants of dangerous sports (Hardie-Bick 2011). Ex-armed robber Razor Smith explains:

I live a whole lifetime in minutes, aware of every breath that leaves my body and every beat of my heart. The world seems to suddenly pop into clear focus and my every sense is heightened...You psyche yourself up to step out of a plane thousands of feet up in the air, knowing that something could go wrong and you are jumping to your death. But you step out anyway, spitting in the face of death and knowing that once you leave the plane there is no changing your mind and turning back. And in the five minutes of free fall, you're aware of everything, but you cannot stop. (R Smith 2005: 83–4)

Armed robbers seldom used the proceeds of their crimes to create permanent alliances or structures (for a couple of intriguing exceptions, see Jennings et al 1991, and the career of Foreman 1996), and most of the professional robbers of the 1960s to 1980s were more concerned with long holidays in Spain and enjoying a lifestyle of conspicuous excess (Taylor 1984). Armed robber Robby Wideman explains:

Straight people don't understand. I mean, they think dudes is after the things straight people got. It aint that at all. People in the life aint looking for no home and grass in the yard and shit like that. We the show people. The glamour people. Come on the set with the finest car the finest woman, the finest wines. Hear people talking about you. Hear the bar get quiet when you walk in the door. Throw down a yard and tell everybody drink up...You make something out of nothing. (Wideman 1985: 131)

Big Hits

Although the emergence of the supergrass destroyed the honorific myth of the underworld, and undoubtedly damaged the armed-robber community, after an initial decrease in the immediate post-Smalls' era armed robbery continued to rise (see Matthews 2002: 53). In 1980 a team of robbers stole 321 ingots of silver valued at £3.4 million which was being transferred by road to Tilbury Docks, and the fallout from the investigation, which again involved testimony from a supergrass, sparked allegations of police corruption (Jennings et al 1991). Robbers also turned their attention to the depots where bullion and cash were stored, and in 1983 a team of robbers from east and south London robbed the Security Express depot of £7 million in cash in a crime that involved careful and extensive planning, and a security guard having petrol poured over him (Knight et al 2003: 10–40). A man responsible for minding some of the money turned informant and the robbery team was convicted. Six months later £26 million of gold bullion was stolen from the Brinks-mat depot at Heathrow (Darbyshire and Hilliard 1993), and the impact of this robbery, which also featured petrol being poured over security guards as a means of gaining compliance (Cater and Tullett 1991), was global. Within 12 hours of the robbery the world's gold markets had reacted and the value of the haul increased by £1 million. The insider who had provided keys and information turned informer, arrests were made, and the violent aftermath of the robbery continues to this day (Pearson 2006: 262–6; T Smith 2005: 149).

In the ten years preceding the Brinks-Mat raid, armed robberies had risen from 380 to 1,772 per annum, an increase of 340 per cent, and while the supergrass system had clearly failed to eliminate armed robbery, it did serve to place an even higher premium upon trust amongst the robbers. The loose-knit teams of the Bertie Smalls' era gave way to tightly bonded units, often with family or neighbourhood connections, and the belief amongst robbers that the police were operating a shoot-to-kill policy impacted upon anyone considering joining an armed robbery firm. In July 1987 two men were shot dead by police during an attempted robbery of a wages van at an abattoir in south London, and in November 1987 a robber was shot dead in a wages snatch at a supermarket in south east London while a television crew filmed (Allison 2009). In April 1989 two men were shot dead during a post office robbery in suburban north London, and in 1990 a robber was shot dead by police in Surrey during an attempted raid on a security van. In a shoot-out near the post office in Brockham near Dorking in August 1992, police injured both the robbery gang and members of the public. The officer in charge was quoted as stating that while he was sorry for any injuries to the public, 'sometimes it was necessary to fight fire with fire' (see Waddington 1991: 24).

However, also key to understanding the decline of professional armed robbery is the fact that the rewards from entrepreneurial pursuits, and in particular drugs, were now so much greater. The underworld had functioned as a network of exchange, controlling and disseminating information (McIntosh 1971; Hobbs 1995: 21), yet it was breaking down as new entrepreneurial opportunities based upon trade emerged, and the unwritten criminal code that provided an ethical framework for a community of professional criminals was proving inadequate to cope with the new market free-for-all (Sutherland 1937: 197; Irwin 1970: 8; cf Cohen and Taylor 1972: Ch 7; Taylor 1984: 79–84, 89–90). Criminal entrepreneurship marked the destruction of all but the highly symbolic debris of the 'underworld', and flagged the inauguration of a mutant variety of enterprise that is fundamentally similar to legitimate commerce, spawning a highly flexible criminal equipped for entrepreneurial engagements, and committed not to a hedonistic self-contained subculture, but to the manipulation of markets and the maximization of profit (Hobbs 1995: 106–24).

Convicted robbers were coming into contact with drug-savvy cellmates, and fugitive robbers basking in the late 1970s' suspension of the extradition treaty between Spain and the UK were made aware of the opportunities of the cannabis trade just a short speedboat trip away across the Strait of Gibraltar. Soon the elite of British armed robbery became commodity brokers at the forefront of the drugs trade, investing in a relatively low-risk business that emerged as central to the concept of contemporary organized crime.[9]

Decline

> ...the risks involved were very real and were not worth it
> (Terry Smith)[10]

Improved security and target hardening, particularly at banks and building societies, has contributed enormously to the decline of armed robbery, and as with the craft criminals that proceeded them, improvements in security technology took their toll: 'voice speaking alarms, exploding boxes with red dye, inaccessible locked safes and satellite tracking devices...CCTV, witness identification techniques and DNA evidence' (T Smith 2005: 296–7; see Matthews 2002). As firearms became easier to acquire, careless, often desper-

---

[9] For an outstanding overview of this shift from predatory crime towards the drug trade, see Dorn et al (1992).

[10] Prodigious armed robber Terry Smith was released from prison in 1995, and commenced a new career as an author and as a consultant to Hollywood (*The Insider*) and the television industry. In early 2010, at the age of 50, he received a 12-year sentence for his role in a series of armed robberies: 'Gangster turned TV pundit jailed for masterminding armed robberies', *Guardian*, 26 February 2010.

ate amateurs (Walsh 1986: Ch 3; Hobbs 1995: 100–2) targeted convenience stores, garages, supermarkets, restaurants, and off-licences (Morrison and O'Donnell 1994; Gill 2001; Matthews 2002).

The 'deskilled' (Matthews 2002), 'dangerous amateur' (Taylor 1984: 92) is now the norm, in an environment where legitimate moneymaking opportunities are sparse within a culture dominated by the 'code of the street' (Anderson 1999) rather than by discrete specialisms. Between 1996 and March 2008, armed robberies at building societies decreased from 144 to 14, and armed robberies of garages and service stations fell from 109 in 2006/07 to 65 in 2008. However, opportunistic robberies of cash in transit (Gill 2000, 2001) have blossomed in recent years as the domain of individualistic or loose-knit, small-group banditry (R Smith 2005; T Smith 2005). There is an especially violent edge to these robberies, which usually target cash couriers when they leave the security van at the point where cash is being transferred. In the course of 836 attacks in 2005 that resulted in losses of £15.4 million, 164 couriers were stabbed, pistol-whipped, and beaten, while six couriers and a member of the public were shot, and in 2009 the cash-in-transit industry suffered over 1000 attacks, leaving 176 crew members and a police officer injured. While the 2010 UK Threat Assessment reports a recent decrease in cash-in-transit robberies, due largely to improved security features such as smoke and dye boxes, vehicle-tracking systems, and face mapping, this activity has acquired a certain kudos, particularly amongst youths and young men adopting a lifestyle 'on road', a 'volatile street-based culture' (Hallsworth and Silverstone 2009: 360; see Gunter 2010: 93–116) unencumbered by the protocols and traditions of professional crime and the underworld that sustained it.

Fantasy and Innovation

It was just like going to work, but easier (Taylor 1984: 88)

Although professional armed robbery as a routinized specialism has all but disappeared, the possibility of capturing a big prize continues to attract professionals with a penchant for project crime. In 2000 an unsuccessful attempt to steal the 'millennium diamonds' involving a JCB digger and a speedboat was caught on camera by a waiting armed police squad (Hollington 2004; Shatford and Doyle

2004). An organized attack on a cash-storage facility in Tonbridge, Kent in February 2006 yielded to date the UK's biggest ever cash haul of £53 million (Sounes 2008), and at the time of writing a number of men have been convicted, while approximately £30 million is still missing (Campbell 2007). The Tonbridge robbery was centred around a cluster of fragile legitimate businesses, and involved personnel from both the traditional south-east London blaggers' heartland, from Albania, and from suburban Kent. Like an earlier cash robbery at a bank in Northern Ireland in 2004 (Bowcott and Oliver 2004), the Kent robbery involved a 'tiger kidnap'[11] in which the family of an employee was taken hostage and threatened in order to force the employee to help the robbers gain access to the storage facility (Sounes 2008).

In turn, drug-use as a lubricant to the edgework of robbery has significantly increased (Matthews 2002: 33–5), creating a high-risk, low-reward, violent drug subculture rather than a quasi-honorific violent specialist elite (R Smith 2005). Consequently, the emergence of much armed robbery as a deskilled, disorganized activity often resembling a drug-addled Ealing comedy makes it tempting to dismiss the robbers as mere dinosaurs. However, the decline of these wide-lapelled denizens of central casting, destined to reside for eternity on a 1970s cop-show loop, enables us to understand the manner in which the storage, distribution, and protection of cash and other high-level goods have driven transgressive innovation through eras of craft and technical invention, via hedonistic camaraderie, teamwork, and brute strength, to deskilling, fragmentation, and individualization.

The craftsman and armed robber were located amongst a criminal fraternity or underworld that marked the frontier of the legal and the illegal, and segregated committed criminal practitioners from dilettantes. They utilized key factors of industrial working-class culture, and refined them into a stylized set of overtly criminal strategies that contributed to the establishment of an exclusive milieu of specialized, explicitly deviant knowledge. Armed robbery holds little appeal to contemporary, career-minded individuals except as a means to create capital,[12] and the unsophisticated

---

[11] The tiger kidnap is so-called due to the way in which the victim of the crime is 'stalked' (Control Risks 2007).

[12] 'Brothers jailed for airport raid. Three brothers who stole £1.2m from Gatwick Airport after executing an elaborate heist have been jailed ... The gang ... turned

often random reality of cash-in-transit robbery is a reminder that this is no longer an exclusive elite, but an all-inclusive community of practice which, despite the brazen banditry bivouacked at its fringes, now embraces entrepreneurship in order to underpin success in marketized arenas where wealth acquisition rather than traditional skills and predispositions is the yardstick of worth and competency.

to crime when rent at the Peacock Gym, in Canning Town, east London, almost tripled…They used the gym's first floor offices to plan raids from Scotland to the Home Counties, with the Gatwick job being the "big one"': *BBC News*, 16 October 2004.

8

The Same Money?: Locating the Entrepreneurial Habitus

Now I know you've got some sort of romantic notion about crime. Yeah, you have Lenny, don't try and deny it. I bet you wish I was a bank robber, something glamorous like that. At the heavy like some sort of modern-day Robin Hood. But it wasn't like that. You see, crime, well what I did, it was just business with the gloves off (Arnott 1999: 311)

The risks are too big...and the money's not that brilliant. One geezer I knew was dropping off 'ozzies' [ounces of cocaine] for this other feller, and he was getting paid £25 for each package...25 quid, that's fuck all. Alright, he's maybe doing, 10, 20, 25 a week...that's maybe three hundred, a monkey [£500] in his hand ....But he's not doing them one by one, you know what I mean, he's always carrying, I don't know, five or seven ounces at any one time...And if it all comes on top, he's the one in the firing line, no one else....and seven ounces of cocaine, you're looking at fucking serious bird ....It's not for me (Joey)

While the activities of craft and project criminals, as well as those of territorially based gangsters, were all locked firmly into the everyday realities of the industrial working class, their occupational status also located them amongst a criminal fraternity or underworld which segregated the legal from the illegal and distinguished the committed professional criminal from the amateur. By utilizing key factors of masculine, industrial, working-class culture and refining them into a stylized set of overtly criminal strategies, the professional criminal could establish an exclusive domain built upon specialized, explicitly deviant knowledge and predatory violence. However, the post-industrial sweep defies such uniformity (Bauman 1992: 52) by emptying out industrial cultures, not only of marketable labour, but also of traditional, informal modes of governance as represented by distinctly criminal subcultures and their associated local applications of extortion and theft. Indeed, the emergence of the marketplace as the primary focus of social life has ushered the last of the doyens of the underworld into the foyer of that great illegal drinking club in the sky, making redundant any analysis of contemporary society restricted to the parameters of traditional cultural forms (Horne and Hall 1995; Hall et al 2008), which have mutated into entrepreneurial associations largely indistinct from those valorized in the entire 'spectrum of legitimacy' (Smith 1980).

Unlike activities such as extortion and armed robbery, contemporary serious crime is not located in fixed terrain, but manifested as both local and global networks of opportunity, featuring ill-defined contours which have shifted the culture of serious crime from the exclusive territory that spawned its most prominent practitioners and their signature modes of organization (King 1991: 6). For as the globalization of legitimate markets has contributed to the erosion of traditional cultures, so the global drug markets that have evolved since the 1970s have contrived to erode the links between traditional criminal territories and the cultures they spawned.

Women are exemplars of these major changes to criminal economies and cultures, and although they remain rarities within this characteristically masculine culture,[1] the drug trade in particular offers opportunities for women that were unimaginable within the male-dominated enclaves of safe-breaking, extortion, and armed robbery (Hobbs 1995). Particularly where industrial processes and their attendant relations have become redundant (Lash and Urry 1987; Piore and Sabel 1984), women are increasingly likely to become involved in illegal trading (Dunlap et al 1994; Fagan 1994), for as Durk and Silverman (1976) have noted, the drug business is an equal opportunity employer.

Via the adoption of mainstream commercial methodologies, female dealers, albeit in a minority, symbolize the breaking-down of taken-for-granted underworld orthodoxies; and the clusters of

---

[1] A UN survey found that crime groups generally viewed women as victims (for example via sexual exploitation), operating in peripheral and lower-ranking expendable roles (for example as couriers), as lower-level operators who may often be unaware of the full extent of the crime groups' activities or who are simply excluded from core and peripheral organized crime groups' activities (UN 2002).

friends, acquaintances, and in particular families[2] who contrive the dealing networks of the contemporary drug trade do not exclude women. Two generations ago Dogtown women often bolstered the distinctly female domestic realm with a little light receiving of stolen goods that was very much in accord with gender expectations in Dogtown, and the territorial-based subcultures that morphed into adult entrepreneurial networks were distinctly masculine zones that mirrored the gender relations of manual labour. However, in the wake of crucial alterations both to the political economy and, in particular, 'the declining status of young men (that) may have diminished their "gatekeeper" and mediating roles in both conventional and street networks in poor neighbourhoods' (Fagan 1994: 186), female engagement within dealing cultures enables a measure of status that had traditionally been denied to women, suggesting that crime networks are altering in accordance with the socio-economic environments that host them.[3]

Miller's Tale

Four women of working age in the Miller family live in three rented flats within 400 yards of each other on an estate now fragmented by the intrusion of owner occupiers, and the prospect of two, near apocalyptic regeneration schemes. The two youngest live together, combining child-rearing with increasingly desperate attempts to get an education. Great-grandmother Zena is a widow in her fifties who spends most of her time minding her grandchildren, and her eldest daughter, Yvonne, is a grandmother in her late thirties who buys kilos of cannabis from a male ex-partner and distributes to one-time neighbours who now live in London's working-class suburbs.

Yvonne has prospered, progressing from 'optional', through 'incidental', before arriving comfortably in the 'professional' crime category (Carlen 1988). She functions as the main source of income for the entire family, keeping the kids well dressed, three homes clean and well furnished, and creating a silo of self-respect, discipline, and well-being in a landscape of fragmentation and uncertainty that

---

[2] The Matrix Knowledge Group report (2007) found that 75 per cent of traffickers entered the drug market via friends and family, rendering facile any attempt to treat the drug market as a mechanistic entity devoid of interactional or cultural context.

[3] Gang 'godmothers' taking over the family business: *Sunday Independent*, 27 November 2011.

features a scarcity of overtly successful men and a dearth of job opportunities for women beyond the fast-food and office-cleaning sectors. Yvonne learnt the business as an enthusiastic teenage smoker who sold to friends, and later from the father of her eldest child who was involved at the edges of an importation network. Her flat is immaculate, and her youngest children are smartly dressed and achieving at school. She now has a male partner who has little involvement with her business, but she is connected to a network that features a number of violent men on its roster, confirming the belief that 'you can't deal on your own as a woman ....It's not safe, you have to have somebody with you, you could get ripped off and it's just not safe. You have to have a bloke' ('Moira' in Hobbs 1995: 26). Nobody is excluded from engagement with this market, and given its flexibility, dealers are unlikely to be lodged into a permanent niche of some rigid patriarchal hierarchy (Ward 2010: Ch 6). Yvonne's career indicates that an association with traditional visceral potential is but one characteristic of her CV, a characteristic that defines neither her nor her business, which she runs discreetly in between school runs and shopping.

Cascading Enterprise

Although academics have attempted to estimate the scale of the drug market (Adler 1985; Reuter and Haaga 1989; Natarajan and Belanger 1998), the 'messy reality' of drug distribution (Johnson et al 1992: 71) suggests that even the most careful estimates should be treated with care.[4] The complexity of this market is due largely to its interconnected layers of brokerage which involve a wide range of intermediaries (Pearson and Hobbs 2001: 17). Other than their operations relying upon 'the instinct which fosters a good eye for profit and the capacity to wheel and deal' (Van Duyne and Levi 2005: 105) and the obvious fact that drug trafficking is commercially driven (Dorn, Levi, and King 2005; Johnson 2005; Barnes et al 2001; Hobbs 1995, 1998),[5] we are somewhat ignorant concerning how the market operates. The UK drugs trade is made up of a series of loosely interlinked

---

[4] Thoumi (2003) cites an unpublished report estimating a worth of US$45 billion and US$280 billion (cited in Davies (in progress)).

[5] This commercial ethic is only partially contradicted by the hedonism that clearly plays a major part in the trajectories of trafficking careers, for ardent hedonists can also be successful traffickers and fervently risk averse (Barnes et al 2001; Dorn et al 2003).

local and regional markets, which do not always resemble each other in terms of operational methods, local and historical roots, or ethnic composition. Consequently, the notion of crime groups as tightly organized, hierarchical entities whose tentacles reach around the globe is not supported by the evidence, and this market should be understood as one that is populated by networks or partnerships of independent traders or brokers (Morselli 2001).

The illegal drug market in Britain is estimated to be one-third the size of the tobacco market and two-fifths the size of the trade in alcohol (Matrix Knowledge Group 2007), and engages the services of 'haulage companies, mariners, serving army officers in South America, bank employees, solicitors, accountants and law enforcement officers' (Matrix Knowledge Group 2007). Generally, drug-dealing enterprises exhibited huge diversity in their structures and operations, with one-fifth of dealers working as sole traders, while the remainder are small or medium-sized. Some enterprises made use of salaried staff; while others had more cooperative and collaborative approaches (Matrix Knowledge Group 2007). The trade is marked by flexibility (Curcione 1997; Jacobs 1999; Williams 1989); and the ability of actors in fluid, constantly mutating networks to move between various levels of operation (Murphy et al 1990; Adler 1985) is a notable characteristic of a complex market that envelopes a substantial cluster of financial relationships and transactions. This market features cascades of debt that flow across regional and geographic boundaries, and where multiple forms of trading relationships can thrive, from orthodox employees to independent traders. Laboratory equipment, precursor chemicals, laboratory location, transportation, warehousing, distribution links, and financial matters were all dealt with by individuals operating discreetly and with little or no knowledge of other individuals or their activities. For instance, in one Turkish importation network, different people were used to organize warehousing, financial transactions, and distribution matters, as well as arrangements for collecting drug supplies from other warehousing arrangements in continental Europe, and transporting heroin in bulk across Europe, making it difficult to locate the centre of such an operation, if indeed there is a centre. To sum up, for a variety of reasons[6] fragmentation is a fundamental

---

[6] Part of this impression of fragmentation is due to the restraints and restrictions imposed upon law enforcement as well as the exigencies of police organizational cultures (Pearson and Hobbs 2001: 55–8).

characteristic of drug markets which are like a 'large jigsaw—but a jigsaw in which each particular piece comes from a different set' (Pearson and Hobbs 2001).

Traffickers[7]

As we can see from the case studies in Appendix 2, involvement with trafficking is clearly dependent on a range of variables, with friends, family, and personal drug-use all impacting upon the level of entry. Many different kinds of people drifted into a business that is unstructured and, unlike the legitimate job market, is marked by a lack of restrictive hierarchies.[8] Drug-use, recreational or addictive, certainly equipped individuals with a basic knowledge of the market at its lowest level, and buying and selling to friends enables individuals to experiment with prices, contacts, and suppliers (Ward 2010). While some were able to fund expensive lifestyles whilst acquiring competencies in markets with few entry restrictions, the pursuit of cash is a quest as complex and varied in terms of its criminal aetiology as in its non-criminal counterpart, and the range of consumption options are clearly more important than the adoption of a clichéd 'criminal lifestyle'.

There are few barriers to entry, and no special skills are required other than a willingness to break the law. A friend in the business was the most likely entry, suggesting that differential association remains a valuable theoretical tool. The role of kinship and ethnicity are important as traditional sources of trust in non-legal business enterprise, and while market principles require that crime networks reach beyond these narrow and traditional means of securing and enforcing trust, and numerous cross-ethnic network linkages are evident, kinship and ethnicity remain vitally important in maintaining viable nodes in international networks. The ethnicity of individuals linked to parts of the world where drugs are harvested or processed is relevant, and, as we can see from the case

---

[7] This section is based upon the Matrix Knowledge Group report (2007), of which I was a co-author. The report is based upon 222 interviews with incarcerated drug traffickers in UK prisons. Appendix 2 is a typology of traffickers and is my personal interpretation of both published and unpublished material gleaned from the Matrix report.

[8] For instance, a group of car dealers with no notable criminal backgrounds pooled their resources and invested in a one-off importation of £30,000 of amphetamine.

studies, can be regarded as a commercial advantage. While prison did not prove to be a major route into trafficking, it was a vital hub for those who entered into the prison system as a result of a drug-related offence. Further, the quality of the contacts made in prison was high, and often these contacts were of an international nature, a fact that relates no doubt to the increasingly cosmopolitan UK prison population (Matrix Knowledge Group 2007).

An entrepreneurial reputation forged in legitimate business constitutes a credible signal that an individual may well be available for drug-market collaboration, blurring the class-specific narratives of the old underworld. For it is not facial scars or time spent stoically in a prison cell, but a business with premises, cash flow, transport, or any of the constituents of an ongoing legitimate enterprise that are indicative of commercial viability, signalling an availability that makes a *'Yellow Pages* for criminal skills or *Corgi* registered getaway drivers' (Chattoe and Hamill 2005) somewhat unnecessary. While friends and family members generate trust relationships, drug cultures generate mutual knowledge of prices, purities, and availability, and while prison can expand the horizons of the guilty, entrepreneurial competence located within the infrastructure of legitimate business signals that an individual is commercially game.

From small-scale enterprises such as newsagents and restaurants, to property and transport companies, there was an entrepreneurial symbiosis associated with a wide range of 'skills, acumen, and logistics' (Morselli and Giguere 2006: 197) common to both criminal and legitimate enterprises. However, although it may be tempting to portray this relationship as the exploitation of a virtuous sector by the unscrupulous and criminally inclined, legitimate actors often 'participated in ways that were well beyond the scope of their legitimate trades' (Morselli and Giguere 2006: 197), suggesting that the quest for profit which is common to both sectors constitutes the most convincing central ethos. Success in the drug trade requires access to resources not exclusive to a redundant alcove of industrial culture, and, as Lea clearly states (2002), entrepreneurial trends in inner-city life have created a blurring of the legitimate and the illegitimate, and the adoption of strategies that are closely related to the formal ethos of late modern urban life.

Overall we can conclude from the Matrix study that drug culture has penetrated British society so thoroughly that few barriers exist to acquiring strategic knowledge, rendering a criminal apprenticeship or a reputation for stoicism in the face of law enforcement, if not irrelevant, then certainly non-essential. Far more important are knowledge of business, transport, prices, weights, and quality, knowledge that is not restricted by class or ethnic origin and does not require the early onset of a criminal career forged in adolescence. Indeed, 'adult starters' whose careers evolved beyond the clichéd constraints of youth were significant (van Koppen et al 2010), and the varied career trajectories of traffickers emphasize that market engagement is a prospect for a wide range of individuals, not all of whom require a platform of early onset chronic offending and serious delinquency (van Koppen et al 2010). Further, late-onset engagement is partly related to the embeddedness of trafficking networks within the enabling environment of ongoing legitimate enterprises, and knowledge gained across a wide range of normative occupations, nurturing transferable skills, connections, and access related to enterprise, feature prominently in this discussion of traffickers. This suggests an emphasis upon the kind of commercial embeddness that comes with maturity, and the ability to function within complementary legal and illegal zones, rather than the adoption of a new and deviant identity.

The impermanence of drug trafficking structures suggests that 'Many traffickers work as individuals, couples and acquaintances, networking to seek out contacts and resources as needed' (Dorn, et al 2005: 16), shifting attention from traditional organizational paradigms towards individuals, business acquaintances, friends, and family members networking in crime markets. The ensuing drug-market transactions stress flexibility, autonomy, and independence, reflecting trends in the organization of legitimate markets (Ruggiero and South 1997; Ruggiero 1995; Chambliss 1978: 8). As a consequence, any quest for the 'fabulous underworld of bourgeois invention' (Benney 1936: 263) amongst the pragmatic coalitions that inhabit the contemporary drug trade will ultimately prove to be in vain. Certainly, the generic adoption of entrepreneurship as both a central ideological prop and a pragmatic strategy of post-industrial society has assisted in the consolidation of both legitimate and illegitimate interests around a central theme of wealth accumulation (Burrows 1991; Heelas and Morris 1992), and the shift towards entrepreneurial action should be regarded as indicative of the duplication of post-industrial interactions within the indistinct parameters of illegal markets.

Team Games: Chris's Tale[9]

> Don't you see that all this underworld business is fictitious at
> bottom? You build up an underworld about you for no reason
> other than to give respectable people the illusion of living in
> an overworld (Benney 1936: 194)

Research based upon offender interviews (Pearson and Hobbs
2001: 5–9; Matrix Knowledge Group 2007) indicated that few
were in possession of detailed information regarding the operational details of dealing networks, and, for many participants, marginality and ignorance were the norm. Consequently, in order to
create some order and make sense of their chaotic lives, individuals
are often heavily reliant upon collaborations and associations
whose levels of coherence are exaggerated. As a mere labourer in
the vineyards of the drug trade, the extent of Chris's knowledge
was limited to the exigencies of the transactions that constituted his
business, and as a consequence the so-called 'higher' levels of the
business were imbued with a considerable amount of awe and fear:
characteristics usually translated as 'respect': 'There is bother [vio-
lence], I am not saying there aint, but it is either the Youth, and that
is really what they always been at. Just boys fighting and this [drugs]
is a reason…That's right, they would do it anyway. At the other
end…the money people, when that goes off at that level of business
people just…They could be abroad, or, the other thing [dead]'.

Chris's connection to the Cash brothers was tenuous. He bought
cocaine from a man who was thought to be one of their associates,
and the subsequent protective cloak of association was reinforced
by rumour and gossip to the extent that Chris was able to assume
the mantle of associate/firm member. This lack of any rigid connection between formal structure and everyday mundane activities is
due to the lack of embeddedness which denies the contemporary
criminal firm a similar status to that of folklore-mandated entities
such as the Kray twins. Further, there is a lack of integration between
the various components of the Cash brothers' enterprise, which
consists largely of a façade adopted by actors for purposes of local
legitimacy, commercial viability, and continuity. Chris accepted his
subordinate position in relation not only to the Cash brothers, but
to others who were regarded as key nodes in the network, and

---

[9] Conversations with Chris took place as an unintended offshoot of Pearson and
Hobbs (2001) during 2006–7.

whose power rested with their close association with the Cash brothers' violent authority. Despite Chris's inability to make any concrete economic connections between these various members, and in particular his failure to link these 'executives' of the firm to his actual dealing activity, he was adamant that he was involved in a coherent enterprise associated with an identifiable and established brand.[10] The Cash brand functions as a form of cultural guarantee, a lightly coded interactional order that has evolved from the local political economy, and which in turn is grounded upon a proletarian entrepreneurship that appears to contradict normative narratives of British working-class culture (Hobbs 1988).

But Chris does not operate in total isolation, and understanding dealing as a team endeavour affords a recognizable cognitive framework to activity which, while not random, is seldom regularized in the manner of legal markets. The collaborative efforts of the drug-dealing team, certainly at the middle-market level experienced by Chris, feature reciprocal dependence that links team-mates to each other (Goffman 1959: 82), and the possibility of cleavage or disruption is balanced by the near certainty of violent retribution guaranteed by the ethereal presence of the Cash firm, thus affording the team some structure in the form of corporate discipline.

The Cash firm retains its symbolic value as an enduring expert system rooted in 'local contextualities' (Giddens 1991: 22), by enabling actors such as Chris to adopt the Cash brand and envelop themselves in tentative connections to a cultural order, and in doing so secure important resources, not least of which is local legitimation. Unlike the intimacies integral to networks of theft, drug dealing generates interactions which, although largely clandestine, are usually simple to the point of banality. Unencumbered by institutional rules, and typified by teamwork, it is the relationships fostered within these teams that constitute the networked activities of so-called organized crime. 'Nobody wants to spoil it so certainly the people I work with...(are) very reliable and steady. Pick ups and deliveries on the button. They all look after their bit of business, pay on time and all that' (Chris). (See Andreas and Wallman 2009: 228.)

---

[10] Even those working at strategic levels have only a partial sight of the overall market. In the main, dealers were knowledgeable of their own operations but had limited knowledge of the activities of others involved (Matrix Knowledge Group 2007: 23).

Although familiarity can develop 'with the passage of time' (Goffman 1959), the clusters of entrepreneurial associations considered here feature high levels of relational flexibility and a willingness to perform pragmatic roles that are flexible or fixed for a specified set of transactions (Goffman 1959: 83). 'You can be doing pick ups for a price, looking after a bit of gear, driving...' Indeed, even within a single transaction, team members may perform several different roles, and status within these flexible collaborations is of less importance than efficient and risk-averse practice: 'It aint good if I go too long without having a (financial) slice of it. Even the jobs, the driving and that, usually I have got (some) dough invested'. Chris, like many of his commercial acquaintances, has performed multiple roles within a number of related collaborations. Couriers, financiers (a rather grand term for 'putting up the money'), warehousemen, security guards, clerks, etc, can be interchangeable roles that should enable the abandonment of the burdensome structural connotations of organized crime, and stress instead the essentially relational arrangements that are produced by illegal enterprises.

Although in Dogtown the political economy no longer offers the traditional, all-inclusive networks of stolen goods that were once central to the everyday interactions of a dockside community (Hobbs 1988), the citizens are still 'at it'. Regardless of the commodities involved, the attractions of a bargain remain a powerful and consistent feature of urban life, and to aspire to the status of dealer or vendor of these desires is merely a working-class rendition of a trend established and valorized (Down 2006) within the normative order (Hobbs 1992; Lea 2002).

The Obvious Distinction of Price

There is a newsagents nestling in one of London's many schizophrenic, low-income, aspirational, cosmopolitan yet racially divided, council-house-dominated, private property hotspot neighbourhoods, where the owner will answer any enquiry concerning the high-value goods on sale behind the counter, for instance a request for a phone card, or for 20 Benson and Hedges, with 'cunt'. Consequently, wherever possible, local shoppers try to restrict their purchases to newspapers and magazines from the easily accessible shelves, and to soft drinks from the refrigerator. When this is not possible they will point to the desired goods. When this does not work and they verbalize their requirements, they will be called a 'cunt'. The one exception to this instinctive resort to profanity is if the shopper asks for 'Albanian Marlboros'. This is a code that triggers the production from below the counter of a range of apparently conventionally branded cigarettes that appear identical to the glossy packets that line the wall behind the shopkeeper's head. The only obvious distinction is the price.

Jack has never been to mainland Europe. In the last few years he has holidayed in Florida and Dubai and once went on a stag weekend to Dublin. As a skilled building worker sub-contracting his skills to property developers in London, Jack has succeeded in acquiring a decent standard of living for his large family. He has no criminal record. He is a hard-working family man who voted for the Labour Party but pines for the Thatcher era. He pays what he feels is a high tax bill and plays golf at the local municipal course:

> My views on crime? With kids (as a father), you are going to be anti drugs. I never did them and I know nothing about them, but they are bad. We have worked on places that have been used by druggies and I don't think you can imagine what their lives are like...My aunt, who is the only one of the older generation left, lives in a flat, one of them Warden assisted places. She has been burgled. Shocking really, so I am glad we live out of it a bit. Having said that, you get trouble round here more and more.

Jack was working on a central London building site and employed a young electrician who sold bootlegged cigarettes to the site's large workforce: 'I can't remember the prices, I don't smoke so it wouldn't mean much to me. But they was cheap...And it was upfront cos it's hardly criminal, the only ones who are suffering are the smokers and they are going to get sick anyway whether they pay full price or not.' The electrician, along with his cousin, travelled to Belgium every two weeks, buying cigarettes legitimately at hypermarkets before returning to England and selling on to friends and acquaintances without paying the excise duty. After working with Jack for about six months, the electrician became employed on a job on the other side of London. However, Jack found many of the electrician's customers were still seeking out their cheap supply: 'I just went back to this Sparks (electrician) and told him that he had a lot of customers looking for him, and he gave me these big old sleeves of fags to go in to work with'. And so, tentatively at first, Jack entered the extremely mundane world of retail contraband. The two cousins worked across Belgium and French hypermarkets, varying their routes and buying-patterns before finding a wholesaler 'who was doing loads of legit booze for the coach parties and that. He put them on to really cheap fags, really cheap, wholesale it was so no tax.'

This was a significant shift from bootlegging (paying local taxes before importing and selling the goods to consumers who avoid paying UK tax). Jack was now involved in smuggling and the avoidance of all taxes; and the opportunity to accrue high profits from this new trade prompted new, ambitious, operational strategies. Jack and his two partners were now bringing in lorries with large amounts of cigarettes hidden amongst legitimate loads: 'Our drivers was always picking up in France, but the fags come from Spain...all the usual brands that you get in the shops.' Jack's role was to locate customers; he found that entrepreneurially minded individuals as well as retail businesses were clamouring for his business. While maintaining his job as a building subcontractor, Jack approached this new business with enthusiasm, and soon found that many hours every day were spent talking to potential customers on the phone.

There was little haggling over prices, and the cigarettes never came near his home since, via a relative, Jack had obtained access to some warehousing facilities on an industrial estate adjacent to a courier firm that operated 24 hours a day, lending the smuggling business flexibility and enabling it to merge seamlessly with legitimate traffic both day and night. Similarly, connections in the transport industry made it easy to recruit lorry drivers who were picking up legitimate loads in continental Europe. Jack's main problem was money: 'I had dough in the fridge, the freezer, behind kitchen units. See for somebody like me used to earning enough to look after the family, having bricks of tenners passed to me was, it sounds strange I know but I didn't always like it...I never put a total on it...all the phone calls did my head in...I am no businessman...it felt kind of serious...well I did start to think about what might happen if it all came on top. The family, kids mortgage, and the other two were so well at it I could never say to them "hang on my bottles going", it just went off on its own.'

Each load was a minimum of a million cigarettes, the drivers were paid £1000, and after rent on the warehouse the profit was split three ways: 'So if we was buying for 50p (for a packet of 20), and at a million sometimes we was, that's £25,000. We would get £2.00 a packet. Take the drivers' chunk and a few quid for rent and extras and we were splitting 60–70 grand three ways.' This trip was made three times in six months, and then one of their customers was arrested for receiving stolen goods, which set in train a series of unconnected arrests of acquaintances for non-smuggling offences. Jack and his fellow smugglers ceased trading. Jack became frightened and told his smuggling partners that he wanted to pull out of the business, provoking an aggressive response from the cousins, who demanded money to pay for what they claimed were outstanding overheads: 'They came on a bit strong with me, nothing happened but I'm worried about my kids and what might happen...So I was not getting into it any more, and that was that. I give them some dough for the lock up (warehouse/storage), but I was out. They went back to buying from the supermarkets so I heard.'

I asked Jack if he had ever considered himself to be an organized criminal. It was the only time that I ever heard him swear: 'Its fucking daft to even think about what we were up to as being anything more than a bit of a scam, a bit of tax dodging really. There is a piece in one of the papers about how footballers avoid tax by making themselves into companies. Our thing was harder work than that, but it's just accepted by most people. If fags was illegal I could see it, but you can buy them anywhere. Having said that my eldest [daughter] smokes and it worries me, the health issue.'

This mundane example indicates how 'global organized crime' is embedded in everyday routines, work, and family life. While cigarette smuggling may not carry the same frisson of dark transgression as drugs, guns, or people, the fact is that smuggling tobacco products is worth £1.3 billion in evaded revenue (HM Revenue and Customs 2008; Joossens and Raw 2003). An estimated 11 billion cigarettes are smuggled into the UK every year (HM Revenue and Customs 2008), and tobacco kills 114,000 in the UK annually (Peto et al 2005). While much of the illegal cigarette trade involves cooperative ventures with legitimate manufacturers operating global brands (Joossens and Raw 2003; van Duyne and Antonopoulos 2009), the global reality of cigarette smuggling is no different from the trade in any other form of contraband. Consequently, the networks that are associated with smuggling are based upon informal and highly local expectations linked to nodules of trust, and jeopardizing the integrity of these expectations can inspire violence or the threat of violence as the most pragmatic and available sanction available (Hornsby and Hobbs 2007).[11]

---

[11] For an outstanding summary of the trade in illegal tobacco products, see L'Hoiry (2012).

Conforming to the Milieu

The onset of post-industrialism and subsequent changes in male employment opportunities (Sassen 2006: 186–7) has, as described in Chapter 5, led to a crisis in the general habitus, which could no longer generate relevant practices, forcing accommodation to an unfamiliar environment whose rules barely distinguish between licensed and unlicensed capitalism. However, as we can see in the case of territorially based neighbourhood collaborations (Chapter 4) and youth groups (Chapter 5), as well as from the trajectories of many of the entrepreneurs detailed in Appendix 2 who were embedded in legitimate commercial practices before seamlessly embarking on careers in trafficking, the dispositions generated by the general habitus of the UK's Dogtowns were easily tweaked, adapted, and ultimately transmuted into the specific habitus of the entrepreneur.

This adaptation, and the subsequent embedding of urban traditions in networks of criminality, have been particularly smooth for individuals who come to activities such as drug dealing with a pre-formed entrepreneurial habitus. For them, 'doing the business' is an ongoing expression of trading competence that bypasses all other personal characteristics, and the transformation of the embedded general habitus into specific dispositions is marked by a ratcheting-up of entrepreneurial action, for instance from petty theft or dealing in stolen goods, to stealing 'lorry loads'; or from buying small amounts of a drug 'for personal use', to dealing. The transformation to the specific habitus can also be marked by engagement with key commodities such as contraband tobacco products or illegal drugs, or by utilizing violence for commercial, as opposed to personal or recreational, reasons. The predatory ethos of entrepreneurial urban culture has 'already laid the groundwork…[and they] come to the setting pre-formed, pre-conditioned' (Desmond 2006: 411) to competent criminal engagement. Those embodying a general entrepreneurial habitus are already acclimated to the relevant protocols and practices, and in this milieu they encounter others of a similar disposition with whom they coordinate their actions, seamlessly, unremarkably, and crucially without the inappropriate emotive façade of 'organized crime'.

As Chris explained when asked if he would give up the drug trade for a legitimate occupation offering the same financial reward: 'The same money? Half the money would do it. Half the money and no ag(ravation). Be ideal, regular hours, no hassle. I can't see how the difference is between what I do and what somebody doing like a dispatching job.'

Fortune's Always Hiding: Dud

Dud's grandfather was a dock worker and trade union shop steward, and two of his three sons also worked in the docks, while Dud's father trained as a butcher, a trade which, along with Dud's mother's clerical job, provided a decent standard of living for their small family. Although he stopped going to school at the age of 15, this was normal where Dud was brought up. Indeed, neither Dud nor his family or friends could discern anything unusual about his early years. His family provided bed, board, and a bi-monthly change of trainers, and the streets and ecology of the locality were sites of play, plunder, and refuge. He became a thief, and did glue, dope, and alcohol—a normal boy growing up in late-twentieth-century urban Britain.

He stole cars and motorbikes, avoided violence at all costs, drank beer and smoked, and dealt dope: 'Just spliff stuff, ounces, half ounces, pocket money really. I was gluing up, doing a bit of black, rolling round and doing houses…especially when there was a bit of dope about and you got paid with it. All any of us, silly kids really was about, was getting off of our faces. That's what money was for and that's where it all went.'

When he was 17 and briefly obsessed with a girlfriend who lived over 200 miles away, he stole a car and crashed it after being chased by the police. For years he claimed that the police beat him up as he lay in the road injured. When they searched him they found a small amount of dope and he received his first prison sentence. In his early twenties, Dud and two friends were convicted of burglary, and on his release he commenced a career as an all-round thief, dealer, buyer, and seller.

He married soon after his release from prison and, with the responsibilities of parenthood that quickly followed, he became more businesslike in his dope-dealing, not allowing customers to smoke on his premises and keeping his stash buried in his parents' garden. However, he was never able to accumulate sufficient capital to expand, and his supplies fluctuated as he constantly scoured the market seeking out a regular outlet willing to deal in comparatively small quantities at low prices. Still in his twenties he and two of his oldest friends stole a lorry and sold the contents to members of a family firm who were in the process of decamping to the suburbs. They were working-class escapees who ran several businesses, and were linked to a transport company with premises in the old neighbourhood. Dud and his friends were, in his words, just 'a bunch of fucking wanky kids…earrings, Escort convertibles'. The lorry load turned out to be only half a lorry load, and the gangsters took Dud and one of his friends into the toilet of a local pub and put guns in their mouths. When Dud soiled his trousers he was taken back into the packed saloon bar and put on display.

By his late twenties Dud was working for associates of the same firm who had humiliated him. He ran errands, delivered bags of cash to strangers, and eventually set himself up as a dealer, first in ecstasy and then cocaine. When he located a contact in the kind of pub that can quickly mutate from a wine bar to an Ibiza beach bar, he became the 'licensed' dealer. By the time he was regularly filling his mother's fridge with used notes, his wife and child were long gone.

A relation was badly injured as the result of a drug debt, and the chaos and violence of the private lives of his friends and business partners overwhelmed him: 'There was a time when people were getting shot and stabbed up all everywhere…I stopped sleeping, and I was well at the gear.' Dud had also briefly been part of a consortium that funded ecstasy importation, but he was 'mugged off' by his partners and lost everything except his car. He did not complain too loudly about being ripped off. The chance of extreme violence being foisted upon him was enough for him to back off: 'I wiped my mouth and walked away' (see Shover 1985: 113–17).

Dud now lives on his own in a high-rise flat that shakes when the wind blows. He is in his mid-forties and separated from his second wife and children, who have started a new life in a new town with a new dad, a clerk who Dud insists used to manage a porn shop:

I never really worked. If that makes sense, cos I am working in a way now I suppose. I buy and sell it ….Yeah it's my business…as it is I could go out and buy anything. Lot of talk about how Es (ecstasy) not the thing anymore and it's this and that, but people still want it. Round here people will do anything, its only another thing, a night out thing…The damage thing is really nothing to do with me, I don't make it so you might as well go to fucking *Johnny Walker* and say to him, 'what about this whiskey thing with all the headaches and that?' Nothing to do with me.

Dud lives on lager and takeaways, and alternates between an optimistic reconciliation with his family and enacting a humiliating revenge. The revenge relates to his relative wealth, and as a non-violent man he wields £10 notes like weapons. Yet his buying power remains latent, money stashed in relatives' fridges, bathroom panels, and kitchen cabinets, the cheap bits of jewellery around his neck are lazy concessions to the lounge lizardom of his fantasy life:

A place where at anytime my girls can come over swim in the pool and that, all down to me. I could live Cyprus or Florida…just a nice place, something with a business so I can earn without working. Just enjoy myself, drink myself fucking silly.

There is only one photograph in Dud's sparse living room. It depicts a pub excursion to the seaside at Margate, the self-conscious smiles of a group of men both young and old are framed by a slightly out-of-focus sign that promises 'Dreamland'.

9
A Sense of Order: Violence, Rumour, and Gossip

> It's the threat of violence that keeps people in line because I mean, that guy...he could say, 'I've took your 25 grand, fuck, I'm off to London, I'm not coming back.' But what happens if I find him in two years time, I'll murder him, or I'll want my mate to murder him, somebody will murder him and he knows that. So it's not worth his while to fuck off with 25 grand (Pearson and Hobbs 2001)

> All London is run by one family. They can do anything. When I was in Highpoint [prison] it was common knowledge, everybody talked about it (Jackie)

The chaotic essence of illegal entrepreneurial culture discussed in Chapter 8 inspires various attempts to create a sense of order. For instance, as described in Chapter 2 in particular, the state is often engaged with imposing order upon the social construct of 'organized crime', and the notion of the underworld is a prime example of an attempt to categorize and order this chaotic, fragmented zone of activity. In addition, those who are active within illegal markets are also concerned to impose some sense of order in a milieu whose signature state is confusion, and this chapter will examine the construction of a sense of order within the culture of illegal trading via the devices of violence, rumour, and gossip.

Violence: Punching Above Weight

Violence is often regarded as a signifier of organized criminal activity, and the ethnographic work that underpins this book has confirmed that, in accord with reviews of the relevant literature (Hagan 1983; Maltz 1976, 1985; Albanese 1996), violence, and the threat of violence are major characteristics of illegal trading networks, as well as being integral to the cultures that nurtured its proponents (Schlegel 1987). Indeed, as Davies notes in relation to the drugs trade, 'by the time imported drugs arrive on our shores, they have almost undoubtedly been party to high levels of violence—real or threatened—from the point of production and at every stage of their journey to the UK' (Davies (in progress)). Consequently, as we can see in the preceding chapters, in relation to a multiplicity of markets and regardless of the sophistication of the methods employed by a crime network, violence will always be regarded as a pragmatic resource (Gambetta 1993: 2), particularly when other forms of social control are absent or have proved inadequate (Falcone 1993: 7–9).

This lack of formal structural arrangements within illegal trading cultures places an emphasis upon 'unofficial history' (Samuel 1994: 3–48), where the chaos of individual lives reflects upon commercial instincts that often have a violent default mode. Indeed, the use of violence to create, protect, and maintain a slice of the market within a densely populated sector inhabited by a multiplicity of networked players is a characteristic of the culture of the illegal marketplace (Arlacchi 1998: 205), and as Catanzaro indicates, 'in the culture this relationship between violence and the accumulation of wealth is socially accepted' (1992: 31). Therefore, 'systemic violence' (Goldstein 1985) is inextricable from the culture of 'violent self help' (Andreas and Wallman 2009: 226) that typifies this disordered fragmented milieu 'which tends to transform impersonal market confrontations into personal antagonisms' (Arlacchi 1986: 157). It is therefore inappropriate to attribute economic rationality to all of the violence performed by individuals who are associated with acquisitive criminal collaborations (Falcone 1993: 97–8).

Consequently, violence should not be regarded exclusively in terms of a 'management technique' (Young 2007: 54) within illegal markets,[1] for violence is also a means of identity construction and maintenance, and it is crucial, therefore, to consider the way in which practitioners of violence transform a personal quest for honour or gratification into a quest to establish some kind of cultural authority (Bauman 1992: 52) which, in turn, may be marketable. The essence of their marketability rests with their willingness to

---

[1] A view vividly expressed by John Gotti, 'And every time we got a partner that don't agree with us, we kill him' (Capeci and Mustain 1992: 27).

invite chaos via the embrace of confrontational options which are the very antithesis of those normative daily strategies that feature the avoidance of conflict (Hobbs 1995: 51; Maas 1998: 53). No matter how sophisticated and market orientated illegal trading is, the viability of traditional visceral resources remains central to the establishment, marketing, regulation, and, most importantly, the culture of entrepreneurially orientated social networks where individuals 'are obligated to respond to a perceived slight to self, or to family with the same level of ferocity and commitment as they would to a threat to their commercial viability' (Hobbs 1995: 122).[2] For the nature of the cultural collateral upon which so much criminal entrepreneurship is grounded ensures that violence becomes an obligation that can be a creative or destructive force; creating identities and reinforcing networks, or destroying temporary working arrangements (see von Lampe 2002: 153).

Although a Home Office study found that only 6 per cent of murder and manslaughter cases were linked to organized crime (Hopkins and Tilley 2007), suggesting that violence is not a major factor of this milieu (van Duyne 1996: 354), these law-enforcement, filtered accounts of *actual* violence associated with loose definitions of organized crime that isolate instrumentality (Bean 2008), are over-simplistic (Smith 1971: 17) since they ignore reputation, threat, intimidation, and the enacted environment of illegal trading which is a social as well as an economic system, and where motivation is complex and business and personal lives are often indistinguishable (Maas 1998; Falcone 1993: 146–52; Pearson 1973: 212–21; Pillegi 1987: 130–4). One of the problems of regarding murder, or any overt act of violence, as an indicator of organized criminal activity is that, as mentioned above, intimidation or the threat of violence is the foundation of many lucrative illicit businesses. For instance, in the US in the list of indictments obtained by the 15 Federal Strike Forces between 1981 and 1989, only 14 feature murder, attempted murder, or conspiracy to murder (Jacobs et al 1994), but most of the remaining indictments feature crimes whose chances of success would be enhanced by being carried out by individuals with violent reputations, for example loan-sharking, illegal gambling, etc.

---

[2] In April 2000, Kenneth Noye, a highly successful British criminal entrepreneur with a reported fortune of £40 million, was convicted of murder following his stabbing of a man in a road rage incident: *Guardian*, 15 April 2000.

During my research I encountered the aftermath of a major crime which, due largely to its apparently non-violent nature, was lauded by both convicted and non-convicted criminals, by law-enforcement personnel, and by the mass media as ingenious and sophisticated. However, one of the unspoken facts underpinning this case was that the crime was closely connected to a well-established crime family with a long-standing and well-deserved reputation for violence, and more than any other factor this reputation ensured that the subsequent sentences handed out by the court were accepted quietly and without complaint by the accused. The parameters of the case merely corralled those 'facts' negotiated by law-enforcement officials and the legal profession as being 'relevant' for successful, albeit token, convictions, and although no violence was actually used, violence underwrote the case, guaranteeing and mediating the level of risk for all of those involved.

Ignoring the cultures that generate illegal trading can spawn some serious misunderstandings, and in particular the true role of violence within illegal trading cultures will be largely invisible if scholars become over reliant upon officially generated data that cannot, by definition, interrogate the role that violence plays within the enabling culture of serious crime. It is not violence per se that is 'bad for business' (Pearson and Hobbs 2001: 45), but the beatings, stabbings, and shootings that come to the notice of law-enforcement agents (and therefore creating 'data' for administratively orientated researchers) that can directly or indirectly threaten the smooth running of illegal capitalism. For instance, one of the drawbacks of placing violent, occasionally psychotic individuals within entrepreneurial fields is that frequent, ferocious, violent action can not only attract the attention of law enforcement, but also deter potential partners and investors. As a highly successful criminal entrepreneur explained when discussing a murderous business associate, 'He became a fucking liability. You are trying to get a deal out of a man, and he is on him cutting and plunging away. He never knew any limits, not what you want out of a moneymaker.'

In addition, it cannot be too forcefully emphasized that drawing a clear line between personal and commercial violence is at best unwise because 'When these webs of relationships are untangled, violence can often acquire personal as opposed to structural characteristics and aims' (Pearson and Hobbs 2001: 45). For instance, an enterprise based upon cannabis and amphetamine importation was enhanced by a car theft and ringing business (changing the identity of stolen cars and selling them on to unsuspecting buyers as legitimate vehicles), two pubs, and a portfolio of property. However, despite this commercial success, when an ex-business partner who, over 15 years previously, had publicly insulted the wife of one of the firm's founder members was released from prison, the man was beaten and stabbed, and the legal and extra-legal fall-out of this violence marked the disintegration of this cluster of entrepreneurship. It is a combination of personal and occupational identities that inform the apparent mayhem of most illegal markets, where an individual's utilization of violence is no more bounded by legal or cultural convention than it is restrained by commercial instrumentality (Hobbs 1995; Katz 1988: 181–5; Presdee 2004: 150).

The Nail Banger

Stewart is a builder by trade who plays down his expertise and training by claiming to be somebody who makes a living by 'banging nails in walls'. When he left school he worked briefly in a clothing factory before the father of a school friend arranged an apprenticeship with a local building firm. Stewart blossomed, made good money, and in his spare time turned his car-repair hobby into a part-time commercial venture. His lock-up garage and skill as a mechanic positioned him as part of a loose-knit network of friends and business acquaintances who, when Stewart became a self-employed builder, provided work in the form of repairs, renovations, and house extensions. This network also provided access to corrupt council officials who granted Stewart permission to build on land whose use was limited to industry or agriculture. In the early 1990s, for £10,000 paid to a clerk or a councillor in a suburban pub car park, Stewart claimed that he could convert a £20,000 plot of land into a £75–100K asset. In common with the money-hungry clerks and planning officials, Stewart was part of an upwardly mobile population fleeing the inner city, and quickly found himself with a great deal of spare cash which he invested in cars, property, and three wives.

By the late 1990s Stewart's life had become increasingly chaotic, and while he paid out to wives and ex-wives, he also over-extended himself in the property market; one business partner was declared bankrupt, owing Stewart over £250,000. The cohort of corrupt public officials who had kick-started his career as a property developer entered retirement or became unreliable, and one man who had received a kick back to grant planning permission proved to be seriously incompetent. As a result, a two-storey house built by Stewart on the back of bank loans had to be demolished. He had run out of money, was drinking to excess, and suffered a number of beatings from relatives of one of his ex-wives. He crashed cars, punched walls, and eventually called on the services of Al.

Hard men 'persevere without limitation until they dominate, then they force others to confront the same choice' (Katz 1988: 100). Such confrontations can take place within public, private, familial, or commercial domains, and may produce outcomes which financially may be either beneficial or calamitous, but the more irrational the level of violence that is utilized, the greater the transcendence of rationality and the more valuable the reputation.

Al was a relative of one of the local bandit icons of the 1970s and had forged a career that was reliant entirely on his willingness to hurt people. A bouncer and degenerate gambler, Al was hired muscle for anyone picking up a bag of shady cash, who needed back-up at a business meeting, squatters evicted, or a debt urgently repaid. Al became the making of the second phase of Stewart's career. They both needed money and Stewart wanted some personal and professional respect. Al started to accompany Stewart whenever a dispute was likely. Cars were torched, a subcontractor and his staff were beaten up, and a number of suburban-based clerical staff were reminded of their obligations. Stewart took Al to meetings with his wives and their families and took to turning up at their places of work in order to 'renegotiate' various property arrangements. If workmates or family members intervened, Al's presence alone was usually enough to ensure order, and for the first time in his life, the unprepossessing Stewart assumed a swagger of invulnerability.

By 2001 Stewart's life was very much in order, settled domestically, and, with a new business partner, Al was seldom required to reinforce Stewart's reputation as a tough and necessarily violent businessman. He ventured increasingly overseas, taking golf holidays and cruises, eventually investing in a building project in Spain, buying a small house in a quiet Mediterranean village, and talking increasingly about one day cashing in and spending his retirement years floating from island to island in the Caribbean.

The swindle put an end to all of this. His business partner disappeared, and his Spanish investment was exposed as a scrap of coastal land, pock marked with discarded breeze blocks and with no building permission. Stewart began drinking heavily and got into a fight with a group of people in his local pub who he insisted were 'travellers'. Three of his drinking friends were convicted of conspiring to import a mixed load of drugs from Holland, his wife left him, and the property market froze, leaving Stewart with a portfolio of debt and a number of expensive habits including a weekend cocaine 'treat' that had morphed into a daily routine. He became morose and increasing aggrieved by ancient slights and perceived insults. One incident in particular became impossible for him to exorcise.

During his mid-twenties Stewart had been buying and selling cars with a group of other young men, and drinking away much of their profits in a pub (now demolished) where they took over the back room. During one heavy session Stewart became embroiled in an argument with a younger man in his late teens, which was probably concerned with football. As neither man had a reputation for fighting the rest of the company ignored them, until the younger man, whose inability to cope with alcohol had made him something of a joke among the amateur car dealers, picked up a glass and made a somewhat half-hearted threat against Stewart. To the amazement of the assembled drinkers Stewart put the man in hospital. Before the stitches had been removed the victim had bought a handgun and flaunted it to a number of friends claiming that he was going to shoot Stewart. Nobody took any notice; the threats were regarded as typical of the young man's eccentricity, and as a consequence Stewart was told neither of gun nor the threat to his life. When Stewart was eventually told about the threat during a boozy evening of reminiscences with his friends some 15 years later, he merely laughed it off and appeared to file it away as part of their communal chaotic youth. Now, a decade later and in his late forties, Stewart's memory of the young man's threat curdled when it came into contact with his current impotence. The man was traced living a blameless family life, and Al broke his arm.

Eventually, Stewart responded to his plight with typical resilience and went back 'on the tools' as a jobbing builder, although his failing health meant that he was increasingly reliant upon his eastern European labour, whom he employed 'off the books'. He invested in a row of suburban shops that boasted generous storage facilities and were due for demolition, and by reconnecting with some of his old drinking circle, Stuart was able to offer these multipurpose premises as a base for a range of illegal activities. By 2009 the shops were sold, he was once again back on top, a wealthy man whose hard graft, manual dexterity, predatory business skills, and astute utility of violent labour had paid off. Al remains available.

Stewart's career spans both the industrial and post-industrial city, and the key to his entrepreneurial career is to be found in urban working-class networks where not only violence, but entrepreneurial endeavour, predatory business acumen, and the exploitation of normative manual skills are highly valued. As we can see from Stewart's life history, violent entrepreneurship is no longer the sole prerogative of an 'underworld' (Haller 1990: 228–9); its precepts, tenets, and methodologies originate in an over-world that leans heavily upon a predatory culture featuring a chaotic subjective backdrop of family, emotional, health, and economic problems that are not exclusive to that of the 'criminal'.

Narratives of Inaction: Criminal Gossip

Roly was a part owner of one of a number of scrap metal yards raided by the police in a high-profile operation against a very successful network of car thieves and ringers. A number of men were convicted. However, Roly was not one of them and his whereabouts became a constant source of speculation:

Asa.   Roly? Gone away, I mean away, fucking gone.
Stan.   What abroad?
Jack.   My Jill saw him at Lakeside with his mum.
Asa.   Gone, Gone, know what I mean?
Rod.   He had a flat in Turkey. Owed fortunes. I reckon he's on his toes over there.
Jack.   Well my Jill reckons he was at Lakeside with his sister.
Stan.   Mum, you said his Mum.
Asa.   He's dead.
Stan.   He used to have some bird in Manchester.

Although omnipresent within illegal markets, albeit in various forms and guises, violence is but one method by which a sense of order, no matter how illusory, is constructed. As we can see in Chapters 4 and 7 in particular, during the era of the underworld, criminal culture was a relatively unambiguous cultural zone, and it is the ambiguity of the contemporary crime market that makes rumour and gossip so central. Within criminal firms the maintenance of order is based largely upon generating a mystique which gives the impression of a clear and unchallenged hierarchy that reacts punitively to internal transgressions, and gossip humanizes those individuals and groups mythologized by rumour. Successful criminal entrepreneurs, like their legitimate counterparts, often rewarded themselves by physically locating in exclusive suburban or rural enclaves remote from the territories of their employees and junior associates. Consequently, their families and social lives were subject to conjecture and fantasy by lower-level operatives. In particular, the sex lives and transgressions of their immediate family were subject to constant speculation, and the drug-taking habits of the children of notable criminal players were of particular interest, as they often indicated an element of vulnerability not apparent in the parents (Rosnow and Fine 1978: 88). So, from fashionable clubs, via bouncers, taxi drivers, and other denizens of the night emanated tales of excess and questionable allegiances that stand at odds with respectable suburban expectations, and a degradation of the beer-soaked, nicotine-stained, heterosexual, stoic hedonism upon which the myths—if not the reality—of the underworld were founded (Saviano 2007: 271).

Rumours of links to iconic, dangerous, or unorthodox individuals and organizations were speculated upon; and to be seen in the company of a white, black, Asian man/woman, with someone speaking a foreign language or with a non-local accent, provoked flights of the imagination that morphed effortlessly into rumours of war, collaboration, triumph, or decline. A sighting on unfamiliar ground, in a bar in Marbella, a football match in Manchester, or a restaurant in Glasgow, could all be interpreted as indicative of an upward or downward business trajectory, a career high, or an imminent retirement. Of particular interest were rumours relating to violence, and especially to gory war stories that involved enemies, grasses, nonces, mugs, and incompetents being cut, beaten, shot, and humiliated.

However, narratives of inaction, although seemingly contradictory, could prove equally potent. In the late 1990s, Peter a 19-year-old landscape gardener and an enthusiastic clubber and part-time ecstasy dealer, was occasionally couriering packages for two men who were associates of the 'Cash Brothers', a very successful criminal group whose name functioned as a highly lucrative brand when linked to a range of criminal pursuits as well as to non-criminal activity—for instance ownership of licensed premises, and local expressions of cultural capital such as boxing, martial arts, and football (Hobbs 2001). Peter 'lost' several thousand pounds, and went missing. On his return he was confronted by the two men who had funded this particular deal, and emerged from the meeting unscathed. However, while the debt was apparently wiped out, the lack of explanation was impossible to forget. Suddenly a young, inexperienced newcomer had become a potential threat. Why had he been let off? What did he know? Was he connected, or even related to somebody with power and influence? Most importantly, what status, jobs, or role should he be afforded in future enterprises? These quandaries were expressed by an associate:

For as long as I could remember, it was always upfront that if something occurred [went wrong], it was down to you to make it right. You heard stories…about a slapping [beating] or worse…But the real thing is you just want things to go smooth so you make money no fuss. When he [Peter] pops up and it was 'forget it no problem'…people were wary obviously.

Peter's ambiguous status assured that he could not be ignored, and he became a popular guest, particularly for individuals lurking on the fringe of Cash enterprises at high-profile football matches and boxing shows. This pardon constituted absolution from on high, and gave Peter's social standing a considerable boost that was unusual to be afforded to one so young by much older and more experienced men. Although he remained a fringe player, and it is doubtful if he was offered any more than mere scraps off the table from any illegal business, his improved status is marked by the fact that he now works for a company that is rumoured to be at least part owned by the Cash family (Bauer and Gleicher 1953: 297–310). When cautionary tales are contradicted, for instance when the dealer who errs continues to deal unharmed by his allegedly violent superiors, existing assumptions are violated, and the moral order of the 'firm' is called to question. However, rather than accept that the firm's authority is built on sand, the deviant is revaluated as a team member, his threat absorbed, and he becomes imbued with a 'special competence' (Katz 1975: 1381) that complements the existing folklore of the firm and imposes a sense of order upon a disorderly and unpredictable environment.

But not all of those missing in action return unscathed, and the expectation of violent action being taken against transgressors is central to the everyday order that enables commercial activity to proceed. Detailed stories of threats, beatings, and rather more vague allusions to killings are relayed across generations as traditional forms of order maintenance, and these folktales survive as long as they engender significant cultural values, central of which is the acceptance of violent authority as an everyday reality. While, as we see in Peter's case above, blame can clearly be negotiated, the periodic exercise of punitive authority serves as a disciplinary device, a visceral social affirmation of the monopoly of force, symbolic or otherwise.[3]

A Rumoured Order

Within criminal firms the context is one of a pervasive atmosphere of chaos, distrust, and suspicion, and rumour-mongering is a problem-solving device that facilitates social control when the existing order is believed to be in jeopardy (Siegel 2008). It is not organization that distinguishes so-called organized crime groups, but the ability of members to create and embellish the rumour and deception that 'is an integral element of how organised crime is experienced, perceived, and reported' (Lacey 1991: 394). As Shibutani (1966) indicates, rumour is an essential part of solving group problems, and in the following passages I will give some examples of the way in which this 'improvised news' is utilized to resist uncertainty and ambiguity in an environment where 'grounds for suspicion and sinister hypotheses are never lacking' (Schneider and Schneider 2003: 91).

Benny and the Trojan Container

Benny had made his name for his role in a highly successful team stealing from and hijacking lorries, and his reputation was based initially upon hard work and reliability. Over time, however, he had assumed more responsibility within a loose-knit network of thieves as someone who could glean information, put together a team, and most importantly get the best price for the stolen goods. Benny also liked to fight, and his multi-scarred face and forearms featured a

---

[3] For instance, when two men stole some heavy plant machinery from an enterprise run by associates of a prominent criminal firm, they were wrapped in a carpet and beaten with scaffolding poles. The beatings were filmed on mobile phone cameras, and proceeded to both entertain and discipline numerous audiences over the next few months.

number of reminders of work-related disputes. Benny made, spent, loaned, and gambled a lot of money. He moved out of Dogtown into a huge seaside house shortly before he was arrested and subsequently convicted for his role in a robbery. He lost most of his money and possessions while in prison, and always expressed his time inside as an invaluable part of his education, although his subsequent career was not so much a glittering cluster of felonious episodes, as a melange of low-level theft, self-employment, and violence, studded with some outstanding successes as part of a team of warehouse robbers.

But the last two years had not been kind. Now middle-aged, he was coming to terms with his fading, once imposing physique by consuming vast quantities of powdered protein drinks as favoured by athletes and body builders. However, a penchant for lager and vodka, and increasingly rare visits to his back bedroom to bench-press plastic-coated concrete discs, had done little to enhance his physical well-being. Consequently, his facial muscles appeared to be melting as he sat at the bar of *The Dog* on a stool that was flanked by a pair of huge, jowly buttocks permanently encased in black track-suit bottoms. Broad shouldered with spam-textured forearms and hooded, permanently bloodshot, eyes, as long as he remains seated Benny presents a formidable figure in *The Dog*, from where, over the past 30 years, his career has encompassed wild-eyed outlaw, provider of cheap goods, custodian of *The Dog*'s moral order, and now grand old man and resident sage.

And then there was the debt. Rent, multiple hire purchase agreements, and electricity and telephone bills were mere institutional bagatelles. The more you could rip off an anonymous company, bank, or local council, so much the better. You just changed address, changed your name, pleaded poverty, then did it all over again. Owing money to institutions was as natural as sucking up a large pint of fizzy chemical lager. However, the personal debt was different. The trick here was never to hit an individual for so much that they were going to come after you and cause a row. So you borrow a ladder and sell it. A set of tools and they 'got stolen'. £250 for repairs to his van, £50 for an IPod for his granddaughter, and on one occasion £800 for a British motor bike, which he bought and immediately sold to a drinking partner for £1000 before borrowing it for the weekend and returning it. When it was returned on the Monday morning it was five years older, 250ccs less powerful, and Japanese.

Benny's reputation was based on over 40 years as a skilled professional thief. He could make trailers, lorries, and 40-foot containers disappear into a vortex of transport yards and industrial estates across east London and Essex, and he had thrived on his willingness to take risks and spot opportunities. Yet he also gained pleasure from giving money, stolen goods, and a great deal of time to old people and local kids. For instance, when times were good he sponsored a local boys' football team, and dozens of sweatshirts were given away to old people and families down on their luck, This generosity was coupled with a fearsome reputation as a fighter, a quality which on occasions was utilized on behalf of noble causes such as protecting a barmaid from amorous strangers, but usually as a response to a perceived challenge or slight. Benny had forged a reputation as a local man of respect, yet with few of the operatic or structural implications suggested by most specialists writing about organized crime. Although he was known and acknowledged by a number of 'faces' he always shunned the now fashionable faux *Goodfellas*' habit of hugging, and generally resented the Guy Ritchie mode of gangsterism that involved little more than a good haircut and the ability to wear an overcoat a size too small. Benny was respected for what he was, an amiable thief and occasionally self-employed man, whose generosity and violence were an integral feature of the local social order.

However, his waning physical powers had resulted in him making increasing demands on his accrued cultural capital. He was no longer borrowing money to fund repairs on his van or to invest in a 'few parcels' of stolen or cheap goods. Loans were funding household bills, rent, and his stool in *The Dog*. The latter posed the biggest problem. Indeed, without half an inch of drinking vouchers tucked into his tracksuit pockets, Benny was disenfranchised from the extensive, albeit fading informal networks that gave his life meaning. For many years his ability and willingness to climb over a fence, break a window, drive through the night, turn the contents of an abandoned warehouse or shop into stock, buy, sell, steal, and scheme had kept him and his family afloat on tide of dreams and stolen microwaves. Now, a £25 loan was all that was keeping Benny from a life of supermarket vodka and daytime television. The range of formal reasons for requiring a loan varied, but equipment (tools, ladders he could not climb, van parts, etc) was the norm. Most people swallowed it when they handed over £200 for Benny to purchase a ladder, only to see him peel off a £20 note and buy a round of drinks; it was part of his brazen charm, he had been doing this for years, and many regarded it as money well spent in exchange for friendship, amiable company, and the fading collateral associated with a man of violence—albeit one of shuffling gait and lager sweat, whose eye whites are yellowing and joints grinding.

Benny borrowed money from friends of his son, young men who had not grown up locally in the shadow of this icon of tough entrepreneurial masculinity. These loans amounting to a few hundred pounds were from men in and out of manual and driving jobs with young families, and who were only differentiated from the trials and tribulations of Benny's life by a generation. Loans should be paid back, and the creditors had no compunction in coming looking for their money publicly, humiliatingly, on Benny's ground. Initially Benny stood firm; he did not have the money, he was waiting for somebody else to pay him for some delivery work that he had done, and when that did not work and his creditors adopted a more aggressive tone, he resorted to a traditional strategy, pointing to his chin and inviting the men to 'take it out of that'. They did not, but kept coming back into *The Dog* asking for repayment, once accompanied by two large men resplendent in bouncer-chic, black nylon Schott jackets. This regular stand-off inspired Benny to carry a Stanley knife on his trips to *The Dog*, and his willingness to up the stakes to a physical confrontation reminded everyone that he was still 'game'. Benny would never have paid the men off even if he had won the lottery. They had attempted to intimidate him on his home ground. After about six weeks of the stand-off the men stopped visiting *The Dog*, and I suspect that unbeknown to his father, Benny's eldest son had reached a monetary compromise with the creditors.

Benny's previous pattern of borrowing continued, but two new business opportunities simultaneously emerged to provide some promise of relief from his cycle of debt. He was approached by an ex-*Dog* customer who had known Benny in his prime. This man had moved away from the area about ten years previously and had lived in various tourist resorts in Spain and the Canary Islands while working as a handyman on British-owned developments. He was now making money from cigarette smuggling and wanted to use a lock-up garage of Benny's for storing the contraband. Benny no longer had the garage but kept this detail to himself as he took delivery of thousands of cigarettes into his living room.

The second business opportunity to come his way was more complex and involved considerable risk. Few middle-class colonists had penetrated Dogtown, which was one of the few parts of London with a local housing market that proved resistible to gentrification. However, a few bold frontiers-folk invested in the ex-council flats and small Victorian terraces before the prospect of sending their children to a local school became too much and the previously resistible mundanity of semi-detached suburbia beckoned. A few of these pioneers even visited *The Dog*, where, in common with most of the clientele, they were generally ignored. However, after several months they began to find the juxtaposition of Benny's increasingly enigmatic Kurtz-like presence with his old-world courtesy one of the few comforting features of their new neighbourhood. Delia was a teacher in a local school. Privately educated, she had deliberately cast aside her extremely privileged background to work with inner-city kids. She dressed in a manner that marked her out from any of the women who drank or worked in *The Dog*. The locals thought of her as 'scruffy' and 'posh', a combination especially disconcerting for those locals with school-age children who were suspicious of anyone deliberately veiling their status. Her partner, Alec, was the son of a upwardly mobile civil servant, and had also been privately educated. In his teens Alec's life had been particularly chaotic, and shoplifting, drinking, and eventually smoking cannabis resulted in expulsion from school at the age of 15, in effect ending his formal education. Periods of living in squats, casual work, and failed attempts at gaining some basic qualifications followed, until, in his mid-twenties, he bluffed his way into a job as a kitchen fitter. Now ten years later he has a small business in a more fashionable part of the East End, but has acquired along the way a sufficiently 'mockney' patina to pass.

Alec and Delia like to smoke dope, and as newcomers to the area had no local supply until Benny stepped in to oblige his new neighbours and occasional drinking partners in their plight. Pleased with the quality and price, Alec and Delia became regular customers, and introduced Benny to a group of their equally bourgeois friends, who within two months were all drinking in *The Dog* and smoking dope provided by Benny. Although at this stage Benny was only earning drinking money, he approached the enterprise with characteristic zeal and imagination, and hatched a plan with the middle-class couple to invest in a mixed load of drugs that he could arrange through one of his old comrades in warehouse theft who was now making regular forays into drugs. Alec and Delia shook hands with Benny, and within a month the money was invested; Benny sold their portion of the consignment and the profit was split three ways. The relationship between Benny, Delia, and Alec was very strong at this time; they met regularly and discussed the possibility of future deals, always with repetitive acknowledgments of Benny's astuteness. This was what Benny had been waiting for: an opportunity to exercise his hard-earned entrepreneurial skill, some risk, and the promise of rewards large enough to transform his life forever. Discarding his tracksuit bottoms he smartened up, his shuffling gait improved, and his back straightened. Clean-shaven and alert, he became charm personified, more Cary Grant than Del Trotter, and more confident than anyone had seen him for at least five years.

The next deal involved a considerable investment by Alec and Delia.[4] This was to finance a part-load of dope that would be sold on their behalf, and word was out that Benny was earning again. A number of people were looking forward to Benny getting paid, including Sam and Sammy, the landlord and landlady of *The Dog*, who had loaned Benny money which had come straight back over the bar, and Ernie, a milkman, who always had a large roll of paper money in his trousers on a Friday night, the one night of the week that he drank in *The Dog*. Ernie had loaned Benny hundreds of pounds, and so had several other people, all of whom were very discreet, for to be otherwise would be to draw attention to Benny's plight. The ease with which Benny was able to move amongst his creditors was undoubtedly enhanced by his current good fortune, and they were content to wait until they were paid out. All except for the cigarette smuggler, who had come looking for his goods only to find a small family saloon where his Benson and Hedges should have been. Benny owed him a lot of money. Then, just at the time that he was due to receive payment for the dope, Benny went missing.

He was away for nearly a fortnight and rumour was rife in *The Dog*. From Spain to his girlfriend's spare bedroom on the other side of Dogtown, everyone had a theory about Benny's disappearance. It says much of his local standing that on his return nobody asked where he had been, and everyone, in particular Delia and Alec, kept their disquiet under control and carried on drinking. Gradually, Benny dropped hints that the importer had yet to pay him, but that he had telephoned and payment was on its way. But disquiet grew, and the cigarette smuggler was seen arguing with Benny in the street. Eventually, one of his youngest creditors broke ranks by asking

---

[4] Some of this money came in the shape of loans from friends.

point blank for his money, using the fact that his wife had just given birth as a tool to both prise the issue open and perhaps to appeal to Benny's well-known sentimentality and love of children. However, after three months the money still had not arrived. Benny again went absent without leave, this time for three weeks.

When he returned, all the bounce and confidence remained, but now there was an uncharacteristic intensity. He volunteered that he had been in hospital with a serious intestinal complaint, which clashed with the accounts given by two members of his family, who had cited business abroad and varicose veins as reasons for his absence. While some people still expected to get paid, others were very privately speculating on how and when Benny would deal with the situation. The word of his good fortune was now out, and debtors from years back, who had long ago written off the money owed to them, were easing back into Benny's life in the hope of being paid off. This was partly due to Benny failing to acknowledge the role of Delia and Alec in the enterprise, an omission for which they were extremely grateful. Benny's role had been largely to act as a lightning conductor for any risk associated with the enterprise, and for this middle-class couple there was no cultural capital to be gleaned. They just wanted their share of the money.

Reefer Madness

When Benny came up with the container story, it produced a mixed reaction. The drugs were in a 22-foot container waiting to be picked up from a lorry park in Essex. The return was going to be huge, and all of Benny's creditors would benefit enormously. A month later Benny announced that the police had the container under surveillance. The ride had come to a shuddering end. He skilfully kept things vague. He had heard that the container was in Tilbury but could not be sure; he thought that the drugs were mixed with boxes of sweets/clothes/shoes, but he did not know. He, after all, was a fellow victim. While a few people hung on waiting for the police to cease their operation, some walked away disappointed, but most seemed to disengage from the fantasy with some relief. Nobody felt obliged to confront Benny who had succeeded in writing off all of his debts whilst simultaneously maintaining, and in some ways enhancing, his status as an entrepreneur.

Delia and Alex ran with the scam and counted themselves as unlucky; if the police had not been so efficient they would have received a substantial chunk of money. But they had enjoyed the buzz of transgression with little of the risk, and had some great nights with Benny. Meanwhile, the ladder-less and bereft of tool maintained a stoic silence, and the petty investors dreamt of what might have been if not for predatory cops lurking in Tilbury. Wiser heads walked away relieved that Benny had offered a way out. By escalating the situation to the level of drug importation and involving undercover police and organized crime, any investment, albeit by proxy, suggested a stage of transgression too far, and by utilizing a rumour of organized crime Benny had called his investors'/creditors' bluff while enhancing his own reputation as someone with contacts in high places. He probably came to an accommodation with the cigarette smuggler, although it is hard to imagine him paying out in full. Ernie was hit by Benny for another £25. Delia and Alex became less-frequent visitors, but had covered some of their losses by borrowing from other risk-averse frontiers folk, who also swallowed their losses when the rumour of police involvement dropped into their stripped-pine lives.

In illegal trading cultures, the void left by official renditions and the constant mutation of relationships serves to intensify gossip and rumour as individuals amplify unverifiable, but culturally feasible vernacular versions of events. The container under surveillance proved to be a highly functional rumour to circulate amongst a community of greedy, yet generally risk-averse individuals who embraced the rumour as a way of resolving the situation without direct confrontation. Given the lack of structure within the culture of illegal trading, ambiguity fed by rumour can be exceptionally functional.

Norman the Dog Killer

Norman was convicted for a serious assault in a club that is known for its cheesy 1970s-style cabaret. On his release from prison he was involved in the theft and damage of cars, threats of violence, at least one arson attack on commercial premises, and the fatal poisoning of a dog guarding a scrap metal yard. Rumours circulated that this activity was due to his enthusiastic feud with a local family who were part of the travelling community. However, the reality was far more complex; the scrapyard was not linked to travellers, but to a group of businessmen who were using the yard to store stolen goods (see Chapter 5). Norman's brother claimed that he had been swindled by the scrapyard owners, and the dog had fallen victim to Norman's quest for revenge. The arson attack was a commercial venture that Norman undertook on behalf of a local man who was seeking repayment of a loan, while the threats of violence were associated with Norman's love life, albeit a love life that involved inter-family loans, and an unfortunate incident featuring a Rottweiler and some patio doors. Although Norman's chaotic life lacked thematic coherence, friends and associates lumped together these tangentially related issues in an attempt to confirm a situational and reputational logic based upon culturally coherent assumptions. This resulted in the manufacture of an easily digested formulaic narrative—in this case 'the feud'. These vernacular interpretations, like the criminal justice data discussed in Chapter 1, tend to veer towards thematic simplicity, and such one-dimensional narratives do not do justice to the complexity of lives whose richness is not diluted but often enhanced by transgression.

Some Sort of Mastermind: Jim, the Quantitative Easer

When nine individuals were sentenced for up to seven years in a major counterfeiting case that allegedly threatened the fiscal well-being of the British state, key players, bit-part players, and entourage members stood shoulder to shoulder in the dock. The case concentrated upon one node of the network and fabricated a simplistic picture of this multi-million pound operation, which, if fully investigated, would have remained open for many years, exposing the ease with which the banking system can be defrauded. Consequently, the police and financial authorities created parameters, limited the case, and padded out the population of proven collaborators with entourage members (Hobbs and Jackson (in progress)). The result is the creation of a community of the guilty, clusters of individuals whose representation is restricted solely to their alleged involvement in a named criminal act or set of acts, feeding the notion of an underworld of exclusively deviant intent motivated by economic gain but drained of cultural or interactional context.

Jim was brought into this network as a result of family associations with a group of counterfeiters who had been active for several years. His role was very specific and involved a process known as 'foiling' and 'finishing'—heat-pressing fake holograms and strips onto pre-printed notes, before a laser printer printed the letters 'land' from 'Bank of England' on top of the hologram. For four months Jim operated the 'foiler': 'I doubt that I made four grand out of it in the end.' Police surveillance of the group had commenced before Jim started work for the counterfeiters, and when his home was raided he was found with one of the counterfeiting machines and a large quantity of forged notes. The reputation of the British banking system relied upon presenting a self-contained, highly publicized case that demanded the spectacle of a competent state taking punitive action against organized criminals. Unable to commit police resources for an indeterminate period in order to track the distribution networks or the whereabouts of the printing plates, police concentrated upon the production process and found suitable enemies amongst some key instigators and an entourage generated by family association (see Hobbs and Jackson (in progress)).

The subsequent worldwide media attention concentrated upon the seriousness of this 'organized crime' and the vast amount of money that had been forged: 'when we walked onto the wing in Pentonville everybody clapped and cheered'. The assumption was that this amiable, exceptionally personable, and articulate man in his late fifties had managed a lucrative, long-term, high-level criminal career, and his fellow inmates assumed 'that I was some sort of fucking mastermind, that I had plenty of dough stashed away and that I had been at it for years and hadn't been nicked. Instead I had just been involved for a few months and never had a pot to piss in.' As a consequence of these assumptions of criminal competence: 'I got offered up all sorts of deals while I was inside. Geezer comes in, a forger, says he wants to meet me and comes on like we was best of pals. Says that I am the business, and that he wants to make one with me when I get out. I tells him no fucking chance.'

However, not all of the rumour and gossip was positive, and Jim was constantly subjected to derogatory remarks from fellow members of the counterfeiting firm and their associates who, knowing of the limited role he had performed, resented the status he was afforded by inmates and staff alike: 'If I got any problems, which when I first went in I did from some of the rest of the firm, they was saying, "he's this and he's that, he was just a wanker but he's giving it the bigun". I had some of the most biggest gangsters, real heavy top, top people saying "Jim, just say and we will stab em up".' In prison Jim was afforded a wisdom that was entirely inappropriate to his actual experience and competence. For decades he had ducked and dived, bought and sold, and survived on the edges of Dogtown's economy, yet his fleeting association with a major crime, and his age, demeanour, and lack of a prison history, enabled Jim to acquire a status amongst staff and inmates alike that was at odds with his actual criminal involvement.

Now out of prison Jim is regarded by many in his local community as a huge success, and driving around the local streets it is clear that his brief period as a threat to global capitalism has inspired a great deal of respect. He goes out of his way not to dispel rumours:

The kids think I am some gangster, and the older ones wish they could have made all the money that I am supposed to have made. I get people saying, 'Jim why didn't you give me some? I would have had some'. But they don't understand they were being sold in batches of a thousand and shifted up north and out of the country ... some French or Italian money changer aint going to ask any questions and look at the metal strip or whatever ... you couldn't say I will have five or ten, you had to take a big batch and even then only certain people would be allowed to buy. But anyway all of that was nothing to do with me, I just had a little job and got on with it. But fuck em if they want to think I am some mastermind that is up to them. But I have been left with fuck all ... they [police] even had [confiscated] my motor and it was 12 years old ... they took my caravan, which was worth about three grand and a few bits of gold that I bought. They wanted to put a confiscation order on me of £1.3 million, and I have got a 12 year old motor and a caravan. I said 'you want all you like but you'll get fuck all off me. I've got fuck all'.

However, Jim also utilizes the assumptions born of the gossip that surrounds him. Playful local youth and feral street entrepreneurs have colonized one tiny, pedestrianized segment of Dogtown that most locals negotiate via a tedious detour, but Jim goes out of his way to walk through the spitting throng, who either avoid his still menacing gaze or acknowledge him with a nod and a grunt. When Jim drove past the boys one hot summer afternoon a youth screamed something unintelligible at the car, and when Jim hit the brakes and wound down the window, the youths stopped playing basketball and looked on expectantly. Jim stared at the youth, who took a step forward and politely explained that he was informing Jim that one of his brake lights was not working. Jim thanked the boy, and looking at the road ahead smiled and said 'good as gold', before driving away.

Jim has also exploited unfounded rumours of his criminality in his dealings with the police. When his house was raided in the middle of the night by police officers looking for one of his relatives, they would not give any details with regard to the nature of the accusation against the relative, so Jim took the officer in charge aside: 'I said, "Don't fucking give me that 'you cant tell me'. Now you know who I am, and you know what I have done. Now what's this about?". Eventually he tells me it's an attempted murder, and the geezer's in a coma, so when they leave I phone up his mum and warn her they are on their way.'

As a short-term, minor member of the counterfeiting team, Jim missed out on the rewards, yet his brief engagement with the business of counterfeiting resulted in him being described in court as a 'lieutenant', a main player integral to 'Britain's biggest ever counterfeiting operation'. The rhetoric of criminal justice ensured that Jim was deprived of his freedom for a considerable amount of time, triggering a series of disastrous consequences from which his family is unlikely ever to fully recover, and rumour and gossip concerning his wealth and criminal competence continue to impact upon his life. However, examination of his actual role, rather than the clichéd presentations by both the police and the media, shrouds the uncomfortable yet mundane reality that the desire to literally make money is common to everyday life rather than an exceptional, transgressive event.

Conclusion: A Rumour of Order

This chapter has looked at the various ways in which violence is utilized within illegal markets, and the role of rumour and gossip in assisting individuals engaging with these markets to gain a sense of order and structure from an environment that is chaotic, disordered, and largely unpredictable. Although the 'maintenance of internal discipline; enforcement of market conditions; and control of competition' (Smith 1971: 17) are generally popular motives expressed for the existence of violence, as the examples above indicate the enacted environment of illegal markets is a social as well as economic system, and such rigidly instrumental motivations understate the chaotic interactional order that pervades within illegal markets grounded in a competitive ethos that dominates both business and personal lives.

The notion of violence being utilized to impose internal discipline is derived largely from Cressey's theory of organized crime as an alternative government, where violence is used as the 'functional equivalent of the criminal law' (Cressey 1969: 166). However, illegal markets are not governments but commercial enterprises, which, above all else, must remain competitive, and violence, whether actual or implied, is used to maintain that competitiveness rather than to enforce abstract laws or codes. The very idea of an alternative government staffed by remnants from *The Godfather* stems from an underworld fantasy which is constituted by the incessant recurrence of sacred myths related to traditional strategies and iconic individuals, and functions to preserve an illusion of an expert system. Even in their most visible and traditional forms (O'Brien and Kurins 1991; Cummings and Volkman 1992), the enacted environments of illegal markets are that of relatively modest cooperative enterprises operating from project to project within an enabling network of cohorts, front-men, and background operators (Reuter 1984; Pileggi 1987), and criminal enterprises do not generally indulge themselves by performing violence on behalf of abstract principles.

They are essentially practical, concerned with profit, and retaining commercial viability by reacting forcefully to any threat to their competitiveness. Illegal markets are highly ambiguous, inclusive entities possessing few elements of structural coherence, and consequently anxiety and stress are constant factors, with rumour often being embraced as an attempt at countering ambiguity by offering a coherent narrative. Within trading cultures which rely upon discretion and highly informal practices, individuals will seek to eliminate chaos and uncertainty by utilizing rumour and gossip in order to provide structure to ongoing uncertainty (Allport and Postman 1947: 501–17), nourish reputations, and manipulate perceptions of both individuals and groups (Gambetta 1988: 168–9). Where information is seldom 'concrete' or its 'truth' subjected to positivistic scrutiny (Radin 1927), reality becomes negotiated via violent folklore, and the resultant negotiated order retains an element of functional fragility; any society deprived of hard news will inevitably rely on rumour and become sceptical and suspicious (Shibutani 1966), which is highly appropriate for social networks heavily reliant upon the 'shading of association' (Simmel 1906: 483).

Violence both promotes order and invites turmoil, while rumour and gossip create an impression of order and coherence in an environment where confusion and disarray is the norm. There is no hidden, secret order to illegal markets, which are marked by fragmentation and the lack of significant enduring monopolies. Physical violence, like law-enforcement activity, can create boundaries over which not all of the diverse, contemporary community of practice who engage with illegal markets are willing to cross. Paranoia and fear of both internal and external dangers dominate the culture of illicit markets for 'the threat of chaos is ubiquitous in the life of illicit action' (Katz 1988: 230). With rumour and gossip about people, families, money, or commodities, as well as the status of redundant or innovative collaborations constantly circulating, the best that scholars can do is to recognize that the illegal market is 'a chaos to be ordered as one likes' (Lukács 1983: 181), and concentrate upon how an internal sense of order is negotiated via a range of both traditional and innovative devices.

10

The Cosmopolitan Criminal

> The cosmopolitanism of our times does not spring from the
> capitalized 'virtues' of Rationality, Universality, and Progress;
> nor is it embodied in the myth of the nation writ large in the
> figure of the citizen of the world. Cosmopolitans today are
> often the victims of modernity, failed by capitalism's upward
> mobility (Pollock et al 2002: 6)

Mapping Crime, Class, and Ethnicity

As discussed in Chapter 2, at key times in the evolution of organized
crime in the UK maps have been introduced to enable audiences to
visualize the 'problem' and valorize the expertise suggested by the
concoction of such data. For instance, during the 1990s mounting
tension regarding the pervasive power of organized crime was
matched by some highly significant newspaper articles[1] that were
often accompanied by national or regional maps with photographs
of the local 'Mr Bigs' imposed. Significantly, Burrell and Levy also
wrote of a meeting of national organized crime figures in a hotel in
Newcastle[2] in a story that uncannily replicated the 'Apalachin Incident' in upstate New York in 1957, which, as part of the dubious
evidential base that constitutes American 'Mafia Studies', went
some way to convince the American public of the existence of an all-
powerful national conspiracy of organized crime (see Albanese 1996:
103–7; Liddick 2007). These stories, and in particular the maps that
accompanied them, served to mutually reinforce the drive by politicians and police that 'something must be done'.[3]

---

[1] Bennetto (1995).

[2] Burrell and Levy (1995).

[3] Burrell and Levy constructed their story from chatting to off-duty police intelligence collators, who, during the 1990s, tended to be experienced officers preparing for retirement (personal communication with Ian Burrell).

Modernity's tendency towards ordering or condensing human activity (Bauman 1989: 44; 1991: 15) via the creation of a meta-order is a key function of globalized law-enforcement culture, structuralizing phenomena that were previously consigned either to localized networks of transgression or to class-bound discourses related to a chaotic clutter of dissenting working-class identities. This obsession with ordering the social world has found its ideal subject matter in organized crime, and the creation of a meta-structure of global conspiracy whose activity is coherent, methodical, and quantifiable imposes order on a chaotic world, rendering the disordered, illegal marketplace rational and predictable (Bauman 1999: 79). By marking, framing, and mapping (Perec 1997: 91), the slippery notion of organized crime is made stable and durable (Latour 1986), and by associating the concept with territory, what is in essence an abstraction is afforded a concrete reality by its colonization of space, lending materiality to a construct which is in a constant imaginary state. Mapping organized crime enables the spacialization of the concept (T Hall 2012), locating an underworld of hostile space and shifting our attentions from the activities of 'the least socially excluded or marginal members of our societies' (Tombs and Hillyard 2004: 31), and focusing instead upon the visceral entrepreneurship of the working class, the excluded, and the dispossessed. Understanding organized crime purely in terms of spatial relations ignores its embeddedness in commercial orthodoxy, and mapping locates the phenomenon within an underworld or 'moral space' (Osborne and Rose 2004: 214) of simplistic, territorially based, binary relationships.[4]

As highlighted throughout this book, the spatial relations that developed from traditional alignment to working-class territories have been vital in understanding the origins of what we have come to understand as organized crime in the UK. However, when these relations are international and the subsequent trading flows are afforded the sobriquet of 'transnational', we are offered more expansive maps (Agozino et al 2009), where hostile spaces are filled exclusively with the unfamiliar, the foreign, and the alien. Extending moral spacialization to the transnational zone enables racial stereotypes to blossom within flows and routes that are illustrated

---

[4] The most obvious presentation of the binary model is the 1960s' rivalry between the Kray twins and the Richardson brothers, whose activities were divided by the Thames.

with extremely broad brushes, dispensing with both the ambiguity of the local and the hypocrisy of indigenous demand, and telling us nothing of the relationships within the cooperative strategies that enable illegal trade to flourish. Further, the mapping of the supply side and its local and global moral spaces are concentrated upon the simplistic valorization of traditional underworld fiefdoms, the banality of illegal harvests, or the source of human contraband, while the moral ambivalence of the demand side, where untaxed hedonism, traditional predatory activities, the commodification of sex, and the demand for cheap labour, are ignored.[5]

As we can see from the Jewish diasporas settlement in east London and the colony cultures of the Chinese in Limehouse and the Italians in Clerkenwell, the social, ethical, and cultural enterprise of cosmopolitanism involves affirmations of familiarity, as well as models of estrangement and alienation. In both industrial and post-industrial cultures newcomers to the UK have found themselves invariably involved in low-paid occupations involving long hours and with little job security; and one of the few areas over which the new arrival has some control is leisure, where the familiar can be affirmed and key aspects of the parent culture are brought to the fore and celebrated. During both the construction of urban America (Hobbs and Antonopoulos (forthcoming)) and at the peak of imperial Britain (Chapter 3), the habits of the cosmopolitan poor inspired fear, revulsion, and special legislation, particularly when their degraded habits were seen as being linked to a shadow global order involving conspiracies of foreigners. One method of threat construction carried out by the state is to corral the cities' abundant forms of acquisitive crimes associated with the working class, and place them into the pot called organized crime; and the cosmopolitan reality of contemporary urban life assures a constant source of new, exotic ingredients to keep the stew simmering (Werbner 1999).

---

[5] 'The United Kingdom Human Trafficking Centre's 2011 baseline assessment concludes that 11% of victims were trafficked for the purposes of domestic servitude; 1% for organ harvesting; 5% for multiple exploitation; 17% for criminal exploitation; 22% for labour exploitation; and 31% for sexual exploitation. The remaining 13% were trafficked for reasons unknown. Klara Skrivankova, Anti-Slavery International's trafficking programme co-ordinator, said: "The UKHTC 2011's assessment shows that more than 50% of trafficking in the UK happens for purposes other than sexual exploitation. The prevalence of trafficking for forced labour in industries like agriculture, construction or food processing is a problem we have been pointing to for a number of years"': *Observer*, 26 August 2012.

Vernacular Cosmopolitanism

As discussed in the early part of this book, foreigners were targeted as both precursors of organized crime and as central to the political construction of the phenomenon in the US, the UK, and beyond. Much of the trope of transnational organized crime has been grounded on the notion of the importation of toxicity across borders and into previously pristine environments. This was particularly relevant to Dogtown, where criminality was embedded in the local political economy, its semi-mythical Camelot coexisting seamlessly with a brief golden age of post-Second World War full employment and prosperity. However, deindustrialization and neighbourhood fragmentation led to the disintegration of stable pragmatic communities and their associated iconic criminal cultures, and the arrival of new communities whose leisure habits and connections with regions supplying the UK's growing demand for drugs and other contraband made them the latest in a long line of non-whites whose involvement in crime was linked entirely to their ethnicity. Crime groups cooperate within flexible networks (Hobbs 1995; Zaitch 2002; UN 2002), and ethnicity, along with family and kinship ties, is useful in the maintenance of trust (see Pearson and Hobbs 2001: Ch 4; Paoli 2003). However, to overstress the importance of ethnicity constitutes little more than racial stereotyping as 'it is possible to assert with some degree of certainty that in the majority of cases criminal groups are not tied together by ethnic linkages' (UN 2002: 23). A 'pick 'n mix' of individuals and groups bring expertise, contacts, and capital to a marketplace that has been enhanced by the relaxation of national boundaries, which has meant that individuals with diverse origins find it increasingly easy to learn from each other's experiences, and indeed to work together (Dorn et al 2005: 22).[6]

Since the closing of the docks and the subsequent decline of related industries, it has been impossible to define Dogtown in terms of common occupational experience, and diverse ethnicity and deprivation now typifies the area. Dogtown's population constitutes a

[6] A group of Pakistani males in the north of England regularly bought four kilos of good quality heroin from a Turkish connection in London. They adulterated this three- or four-fold, then re-packaged the heroin in one-kilo parcels using a press, and sold to customers 'as new'. The group had previously been involved in importation from Pakistan, but found the new arrangement both less risky and more profitable (Pearson and Hobbs 2001).

supra-regional 'community' that is manifested in an overcrowded, youthful, poorly educated, working-class populace, a low proportion of whom are economically active. Many of those who have settled in Dogtown have their own businesses, places of worship, and social centres, and while some also break the law, this does not indicate evidence of transnational crime, but of a warts-and-all cosmopolitanism. In Dogtown, a few Eastern European men are involved with the management of massage parlours, which are part of an emergent vice trade responding to the presence of large numbers of young men who have recently settled in Dogtown in search of cheap housing. Segments of the cannabis and cocaine markets have been partially colonized by African, Asian, and European migrants who are in Dogtown seeking respite from war zones, religious persecution, and economic chaos. Some of them are locked into illegal trafficking networks and labour subcontracting arrangements which are difficult to unravel amongst the complex web of subsistence strategies that thrive within Dogtown's informal labour markets (Rawlinson and Fussey 2010; Sassen 2006: 71). For many individuals the adoption of mainstream identities would exclude them from the only available zone of economic activity, and cloned, forged, and adoptive Dogtown identities are preserved by cross-border migrations that supply labour not only for the sex trade, but for fast-food restaurants and the construction industry (Kelly 2005). In order for these labour markets to function, diasporas must intersect with trafficking groups (Turner and Kelly 2009),[7] and in Dogtown these 'countergeographies of globalization' (Sassen 2000) are played out as glocal phenomena that cast aside the exoticism of the transnational for something more familiar, something that is embedded in East End London's long history of casual labour, and nurtured by the global economy and its associated wings and annexes (Sassen 1998; Bonilla et al 1998).

East London offers cheap accommodation with easy access to employment opportunities in other parts of London, and like generations of sojourners before them, newcomers are fair game for predators within both the host community and the chaotic and ever-mutating networks of their fellow countrymen. This young,

---

[7] The complexities of human trafficking are superbly captured by Turner and Kelly in their attempt to understand these markets, and establish the glocal nature of illegal trade that addresses demand within the context of a fluid cosmopolitan setting. For an overview of the literature, see van Dijck (2005) and AOC (2005).

predominantly male population is exploited by landlords, with up to 20 crammed into small Edwardian terraced houses built for a family of four or five, while others reside in equally cramped conditions in illegally sublet social housing, in illegal extensions built onto back gardens, in shipping containers, and in the store rooms of shops and business (Armstrong et al (in progress)). Some are provided with work by countrymen operating as gangmasters who, come pay day, may disappear or arrive in the designated pub pay station backed up by sufficient muscle to make complaining about short wages a risky enterprise. Although the overwhelming majority of these men are in Dogtown legally, they are escaping poverty and seeking work, and make few demands on local services. They are a relatively isolated community whose version of colony culture resembles those of the Irish in particular, who were also driven by poverty into cramped and insanitary living conditions, engaged in low-paid manual work, and became associated with alcohol-induced disorder. Indeed, alcohol and drug abuse have become a characteristic of this loose-knit community of migrant workers as they seek to attain some relief from exploitative tenuous labour and poor housing.[8]

However, the involvement by a small number of this group with fraud involving the transference of funds back to their homeland has invoked the spectre of transnationality. Funding for international police cooperation designed to target this new organized crime risk was rapidly located, technical and linguistic support recruited, and the problem thrust into the collective consciousness of a range of governmental agencies across Europe.[9] The institutionalization and prioritization of this newly discovered threat convincingly carries the organized crime label, and while the criminal activities of these groups has been exaggerated,[10] the activity is not a fiction, and like the Jewish white slaver, the Chinese opium dealer, and the Maltese pimp, there is real involvement by a small

---

[8] Cushion (2010).

[9] For a concise critique of the evolution of the organized crime threat in Europe, see van Duyne (2011).

[10] 'Migrant crime wave a myth—police study: Acpo report concludes offending no worse than rest of the population…The report finds that, despite newspaper headlines linking new migrants to crime, offending rates among mainly Polish, Romanian and Bulgarian communities are in line with the rate of offending in the general population', *Guardian*, 16 April 2008.

number of newly arrived individuals in this cross-border activity. While the British media have responded in time-honoured fashion,[11] the new architecture of transnational policing has shifted the emphasis from moral transgression to that of a culpable 'threat' to the state, and the perpetrators' engagement with some of the key tools of modernity (electronic communications, knowledge of the banking system, etc) is used to stress the crime's seriousness as well as the inherent cunning of these new devious practitioners.[12]

The sense of wonder that is so often a response to the competent use of everyday technologies, artefacts, and procedures by individuals in the course of committing crime stems from the assumption that within class society crime is performed exclusively by the lower orders who are inherently stupid, incompetent, and unable to utilize the technical and cultural methodologies that are used and exploited by indigenous society.[13] These class-based assumptions are amplified considerably when the perpetrators have difficulty in pronouncing names, have dark skin, and ideally are in the UK illegally, and the alien conspiracy is completed if there is an added moral component, and the crimes involve the exploitation of women, children, or state benefits.[14] The increasingly cosmopolitan sensibilities of migrant communities, often fostered by readily available media and cheap transport, serve to relay opportunities for jobs, housing, and economic vulnerabilities to populations beyond the usual suspects of an indigenous working class population, who themselves often have migrant histories that feature racism and exclusion, and whose labour contributed significantly to every subsequent phase of the industrial era.

The violence, alcohol, and drug abuse that results from this new community's vulnerability to both legal and illegal predators are being addressed by local agencies which are often sympathetic to the latest hard scrabble group to seek sanctuary in the besieged proletarian alcove of Dogtown. However, the potential labelling of this entire community as a profound threat to the UK is founded

---

[11] 'Eastern European immigrants carry out tenth of crime', *Daily Mail*, 2 November 2006.

[12] 'The "money mules" of East London', *BBC News*, 4 February 2011.

[13] 'Police smash gang traficking Poles to UK for benefits scam', *London Evening Standard*, 2 November 2011.

[14] 'Eastern Europe Exports Flesh to the EU', *Le Monde diplomatique* (English-language online edition) December 2001.

largely upon the availability of specially allocated funding as transnational policy networks have encouraged police entrepreneurs (Smith 2008, 2009) to reconfigure the selective transgressions of this migrant group as a potent threat, and in doing so contribute to the illusion of the state's competent management of urban marginality (Wacquant 2009).[15]

Here, illegal trading becomes an 'instrument and a modality of the incorporation of the local into the global' (Diouf 2000: 680–1), illuminating transnationality (Beck and Sznaider 2006: 9), as an uncoordinated set of glocal practices rather than as an exterior, hostile, and essentially alien threat. Illegal entrepreneurial engagements by Dogtown's cosmopolitan population have contributed to the remapping of local space (Beck and Sznaider 2006: 6), reconceptualizing the transnational trope as the cosmopolitan turn. As a consequence of this 'de-nationalisation (of) urban space' (Sassen 2006: 72) the 'basic dualisms such as domestic foreign or national/international...have become ambiguous' (Beck and Sznaider 2006: 1). The fantasy of a fully domesticated realm of illegal activity in the form of a criminal underworld is therefore rendered irrelevant by the porous reality of the nation state and the predominance of cross-border flows of both legal and illegal traffic. However, it is vital that we disregard all aspects of the over-structured essentialism of conventional organized crime narratives for this is not a cosmopolitan political order, but a cosmopolitan reality that is lived 'tenaciously in terrains of historic and cultural transition' (Pollack et al 2002: 4), as a set of interactions involving the appropriation of elements of foreign cultures that serve to create not a threat of alien domination, but a new hybrid of glocalised 'vernacular cosmopolitanism', which in the true sub-cultural tradition is steeped 'in marginality' (Bhabha 1996: 195–6).

It is via this vernacular that seemingly fragmented acts of entrepreneurship are connected by networks of opportunistic imagination that disregard both the commercial irrationality of legal constraints and the efforts of the nation state to reinforce its boundaries. In a world where those responsible for global bankruptcy are rewarded with barely imaginable riches, shifting a few

---

[15] 'Yard rounds up foreign thugs for deportation', *London Evening Standard*, 9 February 2012; 'The Ethnic Connection', *Observer*, 25 May 2003.

boxes or a van-load of people across an invisible border, before distributing its contents to a clientele of eager consumers, seems positively judicious.

Pirates

Every night for a week, two men in their thirties occupy a corner of 'The Rotary' selling leather belts and bags, cannabis, and counterfeit DVDs. The leather goods—'snide' versions of expensive designer products—are identical to those available in nearby street markets and are dispensed openly, while dope transactions are conducted in the gents' toilet. One local watched in bemusement as the two men plied their trade: 'Last week those cunts had DVDs, all old like *Pirates of the Caribbean*, and all that at double what the Chinese geezer does of a Friday...I cant see what they are earning out of it.'

'What they are earning' can be measured in terms of the traditional working-class currency of cultural collateral. Drugs and counterfeit goods are commodities that confirm rather than contradict this rich, self-consciously independent proletarian heritage, a heritage that was central to the informal political economy that formed around the 'little earners', 'parcels', or 'lorry loads' of previous diasporas. This means that the 'Chinese geezer' selling DVDs has almost replaced the traditional shellfish vendor touring the pubs on a Friday night, and the cannabis dealer is no longer a marginalized 'druggie' but your son, my niece, or one of an exceptionally polite group of young West African men who efficiently supply cannabis to a significant portion of Dogtown's student population, or the Polish cocaine dealer offering welcome respite from the dulling effects of lager. He is also your next door neighbour, 'part of the periphery at the core' (Sassen 2006: 196), so make sure you do not slam the front door when you get in late at night, as he has an early start driving down the A13 for his day job as a plasterer.

In particular, the demand for recreational drugs has combined with the area's traditional market for cheap goods, and added to the sense of the area as a '"bazaar" (where) legality and illegality intermingle, and moral boundaries are constantly negotiated' (Ruggiero and South 1997) and where the demise of industrial culture has not eliminated 'ducking and diving', but enhanced it with a cosmopolitan edge, honed in the poverty of warzones, the bald aspiration of transitional states, and the exclusionary logic of postcolonial alcoves (Gilroy 2004).

Cosmopolitan Leisure: Queen's Club

Jamaica's post-colonial economic environment featured high levels of poverty and unemployment inflamed by a housing policy (Henry-Lee 2005) that territorialized deprivation and provided a unique entry into a corrupt political system ridden with violence (Gunst 1995). This resulted in the creation of a Jamaican diaspora, a minority of whom took their market competencies to North America and the UK (Gunst 1995: 22; Pitts 2008: 69–80; Williams and Roth 2011) as they exploited Jamaica's geographically strategic hold on a small but significant portion of the global cocaine trade.[16] In London throughout the 1990s the influence of Jamaican dealing networks and personnel was noticeable, but not in terms of Hollywood-styled ethnic succession,[17] for these groups of young Afro-Caribbean men were engaging with new markets and, consequently, tended not to be in competition with established groups of white illegal entrepreneurs. As a result, racial conflict was not as common as either cooperation[18] or intra-group rivalry which, as with established British criminal culture, was marked by respect or honour-related concerns rather than by purely instrumental violence (Pearson and Hobbs 2001).

Nestling in an alcove of a 1960s' shopping development, Queen's Club developed in the 1980s as an illegal drinking venue where cab drivers, restaurant staff, and other night workers could be guaranteed a game of cards, a quiet drink, and a sandwich at the end of a shift. By the early 1990s Queen's Club had become a predominantly Caribbean venue where gambling was the main activity and where 'Faces' could meet to trade and network. With a fridge, a full set of optics, and a microwave, the club retained a number of cab drivers amongst its clientele and became a important hub for

---

[16] For an outstanding update on the impact of the war on drugs upon the Caribbean that emphasizes the post-colonial flavour of certain aspects of transnationality, see Bowling (2010).

[17] For an example of how the notion of ethnic succession can misfire, see Ianni (1974).

[18] In the mid 1990s a Dogtown-based armed robber was released from prison, and via a Turkish contact he had made while inside, invested what remained of his ill-gotten gains in a part shipment of cocaine. The ex-robber, who had been incarcerated for over a decade during the rise of the 'powder trade', was mystified when his new Turkish partner bought from one firm of Jamaicans and sold most of the consignment to another group of Jamaicans.

mid-level cannabis dealing with a built-in delivery service. It also functioned as a place where men with connections to a large car manufacturer traded in car radios, which for about two years attracted to the Queen's Club a wider ethnic mix than it had previously enjoyed. Briefly, the Queen's Club became closely associated with professional criminals visiting from the Caribbean, and the club acquired some notoriety when several regulars were shot outside an adjacent pub after an argument concerning a gambling debt. By now, the club was all black and all male, a place to be seen if you were an active criminal when most 'villains' pubs' had relocated to Dogtown's predominantly white periphery. Although by the time of its demise a couple of years later Queen's Club had returned to its original function as a drinking club for night workers and the occasional visitor from the Caribbean, it did 'not exist outside (its) own mythical self- representation' (Pollock 2002: 15; Knight 1990; 66–73), crucially lacking a clientele with the kinds of multifarious connections necessary for it to be an exclusively underworld venue.

Particularly in light of the suburbanization of Dogtown's long-established black British population, many of whom cite the area's increasing multiculturalism as evidence of decline, the Queen's Club is best understood as an example of a self-contained cosmopolitan enclave which sits alongside east London's Jewish gambling clubs of the early twentieth century, the Chinese opium dens of nineteenth- and early twentieth-century Limehouse, or the drinking clubs of Clerkenwell's Little Italy, catering to the leisure habits of migrants working irregular hours (see Chapter 4).[19] These 'colony cultures' (Hall et al 1978: 349) of predominantly male migrants working irregular hours are part of the 'survival circuits' (Sassen 2006: 178) that are embedded in the local infrastructures of cosmopolitan society, and, like the suburbanized Dogtowners of Chapter 5, constitute part of the 'reterritorialization of local sub-cultures' (Sassen 2006: 74) that realign key essences of the parent culture on unfamiliar, often hostile ground.

---

[19] Recent arrivals at the bottom of the local labour market include groups of young men from Eastern Europe who have set up drinking clubs, some featuring illegal stills. One of these establishments is in the backroom of a disused shop in Dogtown and run by two men who have quickly forged an alliance with local cab drivers, and a massage parlour managed by men originally from another part of Eastern Europe.

A Turk on the Firm[20]

The British heroin market is typified by extended family connections via various systems of brokerage that reach back to different regions of Turkey, which is the major base for transforming opium and morphine base into heroin intended for the European market. Although South Asian networks were once dominant at importation level, they now more generally occupy a middle-market brokerage role within the UK (Pearson and Hobbs 2001), having ceded during the 1990s to UK-based Turkish, Kurdish, and Turkish Cypriot entrepreneurs with networked connections to individuals, groups, and political entities in Istanbul (Bovenkerk and Yesilgoz 2007), as well as to criminal entrepreneurs all over the UK (Johnson 2007; Ferguson 2006).[21]

Along with the relatively discrete business of drug importation,[22] territorial youth groups, political conflict, and extortion are all apparent within this community,[23] and by the early 1990s the names of competing paramilitary groups in Turkey were being invoked to extort money from London-based Turkish businesses.[24] The London media claimed that extortion was common,[25] and London's self-contained Turkish and Kurdish communities were placed firmly in the public eye in 2002 with a spectacular street fight in north London,[26] followed by a spate of shootings[27] and kidnappings (Pearson and Hobbs 2001) as some prominent north London Turkish businesses were found to be deeply implicated in heroin importation.[28] Up to this point the fact that a south-east London-based Turkish Cypriot family had been prominent in

---

[20] 'At the moment everybody wants to have a Turk on the firm' (SOCA officer, personal communication 2006).

[21] 'Jailed Bristol drug baron thought himself "untouchable"', *BBC News*, 14 July 2010.

[22] 'Gang jailed for £4bn cocaine smuggling plot', *BBC News*, 26 October 2012.

[23] Cohen (2009).

[24] 'Mafia threatens UK Turks and Kurds', *BBC News*, 14 November 2002.

[25] In 2002, the *London Evening Standard* reported the findings of a survey of 200 Turkish and Kurdish shopkeepers in north London claiming that 65 per cent admitted to paying protection money: 'War on the Godfathers', 21 November 2002.

[26] 'London on Cusp of Turf Wars Between Rival drug Dealing Gangs', *Independent*, 21 November 2002.

[27] 'Double murder threatens bloody heroin war', *Independent*, 2 June 2001.

[28] 'Turkish gang jailed for heroin smuggling', *Independent*, 3 August 1996.

armed robbery, drug trafficking, and some murderous old-school feuds with other families for five decades[29] never seems to have established itself as sufficiently 'foreign' to warrant the kind of outrage that has been afforded to other 'alien' groups.

It is vital that the heroin market is not portrayed purely as the domain of non-white, minority ethnic groups such as the Turks, and there is ample evidence of white indigenous groups that trade and collaborate across ethnic boundaries. Indeed, there is a distinctly cosmopolitan flavour to many of these networks which rely upon Dutch nationals to warehouse drugs in Holland and Belgium, and employ British, Dutch, and South Asian drivers to transport heroin into the UK (Pearson and Hobbs 2001). These operations required networked collaborations involving a range of both embedded and arm's-length relationships across local, regional, and international boundaries. For instance, a white British family firm had been buying heroin from the London-based Turkish community for many years and regularly visited their suppliers' homes in northern Cyprus, before establishing their own drug-importation business via a base in Holland using London-based Turkish associates to facilitate importation into the UK (Pearson and Hobbs 2001).

As we can see from the footnoted media headlines, Turkish involvement with heroin smuggling, extortion, and people smuggling can inspire resort to the entire catalogue of organized crime clichés, yet amongst the Hollywood-inspired *Godfather* and Mafia references, there is something unique that deserves a more careful unpacking. In Turkey, a state whose military licenses space to the conventional apparatus of democracy, heroin smuggling is a tried-and-tested method for funding both subversion and its repression (Bovenkerk and Yesilgoz 2007). The rapport between organized crime and the state stands in stark contrast to the simplistic white hat/black hat orthodoxy that typifies so much Western discourse, for the Turkish state has long used a range of criminal actors both to make money and 'to carry out chores (they) don't want to dirty their hands with' (Bovenkerk and Yesilgoz 2007: 23). Particularly in the wake of emigration to the West, this close relationship between the state and organized crime, along with long traditions

---

[29] 'Murder in a tight little manor', *Independent*, 11 August 1991; 'Death at the Bell', *Sunday Times*, 11 August 1991.

of both 'state gangs' (Bovenkerk and Yesilgoz 2007: 211–21) and regional banditry based upon feudal clans (Bovenkerk and Yesilgoz 2007: 222–53), enabled the exploitation of Turkey's strategic position in relation to Afghanistan and the Balkan route into Western Europe. The interests of drug traffickers, right- and left-wing politicians, and civil servants became intertwined, not only as a result of the armed struggle between the Kurdish PKK movement and the Turkish Government, but also as a result of historically grounded relationships that preceded the development of the drug trade (Bovenkerk and Yesilgoz 2007: 68–93). To understand the significance of the Turkish drug trade it is necessary to focus upon the complexity of Turkey's history, the peculiarities of its political culture, and the specificities of its ethnic composition, as well as the strategic importance of a secular state with a majority Muslim population, a fellow member state of NATO bordering the USSR, and a site for Western military installations (Rubin and Çarkoglu 2003).

London's Turkish community is no more typified by transnational organized crime than any of the capital's 50 other non-indigenous communities with a population of more than 10,000,[30] and engagement with illegal trading, like any other aspect of the culture, does not operate in isolation (Murji 2007). In Turkey, illegal trading has become embedded, normalized, and, via political ideology, honorific, and the involvement in drug importation of a small minority of London's Turkish community reflects, along with the tradition of small-scale family-orientated entrepreneurialism, not a global criminal threat, but the cosmopolitan reality of contemporary urban existence that 'pervade(s) the social structure and straddle(s) the boundary between legality and illegality' (Hall 2012: 18).[31]

---

[30] 'London: Every race, colour, nation and religion on earth', *Guardian*, 21 January 2005.

[31] Another UK ethnic minority increasingly linked with illegal trading in the UK is the Vietnamese, who have recently been implicated in the UK-based cultivation and supply of cannabis: 'Commercial Cannabis Cultivation in the UK by Ethnic Vietnamese Organised crime groups', Serious Organised Crime Agency, Joanna Morley, presentation. However, with the exception of the pioneering work of Silverstone and Savage (2010) and Silverstone (2010), Vietnamese engagement with illegal economies is too often blighted by orientalism (Murji 2007: 798), and the mundane, routine provision for indigenous demand by non-British subjects which is central to everyday cosmopolitan life is ignored in favour of a 21st-century version of the 'othering' discussed in Chapter 3 ('Police "can't cope" as Vietnamese flood drugs trade: Gangs make millions by targeting London with cannabis grown in houses rented from unsuspecting landlords', *Observer*, 11 September 2005).

This 'subaltern insurgent cosmopolitanism' (Harvey 2005: 293), which includes engagement with flows of methodologies, labour, and most importantly commodities connected to the country of origin, is merely an acknowledgement of an entrepreneurial field that has been embraced by local operators but with connective nodes across global networks, creating 'multiple loyalties' (Beck-Gernsheim 1999) within transnational flows dominated by marketized cultures and inherited market sensitivities. In Dogtown these sensitivities have inspired durable, transposable dispositions (Bourdieu 1977: 72) that have evolved against the backdrop of post-industrial trauma, and the emergent practices are grounded in powerful, urban, working-class histories as well as cosmopolitan futures. As discussed in Chapter 2, as a consequence of these futures, rather than obsess about criminogenic toxic migration or 'crimmigration' (Welch 2012: 324–44), we should consider that cosmopolitanism has multi-directional flows, and if the liberal conscience can accede that some visitors to British shores will engage in illegal activity, surely the same courtesy should be afforded to Brits abroad, for Dogtown citizens have proved to be bold and astute travellers exporting aspects of their own distinct culture to a global clientele.

Empire of the Sun: Impetigo Bay

I had clearly arrived at Faces bar three decades too late. The pictures on the wall were a mixture of commercially produced prints of long-dead icons of the London underworld, and fading snaps of bar staff posing with smiling, shiny-faced, demi-permed men holding drinks adorned with paper umbrellas. Apart from the length of the clientele's sideburns, little has changed in the bar since the extradition treaty was signed between Spain and the UK a quarter of a century ago, although this part of the Costa del Sol has slipped down the pecking order of desirable bolt holes for thirsty British bandits bursting with bullion. Impetigo Bay has seen better days and the collapse of the Spanish property market and the British pound has created a strange atmosphere where, after dreaming for their entire working lives of a sun-drenched retirement, wizened Brits wander bewildered amongst half-built and deserted housing complexes, where bare wires blossom from street lamps that have never worked, and weeds grow from cracks in untrod pavements.

Notable remnants of the pre-extradition treaty era now reside discreetly in the mountains behind high walls and banks of CCTV cameras, or bestride the golf courses and marinas of Marbella and Puerto Banus. The latter have been joined by a rotating cast of real villains, 'wannabes', and wage slaves from across Europe escaping the rain and seeking out a whiff of Eurotrash glamour. However, back in Faces the haunting odour of the all-day breakfast competes with the Dutch barman's pungent aftershave, as a group of elderly British ex-pats pay their bill before moving on to the Irish pub next door. The barman has no idea who the people in the photos are: the current owner of the bar previously ran a cafe in northern England, and is not in tonight as he works as a barman in an up-market club in Marbella. When the owner's wife later arrives to lock up she explains that they bought the bar from the man who put the photos on the wall and that all she could remember about him was that he chain-smoked when he fried the all-day breakfast.

It is estimated that between 5.5 and 6 million British citizens now live abroad (Sriskandarajah and Drew 2006), and 41 nations have developed communities of at least 10,000 permanent British residents. Although some of these residents live in nostalgic enclaves that replicate the clichéd kitsch of package holidays, with all-day breakfasts and hot-and-cold-running lager, the days when British villains venturing abroad pined for essential comforts such as warm beer, Marmite, baked beans, and rain are long gone. For instance, some of the infamous 'Faces' of the 1960s, were mainly working-class men for whom 'abroad' was a very foreign place, and a number found life in sunny exile difficult to tolerate.[32] However, the inclusive culture of consumption, and in particular the travel, tourism, and property sectors, have made overseas travel, and the commercial opportunities engendered by these sectors, available to a wide range of Britons. The current generation have been reared on cheap holidays and air travel; they enjoy vacations wherever their wallets will take them, buy bars and apartment blocks in Spain and Florida, and dabble with sex tourism in Kenya and Thailand. Indeed, the entrepreneurial careers of a small number of ex-football hooligans have been spectacular, and some can be found running successful businesses in southern Spain, the Canary Islands, and Thailand, In addition, the Costa del Sol, Amsterdam, and Pattaya in particular operate as modern-day Tortugas—pirate

[32] Hobbs, D (1994).

havens boasting hedonistic and entrepreneurial opportunities and hosting thriving expat communities from across the globe, as well as visitors seeking some recreation and a respite from extra-legal retribution on home turf.[33]

Dave Peters

Dave Peters was an all-purpose thief who, in the early 1980s, had organized a team of burglars, and, after serving a short sentence for receiving stolen goods, became closely associated with various coalitions importing cannabis. Dave went on to assist in the management of businesses that at one time formed a chain across London, which introduced him to a group that had financial interests in a number of southern European holiday resorts. In the early 1990s, Dave moved to southern Europe and set up a business dealing primarily with legitimate consignments to holiday resorts catering to a British clientele. Dave owns both commercial and residential property in Spain, and warehouses on the periphery of Dogtown. His willingness to learn Spanish enabled Dave to engage with local businesses, and he became involved with several community organizations.

He operated as a hub for British business networks that were seeking to operate in southern Europe, and his knowledge of various markets and his seamless adoption of the demeanour of a Surrey businessman at play, has proved to be potent in the development of a range of enterprises. He, like the thousands of British citizens who migrate to deal in property, run bars, or jet ski concessions, are merely following economic opportunities (see Pritchard 2008) and their success or failure will depend largely upon their ability to read the local conditions that are integral to global markets, and to exploit, without the self-conscious restraint of previous generations of working-class Brits abroad, the full range of hedonistic opportunities on offer.

Most of the individuals I have met who have made all or part of their livelihood from crime got into the business because the money was good and the hours were even better. They like to dress well, get drunk, use drugs, drive nice cars, and live in salubrious accommodation. In

---

[33] 'Briton Wanted For Gangland Shooting is Gunned Down in Contract Killing on Costa Del Sol', *Daily Mail*, 8 June 2010; 'Britons held in Costa del Crime hashish raid', *Guardian* 17 June 2003.

addition, I know of nobody who has set out in their teens as a burglar, car thief, or drug dealer to create or become a member of a criminal organization. The initial allure and, for some but not all, a continual motivation, is hedonism, and claiming capitalism's prizes without paying the price is a key motivator for engagement with crime. These individuals are inspired by an explicitly hedonistic drive to fund a lifestyle dedicated to variations on the 'Lush Life', which in turn has been enabled and exacerbated by globalization, and is largely indistinguishable from the aspirational leisure of the non-criminal population.

'Doing Well': Brits Abroad

> In an honest service there is thin commons, low wages, and hard labour...No, a merry life and a short one shall be my motto (Bartholomew Roberts, as quoted in Captain Charles Johnson (Daniel Defoe), *The General History of Pirates*, 1724)

At 5am on a spring morning 13 men gather outside a car dealership in a dreary backwater of London's periphery just a dozen miles beyond Dogtown. The men are aged between their early thirties and late fifties and are dressed casually in a variety of styles ranging from Dolce and Gabbana to Marks and Spencer via TK Maxx. Two of the men were born in British colonies and settled in the UK as children, and four were the children of either mothers or fathers of the Windrush generation who arrived from the Caribbean during the immediate post-war era. All of the men are Londoners. There is little conversation, just some muted banter regarding one of the traveller's battered Adidas hold-all. All 13 men load their bags into the back of the mini-bus and climb in. The driver's polyester shirt is a little on the ripe side, and by the time the party arrive at the airport two of the older travellers have found their voices and loudly abuse Jason and Kenny who admit to feeling sick. Once through security and passports presented, the party orders lagers all round, and by 7.45am all but three of the group are engaged in a sit-up competition. The winner buys a replacement for his sweat-sodden cerise Polo shirt, returning with a white Nike t-shirt and a dozen drunk, female office workers from Basildon. The women are off to Tenerife to celebrate a forthcoming wedding, and when the Essex men hear this, Quiet Charlie is pushed to the fore. Within a few minutes a mock wedding has taken place between the softly spoken builder and the prospective bride, the ceremony presided over by thrice-married Bobby with a copy of a motorsport magazine in one hand, and a pint of Carlsberg in the other.

The flight is uneventful, marked only by a dozing Quiet Charlie being reprimanded by an irate flight attendant who insists that he stay awake while the obligatory safety regulations are read out. The men are blasé about the flight; most of them have travelled widely and several own properties in southern Europe, Florida, and Dubai. In their own terms they have all 'done well', having claimed a thin slice of the kind of cosmopolitan entitlement that the bourgeoisie have enjoyed for generations. They are affluent, confident, and at ease with the world. Fifteen years ago such a group would have been exclusively white, but this is not the case in 2007, although the ethnic mix is largely irrelevant to these men, who have made their money grafting on building sites and buying and selling property, cars, and drugs.[34]

Within an hour of arriving at their beachfront hotel, the jet-ski concession that used to be operated by a man with Dogtown connections is visited and cocaine supplies are obtained. Jerry the Plumber is irate; he does not like drugs, in fact he 'doesn't believe in them'. By the evening meal he is more than a little drunk having imbibed from the bottle of Johnny Walker he bought 'for the room' and which he shares with a large, sweating, used-car salesman who talks incessantly about the rent he pays on his car forecourt and his hatred of Birmingham. At the meal Jerry suspects that anyone having a good time is using 'that coke shit', and by the time both drinkers and sniffers are dancing at a nearby bar he has made a comment about 'suntans' to Stanley, who walks with a limp and has an upper body honed from two decades working as a scaffolder. Stanley's mother came from West Africa and his white father from London. He never speaks about the five years he spent in prison for violence, but two more suntan comments and a Frank Bruno reference from Jerry, and Stanley is forced to act. He sits on the plumber's lap and sticks his tongue in his ear. The humiliation is enough, and by the

[34] Another fine example of late-modern cosmopolitan cooperation is to be found in the 2006 Tonbridge robbery discussed in Chapter 7. The robbery team featured a British-born Moroccan national, as well as white and black British and two Albanian men (Sounes 2008).

time most of the party has moved on to a club, Jerry is back in his room alone with his thoughts or, in his case alone, going solo with Johnny Walker.

Next day two of the men take time out to visit some property investments whose value has recently plummeted, while another, who has been deeply involved in a property scam involving corrupt council officials in London's suburbs makes an enquiry about buying 'a little bolt hole away from the coast. Something off a little village square near a nice bar.' A man who has made money from investments in cannabis importation two decades earlier and has served time in prison for receiving stolen goods weeps into his lager as he tells a builder with sunburn about his attempts to adopt a child; and a self-employed lorry driver is sick in a paddling pool after he tries to pick a fight with the hotel's East European security staff. By the end of the trip the group has morphed into a self-congratulatory stew of alcohol, drugs, and golf, where notions of legal and illegal are irrelevant. They live in a world where making money and spending it extravagantly are a cultural expectation. They aggressively claim to be unbound by constraints of class and are unrepentant in their enthusiastic embrace of legal and illegal markets, not as members of the underworld but as part of an affluent network of entrepreneurs utilizing their buying power and finely honed cosmopolitan experience to negotiate obstacles that were previously construed as insurmountable.

Utilizing a habitus that has evolved as a response to the neo-liberal order, the working classes have adapted by abandoning the now-redundant offshoots of traditional communality, and have joined the bourgeoisie in their narcissistic quest to satisfy individual appetites. Dogtown residents have bought 'places' abroad. They have bought into bars, restaurants, and jet-ski businesses, and have invested in property, engaging with the chaos of commerce wherever they hang their hats. Some of these overseas-based opportunities are illegal and their profitability depends upon the establishment and maintenance of brokerage relationships that often span national borders and legislative regimes. Abroad is not foreign any more, as globalization has transformed large, previously exclusive chunks of the planet into their playground. The same formula of post-industrialism, consumerism, the break-down of traditional proletarian conservatism, and the all-pervasive ethos of entrepreneurship that opened up a portal into the suburbs has enabled men and women with roots in and around Britain's former industrial centres to become au fait with the benefits associated with the peculiar political status of Northern Cyprus, the housing market in Croatia, the building regulations in Andalusia, local taxation in Palm Beach, and much more. They no longer visit in wonderment, eyes squinting against the unfamiliar glare of the sun. They belong, for these hot, dry, exotic places are no less 'real' than the ever-churning, constantly fragmenting Dogtown.

Going Missing

> Some people just go missing (Chris)

As discussed in Chapter 9, in illegal firms it is violence rather than dismissal or resort to criminal justice that serves to confirm and create social order, and within criminal collaborations the mere suggestion that somebody has 'gone missing' creates a portal to a zone of mythic possibilities, where individuals are either dead or living a life of global glamour on a beach of warm flesh and cocktails. Either way, it is another country. Chris named a number of people who had 'gone missing', their whereabouts unknown but open to speculation. Beach-front venues were the favoured assumed domiciles for the merely exiled, while for those 'no longer with us', or indeed with anyone, marshes, farmyards, and the seabed were the suspected resting places. However, a return from the dead, or from Benidorm, was not uncommon, and with British citizens enjoying cheap airfares, buying second homes and businesses abroad, their resultant cosmopolitanism has created previously unimaginable opportunities for 'going missing'.

El Plunger

In the 1980s Stevie was a fresh-faced 'Jack the Lad' with a penchant for customized Fords, white wine, and other people's money. As he worked his way through various forms of self-employment, including kitchen and carpet fitting, carpet cleaning, office cleaning, and double glazing installation, his debts piled up. He also worked at the edges of a firm of ex-football hooligans, and when he moved to the Canary Islands to follow his new profession as an ecstasy dealer, he left behind a trail of debt and a lot of sub-standard home improvements. Around 1995 all contact with Stevie was lost, and rumours of a new miasma of unpaid debts, this time involving violent entrepreneurs, filtered back. Murdered by gangsters seemed a good bet, until he started to appear at Essex-based family funerals. Skin the tone and colour of a well-worn horse saddle and driving nothing more noteworthy than a French people carrier, he displayed a business card proclaiming his new profession working as a plumber for ex-pats unwilling to trust their waste disposal and drainage systems to the vagaries of local tradesmen.

Jack Partner

Jack was a party-loving wage slave who 'wanted to be like the cool boys in school'. Unfortunately he was scraping a living somewhere near the bottom of the white collar food chain, a status that he greatly resented. He was a social user of cocaine, consuming a 'cheeky half' at the weekend, and sold to city boys in London buying an eighth (3.5 grams) and stepping on it with herbal tablets (eg New Era) or sinus-clearing tablets to make it up to 4 or 5 grams. Jack's involvement in the cocaine trade mirrored his status in the legitimate world, but it supplemented his clerk's salary and helped alleviate the general mundanity of his everyday existence, a mundanity that was brought home to him every Friday when he watched from his office window affluent diners arriving to lunch at a fashionable eatery. Jack would then leave the office to eat a meagre sandwich and return to his desk. Late in the afternoon, just before he left work for the weekend, Jack would enviously watch the happy, sated diners leaving the restaurant.

Eventually Jack gave up work and went on a month-long holiday to Spain. He stayed for four years. He worked in a bar where he met Reg, an expat British gangster who gave Jack an ounce of cocaine to sell. The cocaine was quickly sold, and when he offered to give Reg his share of the profit, the gangster refused and their future partnership was sealed. Most of Jack's clientele were holidaymakers who were charged above the going rate. Swedish tourists were particularly affluent at this time and were charged £60/gram, £20 over the going rate. Expats received a special discount of £32. Reg was dealing directly with the Columbian community who had 'retired' to Spain, and soon Jack was organizing five or six deals a month of four to five kilos each, with contacts in London, payment arriving in Spain via a Western Union wire. This was, Jack admitted, taking a big risk: 'if something goes wrong you have a huge amount of money to pay—people don't care if your guy got nicked with the drugs—you still owe for the money—everyone knows the risks they are taking'. Jack moved back to London to handle the UK end of the operation, supplying clients in the North, South West and Midlands, most of whom were connected to Reg, who stayed in Spain. Reg and Jack were buying from the Columbians at £18,000 a kilo and selling for £22,000 a kilo, although the prices varied depending on the customer. On a typical 10kg consignment worth £220,000 they would make £40,000 profit (minus expenses) and Reg and Jack would split this 50:50.

Cocaine would come to Spain by boat from Columbia, before the drugs were moved to London, where one of Jack's couriers would pick up the cocaine and deliver it to a customer in the UK. The courier was paid £500 for the journey, plus expenses: 'If you pay people well it keeps them happy.' In London the courier always travelled by black cab, and took the train around the country before checking into a hotel. At some point in the evening Jack would give the courier a phone number to call to make arrangements for the drop-off. The courier could be carrying up to 10kg of cocaine in 'a pikey Nike bag', and Jack would insist that the courier, even in the summer, wore a thin pair of gloves.

The customers would deliver the money to London the following day. Jack used a second worker to collect the money, which might be delivered in any denomination, although Scottish notes were not accepted by the Columbians. This man was paid £250 a day, and worked most days travelling around London in black cabs, before delivering the money to another man, who was also paid £250 a day, to count it. Jack used an elegantly dressed woman to deliver the money to the Columbians in a Louis Vuitton bag to a private address. Jack assumed that this money was then sent somehow to Spain. The woman would then deliver Jack's profits to a friend's house, who would keep the money for an hour before Jack came to collect it. The profits would be split 50:50 with Reg, who, every three weeks, would send people across to the UK to collect his share by strapping the cash around their waists (Matrix Knowledge Group 2007: 34).

Jack was driven around in nothing more ostentatious than a BMW, by a driver who 'wasn't exactly security', but he happened to be large. Jack would instruct the driver to drive to different cafes or bars, each of which would be designated a number between 1 and 10 which the driver had to remember, but not write down. When he wanted to be picked up he would call the driver and ask him to pick him up at number 2, for example. Often the driver would go to the wrong place as he had forgotten what the numbers were, but 'what can you do?' In retrospect Jack is surprised at the way his involvement in the cocaine trade grew, and he claims that he eventually grew bored, finding the business lacking in excitement. Jack emphasized the importance of staying calm, keeping the money, drugs, and employees separate, and having as many links in the chain as possible. As Jack explained, 'It's a very simple business if you have the balls to do it.'[35]

This example of UK citizens taking advantage of cheap travel, and British and Colombian businessmen seeking investment opportunities from bases in Spain, suggests that we should be sceptical of models of organized or serious crime that fail to embrace cosmopolitan complexity. As Robertson notes, 'it makes no good sense to define the global as if the global excludes the local … defining the global in such a way suggests that the global lies beyond all localities, as having systematic properties over and beyond the attributes of units within a global system' (1995: 34). Indeed, the incorporation of South American and Southern and Northern European locales into overlapping networks of enterprise more accurately describes this activity than the melodramatic compression of criminal action into a world order of transnational corporations.

Glocal Crime

Varese (2011) has interrogated the notion of omnipotent transnational criminals operating beyond the territories on which their reputations are founded, and succeeds in presenting a far more complex set of possibilities than the politically inspired xenophobia of the transnational trope, particularly in Europe, where a fearful gaze is forever focused eastwards. It is not a prerequisite for contemporary crime groups to acquire territorial supremacy, and competent criminal businessmen, even those who have made the transition from protector to predatory entrepreneur, rely more upon the cosmopolitan frameworks of legitimacy on which both serious crime networks and legitimate businesses are built, than upon raw muscle. Although market transitions and relocations are not guaranteed to be successful, and some criminal enterprises are restricted by their embeddedness within the territorial concerns

---

[35] Jack's demise occurred as soon as he forgot the golden rule about keeping the drugs and money separate.

upon which crucial reputations were formed (Varese 2011), the market is populated by flexible alliances of 'mobile marauders in the urban landscape alert to institutional weaknesses in both legitimate and illegitimate spheres' (Block 1983: 130–41), who have no need to be located in fixed terrain.

For instance, the remarkable Curtis Warren emerged as a violent, teenaged street criminal at the height of the 1980s recession before quickly moving up to operating a global enterprise spanning five continents (Barnes et al 2000). Warren was arrested in Holland in 1997 and, by the time he was convicted, the *Sunday Times* listed him as the 461st wealthiest individual in the UK, with an estimated fortune of £40 million. Warren's known assets included 'properties in Wales, Turkey, Spain, Gambia, a boat, 200 houses in Liverpool, a brothel and a football club' (Barnes et al 2000: 332). Warren's career is indicative of the way in which methodologies gleaned from the remnants of traditional working-class neighbourhoods can merge with post-industrial commercial concerns to create undertakings based upon the singular pursuit of profit rather than the dominance of territory.

Criminal career trajectories are no longer limited to the highly specific, often stereotyped geographic locations of an urban 'underworld'; their activities are, to paraphrase Latour, 'Local at all points' (Latour 1993), offering a vehicle for transferring from one sphere to another along 'continuous paths that lead from the local to the global, from the circumstantial to the universal, from the contingent to the necessary' (Latour 1993: 117). Although operating within networks which have become part of transnational flows of individuals and groups, relations vary according to demographic dispersal, familial composition, ethnic distribution and integration, commercial practice, trading patterns, the economic backcloth of the legitimate culture, and the particular use of space (King 1991: 111; Soja 1989). While transnational organized crime is an abstract field devoid of relations (Strathern 1995: 179), the interconnected nodes of these markets consist of different kinds of brokerage and ever-mutating, interlocking networks 'featuring a variety of links with similar entities in other neighborhoods—whether located in the same city, or other cities in the same country or abroad' (Sassen 2006: 75).

Mar, an African, worked with Osman, a Turk, who had been in the UK for five years and had a legitimate job as a clerk. Via a distribution system staffed by a mixture of British South Asians and more recent arrivals from Pakistan, they distributed cannabis they had bought from established British importers, and manufactured and distributed amphetamine sulphate from premises owned by an unsuspecting Turkish landlord. Along with a another Turk, Mar operated an entirely separate operation buying, 'stepping on', and distributing cocaine. One of his customers was a British man who was married to a Spanish woman who ran a small clothing manufacturer employing Asian and African women 'off the books'. The sweatshop owner's husband was arrested for dealing ecstasy along with two African men who were paid to occasionally deliver clothing. When the case finally came to court a cluster of legal companies and over a dozen British bank accounts, along with accounts in Spain and Africa, were revealed.[36]

In 2005 60 men and women were jailed in the Caribbean, France, the US, and the UK, including a highly entrepreneurial group of 14 from French Guyana who had arrived in the UK on fake passports and who were jailed for a total of 178 years after allegedly making £3 million a week over a two-year period by producing and selling crack cocaine. Cartier and Rolex watches, diamond jewellery, and designer clothes from Versace and Prada, as well as large quantities of cash were seized in London, along with properties in the Caribbean and Africa. Single mothers were paid £10,000 to fly to the Caribbean to pick up three kilos each of near-pure cocaine hidden in resealed rum bottles, vases, shampoo containers, or toothpaste tubes. The women then flew to Paris or Amsterdam and were guarded overnight before being sent across the Channel to London by coach, ferry, or Eurostar train. Up to three of these couriers— unaware of one another—were used for each trip, and if one was caught the others might slip through the net. Drugs were also sent to the UK via a parcel courier company, where one of the group who worked for the company would intercept the packages that were sent to non-existent addresses, extract the cocaine, and return the packages to the depot as undelivered, before taking the cocaine to the kitchen of a rented Dogtown house where it was converted into crack.[37]

[36] This example was gleaned from interviews and access to a series of documents that were not used in any court case.

[37] 'Fourteen jailed as police smash global crack cocaine network', *Guardian*, 28 February 2006.

Linking dispatching and receiving countries, the character of this highly nuanced market fits well with the notion of glocality (Robertson 1995), and in cosmopolitan sites such as Dogtown, diasporas from the Caribbean, Africa, Asia, and Eastern Europe have joined with established indigenous entrepreneurs in exploiting these alternative circuits of counter-geography. By understanding such 'glocalised cosmopolitanism' (Tomlinson 1999: 198) we can see that it is at the 'glocal' level that crime manifests itself as a tangible process of activity (Hobbs 1998), deflating the mystique of globalization by removing cross-border crime from the virtual zone of transnationality, and placing it on the streets and in the suites of a class-bound, post-industrial society no longer confident of the integrity of its own borders.

Smoking and the Bandits[38]

Tobacco products in the UK can be bought at far cheaper rates elsewhere within the European Union (Joossens and Raw 1998; van Duyne 2003). During the mid 1990s the UK emerged as a major retail market for contraband cigarettes within the European Union (Joossens and Raw 1998; van Duyne 2003; von Lampe 2006). Jason began bootlegging cigarettes in the mid 1990s, making forays into France with coach-loads of day-trippers acting as his 'mules'. These bootleg runs saw Jason operating free coach trips on Channel ferry crossings and providing the mules with money, and shopping-lists of cigarettes and hand-rolling-tobacco brands to purchase in French hypermarkets. On the return leg of the journey into England, the goods were transferred to Jason and the bootleggers were paid in cash for their services. Eventually Jason realized that as he moved further eastwards across Europe, he could buy cigarettes cheaper. From a hotel base in Eastern France, he employed six UK nationals for bootlegging runs into Luxembourg, who returned with vehicles filled with contraband cigarettes and hand-rolling tobacco. The selection of Luxembourg was not driven purely by his search for profit, because by selling the goods on in France to British buyers, Jason was able to distance himself from British law-enforcement attention and improve the odds of remaining undetected. 'So I'm paying for hotel rooms, renting six big French

---

[38] The following example of bootlegging is gleaned from research carried out with Rob Hornsby. Further details can be found in Hornsby and Hobbs (2007).

cars, spending twenty grand a week on the goods, paying the lads a grand each-tax-free-on a weekly basis, and on average I'm making nine grand clear profit a week.'

Jason worked across three national boundaries and within several interlocking networks of trading collaborations at both local and regional levels within mainland Europe and the UK. The crucial trust relationships were dependent upon local contextualities, and labelling this operation as transnational organized crime—'a defining issue of the 21st century as the Cold War was for the 20th century and colonialism was for the 19th' (Shelley 1997)—merely shrouds the enterprise in 'world system' (Wallerstein 1979) rhetorics that exoticize the enacted environment of the innovative but essentially mundane illegal trading that typified the five-year tenure of Jason's business. During 1997, 5,165 million cigarettes were sold in Luxembourg (population 418,000) and it has been estimated that 85 per cent of these transactions were undertaken as cross-border shopping sales (Joossens 1999). Jason and his firm took a considerable slice of that market and, via a range of shrewd risk-assessment strategies, particularly in physically situating the firm some way removed from the possibility of intrusion by HM Customs and Excise, members of the firm succeeded in maintaining an efficient and long-standing commercial operation from a semi-permanent base in France with a knowledge of variable regimes of taxation grounded purely upon experientially acquired wisdom.[39]

European integration has produced 'new zones of ambiguity' (Agamben 1998) that have been exploited by entrepreneurs such as Jason, who operate via flows of networked relations based upon forms of cosmopolitan mobility (Urry and Szerszynski 2002), which were, until recently, unthinkable. As we have established, various forms of trading relationships now dominate the illegal economy, and as globalization has intensified (Robertson 1992, 1995), illegal activities have increasingly mirrored trends in the legitimate economy (Ruggiero 1995; Hobbs 1997, 1998). The introduction of the Single European Market in 1993, and the subsequent relaxation of border controls and the opening-up of national frontiers, resulted in an increase of visits to EU countries by UK residents from 34 million to 42.6 million between 1997 and 2001 (Sriskandarajah and Drew 2006), and this boom in cross-border consumption has enabled

---

[39] Jason only closed down the firm when violent British predators started to pay attention to his enterprise (Hornsby and Hobbs (2007)).

UK-based criminal networks, who should be regarded as integral to this boom, to enter into new arenas.

An Ambiguous Trade

> Analyzing organized crime groups outside of their cultural and social context runs the danger of attributing broadly similar causes for their development in any society, and while these may be accurate, ignores important local causal and contextual issues (UN Centre for International Crime Prevention 2002: 14)

The notion of transnational organized crime exaggerates the connectedness between individuals via the mystification of globalization and the construction of an apocalyptic category which is interpreted as a continuum of a crisis (Bigo 1994), the by-product of 'a political project of universal liberation...the endpoint of a natural evolution' (Bourdieu 2003: 86). From the shadows of the underworld globalization's evil twin, organized crime mimics the everyday routine activities of 'legitimate' trade and commerce, licensing law-enforcement agencies to respond in a state of constant emergency, which, as discussed in Chapter 2, has provided the impetus for the establishment of global norms for the policing of organized crime. Yet crime is not a by-product of globalization, but an aspect of its operationalization featuring flows barely distinct from its legal equivalent. Within the multiple diasporas of the contemporary city crime is an essential part of the quest by the disadvantaged for a stake in survival and autonomy, and it is not feasible to ignore the cultural currency of cosmopolitanism as it impacts upon the citizens of Dogtown. Crime is also part of the complex articulation of cultural and economic conditions that originate beyond the local, and the conceit of a fully domesticated realm of illegal activity in the form of a criminal underworld subsumes crime and its control under the nation state, and offers an explanation in terms of 'domestic/foreign or national/international, which in reality have become ambiguous' (Beck and Sznaider 2006: 1). These dated concepts have clearly been cast aside by the porous nature of the nation state and the predominance of cross-border flows of people and commodities which have impacted upon both the imagery and agency of lawbreakers, as well as upon the nation state's efforts to reinforce its boundaries. However, this is not a cosmopolitan political order, but a cosmopolitan lived reality that offers a more nuanced focus than the mere acknowledgment of connectivity that has acquired voodoo status within the lazy dialogues of Western particularism associated with transnational organized crime.

In this chapter I have referred to the existence of markets where alliances between global and local spaces are negotiated, creating locations that utilize local interpretations of global markets (Robins 1991). Trading relationships between coalitions of individuals, although superseding the constraints of territoriality that marked the industrial era, must involve a recognition of local interests, and it is at the local level that the forms of illegal trading tagged as 'organized crime' are manifested as a tangible process of activity (Korsell 2011: 701–12). The scope of these new networks depends largely upon the extent to which connectivity is established between groups and individuals (Coles 2001), and features interactional mutations that exploit geographic space without being restrained by territorial imperatives (Hobbs 2001). The new criminal entrepreneurs are unfettered by nostalgia, by the shackles of arcane practices, or by national borders, and operate within interwoven networks of 'small, fragmented, and ephemeral enterprises...not large corporate syndicates' (Potter 1994: 13), reflecting disorganized capitalism which is best served by 'vertically disintegrated networks of small firms engaged in transaction rich linkages of market exchanges' (Lash and Urry 1994: 23). Complex affinities between global and local spaces are negotiated via both existing and emergent flows (Nordstrom 2007), and this is where 'the business of crime is planned, contacts are made, some crimes are carried out, the fruits of crime are often enjoyed, and the methodologies for the integration of organised criminals into civil society are established' (Block 1991: 15).

These glocal connections are often manifestations of cosmopolitanism as expressed by a cornucopia of global connections whose roots are to be located as much in the ebbs and flows of urban connectivity as in the acquisitive drives of transgressive global collaborations. Expressed through local trading networks (Dorn et al 1992: 3–59), commercial viability is assured by the continual realignment of local precedents in the context of global markets (cf Hobbs 1995: Ch 5), coordinating relations between individuals and groups (Giddens 1979: 65–6) and involving constant mediations and renegotiations within culturally complex social systems.

Importantly, the entrepreneurial ethic that dominates both legal and illegal markets in post-industrial society does not require a special language, a tattoo of a teardrop on a cheek, or any of the other clichéd exotica of organized crime in order to thrive, for it is large bundles of cash rather than honorific allegiance that keep the whole pot boiling.

11

Conclusion: A Community of Practice

If we wanted to sketch a hypothetical portrait of an especially violent society, it would surely contain these elements: It would separate large numbers of people, especially the young, from the kind of work that could include them securely in community life. It would encourage policies of economic development and income distribution that sharply increased inequalities between sectors of the population. It would rapidly shift vast amounts of capital from place to place without regard for the impact on local communities, causing massive movements of population away from family and neighbourhood supports in search of livelihood. It would avoid providing new mechanisms of care and support for those uprooted, perhaps in the name of preserving incentives to work and paring government spending. It would promote a culture of intense interpersonal competition and spur its citizens to a level of material consumption many could not lawfully sustain (Currie 1985: 278)

Police and Precursors

This book has attempted to trace the construction of the concept of British organized crime during the twentieth and early twenty-first centuries, and to highlight the evolution of various forms of associated criminal collaborations featuring a complex range of competencies, activities, and social relationships. As we can see in Chapter 2, organized crime was constructed by late-modern political institutions as a receptacle for categories of acquisitive crime that pose a 'phantom threat' (van Duyne 1996) of coordinated malevolence by 'others', in particular aliens and those residing within some of the darker alcoves of class society. By presenting organized crime as the product of racial and class pathology, predatory, economically motivated crime is rendered exotic and remote, albeit faintly familiar yet unconnected to the systemic performance of personal accumulation that lies at the heart of late capitalism. Yet the concept has inspired an overwhelmingly US-influenced mandate for action (Hobbs and Antonopoulos (forthcoming)), providing the political justification for a confusing set of enforcement consortiums that function as umbrellas for a multiplicity of local and global concerns.

Yet while the spectre of organized crime, particularly in its transnational form, can always be conjured up when necessary by politicians or entrepreneurial senior police officers, as Chapter 3 indicates, British precursors of the concept pre-date the formal establishment of organized crime as a tool of governance. Indeed, with regard to the UK's current panic concerning globalization and toxic forms of migration, examples from the early twentieth century suggest that 'we overestimate the novelty of our situation' (Knepper 2009: 90). To stress ethnicity to the exclusion of other variables shrouds many distinguishing features of the enacted environments of contemporary socio-economic life that often embrace recreational and economic transgression and are enabled by forms of illegal trade. When viewed from a perspective that regards crime not as separate, exclusive, and essentially removed from normative civil society, but as one of its central props (Chambliss 1978), what emerges is a loose system of power relationships (Albini 1971) interacting seamlessly with both upper and underworlds, and rooted in the evolving class-defined complexities of urban life and the subtleties of criminalization. Alien conspiracy theory lies at the heart of many of the assumptions of law-enforcement agencies, and whether these assumptions are imposed upon local, national, or global realms, they tend to mirror the organizational hierarchies of policing (Reuter 1986), 'creating and supporting a shadow government that manages the rackets' (Chambliss 1978: 92).

As illustrated in Chapter 4, a few, rare athletes of violence drifted from expressive to commodified brutality via extortion, and found that they could generate money as well as fun, excitement, and drama. The industrial era produced street alliances that both protected and extorted the working-class neighbourhood, and while, as documented in Chapter 6, after a brief period of subcultural engagement the majority of youths were eventually absorbed into the industrial project, taking up designated places in class society, a minority extended their reputations beyond their immediate locale and became professional criminals central to an urban underworld that stood in stark opposition to the conformist requirements of Fordism.

Old Wine in New Suburbs

One of the weaknesses of so many academic studies of crime is the tendency to seek out compartmentalized and single-stranded motivations for engaging in illegal activity. However, as Chapter 5 shows, motivations for engagement with illegal markets are multifarious and driven by alterations to the wider political economy, in particular housing policy and the housing market, and the extraordinary fragmentization that has taken place as a result of deindustrialization and the acceleration of globalization. This chapter also emphasizes the shifting significance of territory for crime groups, and the relationship between change and continuity as actors adapt their culture by negotiating with both legal and illegal economic innovations.

Extortionate Platforms

Although beneficial to politicians and law-enforcement agents, the imprecision of the term 'organized crime'[1] makes for an extremely vague category that easily becomes conflated with equally vague constructions such as the mob, firm, or gang. Such terms, along with other emotive, media-nurtured terms, become mere receptacles for class and racial loathing, simplifying vast tracts of complex human activity according to categories devoid of emotional or cultural resonance. As we can see from Chapter 6, the hedonistic territorial violence of industrial-era youth collaborations, which were first highlighted in Chapter 4, served to generate identities which, via the world of work, most protagonists honed into urban maturity in the shape of traditional masculine, working-class inclusion. However, the post-industrial logic that no longer guarantees a half-century stint on a production line has assured that forays into the illegal marketplace are increasingly commonplace, normal, and unremarkable (Hall et al 2008). As Chapter 6 explains, due to their position in drug-trade networks and their prominence on the street,

---

[1] For a list of over 160 definitions of organized crime, see Klaus von Lampe, *Definitions of Organized Crime*, <http://www.organized-crime.de/organizedcrime definitions.htm>.

homegrown, youthful drug entrepreneurs have become integral to the state-constructed trope of transnational organized crime, suggesting a threat that is simultaneously familiar and foreign.

However, embracing entrepreneurship does not mean the abandonment of hedonism—far from it, for the fruits of success guarantee not having to get out of bed in the morning, leaving plenty of time and resources for the good times, which certainly during the early years can feel like one long Friday night. Therefore, it is a mistake to buy into the simplistic fallacy that lies at the heart of so many one-dimensional studies of organized crime in their emphasis upon the rational economic actor (Halstead 1998). Such emphasis artificially excludes cultural practices (Siegel and Nelen 2008) and dilutes the complexity of the constantly evolving social construct of the organized crime phenomenon. As I have tried to stress in previous work (Hobbs 1995), the notion of organized crime resides at the intersection of the cultural and the economic, and while its typical protagonist is neither a monetary programmed 'economic man' (Tobias 1968) nor a slack-jawed hedonist (Shover and Honaker 1991), I suggest that anyone who denies the pleasure to be gained from acquisitive crime has never held in their hand a £10 note they have not had to work for. The search for a blanket aetiology that covers the entirely fabricated amorphous concept of organized crime is doomed to reside forever in the self-contained irrelevancy of yet another academic maze.

Indeed, anyone seeking to impose a cold-blooded economic analysis to illegal entrepreneurs, whether or not youthful, needs to be reminded of the undoubted pleasure that is associated with a deal well struck (Hobbs 1988, 1995), 'of ego enhancement, the thrill of the game, the search for prestige among peers' (Naylor 2004: 19), as well as of the status that is associated with extravagant spending power in a society that regards consumption as central to the creation of identity (see Hall et al 2008). As Hallsworth and Silverstone remind us, 'No-one wants to look stupid. Everyone wants the big chain, everyone wants the big watch, everyone wants a nice car, all the girls, that's how it is' (2009: 369).

Over the Pavement and across the Entrepreneurial Divide

The role of hedonism was also clearly emphasized in Chapter 7 as part of the discussion of armed robbery and its central role in the now-defunct underworld, whose rise and fall was associated with the bandits' relationship to technologies of control. Generations of professional criminals prospered at the edges of class society in networked collaborations that seldom concluded in a Tudor mansion in Surrey, but frequently in a prison cell after a round-up of the usual suspects. The fierce, impudent banditry of the armed-robbery era, along with the mutant proletarianism of Chapter 4, is deeply embossed in the UK's construction of organized crime and serves to preserve a sense of retrospective continuity in an increasingly fractious marketplace.

The demise of armed robbery as a profession embedded in the semi-mythic protocols of the underworld was hastened by the emergence of the vibrant predation of normative entrepreneurship (Down 2006) that signified competent performance particularly in drug-trade-related roles, for, as discussed in Chapter 8 and the accompanying Appendix 2, most engagements with the drug trade do not require the visceral conceits of gangsterdom, and entrepreneurs tend to conduct their business discreetly, with as little fuss as possible. These are not denizens of the underworld, but pragmatic players, often with links to the enabling mechanisms of legitimate business and who are as likely to be spending their ill-gotten gains on double glazing, school fees, child support, paying off the mortgage, or financing the building of a hotel in Croatia, as they are to be joyously shoving their profits down their throats, in their arms, or up their noses (see Mullins 2006: 69–76).

However, although the excitement and fun of doing a deal that is central to the visceral predation of much market engagement can fade (Hobbs 1995: 60–73), given the wide range of agency that is apparent in this new entrepreneurial culture, it would be a grave error to privilege economic considerations over sensuality. As we can see from the case studies in Appendix 2, particularly with regard to drug-use and gambling, it is as unwise to disregard hedonism as an aspect of illegal market engagement, as it would be to ignore the coke-addled, helicopter-riding lifestyles of hedge-fund traders in a consideration of the occupational culture of financial service workers in the City of London (Anderson 2008). The complexity and essentially normative character of the contemporary illegal market demands everyman performances that proceed with neither the industrial era's restraints of hedonistic excess, nor the piratical proletarianism that was associated exclusively with the underworld. The very notion of the underworld had its foundation in proletarian-based networks, which, in the wake of the neoliberal assault, have been fragmented and cast to the winds. As Chapter 9 explains, in its place are ad hoc networks where the threat or reality of violence as well as rumour and gossip create a sense of order amongst a plethora of temporary alliances which operate very much according to free market principles.

Cosmopolitan Community: Crime as an Inclusive Morality

Chapter 10 illustrates that as 'new vernaculars replaced a range of much older cultural practices' (Pollock 2002: 15) many contemporary relationships acquired a certain cosmopolitan awareness that is entirely at odds with the inward-looking, little-Englander stance of the old denizens of the underworld. Illegal trading is merely one example of the 'growing transnational articulation' (Sassen 2006: 78) of UK citizens, which is expressed not in the form of cultural domination by the foreign, but as the appropriation by the local of elements of the foreign in order to formulate new and innovative social and economic forms.

As argued throughout this book, local criminal organization was always deeply entrenched in the cultures of the urban working class, and deindustrialization and the consequent fragmentation of long-established communities resulted in their transformation into disordered mutations of traditional proletarian culture, which in areas such as Dogtown are constantly enlivened by cosmopolitan influences. Part of this disorder involves both individuals and groups clustering around irregular trading relationships that constitute a far less exclusive zone than traditional underworld narratives would suggest, and while a frisson of fear, amazement, and not a little excitement tends to greet actors who apply any form of coherence to their transgressive activities, it is the competence of foreigners in particular that promotes anxiety and apprehension amongst a bewildered host community. However, to attribute organizational mojo to this disparate collection of marketized scavengers is little more than an administrative convenience, for while the big brands of organized crime are not invisible in the UK,[2] the notion of extra-legal governance associated with 'mafias'

---

[2] See Saviano (2007) 259–81; Behan (1996) 125; Allum and Allum (2008) 356.

(see Varese 2010) is not apparent and 'there is no imminent tendency towards the consolidation of large scale modern illegal bureaucracies' (Paoli and Fijnaut 2004: 610).

A Community of Practice

> There was nothing to fear; there were no underworlds or overworlds, only a world (Benney 1936: 350)

The underworlds of gangsters and robbers and the subcultures of urban youth were products of the certainties and consistencies of industrial society that identified the demonic by their reluctance to engage in meaningful labour or by their postures of resistance. While the virtuous embraced the fleeting certainties of Fordism, deindustrialism marked the end of these convenient categories, and the subsequent allure of unfettered hedonism and rampant entrepreneurship has been widely embraced by a population for whom narcissism is no longer the preserve of the wealthy. The contemporary dominance of the market does not suggest a lemming-like, mechanistic abandonment of every human activity other than the accumulation of profit, but it does suggest that in post-industrial society agency is overwhelmingly shaped by market forces and is no longer mediated by the clearly defined inequalities and subsequent communality of industrial society. Given the lack of relevant meta narratives, whether in the shape of Fordism (cf Lipietz 1996) or transnational organized crime, subcultural action—previously the preserve of professional criminals and youths experimenting with territoriality and the quasi-resistance of this week's haircut—now makes perfect sense as a way of operating as a pragmatic, vibrant, informal, communal endeavour within the illegal economy. Although these subcultures may feature expressive and hedonistic activity, they are mediated through market engagement, which is negotiated informally via communities of practice that create 'multiple lateral, horizontal communications, collaborations solidarities and supports' (Sassen 2006: 72).

These communities of practice are typified by ever-fluctuating networks of individuals whose formal identities may or may not be located within categories of transgression. Based upon the pragmatic contribution that an individual can make to the group's aim, communities of practice embrace a wide population including those with access to business and the infrastructures of formal commerce (Mack 1964) and should be considered as integral to entrepreneurial fields that operate within a context of economic, class, and ethnic power relations embracing the entire range of the global marketplace. Consequently, we can see street dealers, wholesalers, and importers in Dogtown and its periphery sharing a domain of interest, not only with regional partners but also with internationally networked nodes—money launderers in Dubai 'warlords', 'oligarchs' (Glenny 2008) and other demonic figures of transnational organized crime. Communities of practice operate according to local conditions, in social arenas that develop repertoires which are coherent with the entrepreneurial habitus of post-industrial society and create collective competencies that are transferred informally and linked via networks of illegal trading to strategically relevant partners (Barnes et al 2000; Taylor 1999: 171–3).

Unlicensed Capitalism

This community of practice is structured around various levels of entrepreneurial performance that are played out within the context of an unlicensed form of capitalism whose fluid parameters are defined by the chaos and fragmentation of deindustrialization. While these networks incorporate ad hoc coalitions of the highly adaptive remnants of industrial society with newcomers to the cosmopolitan city, a consistent feature of this constantly mutating community are professional criminals, whose activities are no longer restricted to an outlaw subculture of theft (Sutherland 1937) but are applied to a vast range of embedded illegal enterprise. Although these professionals, who are defined by their competence and commitment to illegal money-making activity (Hobbs 1995), are no longer restricted to the class-bound restraints of underworld narratives, they have retained a semblance of the traditional 'crime as work' ethos of the proletarian elite of the industrial era (Letkemann 1973) by adapting to the possibilities offered by entrepreneurial engagement with cross-border trading cultures (Junninen 2006).

Barely differentiated from other players in the 'the bland utopia of the free market' (Cohen 2006), this committed core of usual suspects no longer constitutes a subculture in its own right separated from the law-abiding majority by a behaviour system featuring technical skill, consensus via a shared ideology, differential

association, status, and most importantly informal organization
(Sutherland 1937; Hobbs 1995: 4–5). By adopting the notion of a
community of practice, and perceiving the illegal market as a form
of unlicensed capitalism, we can dispense with the arcane concept
of the underworld and break down the mystique of transnational
organized crime with its monolithic, essentially alien threat, and in
their place we can identify independent local units of activity that
are linked via networks that make full use of market society's
embedded licensed infrastructure.

The community of practice comprises a series of discrete, action-
based networks that informally connect individuals whose identities are constructed via full-time, part-time, temporary, or
peripatetic engagement with the full range of profit-driven crimes
(Naylor 2003). Connecting them either practically or abstractly
to communities of practice across the globe, members 'are not
"more alienated" than others, they simply practise the fundamental capitalist exchange relation—to acquire from the other a surplus, as large as possible, in relation to what one gives—in a state
of unrelieved alienation in the raw rather than under the cover of
contrived ethical symbolism' (Hall 2012: 268–9). The predisposi-
tion to acquire profit has informed an increasingly global habitus
that has impacted upon remnants of industrial culture once associated with both resistance and proletarian restraint, and the
involvement of both citizens and fragments of the excluded
diasporic has created shared domains of interest that render
organized crime irrelevant as an analytic category, for both unlicensed capitalism and the community of practice within which it
resides are central to the way that we now live (Levi and Naylor
2000; Ruggiero 2000).

Banal Entitlement

> Ordinary Western Europeans spend an ever-burgeoning
> amount of their spare time and money sleeping with prosti-
> tutes; smoking untaxed cigarettes; snorting coke through E50
> notes up their noses; employing illegal untaxed immigrant
> labour on subsistence wages; stuffing their gullets with caviar;
> admiring ivory and sitting on teak (Glenny 2008: 55)

> The mortality rate of expectations is high, and in a properly
> functioning consumer society it must go on rising steadily
> (Bauman 2005: 82)

During the past three decades the penetration of market forces into British society has enabled the normalization of individualistic and predatory relationships, and a whole range of illegal trades has thrived as a means of acquiring and transacting capital in the void left by legal employment, organized labour, and the enabling institutions of industrial culture. However, Dogtowners' involvement with the trade in illegal commodities originating thousands of miles away does not define them as cogs in global organized crime (Savoie-Gargiso and Morselli 2009), and Dogtowners are no more dupes of global organized crime than they were dupes of capitalism. The complexity of the contemporary population, and the bewildering flow of people, jobs, products, and desires, mean that no individual or group can dominate Dogtown or define its cultural identity: not the hard-working individuals clinging on to the dream of security for their families and a home in the suburbs; not the duckers and divers, thieves, scoundrels, and scallywags living in a world embalmed by an Ealing comedy, central-casting agency; not Dogtown's youth tenuously dipping its trainers into multiple marketplaces; not the self-satisfied gangsters residing in London's periphery; and certainly not the police. The bewildering changes that have swept through the UK during the past four decades have raised unemployment and long-term ill-health, decimated and stigmatized social housing (Jones 2010), impoverished local services, and, via the marketization of social life and the commodification of human agency, created a 'rough, jagged, and uneven world' (Harvey 2009: 58) where communality is a rare and difficult-to-maintain resource (Dorling et al 2007: 87). The unarguable damage that has been created by these changes is the result not of global organized crime, but of global capitalism.

The investment of unlicensed profit is no longer limited to traditional outlets such as pubs, bars, restaurants, nail bars, and other cash-based enterprises, and it is notable that, in 2008, illegally acquired profits served to provide much-needed liquidity for a global financial system that was in meltdown. 'In many instances, the money from drugs was the only liquid investment capital. In the second half of 2008, liquidity was the banking system's main problem and hence liquid capital became an important factor…Interbank loans were funded by money that originated from the drugs trade and other illegal activities…There were signs that some banks were rescued that way' (Antonio Maria Costa, Head of the UN

Office on Drugs and Crime).[3] Indeed, as Chris explained in Chapter 8, 'It's the same money', so why should the beleaguered residents of Dogtown be denied at least some crumbs off the table from the predatory entrepreneurial practices that have become normalized in post-industrial society?[4]

Particularly in the urban centres where the products and services of the illegal market are traded and consumed (T Hall 2012), many residents enthusiastically participate in one of the few segments of market society that is accessible to them, which in turn is closely related to that of its legal free market equivalent, both being driven by insatiable demand (Gilman et al 2011). In these chaotic, post-industrial bazaars where the quest for the 'Lush Life' is everything, the unremarkable demands of competent consumers can run to an ounce of this, a gram of that, 200 'Albanian Marlboro', and a DVD of a yet-to-be-premiered Hollywood blockbuster courtesy of a extremely polite Chinese youth who delivers the goods at 9pm every Friday (Rawlinson 2010: 137), and so much more. These are the banal entitlements of affluence fostering the ambiguity that is central to the urban milieu, and it is this demand for cheap goods and contraband, whether it be drugs, cigarettes, sex, or somebody to pick up the kids from school and do a little light dusting, that drives illegal markets, rather than the administratively convenient demonic catch-all of organized crime.

While high on the hill unearned wealth and cosmopolitan entitlement is the birthright of the bankers and other poster boys of licensed capitalism, in Dogtown the police continue to focus upon loose-knit variations of established citizens, the freshly arrived, and the usual suspects as part of the fallout of illegal trading on the UK's increasingly impoverished streets. The subsequent community of practice is vibrant, attractive, and deeply embedded, and we should not be too surprised that when we abandon human existence to the whims of the marketplace, some will thrive and become adept at its manipulation.

---

[3] *Observer*, 13 December 2009.
[4] For a masterful commentary on the 'institutionalised abuses of the overworld' and the disproportionate emphasis afforded to working-class criminality, see Russo (2001) 491–504.

Appendix 1
Whitwell Road: Five Decades

May 1968

The dances at St Phillips were run by a group of Franciscan Monks who appear to have been handpicked to spread the Lord's word in east London according to their physical rather than spiritual attributes. A fight, followed swiftly by the violent intervention of two or three of the Brothers, was the norm, and added an edge for most of the 15- to 17-year-olds who paid their entrance fee to a large, scowling monk in brown robe and sandals.

In the foyer of St Phillips gathered a group of five young men who were eyeballing new arrivals. One of the men wore a beige Crombie overcoat, beige mohair trousers, and a pair of red, leather, industrial boots with steel toecaps. Three of the men wore newly fashionable Harrington jackets. John was a very dangerous young man who, with his equally violent Crombie-wearing brother, was known for his fighting prowess and willingness to use weapons. The brothers had been at the forefront of local football hooliganism where, before youthful rival fans had regularly threatened the home 'end', they had relished going toe to shiny toe with individual police officers. All of this group were from Plaistow except for one who originated in Canning Town and now lived just a mile away in Stratford. On the street this group presented a highly stylized, violent force who occasionally came together with other small groups to make up a formidable local alliance capable of contesting cafes, parties, parks, streets, and clubs across east London. All six young men had reputations, and their presence assured a real buzz for new arrivals, the more politically astute of whom made sure that they publicly acknowledged John, therefore aligning themselves and their party with what looked and felt like an attack squad, or at least establishing, particularly with the intense Harrington trio, that they offered no threat.

Crombie left soon after, and the evening played itself out in familiar fashion with perhaps 100 teenagers refreshed by little more than a bottle of beer bought at a local off-licence and drunk surreptitiously in the shadow of the dustbin sheds of a nearby block of flats. The dancing, laughing, smoking crowd parted to allow a young man wearing a suit and a Fred Perry shirt to be dragged by his skinny lapel out of the hall by one of the Brothers, while his muscular colleagues patrolled the periphery concentrating their missionary zeal upon the prevention of heavy petting. The St Phillips' dances were renowned for the music that was played, which always featured tasteful selections of Tamla Motown and Stax, and it was during a slow ballad that the evening erupted in an all-too-familiar way. Several young men stumbled in the dark as couples slow danced and voices were raised. A woman screamed and a man shouted. As the music stopped and the lights came up a woman screamed 'he's got a gun', and John and a large young man wearing a black sweater ripped at the neck were squaring up to each other. The man in the black sweater had a split lip. In time-honoured fashion the crowd cleared to form an impromptu arena, and again a woman's voice repeats, 'He's got a gun'. Panic ensued as some people tried to get out of the hall, more screams followed and voices were raised, punches were exchanged, and the Brothers waded in with slaps and cuffs to clear the hall.

From outside there came the sound of fighting, but the three Harringtons remained inside, and as the exit cleared they calmly reached to the inside pockets of their jackets and took out long, thin cases, perhaps six inches long, from which they removed open razors. They placed the cases back in their pockets, opened the razors, and holding the weapons at shoulder height joined the huddle of bodies who were fleeing the hall or joining the fighting. Above the heads of spectators and combatants the razors could be seen slashing down onto heads, faces, and protective hands. In the doorway of some flats a dark bundle received a vigorous kicking, and a running fight took the Harringtons and their prey towards the main road, while the remainder of the St Philips' congregation rapidly dispersed to back streets, bus stops, and chip shops at the end of another Saturday night.

2009 Teenage Stabbing: Two Arrested in London

(*Daily Telegraph*, 25 January 2009)

> The victim, named locally as Steven Lewis, was stabbed to death in Whitwell Road, Plaistow, east London, around 11pm on Saturday night, and taken to the Royal London hospital where he was pronounced dead just before midnight, the Metropolitan Police said. Two boys, thought to be aged 16 and 17, were arrested on suspicion of murder in the early hours of Sunday and were being held at an east London police station....The (Myspace) page suggests the teenager is a member of the 'purple gang'. Next of kin have been informed. The victim, who was found with multiple chest wounds, is the first teenager in the capital to die in a knife attack this year. Last year more than 28 teenagers met violent deaths in and around the capital.
>
> Local residents said the attack followed an earlier incident at a nearby party. A 15-year-old girl from Canning Town, who

wished to remain anonymous, said: 'There was a fund-raising event at St Philips' Church Hall. It was meant to be a party for 16- to 25-year-olds but a fight started so they ended it at 10.30pm. I saw pushing and arms swinging around. Then the bouncers came in and said the party has been knocked off. Everyone came out and there was lots of boys everywhere. I knew there was going to be trouble so I went home. Some people were just hanging around. There was probably over 100 people at the party. I was expecting a fight but I wasn't expecting anyone to get stabbed. There is always a fight, that is why I left early'.

A local man who claimed the victim was his nephew's best friend, said he had recently received a telephone call to warn him that Steven was in danger. 'Steven was threatened and my nephew was threatened' said the man. 'He was a nice lad. He didn't harm anyone. All these kids have got to put down their knives. He was not a knife carrier. He just went to a party to meet his mates. But his mates weren't there and a group of lads came and he got stabbed'.

Stephen had been attending a charity event campaigning against youth violence. Much was subsequently made in the tabloid press of Steven's alleged involvement in a dispute with a rival 'gang' from E16, claiming that the E13-based Dem Man Crew were 'a gang of local youths who sell cannabis and terrorise other youngsters from neighbouring postcodes' (*Daily Mail*, 30 January 2009). A year later an alleged member of the E16 gang was stabbed to death in what was assumed by local people to be a reprisal attack.

At the 1968 dance, it is unclear whether or not anyone had a gun, and open razors can maim but rarely kill. The large young man with the split lip and his friends were from E16, John C's group were from E13 and E15, and this was a traditional territorial dispute probably triggered by a personal slight; the term 'postcode war' had yet to be invented.[1]

Within two years of the 1968 dance one of the youths present at StPhillips was killed in a local pub; a few years later another was jailed for armed robbery; while most of the St Phillips' youths scuffled their way into adulthood engaging variously with violence, theft, stolen goods, and the

---

[1] As Hallsworth and Young (2008) 182 note: 'While the advent of what have been termed "postcode wars" (conflicts over different territories) has been considered by some elements in the media and by control agents as prima facie evidence of gang wars across the UK, this thesis only works if you ignore the historical record. The risk of taking a beating by straying outside your turf has a long history in working class areas that reaches back well beyond the current fascination with territorial conflict (Pearson, 1983).'

emerging markets in drugs. The St Phillips' incident in the early summer of 1968 coincided with the arrest of the Kray twins, an event which held far more relevance to local youths than the bourgeois uprising on the streets of Paris, for a pervasive local mythology relating to gangsters and gangster style fascinated local working-class youths as much in 1968 as it does in the early 21st century. Suits, overcoats, short hair, and the mannered violence of that night at St Phillips were all totally in accord with the activities of adult gangsters, who also used bespoke violence on familiar streets, and on unfamiliar faces from off the manor.

In Plaistow in 1968 nobody called the police, the injured found their own way to hospital, the tabloids stayed away, and nobody attributed the fight to gangs, to the perpetrators' indisputable whiteness, or used it as a racially loaded metaphor for 'Broken Britain'. In Whitwell Road, London, E13 in May 1968, more by luck than judgment, nobody died. In 1968 the end of the post-war boom was marked by a rise in youth unemployment. In 1968 the London Docks started to close down and shed jobs.

Appendix 2
Traffickers

In order to unpack the manner in which individuals locate and engage with the drug trade, the following typology presents a series of role-specific case studies derived from both published and unpublished material based upon interviews with 222 convicted drug traffickers serving over seven years in British prisons (Matrix Knowledge Group 2007; see also Marsh et al 2012).

The Boss

Bosses are seldom problematic drug users, and utilize legitimate business to aid operations, generally dealing in kilograms, and relying upon general networking in order to garner information, which includes collusion with law-enforcement personnel. They have a small number of contacts, and, as well as suppliers and customers, work with individuals undertaking a number of different supporting functions, for instance storers, transporters, and legitimate professionals.

Billy

Billy became involved in the drug trade, not through the stereotypical 'shop floor' or street-dealing route, but via the laundering of money. He was a successful car dealer and nightclub owner, and had also made money from an expanding property portfolio before he was introduced to a group of drug importers who were contemplating how to invest their profits. Attracted by the prospect of easy money, Billy fed these profits through his car dealership, and progressed to become a 'middle man', seeking out buyers for importers. Eventually, he ran the enterprise, becoming embroiled with the day-to-day workings of a large operation consisting of storers, mixers, testers, and legitimate professionals, many of whom were paid a salary. Billy also courted the friendship of police officers who, in exchange for free drinks, would provide him with information and carry out background checks on business associates and employees. He called his associates a 'community of friends', all with their role to play.

Charlie

At 16 Charlie got involved with 'the wrong people', and was storing cannabis for a local dealer. Charlie's family owned a number of newsagents and a transport company, and his older brother was using the newsagents as a front to sell heroin. At the age of 20 Charlie inherited the family hero-in business when his brother married. Charlie described 'transport as the key', and his father's transport business was crucial. He bought 10 to 15 kilos a week from his suppliers who were importing the heroin via Liver-pool, London, and Dover in trucks with carefully concealed compart-ments. His role involved ensuring that everything went smoothly in the UK, and in particular he assumed responsibility for security and anti-sur-veillance, making sure that no one was followed and that phones were not tapped. He also kept the number of people 'in the know' to an absolute minimum, set routes for various operatives, and took an interest in the general appearance of these operatives, emphasizing a low-key, non-extravagant demeanour. On occasions Charlie would personally observe the exchange of drugs by surreptitiously walking his dog nearby. He worked with one supplier, whom he described as a partner, with four main customers, and four workers who were paid salaries.

The Manager

Managers are employees of an enterprise who manage key activities, and this pivotal role locates them in close proximity to both the supplier and the drugs. Managers are involved in logistics, recruitment of 'mules' or couriers, and the collection of drugs. In contrast to the bosses, managers work with fewer types of roles, yet are more personally involved in ensur-ing that tasks are completed than are bosses, which, along with their prox-imity to the drugs and suppliers, places an increased emphasis on risk management (Morselli et al 2007).

Ron

Ron was in his mid-fifties, and had been retired from his job in law enforce-ment for a decade when he first became involved in the drug trade. Ron managed an operation based upon couriers importing cocaine into the UK from Grenada, and his role was to recruit and manage the couriers. He frequented a local casino where he spotted potential couriers from amongst the casino's clientele, tending to target white, middle-aged men, low on money, and 'who needed a holiday'. Ron made all the travel arrangements, purchased the airline tickets, provided the suitcase, and handed over the spending money. He would then instruct the courier to 'behave like a nor-mal holiday maker, don't draw attention to yourself, basically enjoy your holiday'.

The couriers would have their holiday and return with an identical suit-case containing cocaine. On the successful arrival of a consignment into the UK, Ron would collect the case from the courier at the airport and hand the drugs over to his bosses, who would be waiting in a nearby car park. The bosses would then take the bag away to offload the drugs, before returning an hour later with £12,000 in cash, often in shopping bags. Ron would pass £7000 to the courier, who had also enjoyed an all-expenses paid, two-week holiday, and keep £5000 as his payment.[1]

Many inmates of British prisons who receive long sentences are little more than bit-part players in drug-trafficking operations. Couriers, or so-called 'mules',[2] are expendable to dealing networks; for instance, one dealer using mules to import cocaine from the Caribbean estimated that one in four would not get through, while an international transporter importing via road estimated that four out of ten did not get through (Matrix Knowledge Group 2007; see also Green et al 1994; Green 1996).[3]

The International Wholesaler

International wholesalers buy drugs abroad and arrange transportation before selling them within the UK. Most individuals in this section dealt in a wide range of drugs and weights, were flexible in their methodologies, and often had long and quite complex careers that featured prison as a routine hazard. The majority working at this level progressed their careers and attempted to expand, their logistics were sophisticated, and they regularly used professional services and legitimate trade to aid business (Matrix Knowledge Group 2007: 28–9).

Erving

In the late 1970s Erving was serving four years for fraud, and during this sentence he first came into contact with the potential of the drug trade by dabbling in dealing cannabis. Friends of his wife were heroin users, and on his release from prison he commenced selling heroin. Initially he sold £10 bags, but became dissatisfied with his irregular 'hit-and-miss' supply, and apparently hindered by not being a heroin user himself, spent time seeking out reliable suppliers. Once this contact was established, Erving, who described himself as being 'quite ambitious', soon had two to three dealers working for him, and started buying ounces, until his supply went 'haywire' and he bought from three different suppliers.

In 1983 Erving was selling 10-gram bags, and within 18 months he was buying two to three kilos of heroin with 40 to 50 per cent purity, at £21,000 per kilo (£600 per ounce) and selling for £1000 per ounce to old friends, who would in turn sell on to their own networks of users. In 1984 he began

---

[1] Another example of this method was that of a woman who was given a free two-week holiday in the Caribbean and paid £2000 to bring four kilos back to the UK. Having completed a successful run she was employed to recruit couriers herself, which she did, mainly from the local prostitute community.

[2] Individuals, often women, paid to transport drugs across borders.

[3] '[R]ough calculations suggest that, when balancing profits against prison risk, crime does not pay for couriers but can for organizations employing bent lorry drivers' (Caulkins et al 2009).

working with a group of Asian heroin importers, and in 1985–86 he made a huge career leap by travelling to India and meeting some contacts who were networked with his Indian/Pakistani connections. This was his first move into importation, and he described his aim as being to 'cut out the middle man to cut costs and increase quality'. He made two trips during this period, buying two consignments of eight kilos of heroin. The Indians transported the drugs to the UK and Erving picked the drugs up in a suitcase from a pre-arranged address. In 1986 he was arrested by Customs and Excise after a relative, who was arrested picking up a consignment of heroin, had informed on Erving.

After serving his sentence Erving returned to the heroin trade, overseeing the importation of kilos of heroin concealed in passenger luggage from India. Erving explained that this was his favoured method of importation, and that although he did not normally carry out these pick-ups himself, the courier paid to pick up the drugs for Erving on one occasion had failed to turn up. The Indians had told him to go to a hotel to meet the courier who, Erving later discovered, had been arrested at the airport. On his arrival at the hotel, Erving was also arrested, and he served six years in a Belgian prison. It was while serving this sentence that he met some Kurdish and Turkish traffickers who educated Erving, in particular with regard to transportation and smuggling routes.

He was released from prison in 1992, and within a fortnight was working with some of his new Turkish contacts, but this time dealing in hundreds of kilos, supplying new customers in Scotland and the north west of England. Heroin was brought from Turkey to Belgium, and Erving coordinated the leg from Belgium to the UK. At this time he was selling for £1500 per kilo, and between 1995 and 1996 he coordinated about 12 transportations into the UK, while simultaneously buying and selling cannabis, and on one occasion in 10 days making £75,000 profit on a 500-kilo deal.

Dennis

Dennis had been employed at the airport for over a decade in a number of occupations, progressing to be a manager of aircraft cleaners, a job that required security clearance, enabling him access to most areas of the airport, and paying £30,000 to £40,000 per year. He was contacted by a local man asking for information regarding where consignments of cocaine powder might be stored on aircraft coming into the UK from South America and the Caribbean. Dennis explained that there was a flaw in the security system at the airport in that there were no checks on staff driving off the site. He received payment of £20,000 for this information and became a watcher, watching flights coming in from South America and reporting any threatening Customs' activity.

Dennis quickly progressed to removing the drugs from the aircraft and transporting them out of the airport. The cocaine powder cost £1000 a kilo in Colombia and was sold in the UK to regular customers for £18,000 to £22,000, while one-off buyers had to pay £25,000. Dennis and his associates were bringing in ten-kilo consignments and turning the ten kilos into 20 kilos by changing its purity from 95 per cent to around 40 per cent. It took a day and half to 'knock it down' and sometimes he would draft friends in to cut the drugs with 'any white powder', such as bicarbonate of soda, novacone, or manatol, before repackaging and selling on.

Al

Al came to England as a child, and as a young man took over the family Kebab shop when his father returned to Turkey. At this point Al started to gamble, and with his business in decline, he rapidly found himself £7000 in debt, at which point a fellow gambler asked him to store a parcel of heroin. This turned into a regular arrangement for which he received £4000 to £5000 for this service. Al graduated to seeking out customers, and when one of his colleagues was arrested he left the drug trade, but was soon approached by a contact and became a driver for a key London distributor. Al's job was to drive the man to meetings, and interpret for him.

After a couple of years Al took over responsibility for coordinating the distribution of 150 kilos of heroin in two London boroughs He was responsible for paying the storeman, the driver, and the distributor, and every two months he would travel to Turkey to meet with network associates who included lawyers, politicians, and border control police. Information regarding prices was shared with competitors, and Al would go to one of his boss's nightclubs every three to four months to meet with competitors to discuss informants and non-payers. Between 2001 and 2003, Al estimated that he made £400,000.

The National Wholesalers

National wholesalers buy and sell drugs in bulk across the UK. This group were highly adaptable regarding new commodities and innovative methods of transporting and trading drugs. They progressed their careers via small networks that frequently featured salaried employees.

Mr W

Mr W discovered the profitability of heroin while serving a prison sentence for living on immoral earnings: 'They were turning £700, £800 out of an eighth of heroin [3.5 grams] and to me that was big money...All I could see was £signs, it was just too much money to let it go. So I started when I came out.' People were prepared to pay as much as £1000 for an ounce of heroin, which Mr W could buy for £700 or less. At first he was turning over an ounce a day, but he was soon buying kilos for which he paid approximately £17,500 and, at his peak, he was selling five kilos per week. Four women worked for him who were each paid £1500 per week for collecting and delivering parcels of heroin to his five main customers who were based in Manchester, Southampton, Bristol, and London.

This network was based on old friends and family members who happened to live in these different cities, and the financial arrangements were that if he bought one kilo from his supplier, Mr W would receive another kilo on a credit basis, and he would do the same to his customers, who were taking nine-bar (nine ounces) and half-kilo loads on a regular basis. Mr W also bought and sold smaller amounts of cocaine, although this was mainly because he liked to smoke crack 'as a treat'. He reckoned that an ounce of crack cocaine costing £1000 would sell for £3500 on the basis of six or seven £20 'stones' per gram. He was not particularly interested in this retail trade, however, and his main business remained heroin, which funded a lavish lifestyle for himself and his extended family. Mr W knew other small networks that were buying heroin in Amsterdam for £8000 per kilo and importing it via couriers secreting drug-filled packets into body cavities. As for his own position in the market, Mr W said: 'People used to think I'm the boss, and OK I'm that, but I said to myself they should see some of the blokes who I'm dealing with, blokes who I'm giving seventy grand to twice a week, and I'm not his best customer' (Pearson and Hobbs 2001).

Stan

Stan came to England as a small child and was incorporated into the family drug business from an early age. His family had been involved in importing heroin for many years, and he had accrued a general knowledge through 'hearing things' before, at 17, he became actively involved in drug dealing. He had been a recreational user of cannabis since the age of 14, and a recreational cocaine user at age 18. He began selling 1/16th (3.5 grams) ounces of heroin which he purchased for £50 before breaking it down into 12 £10 bag deals, and within six months he was purchasing kilo (36 ounces) quantities of heroin, selling this on in 'ounce' quantities for £900, half nine-bar quantities' (four-and-a-half ounces) at £2400, and 'nine-bar' (nine ounce) amounts at £4800. He attributed his involvement in drug selling to being young and aspiring to a nice lifestyle.

Initially, his customers were drug addicts, but he began asking for introductions to their dealers, and then to the dealers' dealers, who in turn became his customers. When he began buying in larger quantities he handed over his £10-bag business and customer base to someone else, and required them to purchase ounce quantities from him for £900. Aged 18 he was sentenced to three-and-a-half years on a conspiracy to import charge and spent 21 months in prison. After the prison sentence his drug selling resumed and he began purchasing five-kilo quantities from the importers, who were importing in 100- to 350-kilo quantities. Stan then became involved in collecting 350-kilo quantities from different docks around England; three cars would be sent—one to carry the drugs, and the other two to 'ram the police off the road' in the event of the operation being intercepted.

He had 20 to 30 customers from all over the north of England, who included 'suit and tie types', and business people. Some of his customers were friends and others were business associates whom he trusted because 'they knew the rules'. He had four or five people working for him, who were 'family' and were paid £500 a week, fulfilling various roles such as delivering the drugs and collecting money from customers. They acted as look-outs on the street when a hand-over of drugs took place, and sometimes they helped with 'cutting' the heroin. The iron rule for Stan, as for the majority of drug entrepreneurs, was to 'keep the drugs and money separate'.

Steve

Steve was careful who he worked with, and, as a businessman with a legitimate enterprise, he believed that the qualities demanded by the drugs trade were the same as in any other business—integrity, reliability, and trustworthiness. He always trained his employees, equipping them with the knowledge and skills they would need by passing on his own experience.

Steve only ever worked with small units of four to five people, and although trust was important, it was vital that the members of the unit were not so close that they could be connected to each other if caught. New staff would be given easy roles at first, for instance organizing a drop-off or a pick-up. Each time they got through their task successfully they would be given tasks with more responsibility until they proved that they were reliable and trustworthy. Employees were paid on a percentage commission basis according to their role in a successful deal, and if they did well on a particular job they were rewarded with a bigger bonus. Steve did not work with close friends, and he did not employ drug-users, deeming them to be unreliable.

Communication with customers was disguised as part of his legitimate business, which was carried out over the phone. Steve never employed storers, but took responsibility for this role himself, burying the drugs in the ground. Although he lost some drugs in this way, he felt that if the drugs were discovered they would be difficult to trace to him. Steve's role was the buyer, sourcing the goods, and dealing directly with upper-level dealers, while a close associate dealt with the finances. He was never involved with any violence, although he did on occasion feel intimidated by buyers. If he did do business with people who had bad reputations he would only deal small quantities until they proved their trustworthiness, and if he was ripped off, he put it down to experience and avoided any conflict.

The Local Wholesalers

Local wholesalers buy and sell drugs in kilos and ounces within one geographical area. This segment of the market operates in small networks selling multi-commodities.

Gary

At 18 Gary was out of work and started dealing in heroin and cannabis. He commenced with small bags, financing the enterprise by borrowing money from someone he knew would not require paying back, preferring to give the lender some drugs. He despised junkies, considering them to be potential informants, and felt that he was more likely to avoid police attention by moving up-market. Consequently, he moved away from the street and began dealing in kilos, one week selling 26 kilos. Gary also employed 'young soldiers' to grow cannabis, which he would then market.

Gary was very risk-aware, and would only sell to people introduced to him by a trusted source. He had about a dozen customers who he first came into contact with through socializing amongst a small network of people in his home town. New customers were checked out fully, they were followed home, and their family and acquaintances were checked. Gary changed his phone number every week, and had to keep his true source of income from his family. He also worried about creating enemies amongst strangers who threatened violence 'even though you have no idea who they are', and would constantly alter the method of picking up the heroin. For example he would call on a pool of young women whom he paid to take their boyfriends for a day out while picking up the drugs.

Gary worked with the same people he had grown up with, and he always used the same supplier as he was 'good' and Gary trusted him. He worked with four partners in a remarkably cooperative arrangement; although they shared the profits equally, if one of them needed all of the money one week for some reason then he could have it all. Gary employed an accountant, whom he paid in drugs, and a solicitor, while a local police officer would tip him off about police activity.

Joey

Joey was a 33-year-old white English man who had been involved with drugs since the age of 16. Through drinking in his local pub he met people who were involved in various criminal activities, and eventually he was asked to take on the role of delivering heroin, amphetamine, and LSD to various locations, for which he was paid generously. For instance, when delivering heroin he was paid £1000 per kilo, and although sometimes it was 'just' a kilo a week, it could be as much as eight kilos. The people for whom he delivered would put the drugs in a rental car, and Joey would then be told to pick up the car and drive it to a location, where he would leave it for someone else to collect. The car would then be returned to the hire company a week later. Joey would arrive in the area early in order to survey the surrounding area for police or surveillance activity. 'If it did not 'feel right', he would walk away.

Joey progressed from being a driver, and by the age of 23 was buying kilos and setting people up to sell for him. He had a close business associate who was a good friend with whom he 'trusted his life', and they moved to different areas of the country to establish customer bases and to avoid police detection, gaining local intelligence by drinking in pubs and talking to people involved in the drug trade. When they left an area because 'things were getting on top', they would set someone else up to take over the business, passing on their clients and supplying the new dealer with an eighth of heroin and building up from there. If the new dealer could prove that they could reliably pay back the cost of the eighth, they would be supplied with a larger amount.

Through being in social environments where drugs were voraciously consumed, from around the age of 25 Gary had become a daily heroin user and four years later he was a crack addict with a £2000-a-week habit. When he became addicted Joey lost his reputation as a competent dealer; he was no longer reliable and resorted to robbery and burglary to fund his habit. He was arrested in a car he had stolen.

Dee

Dee's uncles had been involved in the drug trade since the 1980s. In the mid-1990s Dee joined the family business and was given a kilo of heroin on credit, which he sold within two months. Dee quickly progressed to selling between nine ounces and a kilo per week, collecting the drugs from his supplier in Yorkshire once or twice a week, storing the drugs in his house and car, and selling directly to over 100 customers who were both users and dealers. After only three months he employed four workers to help him, and began working across a wide area of northern England. The four workers were of Afghani and Turkish origin and in their mid-twenties, and Dee felt that the trust that existed between himself and these men was due to the fact that they came from the same community.

Having a constant supply of good quality heroin and a line of credit with the wholesaler helped his business expand. His suppliers were delivering the drugs by taxi once or twice a week, and using six safe houses where the dealers bagged and sold the drugs. During this time Dee invested his profits in a number of legitimate businesses importing cars from Dubai, renting property, and running a post office, as well as buying and selling contraband cigarettes and alcohol from France.

Greg

Greg was a self-employed importer who earned an 'above average income', and although he did not use drugs himself, he socialized with a middle-class group of friends who used cocaine at weekends. When their supplier let them down, Greg called a dealer whom he had once met at a party, and purchased two ounces of cocaine for £1500. While Greg's girlfriend tested the drugs, the supplier explained that it was possible to make £26,000 profit on a kilo of cocaine, which inspired Greg to commence dealing.

Encouraged by his girlfriend, he purchased a kilo of cocaine for £25,000 cash from the original supplier. Charging £600 per ounce to 12 of his close friends, he assumed the kilo would last for three months, but he sold out in six weeks. Two months later he purchased five kilos for £125,000, and from then on purchased ten kilos per month. By selling larger quantities to his friends, he created a fresh dealing network as his friends were selling to their friends, work colleagues, and others within their social circle. As Greg, who became a user three months into his dealing, explained: 'It was a social network.'

Although Greg continued to work in his legitimate business, he was soon purchasing 50 kilos four times a year, which he sold for £600 per ounce. His supplier had now moved to Spain, where Greg would travel to pay for the drugs. Greg started with 12 customers, and six months later had 200 customers. He would reduce the price from £600 to £500 an ounce for customers buying a kilo or more, and reported up to a threefold increase in demand over the Christmas and New Year period.

The Specialist

Specialists are individuals who bring to the drug market particular skills and knowledge that have been acquired in a normative environment.

Tommy Atkins

Tommy Atkins is now in his early fifties, and after leaving the Army after over 20 years' service had spent six years trying various occupations before entering the drugs trade through a friend, who paid him £1000 to carry out a 'money-out' trip. After regularly delivering money to an address in France for six months, he felt sufficiently confident to branch out as an independent. His business was to organize the transport of drugs across the English Channel, warehouse to warehouse, and pay the driver. Atkins explained that the various human links in the drug importation chain had no need to be acquainted, and claimed to be willing to move anything except heroin and people. For him, people-trafficking was tantamount to slavery, and two close members of his family had become heroin addicts.

Atkins stressed that although in his business there was virtually no violence, gangs had emerged to target money-out trips, and occasionally the supplier's own men would try to rob the shipment before it was loaded. However, these incidents were exceptional, and most of the violence was committed at the bottom of the chain, with petty villains robbing small-time dealers. Atkins dealt with both large and small loads. A large load was 100 kilos of cocaine or 120 kilos of amphetamine, transported by vehicle, while small loads, five kilos of cocaine, were 'walked through' by foot passengers on ferries. The cost of moving one kilo of anything across the Channel was £2000. Atkins made £500 per kilo and the rest went to his personnel. As an example he would charge £200,000 to move 100 kilos of cocaine, and his personal profit would be £50,000. The value of the load would be around £4.5 million.

Atkins recruited ex-military personnel whenever possible, and spent considerable amounts of time talking to potential collaborators, making sure that they were genuine and that they really wanted to do this sort of work. Interestingly, he was also concerned to ascertain whether or not he liked them, as he had no wish to work with someone that he could not get on with. Atkins maintained a strict wage structure, and all of his personnel were paid £500 per week whether or not a job had been completed. Although from mid-December to February the trade was slow, 'everyone gets paid and for holidays'. Atkins expected to be arrested at some point in his career, and so made provision for that event, a provision that resulted in him raising the price of his service. He also applied this principle to his employees, and when two of his personnel were arrested he made provision for their wives so that they continued to be supported while their partners were in prison.

Atkins would receive a coded call from a wholesaler telling him to use a payphone for a detailed conversation, and a face-to-face meeting was arranged either in the UK or elsewhere. At that meeting details of the transaction were discussed, in particular the nature and size of the load and the timing of the deal. All money for expenses would be paid up-front. Atkins would develop a plan and contact and brief his personnel. This would take two days, after which he would agree the pick-up and final destination details with the wholesaler, and arrange and rendezvous with the driver and supplier to load the consignment, although making sure that he was not present during the actual loading.

Atkins operated a cell-type structure where only a very few people actually knew each other; there were few face-to-face meetings, with an understudy in another cell ready to take over in case of any emergency. Atkins would then cross the Channel to the UK, confirm the details regarding unloading, and wait for the load to come through on the ferry. He would know the ferry number in advance and the registration of the vehicle, the driver going to a prearranged location near to the final drop point. Atkins would meet the wholesaler and receive the transport fee before phoning the driver to tell him the final destination point. He would then meet the driver at another location to pay him off. Atkins felt no need to bribe officials as the loads always looked legitimate even when searched—the drugs were imported as part of a load often bound for wholesale fruit and vegetable markets, or hidden in consignments of frozen fish.

Bibliography

ACPO (1985) Final Report of the Working Party on Drugs Related Crime ('the Broome Report') (unpublished).

ACPO (2012) *UK National Problem Profile for the Commercial Cultivation of Cannabis* London: Association of Chief Police Officers.

Adler, PA (1985) *Wheeling and Dealing: An Ethnography of an Upper-Level Drug Dealing and Smuggling Community* New York: Columbia University Press.

Agamben, G (1998) *Homo Sacer. Sovereign Power and Bare Life* California: Stanford University Press.

Agozino, B (2000) 'Theorizing Otherness, the War on Drugs and Incarceration', *Theoretical Criminology* 4(3): 359–76.

Agozino, B, Bowling, B, Ward, E, and St Bernard, G (2009) 'Guns Crime and Social Order in the West Indies', *Criminology and Criminal Justice* 9(3): 287–305.

Albanese, J (1996) *Organised Crime in America* (3rd edn) Cincinnati: Anderson.

Albini, J (1971) *The American Mafia: Genesis of a Legend* New York: Appleton-Century-Crofts.

Aldis, A and Herd, G (2005) 'Managing Soft Security Threats: Current Progress and Future Prospects', in G Herd and A Aldis (eds), *Soft Security Threats and European Security* London: Routledge 169–76.

Aldridge, J and Medina, J (2008) *Youth Gangs in an English City* University of Manchester.

Aldridge, J, Ralphs, R, and Medina, J (2011) 'Collateral Damage', in Barry Goldson (ed), *Youth in Crisis?* London: Routledge 72–88.

Aldridge, J, Shute, J, Ralphs, R, and Medina, J (2009) 'Blame the Parents? Challenges for Parent-focused Programmes for Families of Gang-involved Young People', *Children and Society* 1: 11.

Alexander, C (2000) *The Asian Gang: Ethnicity, Identity, Masculinity* Oxford: Berg.

Alexander, C (2008) *(Re)Thinking 'Gangs'* London: Runnymede Trust.

Alexander, I, Millen, J, and Fallows, D (2003) *Global AIDS: Myths and Facts* Cambridge: South End Press.

Allison, E (2009) 'Obituary: Ronnie Easterbrook', *Guardian*, 20 May.

Allport, GW and Postman, LJ (1947) 'An Analysis of Rumour', *Public Opinion Quarterly* 10: 501–17.

Allum, F and Allum, P (2008) 'Revisiting Naples: Clientelism and Organized Crime', *Journal of Modern Italian Studies* 13(3): 340–65.

Anastasia, G (1991) *Blood and Honor* New York: Zebra Books.

Anderson, E (1999) *The Code of the Street: Decency, Violence and the Moral Life of the Inner City* New York: William W Norton & Co.

Anderson, G (2008) *Cityboy: Beer and Loathing in the Square Mile* London: Headline.

Anderson, M (1994) 'The United Kingdom and Organised Crime—The International Dimension', *European Journal of Crime, Criminal Law and Criminal Justice* 1(4): 292–308.

Andreas, P and Nadelmann, N (2006) *Policing the Globe—Criminalization and Crime Control in International Relations* Oxford: Oxford University Press.

Andreas, P and Wallman, J (2009) 'Illicit Markets and Violence: What is the Relationship?', *Crime Law and Social Change* 52(3): 225–9.

AOC Assessing (Organised Crime Consortium) (2005) *Provisional Situation Report on People Smuggling in the EU* Brussels: EEC.

Arlacchi, P (1986) *Mafia Business: The Mafia Ethic and the Spirit of Capitalism* London: Verso.

Arlacchi, P (1998) 'Some Observations on Illegal Markets', in V Ruggiero, N South, and I Taylor (eds), *The New European Criminology* London: Routledge 203–15.

Arlacchi, P and Calderone, A (1992) *Men of Dishonor. Inside the Sicilian Mafia. An Account of Antonio Calderone* New York: William Morrow & Co.

Armstrong, G, Gulianotti, R, Hales, G, and Hobbs, D (in progress) *A Sociology of Policing and Police-Community Relations at the London 2012 Olympics.*

Arnott, J (1999) *The Long Firm* Sceptre: London.

Augé, M (1992) *Non-places: Introduction to an Anthropology of Supermodernity* London: Verso.

Ayres, T and Treadwell, J (2012) 'Bars, Drugs and Football Thugs: Alcohol, Cocaine Use and Violence in the Night Time Economy among English Football Firms', *Criminology and Criminal Justice*, February 2012.

Back, L (2007) *The Art of Listening* Oxford: Berg Publishers.

Balcaen, A, Vander Beken, T, van Dijck, M, van Duyne, P, Hobbs, D, Hornsby, R, von Lampe, K, Markina, A, and Verpoest, K (2006) *Assessing Organised Crime by a New Common European Approach: Final Report* Brussels: European Commission.

Ball, J et al (1978) *Cops and Robbers* London: Andre Deutsch.

Ball, R and Curry, D (1995) 'The Logic of Definition in Criminology: Purposes and Methods for Defining "Gangs"', *Criminology* 33(2): 225–45.

Bancroft, A (2009) *Drugs, Intoxication and Society* Cambridge: Polity.

Barnes, T, Elias, R, and Walsh, P (2001) *Cocky: The Rise and Fall of Curtis Warren Britain's Biggest Drug Baron* London: Milo.

Barrett, D (2008) 'Organised Crime Chief Attacks "Disgraceful" Staff', *Independent*, 15 May.

Barrett D and Nowak M (2009) 'The United Nations and Drug Policy: Towards a Human Rights-based Approach', in A Constantinides and N Zaikos (eds), *The Diversity of International Law: Essays in Honour of Professor Kalliopi Koufa* The Hague: Martinus Nijhoff 449–77.

Bauer, RA and Gleicher, DB (1953) 'Word-of-mouth Communication in the Soviet Union', *Public Opinion Quarterly* 17: 297–310.

Bauman, Z (1989) *Legislators and Interpreters* Cambridge: Polity.

Bauman, Z (1991) *Modernity and Ambivalence* Ithaca, NY: Cornell University Press.

Bauman, Z (1992) *Intimations of Postmodernity* London: Routledge.

Bauman, Z (1993) *Modernity and Ambivalence* Cambridge: Polity.

Bauman, Z (1998) *Globalisation: The Human Consequences* Cambridge: Polity.

Bauman, Z (1999) *In Search of Politics* Cambridge: Polity.

Bauman, Z (2000) *Liquid Modernity* Cambridge: Polity.

Bauman, Z (2005) *Liquid Life* Cambridge: Polity.

Beames, T (1852) *The Rookeries of London: Past, Present, and Prospective* London: Thomas Bosworth.

Bean, JP (1981) *The Sheffield Gang Wars* Sheffield: D and D Publications.

Bean, P (2008) *Drugs and Crime* Cullompton: Willan.

Beck, U (1992) *Risk Society* London: Sage.

Beck, U and Sznaider, N (2006) 'Unpacking Cosmopolitanism for the Social Sciences: a Research Agenda', *British Journal of Sociology* 57: 1.

Beck-Gernsheim, E (1999) *Schwarze gibt es in allen Hautfarben* Frankfurt/ M: Suhrkamp.

Behan, T (1996) *The Camorra* London: Routledge.

Bell, D (1961) *The End of Ideology* London: Free Press/Collier-Macmillan.

Bell, D (1963) 'The Myth of the Cosa Nostra', *The New Leader* 46(26), 12–15 (23 December).

Bennett, W (1991) 'The Plea to Legalize Drugs is a Siren Call to Surrender', in M Lyman and G Potter (eds), *Drugs in Society* Cincinatti: Anderson.

Bennetto, J (1995) 'Caution: You Are About to Enter Gangland Britain', *Independent*, 21 August.

Benney, M (1936) *Low Company* (facsimile edn) Caliban Books: Sussex (1981).

Bermant, C (1975) *London's East End: Point of Arrival* London: Eyre Methuen.

Berridge, V (1978) 'East End Opium Dens and Narcotic Use in Britain', *The London Journal* 4(1): 2–28.

Berridge, V and Edwards, G (1981) *Opium and the People: Opiate Use in Nineteenth-century England* New York: St Martin's.

Best, J (1990) *Threatened Children, Rhetoric and Concern About Child-Victims* Chicago: University of Chicago Press.

Bewley-Taylor, D (1999) *The United States and International Drug Control, 1909–1997* London: Pinter.

Bhabha, HK (1996) 'Unsatisfied: Notes on Vernacular Cosmopolitanism', in L Garcia-Moreno and PC Pfeiffer (eds), *Text and Nation: Cross-Disciplinary Essays on Cultural and National Identities* Columbia, SC: Camden House 191–207.

Biggs, R (1981) *His Own Story* London: Sphere Books.

Bigo, D (1994) 'The European Internal Security Field: Stakes and Rivalries in a Newly Developing Area of Police Intervention', in M Anderson and den Boer (eds), *Policing Across National Boundaries* London: Pinter 161–73.

Bigo, D (2000) 'When Two Becomes One: Internal and External Securitizations in Europe', in M Kelstrup and MC Williams (eds), *International Relations Theory and the Politics of European Integration. Power, Security and Community* London-New York: Routledge 173–4.

Bland, L (1995) *Banishing the Beast: English Feminism and Sexual Morality 1885–1914* Penguin: Harmondsworth.

Blauner, P (1992) *Slow Motion Riot* New York: William Morrow.

Block, A (1983) *East Side-West Side: Organizing Crime in New York, 1930–1950* Newark, NJ: Transaction.

Block, A (1991) *Masters of Paradise* New Brunswick: Transaction.

Block, A (1994) *Space Time and Organised Crime* New Brunswick: Transaction.

Blok, A (1972) 'The Peasant and the Brigand: Social Banditry Reconsidered', *Comparative Studies in Society and History* 14(4): 494–503.

Blok, A (1974) *The Mafia of a Sicilian Village* New York: Harper.

Bonilla, F, Melendez, E, Morales, R, and Torres, Maria de los Angeles (eds) (1998) *Borderless Borders* Philadelphia: Temple University Press.

Booth, C (1889) *Life and Labour of the People. Vol 1* London: Williams and Norgate.

Booth, D (1969) 'Law Enforcement in Great Britain', *Crime & Delinquency* 15(3), 407–14.

Bourdieu, P (1977) *Outline of a Theory of Practice* Cambridge: Cambridge University Press.

Bourdieu, P (1997) *Pascalian Meditations* Stanford, CA: Stanford.

Bourdieu, P (2003) *Firing Back: Against the Tyranny of the Market* London: Verso.

Bourgois, P (1995) *In Search of Respect* Cambridge: Cambridge University Press.

Bourgois, P (2003) 'Crack and the Political Economy of Social Suffering', *Addiction Research and Theory* 11(1): 31–37.

Bovenkerk, F and Yesilgoz, Y (2007) *The Turkish Mafia* Liverpool: Milo.

Bovenkerk, F, Siegel, D, and Zaitch, D (2003) 'Organised Crime and Ethnic Reputation Manipulation', *Crime, Law & Social Change* 39: 23–38.

Bowcott, O and Oliver, T (2004) '£20m stolen in UK's biggest bank robbery—was it paramilitaries or common criminals?', *Guardian*, 22 December.

Bowling, B (1999) 'The Rise and Fall of New York Murder', *The British Journal of Criminology* 39(4): 531–54.

Bowling, B (2010) *Policing the Caribbean* Oxford: Oxford University Press.

Bowling, B and Ross, J (2006) 'The Serious Organised Crime Agency: Should We Be Afraid?', *Criminal Law Review*, December 2006, 1019–34.

Brotherton, D and Barrios, L (2004) *The Almighty Latin King and Queen Nation: Street Politics and the Transformation of a New York Gang* New York: Columbia University Press.

Broughton, F and Brewster, B (2009) *'Boy's Own', the Complete Fanzines 1986–92: Acid House Scrapes and Capers* Djhistory.com.

Brown, R (1991) *No Duty to Retreat: Violence and Values in American History and Society* New York: Oxford University Press.

Brustein, W (2003) *The Roots of Hate: Anti-Semitism in Europe Before the Holocaust* Cambridge: Cambridge University Press.

Brzezinski, M (2002) 'Re-engineering the drug business', *New York Times Magazine*, 24 June.

Bullock, K, Chowdury, R and Hollings, P (2009) *Public Concerns About Organised Crime*, Home Office Research Report 16. London: Home Office.

Burrell, I (1996) 'Leak reveals contempt for British "FBI"', *Independent*, 11 October.

Burrell, I and Levy, A (1995) 'Men Who Run Crime UK', *Sunday Times*, 15 January.

Burrows, R (ed) (1991) *Deciphering the Enterprise Culture* London: Routledge.

Bursik, RJ (1986) 'Ecological Stability and the Dynamics of Delinquency', in AJ Reiss and M Tonry, *Communities and Crime* Chicago: University of Chicago Press.

Butler, T, Hamnett, C, and Ramsden, M (2008) 'Inward and Upward: Marking out Social Class Change in London, 1981–2001', *Urban Studies* 45(1): 67–88.

Buzan, B, Wæver, O, and de Wilde, J (1998) *Security: A New Framework for Analysis* Boulder, CO: Lynne Rienner.

Cabinet Office (2008) *The National Security Strategy of the United Kingdom: Security in an Interdependent World* London: The Stationery Office.

Cabinet Office Strategy Unit (2009) *Extending our Reach: A Comprehensive Approach to Tackling Serious Organised Crime* Norwich: The Stationery Office.

Calvi, F (1993) *Het Europa Van de Peetvaders. De Mafia Verovert een Continent* Leuven: Kritak Balans.

Campbell, A and Muncer, S (1989) 'Them and Us: A Comparison of the Cultural Context of American Gangs and British Subcultures', *Deviant Behaviour* 10: 271–88.

Campbell, D (1994) *The Underworld* London: BBC Books.

Campbell, D (2007) 'Greed, Pure and Simple—Court Told of Gang's Motive for £53m Robbery', *Guardian*, 27 June.

Capeci, J and Mustain, G (1996) *Gotti: Rise and Fall* New York: Onyx

Carlen, P (1988) *Women, Crime and Poverty* Milton Keynes: Open University Press.

Carr, M (2006) 'You are Now Entering Eurabia', *Race and Class* 48: 1.

Castells, M (1996) *The Rise of the Network Society* Oxford: Blackwell.

Catanzaro, R (1992) *Men of Respect* New York: Free Press.

Catanzaro, R (1994) 'Violent Regulation: Organised Crime in the Italian South', *Social and Legal Studies* 3(2): 267–70.

Cater, F and Tullett, T (1991) *The Sharp End* London: HarperCollins.

Caulkins, J, Burnett, H, and Leslie, E (2009) 'How Illegal Drugs Enter an Island Country: Insights from Interviews with Incarcerated Smugglers', *Global Crime* 10: 1–2.

Cesarani, D (1993) 'An Alien Concept? The Continuity of Anti-Alienism in British Society before 1940', in D Cesarani and T Kushner (eds), *The Internment of Aliens in Twentieth Century Britain* London: Frank Cass 25–42.

Cesarani, D (1994) *The Jewish Chronicle and Anglo-Jewry 1841–1991* Cambridge: Cambridge University Press.

Chambliss, W (1972) *Box Man* New York: Harper and Row.

Chambliss, W (1978) *On the Take* Bloomington: Indiana University Press.

Chaney, D (1994) *The Cultural Turn* London: Routledge.

Chattoe, E and Hamill, H (2005) 'It's Not Who You Know—It's What You Know About People You Don't Know That Counts: Extending the Analysis of Crime Groups as Social Networks', *British Journal of Criminology* 45(6): 860–76.

Chinn, C (1991) *Better Betting With a Decent Feller* Hemel Hempstead: Harvester Wheatsheaf.

Chomsky, N (1998) 'The Drug War Industrial Complex. Noam Chomsky interviewed by John Veit', *High Times*, April.

Christie, N (1993) *Crime Control as an Industry. Gulags Western Style?* London: Routledge.

Clarke, G (1982) 'Defending Ski-jumpers: A Critique of Theories of Youth Sub-cultures', Special Paper 72, Centre for Contemporary Cultural Studies, University of Birmingham.

Clarkson, W (2004) *Moody* London: Mainstream Publishing.

Cloward, R and Ohlin, L (1960) *Delinquency and Opportunity: A Theory of Delinquent Gangs* New York: Free Press.

Cohen, AK (1955) *Delinquent Boys. The Culture of the Gang* New York: Free Press.

Cohen, D (2009) 'Heroin Wars, loan Sharks and executions: the Turkish gangs terrorising north London', *London Evening Standard*.

Cohen, P (1972) 'Subcultural Conflict and Working Class Community', *Working Papers in Cultural Studies*, No 2, Centre for Contemporary Studies, University of Birmingham.

Cohen, S (1973) *Folk Devils and Moral Panics* London: Paladin.

Cohen, S (1980) 'Introduction', in *Folk Devils and Moral Panics* (2nd edn) London: Martin Robertson.

Cohen, S (2006) 'Don't Look Back', *New Humanist* 121(4) July/August.

Cohen, S and Taylor, L (1972) *Psychological Survival* Harmondsworth: Penguin.

Coles, N (2001) 'It's Not What You Know, It's Who You Know that Counts: Analysing Serious Crime Groups as Social Networks', *British Journal of Criminology* 41: 580–94.

Collin, M (1997) *Altered State: The Story of Ecstasy Culture and Acid House* London: Serpent's Tail.

Condon, P (1995) 'Crime 2000', *Police Review*, 15/10/1995: 26–9.

Connor, M (2003) *The Soho Don* Edinburgh: Mainstream.

Control Risks (2007) *Tiger Kidnap—The Threat to the UK Banking Sector* London: Control Risks.

Cook, PJ (1987) 'Robbery Violence', *Journal of Criminal Law and Criminology* 78: 357–76.

Cooke, P (1988) 'Modernity, Postmodernity and the City', *Theory Culture and Society* 5(2)–(3): 472–92.

Cooke, P and Morgan, K (1993) 'The Network Paradigm', *Society and Space* 11: 543–64.

Coomber, R (2006) *Pusher Myths: Re-Situating the Drug Dealer* London: Free Association Books.

Cornish, W (1935) *Cornish of the Yard* London: Bodley Head.

Corrigan, P (1979) *Schooling the Bash Street Kids* London: Macmillan.

Courtwright, D (1996) *Violent Land: Single Men and Social Disorder from the Frontier to the Inner City* Cambridge, MA: Harvard University Press.

Cox, B, Shirley, J, and Short, M (1977) *The Fall of Scotland Yard* Harmondsworth: Penguin.

Craine, S (1997) 'The Black Magic Roundabout: Cyclical Transitions, Social Exclusion and Alternative Careers', in R MacDonald (ed), *Youth, the 'Underclass' and Social Exclusion* London: Routledge.

Cressey, D (1969) *Theft of the Nation: The Structure and Operations of Organized Crime in America* New York: Harper and Row.

Critchley, TA (1967) *A History of the Police in England and Wales: 1900–1966* London: Constable.

Cummings, J and Volkman, E (1992) *Mobster* London: Warner.

Curcione, N (1997) 'Suburban Snow Men: Facilitating Factors in the Careers of Middle Class Coke Dealers', *Deviant Behavior* 18: 233–53.

Currie, E (1985) *Confronting Crime: an American Challenge* New York: Pantheon.

Currie, E (1993) 'Towards a Policy on Drugs', *Dissent* (Winter): 65–71.

Cushion, J (2010) 'Engaging Eastern European communities to tackle problems in the night time economy', BME National Workshop, Peterborough, 6 July.

Damer, S (1974) 'Wine Alley: The Sociology of a Dreadful Enclosure', *Sociological Review* 22.

Darbyshire, N and Hilliard, B (1993) *The Flying Squad* London: Headline.

Davies, A (2008) *The Gangs of Manchester* Liverpool: Milo Books.

Davies, N (1998) *Dark Heart: The Shocking Truth About Hidden Britain* London: Vintage.

Davies, N (2011) 'Farewell youth clubs, hello street life—and gang warfare', *Guardian*, 29 July.

Davies, T (in progress) 'Homicide, Sub lethal Violence and the Illegal Economy in London: A Three Borough Study', PhD Dissertation, University of Essex.

Davis, M (1990) *City of Quartz* London: Verso.

De Polnay, P (1970) *Napoleon's Police* London: WH Allen.

Decker, S and van Winkle, B (1996) *Life in the Gang* Cambridge: Cambridge University Press.

Decorte, T, Potter, G, and Bouchard, M (2011) *World Wide Weed: Global Trends in Cannabis Cultivation and Its Control* London: Ashgate.

Dench, G (1991) *Crime in a Minority Situation: The Maltese Case* London: Institute of Community Studies.

Desmond, M (2006) 'Becoming a Firefighter', *Ethnography* 7: 387–421.

Dickson, J (1986) *Murder Without Conviction: Inside the World of the Krays* London: Sidgwick and Jackson.

Dikotter, F (2003) 'Patient Zero: China and the Myth of the Opium Plague', School of Oriental and African Studies (SOAS): <http://web.mac.com/dikotter>.

Diouf, M (2000) 'The Senegalese Murid Trade Diaspora and the Making of a Vernacular Cosmopolitanism', *Public Culture* 12(3): 679–702.

Divall, T (1929) *Scallywags and Scoundrels* London: Ernest Benn.

Doctorow, E (1989) *Billy Bathgate* London: Picador.

Donoghue, A and Short, M (1995) *The Krays' Lieutenant* London: Smith Gryphon.

Dorling, D, Rigby, J, Wheeler, B, Ballas, D, Thomas, B, Fahmy, E, and Gordon, D (2007) *Poverty and Wealth in Britain, 1968 to 2005* Bristol: Policy Press/JRF.

Dorn, N, Bucke, T, and Goulden, C (2003) 'Traffick, Transit and Transaction: A Conceptual Framework for Action against Drug Supply', *The Howard Journal* 2(4): 348–65.

Dorn, N, Levi, M, and King, L (2005) *Literature Review on Upper Level Drug Trafficking* London: HMSO.

Dorn, N, Murji, K, and South, N (1992) *Traffickers* London: Routledge.

Douglas, M (1966) *Purity and Danger* London: Routledge and Kegan Paul.

Douglas, M (1995) 'Forgotten Knowledge', in M Strathern (ed), *Shifting Contexts: Transformations in Anthropological Knowledge* London: Routledge.

Down, S (2006) *Narratives of Enterprise: Crafting Entrepreneurial Self Identity in a Small Firm* Cheltenham: Edward Elgar.

Downes, D (1966) *The Delinquent Solution: A Study in Subcultural Theory* London: Routledge and Kegan Paul.

Dumenil, G and Levy, D (2004) *Capital Resurgent: Roots of the Neoliberal Revolution* Boston: Harvard University Press.

Dunlap, E, Johnson, B, and Manwar, A (1994) 'A Successful Female Crack Dealer: Case Study of a Deviant Career', *Deviant Behaviour* 15: 1–25.

Dunnighan, C and Hobbs, D (1996) *A Report on the NCIS Pilot Organised Crime Notification Survey* London: Home Office (unpublished).

Durk, A and Silverman, I (1976) *The Pleasant Avenue Connection* New York: Harper & Row.

Earle, P (2004) *Pirate Wars* London: Methuen.

Edwards, A and Gill, P (eds) (2003) *Transnational Organised Crime: Perspectives on Global Security* London: Routledge.

Edwards, A and Levi, M (2008) 'Researching the Organisation of Serious Crimes', *Criminology and Criminal Justice* 8(4): 363–88.

Edwards-Jones, I (1994) 'The Russians are Coming', *Evening Standard*, 15 April, 8–10.

Ehrenreich, B (1990) *The Worst Years of Our Lives* New York: Pantheon.

Elvins, M (2003) 'Europe's Response to Transnational Organised Crime', in A Edwards and P Gill (eds), *Transnational Organised Crime: Perspectives on Global Security* London: Routledge.

Emsley, C (1996) *The English Police: A Political and Social History* Harlow: Harvester Wheatsheaf.

Emsley, C (2005) *Hard Men: Violence in England since 1750* London: Hambledon.

Engels, F (1987) *The Condition of the Working Class in England* Harmondsworth: Penguin Classics.

Fabian, R (1954) *Fabian of the Yard: An Intimate Record* (5th edn) London: Naldrett Press.

Fagan, J (1994) 'Women and Drugs Revisited: Female Participation in the Cocaine Economy', *The Journal of Drug Issues* 24(2): 179–225.

Fagan, J (1990) 'Social Processes of Drug Use and Delinquency among Gang and Non-Gang Youths', in C Ronald Huff (ed), *Gangs in America* Newbury Park CA: Sage Publications 183–222.

Fagan, J and Wilkinson, D (1998) 'Guns, Youth Violence, and Social Identity in Inner Cities', in M Tonry and MH Moore (eds), *Youth Violence. Crime and Justice: A Review of Research* Chicago: University of Chicago Press.

Falcone, G (1993) *Men of Honour* London: Warner.

Farley, M, Bindel, J, and Golding, JM (2009) *Men Who Buy Sex: Who They Buy and What They Know* London: Eaves.

Feheney, JM (1983) 'Delinquency among Irish Catholic Children in Victorian London', *Irish Historical Studies* 23(92): 319–29.

Feldman, D (2003) 'Was the Nineteenth Century a Golden Age for Immigrants?', in A Fahrmeir et al (eds), *Migration Control in the North Atlantic World: The Evolution of State Practices in Europe and the United States from the French Revolution to the Inter-War Period* Oxford: Berghahn Books 167–77.

Fellstrom, C (2010) *Hoods: The Gangs of Nottingham* Liverpool: Milo Books.

Ferguson, H (2006) *Lima 3: Taking on the Heroin Traffickers* London: Bloomsbury.

Ferrell, J (1999) 'Cultural Criminology', *Annual Review of Sociology* 25: 395–418.

Ferrell, J, Hayward, K, and Young, J (2008) *Cultural Criminology: An Invitation* London: Sage.

Fieldhouse, EA (1999) 'Ethnic Minority Unemployment and Spatial Mismatch: The Case of London', *Journal of Urban Studies* 36: 1569–96.

Fields, I (2004) 'Family Values and Feudal Codes: The Social Politics of America's Twenty-First Century Gangsters', *The Journal of Popular Culture* 37(4): 611–33.

Fijnaut, C (1989) *Researching Organized Crime. Policing Organized Crime and Crime Prevention* Bristol: Bristol and Bath Centre for Criminal Justice 75–85.

Fijnaut, C and Paoli, L (2004) 'Sources and Literature', in C Fijnaut and L Paoli, *Organised Crime in Europe* Netherlands: Springer 239–63.

Findlay, M (2008) *Governing through Globalised Crime* Cullompton: Willan.

Finmore, HL (1951) *Immoral Earnings* London: MH Publications.

Fishman, R (1987) *Bourgoise Utopias; The Rise and Fall of Suburbia* New York: Basic Books.

Fishman, W (1975) *East End Jewish Radicals 1875–1914* London: Duckworth.

Fishman, W (1979) *The Streets of East London* London: Duckworth.

Fishman, W (1988) *East End 1888: Life in a London Borough Among the Labouring Poor.* London: Duckworth (2nd edn, 2001: London: Five Leaves).

Fitch, HT (1933) *Traitors Within: The Adventures of Detective Inspector Herbert T. Fitch* London: Hurst & Blackett.

Fordham, P (1965) *The Robbers' Tale* London: Hodder and Stoughton.

Foreman, F (1996) *Respect* London: Century.

Fraser, A (2011) 'Growing through Gangs: Young People, Identity and Social Change in Glasgow', PhD Thesis, University of Glasgow.

Fraser, F (1994) *Mad Frank* London: Little Brown.

Fraser, F (1998) *Mad Frank and Friends* London: Little Brown.

Friman, H (1991) 'The United States, Japan, and the International Drug Trade: Troubled Partnership', *Asian Surv* 31(9): 875–90.

Gachevska, K (2009) 'Building the New Europe: Soft Security and Organised Crime in EU Enlargement', unpublished PhD Thesis, University of Wolverhampton.

Gainer, B (1972) *The Alien Invasion: The Origins of the Aliens Act of 1905* London: Heinemann.

Gambetta, D (1988) 'Fragments of an Economic Theory of the Mafia', *Archives Europeennes de Sociologie* 29: 127–45.

Gambetta, D (1993) *The Sicilian Mafia: The Business of Private Protection* Cambridge, MA: Harvard University Press.

Gambetta, D (2009) *Codes of the Underworld: How Criminals Communicate* New Jersey: Princeton University Press.

Gambetta, D and Reuter, P (1995) 'Conspiracy among the Many: The Mafia in Legitimate Industries', in G Fiorentini and S Peltzman (eds), *The Economics of Organized Crime* Cambridge: Cambridge University Press 116–36.

Garbett, C (1931) *In the Heart of South London* London: Longman.

Gardner, D (1987) 'Black Mafia in Gang War', *Daily Mail*, 28 December.

Garland, D (1996) 'The Limits of the Sovereign State: Strategies of Crime Control in Contemporary Society', *British Journal of Criminology* 36(4): 445–7.

Garland, D (2001) *The Culture of Control* Oxford: Oxford University Press.

Gavan, P (1985) 'Drug threat is worst we face', *London Standard*, 23 May.

Gavron, K, Dench, G, and Young, M (2006) *The New East End: Kinship, Race and Conflict* London: Profile.

Gibbens, T and Ahrenfeldt, R (eds) (1966) *Cultural Factors in Delinquency* London: Tavistock.

Giddens, A (1979) *Central Problems in Social Theory* London: Macmillan.

Giddens, A (1990) *The Consequences of Modernity* Cambridge: Polity.

Giddens, A (1991) *Modernity and Self-Identity* Cambridge: Polity.

Gill, M (2000) *Commercial Robbery: Offenders' Perspectives on Security and Crime Prevention* London: Blackstone Press.

Gill, M (2001) 'The Craft of Robbers of Cash-in-transit Vans: Crime Facilitators and the Entrepreneurial Approach', *International Journal of the Sociology of Law* 29(3): 277–91.

Gill, O (1977) *Luke Street: Housing Policy, Conflict and the Creation of the Delinquent Area* London: Macmillan.

Gilman, M (1994) 'Football and Drugs: Two Cultures Clash', *The International Journal of Drug Policy* 5(1): 40–51.

Gilman, N, Weber, S, and Goldhammer, J (2011) *Deviant Globalization* London: Continuum International Publishing Group.

Gilroy, P (1987) *There Ain't No Black in the Union Jack* London: Hutchinson.

Gilroy, P (2004) *After Empire: Multiculture or Postcolonial Melancholia* London: Routledge.

Glenny, M (2008) *McMafia: Crime Without Frontiers* London: Bodley Head.

Godson, R and Olson, W (1993) *International Organised Crime: Emerging Threat to U.S. Security* Washington: National Strategy Information Center.

Goffman, E (1952) 'On Cooling the Mark Out: Some Aspects of Adaptation to Failure', *Psychiatry* 15: 451–63.

Goffman, E (1959) *The Presentation of Self in Everyday Life* New York: Doubleday Anchor.

Gold, M and Levi, M (1994) *Money Laundering in the UK. An Appraisal of Suspicion-Based Reporting* London: Police Foundation.

Goldson, B (ed) (2011) *Youth in Crisis?: 'Gangs', Territoriality and Violence* London: Routledge.

Goldstein, PJ (1985) 'The Drugs/violence Nexus: A Tripartite Conceptual Framework', *Journal of Drug Issues* 15: 493–506.

Goode, E and Ben-Yehuda, N (1994) *Moral Panics: The Social Construction of Deviance* Cambridge, MA: Blackwell Publishers.

Gottfredson, MR and Hirschi, T (1990) *A General Theory of Crime* Stanford: Stanford University Press.

Gottschalk, E (2009) *Public Perception on Organised Crime—Results from an Opinion Poll* London: Home Office/Mori; <http://webarchive.nationalarchives.gov.uk/20100413151441/http://www.crimereduction.homeoffice.gov.uk/organisedcrime/organisedcrime017.pdf>.

Green, P (1996) *Drug Couriers: A New Perspective* London: Howard League Green.

Green, P, Mills, C, and Read, T (1994) 'The Characteristics and Sentences of Illegal Drug Importers', *The British Journal of Criminology* 34(4): 479–86.

Greene, G (1943) *Brighton Rock* Harmondsworth: Penguin.

Greeno, E (1960) *War on the Underworld* London: John Long.

Greenslade, R (2008) 'People Power', *British Journalism Review* 19(1): 15–21.

Greenwood, J (1883) 'An Opium Smoke in Tiger Bay', in *In Strange Company: Being the Experiences of a Roving Correspondent* (2nd edn) London: Vizetelly & Co.

Gregory, F (2003) 'Classify, Report and Measure: the UK Organised Crime Notification Scheme', in A Edwards and P Gill (eds), *Transnational Organised Crime* London: Routledge 78–96.

Grieveson, L (2005) 'Gangsters and Governance in the Silent Era', in L Grieveson et al (eds), *Mob Culture: Hidden Histories of American Gangster Film* Oxford: Berg.

Gunst, L (1995) *Born Fi' Dead: A Journey Through the Jamaican Posse Underworld* New York: Holst

Gunter, A (2010) *Growing Up Bad? Road Culture, Badness and Black Youth Transitions in an East London Neighbourhood* London: Tufnell Press.

Hacking, I (1999) *The Social Construction of What?* Cambridge, MA: Harvard University Press.

Hadfield, P (2006) *Bar Wars* Oxford: Oxford University Press.

Hagan, F (1983) 'The Organized Crime Continuum: A Further Specification of a New Conceptual Model', *Criminal Justice Review* 8: 52–7.

Hagedorn, J (1988) *People and folks: Gangs, crime and the underclass in a rustbelt city* Chicago: Lake View.

Hagedorn, J (2007) *Gangs in the Global City: Alternatives to Traditional Criminology* Chicago: University of Illinois Press.

Hagedorn, JM (1998) 'Gang Violence in the Post-industrial Era', in M Tonry and M Moore (eds), *Youth Violence*, Crime and Justice Series, Vol 24 Chicago: University of Chicago.

Hales, G, Lewis, C, and Silverstone, D (2006) *Gun Crime: The Market in and Use of Illegal Firearms*. Home Office Research Study 298, London: Home Office.

Hall, PG (1962) *The Industries of London since 1861* London: Hutchinson.

Hall, S (1997) 'Visceral Cultures and Criminal Practices', *Theoretical Criminology* 1(4): 453–78.

Hall, S (2012) *Theorizing Crime and Deviance: A New Perspective* London: Sage.

Hall, S and Jefferson, T (eds) (1976) *Resistance through Rituals* London: Hutchinson.

Hall, S, Critcher, S, Jefferson, T, and Clarke, J (1978) *Policing the Crisis: Mugging, the State, and Law and Order* London: MacMillan.

Hall, S, Winlow, S, and Ancrum, C (2008) *Criminal Identities and Contemporary Culture* Cullompton: Willan.

Hall, T (2012) 'The Geography of Transnational Organised Crime: Spaces, Networks and Flows', in F Allum and S Gilmour (eds), *The Handbook of Transnational Organized Crime* London: Routledge 173–85.

Haller, M (1990) 'Illegal Enterprise: A Theoretical and Historical Interpretation', *Criminology* 28(2): 207–35.

Hallsworth, S (2005) *Street Crime* Cullompton: Willan.

Hallsworth, S (2011) 'Academic seeks new understanding of rioters', *Guardian*, 20 November.

Hallsworth, S and Silverstone, D (2009) '"That's Life Innit" A British Perspective on Guns, Crime and Social Order', *Criminology and Criminal Justice* 9(3): 359–77.

Hallsworth, S and Young, T (2008) 'Gang Talk and Gang Talkers: A Critique', *Crime Media Culture* 4(2): 175–95.

Halstead, B (1998) 'The Use of Models in the Analysis of Organised Crime and Development of Policy', *Transnational Organized Crime* 4(1): 1–24.

Hamid, A (1990) 'The Political Economy of Crack Related Violence', *Contemporary Drug Problems*, 17: 31–78.

Hamilton-Smith, N and Mackenzie, S (2010) 'The Geometry of Shadows: A Critical Review of Organised Crime Risk Assessments', *Policing and Society*, 20(3): 257–79.

Hancock, L (2006) 'Urban Regeneration, Young People, Crime and Criminalisation', in B Goldson and J Muncie (eds), *Youth Crime and Justice* London: Sage.

Hanes, WT and Sanello, F (2003) *Opium Wars: The Addiction of One Empire and the Corruption of Another* London: Robson Books.

Hardie-Bick, J (2011) 'Sky-diving and the Metaphorical Edge', in D Hobbs, *Ethnography in Context Vol 3, Leisure. Sage Benchmarks in Social Research Methods* London: Sage 183–204.

Harfield, C (2006) 'Soca: A Paradigm Shift in British Policing', *British Journal of Criminology* 46: 743–61.

Harfield, C (2008) 'Paradigms, Pathologies, and Practicalities—Policing Organized Crime in England and Wales', *Policing* 2(1): 63–73.

Hart, ET (1993) *Britain's Godfather* London: True Crime Library.

Harvey, D (2005) *A Brief History of Neoliberalism* New York: Oxford University Press.

Harvey, D (2009) *Cosmopolitanism and the Geographies of Freedom* New York: Columbia University Press.

Hawdon, J (2001) 'The Role of Presidential Rhetoric in the Creation of a Moral Panic: Reagan, Bush and the War on Drugs', *Deviant Behaviour*, 22: 419–45.

Hayter, A (1968) *Opium and the Romantic Imagination* Berkeley: University of California Press.

Hayward, K and Hobbs, D (2007) 'Beyond the Binge in "Booze Britain": Market-led Liminalization and the Spectacle of Binge Drinking', *The British Journal of Sociology* 58(3): 437–56.

Hebdige, D (1979) *Subculture: The Meaning of Style* London: Methuen.

Heelas, P and Morris, P (eds) (1992) *The Values of the Enterprise Culture* London: Routledge.

Hellawell, K (2002) *The Outsider: The Autobiography of One of Britain's Most Controversial Policemen* London: Harper Collins.

Hencke, D (1985) 'MPs urge harsher heroin penalties', *Guardian*, 24 May.

Henriques, URQ (1968) 'The Jewish Emancipation Problem in Nineteenth Century Britain', *Past and Present* 40: 126–46.

Henry-Lee, A (2005) 'The Nature of Poverty in the Garrison Constituencies in Jamaica', *Environment and Urbanization* 17(2) October: 83–99.

Her Majesty's Inspectorate of Constabulary (2009) *Getting Organised: A Thematic Report on the Police Service's Response to Serious and Organised Crime* London: HMIC.

Hickman, M (1995) *Religion, Class and Identity: The State, the Catholic Church and the Education of the Irish in Britain* London, Aldershot: Avebury.

Hill, B (1955) *Boss of Britain's Underworld* London: Naldrett Press.

Hill, C (1969) *Reformation to Industrial Revolution* Harmondsworth: Pelican.

Hill, S (1976) *The Dockers* London: Heinemann.

HM Revenue and Customs (2008) *Tackling Tobacco Smuggling Together: An Integrated Strategy for HM Revenue & Customs and the UK Border Agency* The Stationery Office Limited.

Hobbs, D (1988) *Doing the Business: Entrepreneurship, Detectives and the Working Class in the East End of London* Oxford: Clarendon Press.

Hobbs, D (1991) 'A Piece of Business: The Moral Economy of Detective Work in East London', *The British Journal of Sociology* 42(4): 597–608.

Hobbs, D (1992) 'Enterprise Culture: A Review', *Journal of Work and Employment* 6(2): 303–8.

Hobbs, D (1994) 'Buster Edwards (Obituary)', *Independent*, 1 December.

Hobbs, D (1995) *Bad Business: Professional Criminals in Modern Britain* Oxford: Oxford University Press.

Hobbs, D (1995) 'Obituary: Ron Kray', *Independent*, 18 March.

Hobbs, D (1996) 'Obituary: Gerald McArthur', *Independent*, 17 September.

Hobbs, D (1997) 'Professional Crime: Change, Continuity and the Enduring Myth of the Underworld', *Sociology* 31(1), February: 57–72.

Hobbs, D (1998) 'Going Down the Glocal: The Local Context of Organised Crime', *The Howard Journal*, Special Issue on Organised Crime 37(4): 407–22.

Hobbs, D (2000a) 'Obituary: Reg Kray', *Independent*, 2 October.

Hobbs, D (2000b) 'Obituary: Charlie Kray', *Independent*, 6 April.

Hobbs, D (2001) 'The Firm: Organizational Logic and Criminal Culture on a Shifting Terrain', *British Journal of Criminology* 41(4): 549–60.

Hobbs, D (2004) 'Organised Crime in the UK', in C Fijnaut and L Paoli (eds), *Organised Crime in Europe* Netherlands: Springer 413–34.

Hobbs, D (2006) 'East Ending: Dissociation, De-industrialisation and David Downes', in T Newburn and P Rock (eds), *The Politics of Crime Control* Oxford: Oxford University Press.

Hobbs, D (2008) 'Obituary: Bertie Smalls', *Independent*, 1 March.

Hobbs, D (2012) 'It was Never about the Money: Market Society, Organised Crime and UK Criminology', in S Hall and S Winlow (eds), *New Directions in Criminological Theory* London: Routledge.

Hobbs, D and Antonopoulos, GA (2012) 'How to Research Organized Crime', in L Paoli (ed), *Oxford Handbook of Organized Crime* New York: Oxford University Press.

Hobbs, D and Antonopoulos, GA (forthcoming) *Endemic to the Species: Ordering the 'Other' via Organised Crime* Global Crime.

Hobbs, D and Dunnighan, C (1997) *Serious Crime Networks*, Final Report to the ESRC.

Hobbs, D and Dunnighan, C (1998a) 'Organised Crime and the Organisation of Police Intelligence', in P Carlen and R Morgan (eds), *Crime Unlimited* London: Routledge.

Hobbs, D and Dunnighan, C (1998b) 'Glocal Organised Crime: Context and Pretext', in V Ruggiero, N South, and I Taylor (eds), *The New European Criminology* London: Routledge 289–303.

Hobbs, D and Hobbs, S (2012) 'A Bog of Conspiracy: The Institutional Evolution of Organised Crime in the UK', in F Allum and S Gilmour (eds), *The Handbook of Transnational Organized Crime* London: Routledge.

Hobbs, D and Jackson, T (in progress) *A Good Earner*.

Hobbs, D, Hadfield, P, Lister, S, and Winlow, S (2003) *Bouncers: Violence, Governance and the Night time Economy* Oxford: Oxford University Press.

Hobsbawm, E (1972) *Bandits* Harmondsworth: Pelican.

Hoggart, R (1957) *The Uses of Literacy* London: Chatto and Windus.

Hohimer, F (1981) *Violent Streets* London: Star.

Hollington, K (2004) *Diamond Geezers—The Inside Story of the Crime of the Millennium* London: Michael O'Mara Books Ltd.

Home Affairs Committee (1994) *Organised Crime: Minutes and Memoranda* London: Home Office.

Home Office (2004) *One Step Ahead: A 21st Century Strategy to Defeat Organised Crime*; <http://www.homeoffice.gov.uk/documents/cons-organised-crime-300704/>.

Home Office (2008) *Saving Lives. Reducing Harm. Protecting the Public: An action plan for tackling violence* London: Home Office.

Home Office (2010) *Policing in the 21st Century: Reconnecting Police and the People* London: Home Office.

Home Office (2011a) *Tackling Organised Crime Through a Partnership Approach at the Local Level: a process evaluation*, Home Office Research Report 56.

Home Office, (2011b) *Local to Global: Reducing the Risk from Organised Crime* <http://www.homeoffice.gov.uk/publications/crime/organised-crime-strategy?view=Binary>.

Hopkins, M and Tilley, N (2007) *Exploring the Links between Homicide and Organised Crime*, Home Office Research Report 54.

Horne, R and Hall, S (1995) 'Anelpis: A Preliminary Expedition into a World without Hope or Potential', *Parallex* 1: 81–92.

Hornsby, R and Hobbs, D (2007) 'A Zone of Ambiguity: The Political Economy of Cigarette Bootlegging', *British Journal of Criminology* 47(4): 551–71.

Horowitz, L and Liebowitz, M (1968) 'Social Deviance and Political Marginality', *Social Problems* 15: 280–96.

Houlbrook, M. (2007) '"The Man with the Powder Puff" in Interwar London', *Historical Journal* 50: 145–71.

Howard, M (1996) Speech as Home Secretary to ACPO summer Conference. London: Conservative Central Office.

Howell, J and Gleason, D (2001) 'Youth Gang Drug Trafficking', in J Miller, CL Maxson, and MW Klein, *The Modern Gang Reader* (2nd edn) Los Angeles: Roxbury.

Huggins, M (2003) *Horseracing and the British 1919–39* Manchester: Manchester University Press.

Humphreys, C (1946) *Criminal Days: Recollections and Reflections* London: Hodder and Stoughton.

Ianni, F (1971) 'Formal and Social Organisation in an Organised Crime "Family": A Case Study', *University of Florida Law Review* 24: 31–41.

Ianni, F (1974) *Black Mafia: Ethnic Succession in Organized Crime* New York: Simon and Schuster.

Ianni, F and Ianni, ER (1972) *A Family Business: Kinship and Social Control in Organized Crime* New York: Russel Sage.

Inciardi, J (1976) 'The Pickpocket and his Victim', *Victimology* (1) Fall: 141–9.

Irwin, J (1970) *The Felon* Englewood Cliffs, NJ: Prentice Hall.

Jacobs, JB (1999) *Gotham Unbound* New York: New York University Press.

Jacobs, JB, Panarell C, and Worthington, J (1996) *Busting the Mob: United States v. Cosa Nostra* New York: New York University Press.

Jamieson, A (2001) 'Transnational Organized Crime: A European Perspective', *Studies in Conflict & Terrorism* 24: 377–87.

Janson, H (1959) *Jack Spot: Man of a Thousand Cuts* London: Alexander Morning.

Jenks, C and Lorentzen (1997) 'The Kray Fascination', *Theory Culture and Society* 14(3): 87–107.

Jennings, A, Lashmar, P, and Simson, V (1991) *Scotland Yard's Cocaine Connection* London: Arrow.

Johnson, BD, Hamid, A, and Sanabria, H (1992) 'Emerging Models of Crack Distribution', in T Mieczkowski (ed), *Drugs, Crime and Social Policy* Boston: Allyn and Bacon.

Johnson, C (1724) *A General History of the Robberies and Murders of the Most Notorious Pyrates* (copy available on the website of Eastern North Carolina Digital Library).

Johnson, G (2005) *Powder Wars: The Supergrass who Brought Down Britain's Biggest Drug Dealers* London: Mainstream.

Johnson, G (2007) *Druglord: Guns, Powder and Pay-Offs* London: Mainstream.

Johnston, L, MacDonald, R, Mason, P, Ridley, L, and Webster, C (2000) *Snakes & Ladders: Young People, Transitions and Social Exclusion* Bristol: Policy Press.

Jones, C (2010) 'The Right to Buy', in P Malpass and R Rowlands (eds), *Housing, Markets and Policy* London: Routledge 59–75.

Jones, T and Newburn, T (2002) 'Policy Convergence and Crime Control in the USA and the UK: Streams of Influence and Levels of Impact', *Criminology and Criminal Justice* 2(2): 173–203.

Joossens, L (1999) *Smuggling and Cross-border Shopping of Tobacco Products in the European Union* London: Health Education Authority.

Joossens, L and Raw, M (1998) 'Cigarette Smuggling in Europe: Who Really Benefits?', *Tobacco Control* 7(1): 66–71.

Joossens, L and Raw, M (2003) 'Turning off the Tap: The Real Solution to Cigarette Smuggling', *The International Journal of Tuberculosis and Lung Disease* 7(3): 214–29.

Junninen, M (2006) *Adventurers and Risk-Takers: Finish Professional Criminals and their Organisations in 1990's Cross-border Criminality* Helinski: HEUNI.

Kadish, S (1992) *Bolsheviks and British Jews: The Anglo-Jewish Community, Britain and the Russian Revolution* London: Frank Cass.

Katz, J (1975) 'Essences as Moral Identities: On Verifiability and Responsibility in Imputations of Deviance and Charisma', *American Journal of Sociology* 80 (May): 1369–90.

Katz, J (1988) *Seductions of Crime* New York: Basic Books.

Katz, J and Jackson-Jacobs, C (2004) 'The Criminologists Gang', in C Sumner (ed), *The Blackwell Companion to Criminology* Oxford: Blackwell: 91–124.

Kelland, G (1986) *Crime in London* London: Bodley Head.

Kelly, L (2005) 'Inside Outsiders: Mainstreaming Gender into Human Rights…of the Human Trafficking Chain', *British Journal of Criminology* 49(2): 184–201.

Kelly, L and Regan, L (2000) *Stopping Traffic: Exploring the Extent of, and Responses to, Trafficking in Women for Sexual Exploitation in the UK* Police Research Series.

Kempe C et al (eds) (1980) *The Abused Child in the Family and in the Community: Selected Papers from the Second International Conference on Child Abuse and Neglect* Oxford: Pergamon.

Keohane, R (1984) *After Hegemony: Cooperation and Discord in the World Political Economy* Princeton: Princeton University Press.

Kershen, AJ (1995) *Uniting the Tailors: Trade Unionism Amongst the Tailoring Workers of London* London: Frank Cass.

King, AD (1991) 'Introduction', in AD King (ed), *Culture Globalisation and the World System* London: Macmillan.

Kirby, T (1993) 'Russian gangs pose threat to British cities', *Independent*, 25 May.

Kitsuse, J and Cicourel, A (1963) 'A Note on the Uses of Official Statistics', *Social Problems* 11(2): 131–9.

Kleemans, ER (2007) 'Organized Crime, Transit Crime, and Racketeering', in M Tonry and CJC Bijleveld (eds), *Crime and Justice in the Netherlands* Chicago, University of Chicago Press 163–215.

Klein, M (1995) *The American Street Gang: Its nature, Prevalence, and Control* New York/Oxford: Oxford University Press.

Klein, M (2005) 'The Value of Comparisons in Street Gang Research', *Journal of Contemporary Criminal Justice* 21(2): 135–52.

Knepper, P (2007) 'British Jews and the Racialisation of Crime in the Age of Empire', *British Journal of Criminology* 47(1): 61–79.

Knepper, P (2008) 'The Other Invisible Hand: Jews and Anarchists in London before the First World War', *Jewish History* 22(3): 295–315.

Knepper, P (2009) *The Invention of International Crime: A Global Issue in the Making, 1881–1914* Basingstoke: Palgrave Macmillan.

Knepper, P and Azzopardi, J (2011) 'International Crime in the Interwar Period: A View from the Edge', *Crime Law Soc Change* 56: 407–19.

Knight, R (1990) *Black Knight* London: Century.

Knight, R, Knight, J, and Wilton, P (2003) *Gotcha: The Untold Story of Britain's Biggest Cash Robbery* London: Pan.

Kohn, M (1992) *Dope Girls. The Birth of the British Drug Underground* London: Lawrence and Wishart.

Korsell, L (2011) 'Local Organised Crime. The Swedish Example', in T Spapens, M Groenhuijsen, and T Kooijmans (eds), *Universalis. Liber Amicorum Cyrille Fijnaut* Intersentia: Antwerp.

Kray, C and Sykes, J (1977) *Me and My Brothers* London: Everest.

Kray, R and Dineage, F (1994) *My Story* London: Pan.

Kray, R and Kray, R (1988) *Our Story* London: Pan.

Kuhn, G (2010) *Life under the Jolly Roger* Oakland: CA: PM Press.

L'Hoiry, X (2012) 'Policing "Organised Crime"—Blurring the Image', PhD Thesis, University of Teeside.

Labrousse, A and Wallon, A (eds) (1993) *La Planete des Drogues* Paris: Seuil.

Lacey, R (1991) *Little Man* New York: Little Brown.

Lambrianou, T (1992) *Inside the Firm* London: Pan.

Landesco, J (1968), (1929) *Organised Crime in Chicago* (2nd edn) Chicago: University of Chicago Press.

Langford, B (2005) *Film genre: Hollywood and beyond* Edinburgh: Edinburgh University Press Ltd.

Larke, GS (2003) 'Organised Crime: Mafia Myths in Film and Television', in P Mason (ed), *Criminal Visions* Cullompton: Willan 116–32.

Lasch, C (1979) *The Culture of Narcissism: American Life in an Age of Diminishing Expectations* New York: Norton.

Lash, S and Urry, J (1987) *The End of Organised Capitalism* Cambridge: Polity Press.

Lash, S and Urry, J (1994) *Economies of Signs and Space* London: Sage.

Lashmar, P (2008) 'Britain's FBI "is a dismal failure"', *Independent on Sunday,* 18 May.

Latour, B (1986) '"Visualization and Cognition: Thinking with Eyes and Hands"', in H Kukli and E Long, *Knowledge and Society: Studies in the Sociology of Culture Past and Present,* Vol 6 Greenwich, CT: JAI Press 1–40.

Latour, B (1993) *We Have Never Been Modern* London: Harvester Wheatsheaf.

Lea, J (1999) 'Social Crime Revisited', *Theoretical Criminology* 3(3): 307–25.

Lea, J (2002) *Crime and Modernity* London: Sage.

Leach, C (2003) *Muscle* London: Blake.

Lebzelter, G (1981) 'Anti-Semitism—A Focal Point for the British Radical Right', in P Kennedy and A Nicholls (eds), *Nationalist and Racialist Movements in Britain and Germany before 1914* London: Macmillan.

Leeson, B (1934) *Lost London* London: Stanley Paul and Co.

Letkemann, P (1973) *Crime as Work* New Jersey: Prentice Hall.

Levi, M (1981) *The Phantom Capitalists* Aldershot: Gower.

Levi, M (2002) 'The Organisation of Serious Crime', in Maguire, Morgan, and Reiner (eds), *The Oxford Handbook of Criminology* Oxford: Oxford University Press.

Levi, M (2004) 'The Making of the United Kingdom Organised Crime Control Policies', in C Fijnaut and L Paoli (eds), *Organised Crime in Europe* Netherlands: Springer 823–52.

Levi, M (2010) 'Combating the Financing of Terrorism: A History and Assessment of the Control of "Threat Finance"', *British Journal of Criminology* Special Issue, *Terrorism: Criminological Perspectives* 50(4): 650–69.

Levi, M and Naylor, T (2000) *Organised Crime, the Organisation of Crime and the Organisation of Business*, Essay for the Crime Foresight Panel, London: Department of Trade and Industry.

Levine, HG (2003) 'Global Drug Prohibition: Its Uses and Crises', *Int J Drug Pol* 14: 145–53.

Liddick, DR (2007) 'Canada Dry Wiseguys at Apalachin: Politics and the Social Construction of a Crime Problem', *Trends in Organized Crime*, 10(4): 16–38.

Linebaugh, P (1993) *The London Hanged* London: Penguin.

Lipietz, A (1996) 'The Next Transformation', in M Cangiani (ed), *The Milano Papers: Essays in Societal Alternatives* Montreal: Black Rose Books 116–17.

Lipman, VD (1990) *A History of the Jews in Britain since 1858* Leicester: Leicester University Press.

Lippmann, W (1967) (1931) 'The Underworld as Servant', in G Tyler (ed), *Organized Crime in America* Detroit: University of Michigan Press 58–69.

Lloyd, D (1988) 'Assemblage and Subculture: The Casuals and their Clothing', in J Ash and L Wright, *Components of Dress: Design, Manufacturing, and Image-making in the Fashion Industry* London: Routledge 100–6.

Loader, I (2002) 'Policing, Securitization and Democratization in Europe', *Criminology and Criminal Justice* 2(2): 125–53.

Loseke, D (1999) *Thinking About Social Problems: An Introduction to Constructionist Perspectives* New York: Aldine de Gruyter.

Lucas, N (1969) *Britain's Gangland* London: Pan.

Luckenbill, D (1981) 'Generating Compliance: The Case of Robbery', *Urban Life* (10) April: 25–46.

Lukács, G (1983) (1937) *The Historical Novel* Nebraska: University of Nebraska Press.

Lupsha, P (1986) 'Organised Crime in the United States', in R Kelly (ed), *Organised Crime: A Global Perspective* Totowa, NJ: Rowman and Littlefield.

Lupton, R, Wilson, A, May, T, Warburton, H, and Turnbull, PJ (2002) *A Rock and a Hard Place: Drug Markets in Deprived Areas*, Home Office Research Study 240.

Lyng, S (1990) 'Edgework: A Social Psychological Analysis of Voluntary Risk Taking', *American Journal of Sociology* 95(4): 851–86.

Maas, P (1998) *Underboss: Sammy The Bull Gravano's Story of Life in the Mafia* New York: Harper Collins.

MacAllister, W (2000) *Drug Diplomacy in the Twentieth Century: An International History* London: Routledge.

MacDonald, R (1997) 'Informal Working, Survival Strategies and the Idea of an Underclass', in R Brown (ed), *The Changing Shape of Work* Basingstoke: Macmillan.

MacDonald, R (1998) 'Youth, Transitions and Social Exclusion: Some Issues for Youth Research in the UK', *Journal of Youth Studies* 1(2): 163–76.

Macintyre, B (2007) *Operation Zig Zag* London: Bloomsbury.

Mack, J (1964) 'Full-time Miscreants, Delinquent Neighbourhoods and Criminal Networks', *British Journal of Sociology* 15: 38–53.

MacRaild, D (1999) *Irish Migrants in Modern Britain, 1750–1922* London: Macmillan.

Makarenko, T (2004) 'The Crime–Terror Continuum: Tracing the Interplay between Transnational Organised Crime and Terrorism', *Global Crime* 6(1): 129–45.

Maltz, M (1976) 'On defining "organized crime"', *Crime and Delinquency* 22: 338–46.

Maltz, M (1985) 'Towards Defining Organized Crime', in H Alexander and G Caiden (eds), *The Politics and Economics of Organized Crime* Lexington, MA: DC Heath.

Mann, M. (1997) 'Has Globalization Ended the Rise and Rise of the Nation-State?', *Review of International Political Economy* 4(3): 472–96.

Mannheim, H (1955) *Group Problems in Crime and Punishment* London: Routledge and Kegan Paul.

Manning, PK (1997) *Police Work: The Social Organization of Policing* Prospect Heights: Waveland Press.

Mark, R (1978) *In the Office of Constable* London: Collins.

Marks, L (1996) 'Race, Class and Gender: The Experience of Jewish Prostitutes and Other Jewish Women in the East End of London at the Turn of the Century', in J Grant, *Women, Migration and Empire* Staffordshire: Trentham Books.

Marotta, V (2002) 'Zygmunt Bauman: Order, Strangerhood and Freedom', *Thesis Eleven*, Number 70, August 2002: 36–54.

Marsh, K, Wilson, L, and Kenehan, R (2012) 'The Impact of Globalization on the UK Market for Illicit Drugs: Evidence from Interviews with Convicted Drug Traffickers', in C Costa Storti and P De Grauwe (eds), *Illicit Trade and the Global Economy* Cambridge MA: MIT Press.

Marx, GT and Corbett, R (1991) 'Critique: No Soul in the New Machine: Technofallacies in the Electronic Monitoring Movement', *Justice Quarterly* 8(3): 399–414.

Mason, E (1994) *Inside Story* London: Pan.

Matrix Knowledge Group (2007) *The Illicit Drug Trade in the United Kingdom*, Home Office Online Report 20/07, London: Home Office.

Matthews, R (2002) *Armed Robbery* Devon: Willan.

Matthews, R (2008) *Prostitution, Politics, and Policy* Abingdon: Routledge-Cavendish.

Matza, D (1969) *Becoming Deviant* Englewood Cliffs: Prentice Hall.

Maurer, DW (1955) *The Whizz Mob* New Haven: College and University Press.

Mawby, RC and Wright, A (2003) 'The Police Organisation', in T Newburn (ed), *The Handbook of Policing* Cullompton: Willan Publishing 169–95.

Maxson, CL and Klein, MW (1995) 'Investigating Gang Structures', *Journal of Gang Research* 3(1): 33–40.

Mayhew, H (1861) (1981) *The Morning Chronicle Survey of Labour and the Poor: The Metropolitan Districts, Vol 2* London: Caliban Books.

Mayhew, H and Binney J (1862) (1968) *The Criminal Prisons of London and Scenes of Prison Life* London: Frank Cass.

McClintock, FH and Gibson, ER (1961) *Robbery in London* London: Macmillan.

McCracken, G (1988) *Culture and Consumption* Indiana UP: Bloomington.

McCright, AM and Dunlap, RE (2000) 'Challenging Global Warming as a Social Problem: An Analysis of the Conservative Movement's Counter-Claims', *Social Problems*, 47: 499–522.

McDonald, B (2002) *Elephant Boys* Edinburgh: Mainstream.

McIntosh, M (1971) 'Changes in the Organisation of Thieving', in S Cohen (ed), *Images of Deviance* Harmondsworth: Penguin.

McIntosh, M (1975) *The Organisation of Crime* London: Macmillan.

McLaughlan, E and Redhead, S (1985) 'Soccer Style Wars', *New Society*, 16 August, 225–8.

McLean, L (1998) *Guv'nor* London: Blake Publishing.

McManus, M (1994) 'Folk Devils and Moral Panics? Irish Stereotyping in Mid-Victorian Durham', *Durham County Local History Society Bulletin 53*.

McMullan, J (1982) 'Criminal Organisation in Sixteenth and Seventeenth Century London', *Social Problems* 29: 311–23.

McMullan, J (1984) *The Canting Crew: London's Criminal Underworld, 1550–1700* New Brunswick, NJ: Rutgers University Press.

McVicar, J (1979) *McVicar By Himself* London: Arrow.

Medina, J, Aldridge, J, and Ralphs, R (2011) 'Gang Transformation, Changes or Demise', in J Hazen and D Rodgers (eds), *Global Gangs* Minnesota: University of Minnesota Press.

Meier, WM (2011) *Property Crime in London, 1850–Present* London: Palgrave Macmillan.

Mena, F and Hobbs, D (2010) 'Narcophobia: Drugs Prohibition and the Generation of Human Rights Abuses', *Trends in Organised Crime* 13(1): 60–74.

Mercer, K (1987) 'Black Hair/Style Politics', *New Formations* 3 (Winter): 33–56.

Metropolitan Police Service (2010) *Internal Statistics* (unpublished).

Mieczkowski, T (1990) 'Crack Distribution in Detroit', *Contemporary Drug Problems* 17: 9–30.

Miller, D (2008) *The Comfort of Things* Cambridge: Polity.

Miron, JA (2004) *Drug War Crime* Oakland, California, Washington: Independent Institute.

Mitsilegas, V (2003) 'From National to Global, From Empirical to Legal: The Ambivalant Concept of Transnational Organised Crime', in ME Beare (ed), *Critical Reflections on Transnational Organised Crime, Money Laundering and Corruption* Toronto: University of Toronto Press.

Mitsilegas, VJ, Monar, J, and Rees, W (2003) *The European Union and Internal Security* Basingstoke: Palgrave/Macmillan Global Academic Publishing.

Moore, J (1991) *Going Down to the Barrio* Philadelphia: Temple University Press.

Moore, W (1974) *Kefauver and the Politics of Crime* Columbus: University of Missouri Press.

Morgan, G, Dagistanli, S, and Martin, G (2010) 'Global Fears, Local Anxiety: Policing, Counter-Terrorism and Moral Panic over "Bikie Gang Wars" in New South Wales', *Australian and New Zealand Journal of Criminology*, 43(3): 580–99.

Morgan, J, McCullough, L, and Burroughs, J (1986) *Central Specialist Squads. A Framework for Monitoring and Evaluation* London: Home Office, Police Research Series Paper 17.

Morrison, S and O'Donnell, I (1994) 'Armed Robbery: A Study in London', Occasional Paper Number 15, Oxford Centre for Criminological Research.

Morselli, C (2001) 'Structuring Mr. Nice: Entrepreneurial Opportunities and Brokerage Positioning in the Cannabis Trade', *Crime, Law and Social Change* 35(3): 203–44.

Morselli, C (2005) *Contacts, Opportunities, and Criminal Enterprise* Toronto: University of Toronto Press.

Morselli, C and Giguere, C (2006) 'Legitimate Strengths in Criminal Networks', *Crime, Law and Social Change* 45(3): 185–200.

Morselli, C, Giguere, C, and Petit, K (2007) 'The Efficiency/Security Trade-off in Criminal Networks', *Social Networks* 29: 143–53.

Morton, J (1992) *Gangland: London's Underworld* London: Little Brown.

Morton, J (2000) *East End Gangland* London: Little Brown.

Morton, J (2001) 'Obituary of Lord Justice Lawton', *Guardian*, 5 February.

Mullins, C (2006) *Holding Your Square: Masculinities, Streetlife and Violence* Cullompton: Willan.

Munsche, P (1981) *Gentlemen and Poachers* Cambridge: Cambridge University Press.

Murji, K (1999) 'Wild Life: Constructions and Representations of Yardies', in J Ferrell and N Websdale (eds), *Making Trouble: Cultural Constructions of Crime, Deviance, and Control* New York: Aldine de Gruyter 179–201.

Murji, K (2007) 'Hierarchies, Markets and Networks: Ethnicity/Race and Drug Distribution', *Journal of Drug Issues* 37(4): 781.

Murphy, R (1993) *Smash and Grab: Gangsters in the London Underworld, 1920–60* London: Faber and Faber.

Murphy, S, Waldorf, D, and Reinarman, C (1990) 'Drifting into Dealing: Becoming a Cocaine Seller', *Qualitative Sociology*, 13(4): 321–43.

Nadelmann, E (1990) 'Global Prohibition Regimes: The Evolution of Norms in International Society', *Int Organ* 44(4): 479–526.

Nadelmann, E (1993) *Cops across Borders: The Internationalization of U.S. Criminal Law Enforcement* University Park: Penn State Press.

Napper, L (1997) 'A Despicable Tradition: Quota Quickies in the 1930s', in R Murphy (ed), *The British Cinema Book* London: British Film Industry.

Natarajan, M (2000) 'Understanding the Structure of a Drug Trafficking Organization: A Conversational Analysis', in M Natarajan and M Hough (eds), *Illegal Drug Markets: From Research to Policy*, Crime Prevention Studies Volume 11, Monsey, NY: Criminal Justice Press 273–98.

Natarajan, M (2006) 'Understanding the Structure of a Large Heroin Distribution Network: A Quantitative Analysis of Qualitative Data', *Quantitative Journal of Criminology* 22(2): 171–92.

Natarajan, M and Belanger, M (1998) 'Varieties of Upper-Level Drug Dealing Organisations: A Typology of Cases Prosecuted in New York City', *Journal of Drug Issues* 28(4): 1005–26.

Naylor, R (2003) 'Towards a General Theory of Profit Driven Crimes', *British Journal of Criminology* 43(1): 81–101.

Naylor, R (2004) *Wages of Crime: Black Markets, Illegal Finances, and the Underworld Economy* London: Cornell University Press.

Naylor, R (2007) 'Criminal Profits, Terror Dollars and Nonsense', *Crime and Justice International Magazine* 23(101): 27–33.

NCIS (1993a) *An Outline Assessment of the Threat and Impact by Organised/Enterprise Crime Upon United Kingdom Interests* London: NCIS.

NCIS (1993b) *Organised Crime Conference: A Threat Assessment* London: NCIS.

NCIS (2000) *An Outline Assessment of the Threat and Impact by Organised/Enterprise Crime Upon United Kingdom Interests* London: NCIS.

Nellis, M (2000) 'Law and Order: The Electronic Monitoring of Offenders', in D Dolowitz, R Hulme, M Nellis, and F O'Neil (eds), *Policy Transfer and British Social Policy: Learning from the USA* Buckingham: Open University Press.

Newburn, T and Sparks, R (2004) 'Criminal Justice and Political Cultures', in T Newburn and R Sparks (eds), *Criminal Justice and Political Cultures* Cullompton: Willan 1–15.

Newburn, T, Taylor, M, and Ferguson, B, 'What is a gang?', *Guardian*, 7 December.

Newman, A (ed) (1981) *The Jewish East End 1840–1939* London: The Jewish Historical Society of England.

Ng, KC (1968) *The Chinese in London* Oxford: Oxford University Press, for the Institute of Race Relations.

Nordstrom, C (2007) *Global Outlaws*. Berkeley: University of California Press.

Nutt D (2009) 'Government vs Science over Drug and Alcohol Policy', *Lancet* 374: 1731–3.

Nutt, D (2010) 'Science and Non-science in UK Drug Policy', *Addiction* 105: 1154.

O'Brien, J and Kurins, A (1991) *Boss of Bosses* New York: Simon and Schuster.

O'Brien, M, Tzanelli, R, and Yar, M (2005) 'Kill-n-tell (& all that jazz): The seductions of crime in Chicago', *Crime Media Culture* 1(3): 243–61.

O'Byrne, D (1997) 'Working Class Culture: Local Community Under Global Conditions', in J Eade (ed), *Living the Global City* London: Routledge.

O'Connor, D (2005) *Closing the Gap: A Review of the 'Fitness for Purpose' of the Current Structure of Policing in England and Wales* HMIC.

O'Connor, J and Wynne, D (1996) 'Introduction', in J O'Connor and D Wynne (eds), *From the Margins to the Centre: Cultural Production and Consumption in the Post-Industrial City* Aldershot: Arena.

O'Day, A (1996) 'Varieties of anti-Irish behaviour, 1846–1922', in P Panayi (ed), *Racial Violence in Britain in the Nineteenth and Twentieth Centuries* Leicester: Leicester University Press.

O'Dell, R (1965) *Jack the Ripper in Fact and Fiction* London: Harrap.

O'Donnell, I and Morrison, S (1997) 'Armed and Dangerous? The Use of Firearms in Robbery', *The Howard Journal of Criminal Justice* 36(3): 305–20.

O'Mahoney, B (1997) *So This Is Ecstasy?* Edinburgh: Mainstream Publishing.

O'Mahoney, M and Wooding, D (1981) *King Squealer: True Story of Maurice O'Mahoney* London: Sphere.

O'Neill, S (2008) 'Soca abandons hunt for crime lords', *The Times Online*; <http://www.timesonline.co.uk/tol/news/uk/crime/article3919686.ece>.

Osborne, T and Rose, N (2004) 'Spatial Phenomenotechnics: Making space', with C Booth and P Geddes, *Environment and Planning D: Society and Space* 22: 209–28.

Padilla, F (1992) *The Gang as an American Enterprise* New Brunswick, NJ: Rutgers University Press.

Pakulski, J and Walters, M (1996) *The Death of Class* London: Sage.

Paoli, L (2003) *Mafia Brotherhoods: Organized Crime, Italian Style* New York: Oxford University Press.

Paoli, L and Fijnaut, C (2004) 'Comparative Synthesis of Part 2', in L Paoli and C Fijnaut (eds), *Organised Crime in Europe* Netherlands: Springer 603–24.

Paoli, L and Fijnaut, C (2006) 'Organised Crime and its Control Policies', *European Journal of Criminal Law and Criminal Justice* 13(3): 307–27.

Parker, H (1974) *View from the Boys, A Sociology of Down Town Adolescents* Newton Abbott: David and Charles.

Parker, M (2012) *Alternative Business: Outlaws, Crime and Culture* London: Routledge.

Parker, R (1981) *Rough Justice* London: Fontana.

Patrick, J (1973) *A Glasgow Gang Observed* London: Eyre Methuen.

Payne, L (1973) *The Brotherhood* London: Michael Joseph.

Pearson, G (1983) *Hooligan: a History of Respectable Fears* London: Macmillan.

Pearson, G and Hobbs, D (2001) *Middle Market Drug Distribution*, Home Office Research Study No 227, London: Home Office.

Pearson, J (1973) *The Profession of Violence* London: Granada.

Pearson, J (2001) *The Cult of Violence* London: Orion.

Pearson, J (2010) *Notorious: The Immortal Legend of the Kray Twins* London: Century.

Pearson, W (2006) *Death Warrant* London: Orion.

Pellew, J (1989) 'The Home Office and the Aliens Act, 1905', *The Historical Journal* 32(2): 369–85.

Pennant, C (2003) *Congratulations You Have Just Met The ICF* London: Blake.

Perec G (1997) *Species of Spaces and Other Pieces* Harmondsworth: Penguin.

Persaud, R and Lusane, C (2000) 'The New Economy, Globalisation and the Impact on African Americans', *Race and Class* 42(1): 21–34.

Peto, R Lopez, AD, Boreham J, and Thun, M (2005) *Mortality from Smoking in Developed Countries 1950–2000* (2nd edn) Oxford: Oxford University Press.

Pileggi, N (1987) *Wise Guy* London: Corgi.

Piore, M and Sabel, C (1984) *The Second Industrial Divide* New York: Basic Books.

Pitts, J (2008) *Reluctant Gangsters: The Changing Face of Youth Crime* Cullompton: Willan.

Pollard-Urquhart, W (1862) 'The Irish Labourers in London' in *Transactions of the National Association for the Promotion of Social Science, 1861* London; cited in Feheney, JM (1983) 'Delinquency among Irish Catholic Children', *Victorian London Irish Historical Studies* 23(92): 319–29.

Pollock, S (2002) 'Cosmopolitanism and Vernacular in History', in C Breckenridge, S Pollock, H Bhabha, and D Chakrabarty (eds), *Cosmopolitanism* Durham: Duke University Press 15–53.

Pollock, S, H Bhabha, C Breckenridge, and D Chakrabarty, D (2002) 'Cosmopolitanism', in C Breckenridge, S Pollock, H Bhabha, and D Chakrabarty (eds), *Cosmopolitanism* Durham: Duke University Press 1–14.

Porter, B (1987) *The London Metropolitan Police Special Branch Before the First World War* London: The Boydell Press.

Potter, G (2010a). 'You Reap What You Sow: Profit, Pleasure and Pain in Domestic Cannabis Cultivation', in T Decorte and J Fountain (eds), *Pleasure, Pain and Profit: European Perspectives on Drugs* Lengerich: Pabst Science Publishers 134–51.

Potter, G (2010b) *Weed, Need and Greed: A Study of Domestic Cannabis Cultivation* London: Free Association Books.

Potter, GW (1994) *Criminal Organisations* Illinois: Waveland Press.

Pountain, D and Robins, D (2007) 'Immoral Support', *Guardian*, 20 June.

Presdee, M (2004) *Cultural Criminology and the Carnival of Crime* London: Routledge.

President's Commission on Organized Crime (1983) *Organized Crime: Federal Law Enforcement Perspective* Washington DC: Government Printing Office 4–6.

Pritchard, A (2008) *Urban Smuggler* Edinburgh: Mainstream.

Punch, M (1991) 'In the Underworld: An Interview with a Dutch Safe-Breaker', *The Howard Journal* 30(2): 121–39.

Radin, P (1927) *Primitive Man as a Philosopher* New York: Appleton.

Raine, L and Cilluffo, F (eds) (1994) *Global Organized Crime: The New Empire of Evil* Washington DC: Center for Strategic and International Studies.

Ralphs, R, Medina, J, and Aldridge, J (2009) 'Who Needs Enemies with Friends Like These? The Importance of Place for Young People Living in Known Gang Areas', *Journal of Youth Studies* 12(5): 483–500.

Rawlinson, P (2010) *From Fear to Fraternity: A Russian Tale of Crime, Economy and Modernity* London: Pluto Press.

Rawlinson, P and Fussey, P (2010) 'Crossing Borders', *Criminal Justice Matters* 6–7: 79–1.

Read, L and Morton, J (1991) *Nipper* London: McDonald.

Read, PP (1978) *The Train Robbers* London: WH Allen.

Reuter, P (1984) *Disorganised Crime: Illegal Markets and the Mafia* Cambridge, MA: MIT Press.

Reuter, P (1985), *The Organisation of illegal Markets: An Economic Analysis* Washington, DC: US Department Of Justice.

Reuter, P (1986) 'Methodological and institutional problems in organized crime research', Paper prepared for the conference on Critical Issues in Organized Crime Control, Washington DC: The Rand Corporation.

Reuter, P (2009) 'Systemic Violence in Drug Markets', *Crime Law and Social Change* 52(3): 275–84.

Reuter, P and Haaga, J (1989) *The Organization of High-Level Drug Markets: An Exploratory Study* Santa Monica, CA: RAND.

Reynolds, B (2000) *The Autobiography of a Thief* London: Virgin.

Richardson, C (1992) *My Manor* London: Pan.

Richardson, E (2005) *The Last Word: My Life as a Gangland Boss* London: Headline Book Publishing.

Rietveld, H (1993) 'Living the Dream', in S Redhead (ed), *Rave Off: Politics and Deviance in Contemporary Youth Culture* Aldershot: Avebury 41–78.

Robertson, R (1992) 'Globality and Modernity', *Theory Culture and Society* 9(2): 153–61.

Robertson, R (1995) 'Glocalisation: Time-Space and Homogeneity-Heterogeneity', in M Featherstone, S Lash, and R Robertson (eds), *Global Modernities* London: Sage.

Robins, K (1991) 'Tradition and Translation: National Culture in its Global Context', in J Corner and S Harvey (eds), *Enterprise and Heritage: Crosscurrents of National Culture* London: Routledge.

Robson, G (1997) *Class, Criminality and Embodied Consciousness: Charlie Richardson and a South East London Habitus* London: Goldsmiths College.

Rohmer, S (1998) *The Fu-Manchu Omnibus* London: Alison and Busby.

Rose, A (1962) *Human Behaviour and Social Processes* London: Routledge and Kegan Paul.

Rosnow, RL and Fine, GA (1976) *Rumor and Gossip: The Social Psychology of Hearsay* New York: Elsevier.

Rosow, E (1978) *Born to Lose: The Gangster Film in America* New York: Oxford University Press.

Ross, C (2010) *Death of the Docks* Milton Keynes: Author House.

Rubin, BM and Çarkoglu, A (2003) *Turkey and the European Union: Domestic Politics, Economic Integration, and International Dynamics* London: Routledge.

Rugby, K and Thompson, T (2000) *Bloggs 19* London: Time Warner Paperbacks.

Ruggiero, V (1993) 'Brixton, London: A Drug Culture without a Drug Economy?' *International Journal of Drug Policy* 4(2): 83–90.

Ruggiero, V (1995) 'Drug Economics: A Fordist Model of Criminal Capital', *Capital and Class* 55: 131–50.

Ruggiero, V (1996) *Organised Crime and Corporate Crime in Europe* Dartmouth: Aldershot.

Ruggiero, V (2000) *Crime and Markets* Oxford: Oxford University Press.

Ruggiero, V and Khan, K (2006) 'British South Asian Communities and Drug Supply Networks in the UK: A Qualitative Study', *The International Journal of Drug Policy* 17: 473–83.

Ruggiero, V and South, N (1997) 'The Late Modern City as a Bazaar', *British Journal of Sociology* 48(1): 54–70.

Rumbelow, D (1973) *The Houndsditch Murders* London: Macmillian.

Russo, G (2001) *The Outfit* London: Bloomsbury.

Rustin, M (1996) 'Perspectives on East London: An Introduction', in T Butler and M Rustin (eds), *Rising in the East: The Regeneration of East London* London: Lawrence and Wishart.

Ryder, M (2009) 'The pursuit of riches destroys the lives of young black men', *Observer*, 9 August.

Samuel, R (1981) *East End Underworld: The Life and Times of Arthur Harding* London: Routledge & Kegan Paul.

Samuel, R (1994) *Theatres of Memory* London: Verso.

Sanchez-Jankowski, M (1991) *Islands in the Street: Gangs in American Urban Society* Berkeley: University of California Press.

Sanders, TLM (2008) *Paying for Pleasure: Men Who Buy Sex* Cullompton: Willan.

Sandu, S (2003) 'Come Hungry, Leave Edgy', *London Review of Books*, 9 October.

Sassen, S (1998) *Globalisation and its Discontents: Essays on the New Mobility of People and Money* New York: The New Press.

Sassen, S (2000) 'Women's Burden: Counter-geographies of Globalization and the Feminization of Survival', *Journal of international affairs* 53(2): 504–24.

Sassen, S (2006) *Cities in a World Economy* (3rd edn) Thousand Oaks: Pine Forge.

Saul, JS (1992) *Voltaire's Bastards: The Dictatorship of Reason in the West* Toronto: Penguin Books.

Saviano, R (2007) *Gomorrah: Italy's Other Mafia* London: Macmillan.

Savoie-Gargiso, I and Morselli, C (2009) 'Lady's Man: The Pimp and his Place Among Prostitutes', Presentation at the 9th European Society of Criminology conference, Ljubljana, Slovenia, 9–12 September.

Schatz, T (1981) *Hollywood Genres: Formulas, Filmmaking and the Studio System* New York: Random House.

Schelling, T (1984) *Choice and Consequences* Harvard: Harvard University Press.

Scherrer, A (2008) 'The G8 and Transnational Organized Crime: The Evolution of G8 Expertise on the International Stage', presentation for the Munk Centre for International Studies, Toronto, 21 January; <http://www.g7.utoronto.ca/speakers/scherrer2008.htm>.

Schlegel, K (1987) 'Violence in Organized Crime: A Content Analysis of the De Cavalcante and De Carlo Transcripts', in TS Bynum (ed), *Organized crime in America: Concepts and Controversies* Monsey, New York: Criminal Justice Press 55–70.

Schneider, E (1999) *Vampires, Dragons, and Egyptian Kings: Youth Gangs in Postwar New York* Princeton, NJ: Princeton University Press.

Schneider JT and Schneider, PT (2003) *Reversible Destiny: Mafia, Antimafia, and the Struggle for Palermo* Berkeley: University of California Press.

Schur, E (1957) 'A Sociological Analysis of Confidence Swindling', *Journal of Criminal Law, Criminology and Police Science* 48: 296–304.

Scott, H (1954) *Scotland Yard* London: Andre Deutsch.

Scott, P (1995) *Gentleman Thief: Recollections of a Cat Burglar* London: Harper Collins.

Seed, J (2006) '"Limehouse Blues": Looking for Chinatown in the London Docks, 1900–1940', *History Workshop Journal* 62: 58–85.

Sennett, R (1994) *Flesh and Stone: The Body and the City in Western Civilization* New York: Norton.

Sennett, R (1998) *The Corrosion of Character* New York: Norton.

Sharp, C, Aldridge, J, and Medina, J (2006) *Delinquent Youth Groups and Offending Behaviour: Findings from the 2004 Offending, Crime and Justice Survey*, Home Office Online Report 14/06.

Sharpe, FD (1938) *Sharpe of the Flying Squad* London: John Long.

Sharpe, J (1999) *Crime in Early Modern England 1550–1750* London: Longman.

Shatford, J and Doyle, W (2004) *Dome Raiders—How Scotland Yard Foiled the Greatest Robbery of All Time* London: Virgin Books.

Shaw, C and McKay, H (1942) *Juvenile Delinquency and Urban Areas* Chicago: University of Chicago Press.

Shelley, L (1997) Congressional Testimony Before the House Committee on International Relations: Threat From International Organized Crime and Terrorism; <http://www.fas.org/irp/congress/1997_hr/h9710011s.htm>.

Sheptycki, J (1995) 'Transnational Policing and the Making of a Postmodern State', *British Journal of Criminology* 35(4): 613–35.

Sheptycki, J (1998) 'The Global Cops Cometh: Reflections on Transnationalisation, Knowledge Work and Police Subculture', *British Journal of Sociology* 49(1): 57–74.

Sheptycki, J (2000) 'The Drug War: Learning from the Paradigm Example of Transnational Policing', in J Sheptycki (ed), *Issues in Transnational Policing* London: Routledge 201–28.

Sheptycki, J (2003) 'Against Transnational Organised Crime', in ME Beare (ed), *Critical Reflections on Transnational Organised Crime, Money Laundering and Corruption* Toronto: University of Toronto Press 120–44.

Sheptycki, J (2004) 'The Accountability of Transnational Policing Institutions: The Strange Case of Interpol', *Canadian Journal of Law and Society* 19: 107–34.

Sherry, F (1986) *Raiders and Rebels* New York: Hearst Marine Books.

Shibutani, T (1966) *Improvised News A Sociological Study of Rumor* New York: Irvington Publishers.

Shildrick, TA and MacDonald, R (2007) 'Street Corner Society: Leisure Careers, Youth (Sub)culture and Social Exclusion', *Leisure Studies* 26(3): 399–55.

Shore, H (2007) '"Undiscovered Country": Towards a History of the "Criminal Underworld"', *Crimes and Misdemeanours: Deviance and the Law in Historical Perspective* 1(1): 41–68.

Shore, H (2012) 'Criminality and Englishness in the Aftermath: The Racecourse Wars of the 1920s', *Twentieth Century British History* 22(4): 474–97.

Short, M (1991) *Lundy: The Destruction of Scotland Yard's Finest Detective* London: HarperCollins.

Shover, N (1973) 'The Social Organisation of Burglary', *Social Problems* 20: 499–514.

Shover, N (1985) *Aging Criminals* Beverly Hills, CA: Sage.

Shover, N and Honaker, D (1992) 'The Socially Bounded Decision Making of Persistent Property Offenders', *The Howard Journal* 31: 276–93.

Sibley, D (1995) *Geographies of Exclusion* London: Routledge.

Siegel, D (2008) 'Conversations with Russian Mafiosi', *Trends in Organised Crime* 11: 21–9.

Siegel, D and Nelen, H (2008) 'Introduction', in D Siegel and H Nelen (eds), *Organized Crime: Culture, Markets, and Policies* New York: Springer 1–3.

Silke, A (2000) 'Drink, Drugs and Rock 'n' Roll: Financing Loyalist Terrorism in Northern Ireland—Part Two', *Studies in Conflict and Terrorism* 23(2): 107–27.

Sillitoe, P (1955) *Cloak Without Dagger* London: Cassells & Co.

Silverstone, D (2010) 'The Policing of Vietnamese Organized Crime within the UK', *Policing* 4(2): 132–41.

Silverstone, D (forthcoming) *Drugs, Clubs and Regulation* London: Routledge.

Silverstone, D and Savage, S (2010) 'Farmers, Factories and Funds: Organised Crime and Illicit Drugs Cultivation within the British Vietnamese Community', *Global Crime* 11(1): 16–33.

Simmel, G (1906) 'The Sociology of Secrecy and of Secret Societies', *American Journal of Sociology* 11: 441–98.

Simmel, G (1955) [1908/1922] *Conflict & The Web of Group-Affiliations* New York: The Free Press.

Simon, D and Burns, E (2009) (1997) *The Corner: A Year in the Life of an Inner-City Neighborhood* Edinburgh: Canongate.

Sims, GR (1911) *Off the Track in London* London: Jarrold & Sons.

Sinclair, I (1997) *Lights Out for the Territory: 9 Excursions in the Secret History of London* London: Granta Books.

Slater, S (2007) 'Pimps, Police and Filles de Joie: Foreign Prostitution in Interwar London', *The London Journal* 32(1): 53–74.

Slater, S (2009) 'Prostitutes and Popular History: Notes on the Underworld, 1918–1939', *Crime History and Societies* 13(1): 25–48.

Slater, S (2010) 'Containment: Managing Street Prostitution in London 1918–1959', *Journal of British Studies* 49(2): 332–57.

Slaughter, P (2003) 'Of Crowds, Crimes, and Carnivals', in R Matthews and J Young (eds), *The New Politics of Crime and Punishment* Cullompton: Willan 178–98.

Smart, C (1981) 'Law and the Control of Women's Sexuality: The Case of the 1950s', in B Hutter and G Williams (eds), *Controlling Women* London: Croom Helm.

Smith, D (1975) *The Mafia Mystique* New York: Basic Books.

Smith, D Jr (1971) 'Some Things that may be More Important to Understand about Organized Crime than Cosa Nostra', *University of Florida Law Review* 24: 1–30.

Smith, D Jr (1980) 'Paragons, Pariahs, and Pirates: A Spectrum-Based Theory of Enterprise', *Crime and Delinquency* 26: 358–86.

Smith, R (2005) *A Few Kind Words and a Loaded Gun* London: Penguin.

Smith, R (2008) 'Exploring the Policing–Entrepreneurship Nexus', Scottish Institute of Policing Research—Briefing Paper 2.

Smith, R (2009) 'Entrepreneurial Policing', *Police Professional*, February: 23–5.

Smith, T (2005) *The Art of Armed Robbery* London: Blake.

Smithies, E (1982) *Crime in Wartime* London: Allen and Unwin.

SOCA (2009) *Annual Report 2008/2009* London: Home Office.

Soja, E (1989) *Postmodern Geographies* London: Verso.

Solana, J (2004) *A secure Europe in a better world—the European Security Strategy in Civilian Perspective or Security Strategy?* European Development Policy Confronting New Challenges in Foreign and Security Policy International Conference Berlin, 23 November 2004, Friedrich-Ebert-Stiftung, 52–7.

Sounes, H (2008) *Heist: The True Story of the World's Biggest Cash Robbery* London: Simon & Schuster.

Sparks, R (2001) 'Degrees of Estrangement: The Cultural Theory of Risk and Comparative Penology', *Theoretical Criminology* 5(2): 159–76.

Sparrow, MK (1991) 'Network Vulnerabilities and Strategic Intelligence in Law Enforcement', *International Journal of Intelligence and Counter Intelligence* 65: 255–74.

Spencer, J and Broad, R (2010) 'Lifting the Veil on SOCA and the UKHTC: Policymaking Responses to Organised Crime', in PC van Duyne, A Maljevic, M van Dijck, K von Lampe, and J Harvey (eds), *Cross-border Crime Inroads on Integrity*, Nijemgen: Wolf Legal publishers.

Sponza, L (1988) *Italian Immigrants in Nineteenth-century Britain* Leicester: Leicester University Press.

Sponza, L (1993) 'The British Government and the Internment of Italians', in Cesarani and Kushner (eds), *The Internment of Aliens in Twentieth Century Britain* London: Routledge 125–45.

Sriskandarajah, D and Drew, C (2006) *Brits Abroad: Mapping the Scale and Nature of British Emigration* London: Institute for Public Policy Research.

Stanko, E (2009) *Serious Youth Violence: Learning from 2007/2008. Homicides of Children and Young People*, unpublished presentation to the Serious Youth Violence Board, Strategic Research and Analysis Unit, Metropolitan Police: London.

Stedman-Jones, G (1971) *Outcast London* Oxford: Oxford University Press.

Stelfox, P (1996) *Gang Violence: Strategic and Tactical Options* London: Home Office, Police Research Group.

Sterling, C (1994) *Crime Without Frontiers* London: Little Brown.

Strathern, M (1995) 'Afterword: Relocations', in M Strathern, *Shifting Contexts: Transformations in Anthropological Knowledge* London: Routledge 177–85.

Styles, J (1980) 'Our Traitorous Moneymakers', in J Brewer and J Styles (eds), *An Ungovernable People* London: Hutchinson.

Sugden, J (2002) 'Scum Airways', *Observer*, 17 November.

Sullivan, M (1989) *Getting Paid* Ithaca NY: Cornell University Press.

Sutherland, E (1937) *The Professional Thief* Chicago: University of Chicago Press.

Suttles, G (1968) *The Social Order of the Slum* Chicago: University of Chicago Press.

Sweeney, J, Connett, D, Clark, V, Gillard, M, Doyle, L, Meek, J, and Bhatia, S (1996) 'Russian mafiya invades Britain', *Observer*, 15 December.

Taylor, C (1990) *Dangerous Society* East Lansing: Michigan State University Press.

Taylor, I (1971) 'Soccer Consciousness and Soccer Hooliganism', in S Cohen (ed), *Images of Deviance* Harmondsworth: Penguin.

Taylor, I (1999) *Crime in Context* Cambridge: Polity.

Taylor, I and Hornsby, R (2000) *Replica Firearms: A New Frontier in the Gun Market* London: INFER Trust.

Taylor, I, Walton, P, and Young, J (1973) *The New Criminology* London: RKP.

Taylor, L (1984) *In the Underworld* Oxford: Blackwell.

Tendler, S (2002) 'Albanian gangs use Balkan violence to invade underworld', *The Times Online*, 25 November.

Thomas, D (2003) *An Underworld at War* London: John Murray.

Thompson, EP (1974) *The Making of the English Working Class* Harmondsworth: Penguin.

Thornberry, TP, Krohn, MD, Lizotte, AJ, Smith, CA, and Tobin, K (2003) *Gangs and Delinquency in Developmental Perspective* Cambridge: Cambridge University Press.

Thornton, P (2003) *Casuals: Football, Fighting & Fashion* Liverpool: Milo.

Thoumi, T (2003) 'The Numbers' Game: Let's All Guess the Size of the Illegal Drugs Industry!', Paper TNI Seminar, 5–6 December.

Thrasher, F (1927) *The Gang* Chicago: University of Chicago Press

Tobias, J (1968) 'The Crime Industry', *British Journal of Criminology*, 2: 247–58.

Tombs, S and Hillyard, P (2004) 'Towards a Political Economy of Harm: States, Corporations and the Production of Inequality', in P Hillyard, C Pantazis, S Tombs, and D Gordon (eds), *Beyond Criminology: Taking Harm Seriously* London: Pluto Press 30–54.

Tomlinson, J (1999) *Globalisation and Culture* Cambridge: Polity Press.

Toy, J (2008) *Die Another Day* London: London Borough of Southwark.

Travis, A (2006) 'Crime-busting ideas imported from the US', *Guardian*, 4 April.

Tsoukala, A (2008) 'Boundary-creating Processes and the Social Construction of Threat', *Alternatives: Global, Local, Political* 33(2): 139–54.

Turner, J and Kelly, L (2009) 'Trade Secrets: Intersections between Diasporas and Crime Groups in the Constitution of the Human Trafficking Chain', *British Journal of Criminology* 49(2): 184–201.

Tyler, A (1985) '2nd Opinion', *Time Out*, 30 May.

Uglow, S and Trelford, V (1997) *The Police Act 1997* London: Jordans.

UN Centre for International Crime Prevention (2002) *Towards a Monitoring System for Transnational Organized Crime Trends: Results of a Pilot Survey of 40 Selected Organized Criminal Groups in 16 Countries* Vienna: UN.

Ungar, S (2005) 'The Rise and (Relative) Decline of Global Warming as a Social Problem', *Sociological Quarterly* 33:4, 483–501.

United States Senate (1951) *Special Committee to Investigate Organized Crime in Interstate Commerce* New York: Didier.

Urry, J and Szerszynski, B (2002) 'Cultures of Cosmopolitanism', *Sociological Review* 50: 461–81.

van Dijck, M (2005) *Trafficking in Human Beings: A Literature Survey* Brussels: Assessing Organised Crime Project, European Commission.

van Duyne, PC (1996) 'The Phantom and Threat of Organized Crime', *Crime, Law and Social Change* 24(4): 341–77.

van Duyne, P (2003) 'Organizing Cigarette Smuggling and Policy Making, Ending Up in Smoke', *Crime Law and Social Change* 39: 285–317.

van Duyne, PC (2011) '(Transnational) Organised Crime, Laundering and the Congregation of the Gullible', Valedictory, 14 March 2011, Tilburg University.

van Duyne, PC and Antonopoulos, GA (eds) (2009) *The Criminal Smoke of Tobacco Policy Making: Cigarette Smuggling in Europe* Nijmegen: Wolf Legal Publishers.

van Duyne, P and Levi, M (2005) *Drugs And Money: Managing the Drug Trade and Crime Money in Europe* London: Routledge.

van Duyne, P and Nelemans, M (2011) 'Transnational Organized Crime: Thinking in and Out of Plato's Cave', in F Allum and S Gilmour (eds) (2011) *Handbook of Transnational Organized Crime* London: Routledge 36–51.

van Koppen, MV, de Poot, CJ, Kleemans, RR, and Nieuwbeerta, R (2010) 'Criminal Trajectories in Organised Crime', *British Journal of Criminology* 50, 102–23.

Vander Beken, T and Verfaillie, K (2010) 'Assessing European Futures in an Age of Reflexive Security', *Policing and Society* 20(2): 187–203.

Varese, F (2010) 'What is Organised Crime?', introduction to F Varese (ed), *Organised Crime* London: Routledge 1–35.

Varese, F (2011) *Mafias on the Move: How Organized Crime Conquers New Territories* New York: Princeton University Press.

Varese, F (2012) 'How Mafias Take Advantage of Globalisation: The Russian Mafia in Italy', *British Journal of Criminology*, 52: 235–52.

Verpoest K and Vander Bekan T (2005) 'The European Methodology for Reporting on Organised Crime', in *The European Methodology for Reporting Crime, A report for Sixth Framework Project 'Assessing Organised Crime: Testing the Feasibility of a Common European Approach in a Case study of the Cigarette Black Market in the EU'*; <http://www.sprinxdata.com/AOC/publications/AOC-DLV-EU-methodology-vFI.pdf>.

Vigil, J (1988) *Barrio Gangs: Street Life and Identity in Southern California* Austin: University of Texas Press.

von Lampe, K (1995) 'Understanding Organised Crime: A German View', Paper presented at the Academy of Criminal Justice Sciences in Boston, 7–11 March 1995.

von Lampe, K (2001) 'Not a Process of Enlightenment: The Conceptual History of Organized Crime in Germany and the United States of America', *Forum on Crime and Society* 1(2): 99–116.

von Lampe, K (2002) 'The Trafficking in Untaxed Cigarettes in Germany: A Case Study of the Social Embeddedness of Illegal Markets', in P van Duyne, K von Lampe, and N Pasas (eds), *Upperworld and Underworld in Cross Border Crime* Nijmegan: Wolf Legal Publishers 141–61.

von Lampe, K (2006) 'The Cigarette Black Market in Germany and in the United Kingdom', *Journal of Financial Crime* 13(2): 235–54.

Wacquant, L (1994) 'The New Urban Color Line: The State and Fate of the Ghetto in Postfordist America', in J Craig (ed), *Social Theory and the Politics of Identity* Oxford: Blackwell 231–76.

Wacquant, L (2009) *Punishing the Poor: The Neoliberal Government of Social Insecurity* Durham: Duke University Press.

Waddington, PAJ (1991) *The Strong Arm of the Law: Armed and Public Order Policing* Oxford: Clarendon Press.

Wade, G (1900) 'The Cockney John Chinaman', *The English Illustrated Magazine* (July): 301–7, Chinatown File, Local History Archive, Tower Hamlets Central Library.

Waldorf, D and Lauderback, D (1993) *Gang Drug Sales in San Francisco: Organized orFreelance?* Alameda, CA: Institute for Scientific Analysis.

Walklate, S and Mythen, G (2008) 'How Scared are We?', *British Journal of Criminology* 48: 209–25.

Walkowitz, J (1992) *City of Dreadful Delight: Narratives of Sexual Danger in Late-Victorian London* Chicago: University of Chicago Press.

Wallerstein, I (1979) *The Capitalist World Economy: Essays by Immanuel Wallerstein* Cambridge: Cambridge University Press.

Walsh, D (1986) *Heavy Business* London: Routledge.

Walton, S (2002) *Out of It: A Cultural History of Intoxication* New York: Three Rivers Press.

Ward, H (1974) *Buller* London: Hodder and Stoughton.

Ward, J (2010) *Flashback: Drugs and Dealing in the Golden Age of the London Rave Scene* Cullompton: Willan.

Warshow, R (1948) 'The Gangster as Tragic Hero', *The Partisan Review*, 240–4.

Watts, M (1960) *The Men in My Life* London: Christopher Johnson.

Webb, B (1993) *Running with the Krays* Edinburgh: Mainstream.

Webb, D (1953) *Crime is my Business* London: Muller.

Welch, M (2012) 'The Sonics of Crimmigration: Wall of Noise and Quiet Manoeuvring', *British Journal of Criminology*, 52: 324–44.

Wensley, F (1931) *Detective Days* London: Cassell and Co.

Werbner, P (1999) 'Global Pathways. Working Class Cosmopolitans and the Creation of Transnational Ethnic Worlds', *Social Anthropology* 7(1): 17–35.

White, J (1980) *Rothschild Buildings: Life in an East End Tenement Block 1887–1920* London: Routledge and Kegan Paul.

White, J (2001) *London in the 20th Century: A City and Its People* London: Vintage.

White, J (2008) *London in the 19th Century: A Human Awful Wonder of God* London: Vintage.

Whyte, W (1943) *Street Corner Society: The Social Organisation of a Chicago Slum* Chicago: University of Chicago Press.

Wickstead, B (1985) *Gangbuster* London: Futura.

Wideman, J (1985) *Brothers and Keepers* New York: Penguin.

Wilk, R (1995) 'Learning to be Local in Belize: Global Systems of Common Difference', in D Miller (ed), *Worlds Apart: Modernity Through the Prism of the Local* London: Routledge 110–33.

Willets, P (2010) *Members Only: The Life and Times of Paul Raymond* London: Serpent's Tail.

Williams, C and Roth, MP (2011) 'The Importation and Re-exportation of Organized Crime: Explaining the Rise and Fall of the Jamaican Posses in the United States', *Trends in Organized Crime* 14(4): 298–313.

Williams, P and Savona, E (eds) (1995) 'The United Nations and Transnational Organised Crime', Special Issue of *Transnational Organised Crime* 1(3).

Williams, T (1989) *The Cocaine Kids* Reading, MA: Addison-Wesley.

Williams, T (1992) *Crack House* Reading, MA: Addison-Wesley.

Willis, P (1977) *Learning to Labour: How Working Class Kids Get Working Class Jobs* London: Saxon House.

Willoughby, W (1976) *Opium as an International Problem* Baltimore: Johns Hopkins University Press.

Wilson, AH (2002) *24 Hour Party People* London: Channel 4 Books.

Wilson, WJ (1987) *The Truly Disadvantaged* Chicago: University of Chicago Press.

Winlow, S (2001) *Badfellas: Crime Tradition and New Masculinities* Oxford: Berg.

Winlow, S and Hall, S (2006) *Violent Night: Urban Leisure and Contemporary Culture* Oxford: Berg.

Witchard, AV (2009) *Thomas Burke's Dark Chinoiserie: Limehouse Nights and the Queer Spell of Chinatown* Basingstoke: Ashgate.

Wobble, J (2009) *Memoirs of a Geezer: The Autobiography of Jah Wobble* London: Serpents Tale.

Woodiwiss, M (1988) *Crime, Crusades and Corruption: Prohibitions in the United States, 1900–1987* London: Pinter.

Woodiwiss, M (2012) 'Organised Crime, the Mythology of the Mafia, and the American/Anglo Response', *History and Policy*.

Woodiwiss, M and Bewley-Taylor, D (2005) *The Global Fix: The Construction of a Global Enforcement Regime* Amsterdam: Transnational Institute; <http://www.tni.org/detail_pub.phtml?&know_id=68>.

Woodiwiss, M and Hobbs, D (2009) 'Organized Evil and the Atlantic Alliance: Moral Panics and the Rhetoric of Organized Crime Policing in America and Britain', *British Journal of Criminology* 49(1): 106–28.

Wright, A (2006) *Organised Crime* Cullompton: Willan.

Wright, A, Waymont, A, and Gregory, F (1993) *Drug Squads: Drugs Law Enforcement and Intelligence in England and Wales* London: Police Foundation.

Wright, JD and Rossi, PH (1985) *The Armed Criminal in America* Washington, DC: US Department of Justice.

Wright, R and Decker, S (1997) *Armed Robbers in Action* Boston: North Eastern University Press.

Yablonsky, L (1962) *The Violent Gang* New York: Macmillan.

Young, J (1971) *The Drugtakers: The Social Meaning of Drug Use* London: Paladin.

Young, J (2004) 'Voodoo Criminology and the Numbers Game' in J Ferrell, J Hayward, W Morrison, and M Presdee (eds), *Cultural Criminology Unleashed* London: Routledge 13–28.

Young, J (2007) *The Vertigo of Late Modernity* London: Sage.

Young, J (2009) 'Moral Panic: Its Origins in Resistance, Resentment and the Translation of Fantasy into Reality', *British Journal of Criminology* 49(1): 4–16.

Young, M and Willmott, P (1957) *Family and Kinship in East London* London: Routledge and Kegan Paul.

Young, T, FitzGerald, M, Hallsworth, S, and Joseph, I (2007) *Groups, Gangs and Weapons. Full Report* London: Youth Justice Board.

Zaitch, D (2002) *Trafficking Cocaine: Colombian Drug Entrepreneurs in the Netherlands* The Hague: Kluwer.

Zaluar A (2001) 'Violence in Rio de Janeiro: Styles of Leisure, Drug Use and Trafficking', *International Social Science Journal* 53: 369–78.

Zedner, L (2009) *Security* London: Routledge.

Zizek, S (2003) *The Puppet and the Dwarf: The Perverse Core of Christianity* Cambridge, MA: MIT Press.

Zorbaugh, H (1929) *The Gold Coast and the Slum* Chicago: University of Chicago Press.

Index